THE SOCIOLOGY OF
URBAN REGIONS

SOCIOLOGY SERIES
Edited by John F. Cuber

ALVIN BOSKOFF
Emory University

THE SOCIOLOGY OF
URBAN REGIONS

New York

APPLETON-CENTURY-CROFTS
Division of Meredith Publishing Company

TO

Students of, and Participants in, Urban Living

AND

the Embattled Urban Planners

WHO

are on the frontiers of a barely visible new urban realm

Preface

An understanding of modern man's increasingly typical habitat—the city and the urban region—is a practical necessity for almost everyone. But this is by no means a simple problem. Studies of virtually every aspect of city life, from a number of standpoints, are already overwhelming in quantity and quite confusing in their findings and implications. Sociologists are intensely interested in urban life and its extension for several reasons, but perhaps most significantly because so many sociological questions are increasingly (if not exclusively) matters of human behavior and relationships in an urban setting. Marriage and family problems, child rearing, crime, delinquency, migration, race relations, old age, mental health, social class, religion, education, and public opinion trends are only a sprinkling of the crucial problems that are found in, or derive from, an urbanized way of life.

In this work, I have tried to present an organized review and interpretation of the sociologist's work on the nature of contemporary urban regions as clusters of areas that seem to form a new kind of community. Specifically, considerable attention has been given to: (1) the unique features of urban communities; (2) the historical background of modern urbanism; (3) the continuous changes and adjustments in values and organization that accompany urban development; and (4) the rise of urban planning as an attempt to preserve the essence of urban life under conditions of rapid social and cultural change. Where possible, examples have been drawn from urban regions in various parts of the world; however, the primary focus is on the United States and modern European settings.

As indicated in numerous places throughout the book, I am indebted to many investigators of urban life for important information and helpful viewpoints. My students in classes on Urban Sociology through the years have also been unwitting but extremely necessary collaborators in discussions of many issues that await the reader. Also, I gratefully acknowledge permission to use various materials from the following publishers, periodicals, or individuals: The Free Press of Glencoe, Inc.; Princeton University Press; University of California Press; University of Michigan Press; University of Chicago Press; Jonathan Cape, Ltd.; King's Crown Press; Russell Sage Foundation; Twentieth Century Fund; The Macmillan Company; Harcourt Brace & World; Thomas Y. Crowell Company; *Social Forces;*

American Sociological Association; International City Managers Association; John Wiley and Sons, Inc.; Morris Axelrod; Herbert H. Hyman; Wendell Bell; Morris Janowitz.

A.B.

Emory University

Contents

PART IV

Urban Planning and Social Problems

List of Illustrations

List of Tables

PART I

Orientation To
Human Communities

CHAPTER 1

The Sociological Approach
to the Community
and Region

THE HUMAN COMMUNITY, in its various forms, is one of man's most intriguing *inventions*. Since community is a hoary creation—so ancient that man without community is inconceivable—perhaps we might add that, throughout the long history of the human species, man has been changing the nature of his communities in a number of ways. These changes, which reflect the vicissitudes and achievements of human history, constitute a series of sociocultural *experiments* in providing a suitable context for the persistence of the species and a thrilling but checkered quest for the limits of man's potentialities.

No complexity of argument is needed to acknowledge not only the *practical* significance of community, but also its *intellectual* and *emotional* significance for humans. In their distinctive ways, religion, philosophy, art and literature, economics, geography, politics and political science, anthropology, and welfare movements have concerned themselves to some degree with the nature and problems of this constantly evolving invention. We owe a great deal to their respective insights and their efforts to focus man's attention on the community context. However, these contributions are understandably incidental to the more specialized objectives of each of these fields. From the very nature of human communities, the major (but not exclusive) responsibility for their analysis and understanding rests on the unique skills and viewpoint of sociology, which in the last thirty years has emphasized its obligation through a Himalayan mass of relevant researches

3

and analyses. At the present time, therefore, we may justifiably conclude that a genuine, comprehensive study of community and the sociology of the community are virtually synonymous.

Community and Its Dimensions

Since general usage of this important term is often vague and sometimes contradictory, we can best open the sociological approach by offering an initial, orienting definition of community and exploring the relations between community and region in complex societies. In the most general sense, we may define the community as a *relatively self-contained constellation of variably interdependent social groups within a definite, manageable geographic area, which, through their interrelated functioning, provide minimal satisfaction of the basic and acquired needs of their members.* However, a definition is an *invitation,* not a consummation; it requires elaboration, specification, and additional explanation.

Implicit in this definition is the conception of human communities as products of interacting "parts," factors, or dimensions of human experience. First and most obvious is the character of the *population* —the socially relevant physical traits of the social aggregate (numbers, density, sex, age, etc.). Second, and likewise obvious, is the nature and extent of the *land area* (size, soil fertility, climate, resources, topology) occupied by a definite population. Third, we must recognize (*a*) a constant set of biological or basic needs or drives common to all normal human organisms, making proper allowances for age and sex differences, and (*b*) an infinitely variable set of learned needs (values, norms, goals, etc.—in short, *culture*), which serve to modify and often dominate the purely biological drives. Fourth, and closely related to (*b*), there is a more or less distinct distribution of specific technical skills, which are developed and employed to implement the satisfaction of biological and acquired needs. Finally, every community exhibits a typical *social organization*—composed of definite social groups and their interaction—which organizes and coordinates the potentialities of the previously mentioned factors and thus sustains an *identity* visible both to participants and observers.

Community as a Level of Analysis

The detailed description of these dimensions and their empirical combinations in the urban community and region are focal and continuing objectives of this book. Therefore, we may now comfortably resist the temptation to anticipate discussions in later chapters. Instead, it may be helpful at this point to conceive of the community (defined in terms of these five dimensions) as a level of *social reality*. For those who might be perturbed by the epistemological implications of this term, let us therefore define "level of social reality" as the level or context of social *experience*—*i.e.*, the level of meaningful stimuli, of the conscious or implicit "projection" of social behavior, and the level of consequences generated by such behavior. To develop perspective for analyzing the community (and particularly the urban community), let us consider the following simplified typology of social levels:

1. The *group* level. At this level, interest is focused on the structure and operation of analytically isolated sets of interaction—a family, a gang, an office clique, a governmental agency, etc. This is the realm in sociology and social psychology of "group dynamics," small group research, formal organization, and socialization. On this level, groups are conceived as "closed" systems, legitimately abstracted from wider contexts.
2. The *community* level, as defined above.
3. The *regional* level.
4. The *societal* level.
5. Potentially, the level of *intra-planetary society*.

For present purposes, we may ignore levels 1, 4, and 5 and attempt to establish a crucial connection between the community and regional levels.

Region as Extension of Community

Our earlier definition treated community as a "relatively self-contained constellation" of interrelated social groups. This was meant to be an orienting definition to community in general and therefore must be appropriately modified to take account of variations in *types* of community. Clearly, such a definition refers principally to small, agricultural communities in slowly changing societies, and in an overwhelming proportion of man's residence on this planet. However, the *urban* community type (and its subtypes) in antiquity, and with even more salience in modern society, is by its very nature an accessible and peculiarly dependent entity. As we shall see later in more detail (Chapter 7), the urban community characteristically stimulates the creation (or the modification) of surrounding communities in a network of interdependencies that constitute a complex innovation in human experience. This constellation of communities about a politically delimited urban center might be called a "supercommunity," but we shall refer to it throughout this book as an *urban region*. Increasingly, study of human behavior in the urban center is inseparable from behavior and social organization in the urban region. Hence the title of this book: *The Sociology of Urban Regions*.

Indeed, the nature of the urban community type and its product—the urban region—subtly provides added significance to the community context of human experience. Whereas pre-urban community types functioned as rather isolated shells for their inhabitants—so that community and society were almost identical—the urban region now appears to be a two-way intermediary link between its component groups on the one hand and the environing society and the world, on the other hand. As a consequence, the impact of changes within the urban region and in the broader social structures is quickly communicated to persons participating in both contexts. The urban region, therefore, becomes the crucial focus for understanding the complexities, the problems, achievements, and the limitations of modern society.

UNDERSTANDING THE COMMUNITY

Most readers are of course familiar with several concrete examples of the urban community and the urban region. They know its various parts through personal experience or through the media of magazines, films, and newspapers. Slum area, "Chinatown," "Beacon Hill," "the Gold Coast," downtown, suburbia, the freeway, "Wall Street," the university campus, mammoth shopping centers, the City Hall, hobohemia, the country club—these are not merely *places,* but *symbols* [1] of a wide range of activities and of the heterogeneous people who live, work, and expire in the urban region. But how do these interesting fragments unite to form the fascinating amalgam of communities called the urban region?

Essentially, this question simultaneously poses the underlying problem of this book and of the sociology of urban regions: understanding

[1] Kevin Lynch, *The Image of the City* (Cambridge, Mass., Harvard University Press, 1960).

and explaining the peculiarities of the urban community and region in the modern world. This is obviously a large order, which can be filled most effectively with separable aspects of the basic problem. Indeed, research experience and serious thinking seem to distinguish four relevant foci of attention, investigation, and generalization. First, we may mention problems in the emergence and specific *location* of urban centers. This will be reviewed in Chapter 5. Second, there is the problem of analyzing the unfolding of community and regional development through the *differentiation* of their component parts in a complex sociogeographic division of labor. Chapters 5 and 6 are primarily concerned with this aspect. Third, an understanding of the urban region requires explicit and careful concern for the special mechanisms by which these component parts are organized and co-ordinated into a recognizable and unique entity. This is perhaps the most difficult and least understood facet of our larger problem; it will be given some discussion in Chapters 7, 14. Finally, and perhaps most characteristically, there is the necessity of acquiring and deepening our understanding of social and cultural change in the urban region, of the practical difficulties and potentialities accompanying such changes, and of the typical readjustments which have either been devised or which can be reasonably predicted. To this important set of problems we devote all of Part IV.

A Basic Sociological Approach

The sociological approach to these problems, which is basic to the discussions that follow, deals with the urban region as a relatively "closed" system of social structures and cultural patterns,[2] which operate to create and sustain the identity of the region and likewise produce variations and changes in its organization. This approach should be conceived as an attempt to provide a useful, broad, orienting hypothesis—a reference point for investigation and analysis—rather than a mental strait jacket. Because of the complexity of the urban region, we would expect both a realm of organization and consistency, and a puzzling component of unarticulated, nonconnectable activities and values. We take the tentative position that an over-

[2] This viewpoint is persuasively discussed by Florian Znaniecki, *The Method of Sociology* (New York, Rinehart & Co., 1934), Chap. I. See also Harry M. Johnson, *Sociology: A Systematic Introduction* (New York, Harcourt, Brace, and World, 1960), Chap. III.

whelming proportion of social behavior in urban regions is amenable to understanding, with proper analysis, against the backdrop of the larger and more complex "system." Pockets of inconsistency, however, do exist and we shall take note of them whenever necessary.

In considering the urban region as a sociological "system," we shall find it necessary to distinguish its parts and their interconnections (structure) in a meaningful way. Familiar and indispensable sociological concepts—social relations, social role, primary group, secondary group, status, class, elite, ethnic category, etc.—are therefore important means of sifting and organizing the multitudinous facts of urban life. But we must recognize that these facts have both genesis and consequences, that persons and groups in the urban system engage in *social actions* (behavior directed toward other persons and groups) which exhibit developments and variations in specific time periods and in definable units of space. Therefore, we shall use two kinds of sociological concepts to capture the *dynamic* element in urban regional systems. On the one hand, we shall have reference to *social processes* (such as cooperation, conflict, accommodation) as relatively conscious and clear-cut means of implementing values and pursuing social needs. To give proper prominence to the unintended effects of social processes, on the other hand, we shall attempt to analyze the *latent functional consequences* of urban behavior patterns—and particularly as these consequences are embodied in *adaptive sociocultural innovations*.[3] For example, the frequently studied ecological processes (competition, centralization, invasion, and succession) are best understood, from the sociological standpoint, as latent consequences of numerous social action processes.[4]

A final sociological concept is imperative in the study of urban regions: social change. This term has suffered from so many abuses and permutations of meaning that consensus among sociologists is still difficult to achieve. However, since social organization is a dominating dimension of the urban region and since numerous variations in behavior and organization are repeatedly found by participants and

[3] Robert K. Merton, *Social Theory and Social Structure*, revised and enlarged edition (New York, The Free Press of Glencoe, 1957), Chaps. I, IV, V.

[4] These processes are discussed by James A. Quinn, *Human Ecology* (Englewood Cliffs, N.J., Prentice-Hall, 1950), Part III; and Amos H. Hawley, *Human Ecology* (New York, Ronald Press, 1950), Parts III and IV. See also Otis D. Duncan and Leo F. Schnore, "Cultural, Behavioral, and Ecological Perspectives in the Study of Social Organization," *American Journal of Sociology,* 65 (September, 1959), pp. 132–146.

observers, a concept of social change is required to aid in distinguishing and analyzing these phenomena. For reasons that are developed elsewhere,[5] *social change* will be used to refer to significant variations or alterations in the organization, functioning, and interrelations of social groups in a given community, region, or society. The study of social change in the urban region consequently demands attention to four related aspects: (*a*) the description of specific social change processes; (*b*) the search for explanatory factors in production of social changes; (*c*) the patterns of initial reactions to such changes—maladjustments, conflicts, etc.; and (*d*) the processes of adaptation and incorporation of social changes.

The Need For Auxiliary Approaches

While the sociological orientation sketched in the preceding pages is conceived to be basic to the understanding of urban regions, the complexity of urban regions appears to justify the use of several auxiliary approaches. On hindsight, these are most profitably employed, not as alternatives or competitors, but as supplements to the sociological approach. Indeed, it is suggested that they be used whenever one or more of these supplementary viewpoints seems to be appropriate for *specific* problems in the study of urban regions. The most important auxiliary approaches are:

1. The *historical*. To provide perspective as well as rich comparative materials on earlier forms of the urban community, the historical approach has much to offer. Sociologists have often ignored historical materials in recent decades for several reasons; but it is becoming increasingly evident that this attitude closes off a broad avenue of information on *processes* of community and regional development.[6] Incidentally, the recent emergence of an urban historical interest

---

[5] Alvin Boskoff, "Social Change: Major Problems in the Emergence of Theoretical and Research Foci," in Howard Becker and Alvin Boskoff, eds., *Modern Sociological Theory* (New York, Dryden Press, 1957), pp. 263–267.

[6] See especially Max Weber, *The City*, trans. by Don Martindale (New York, The Free Press of Glencoe, 1958); Carl Bridenbaugh, *Cities in the Wilderness* (New York, Ronald Press, 1938) and *Cities in Revolt* (New York, Alfred A. Knopf, 1945); Richard M. Morse, *From Community to Metropolis* (Gainesville, University of Florida Press, 1958); Richard C. Wade, *The Urban Frontier* (Cambridge, Mass., Harvard University Press, 1959); Eric F. Goldman, ed., *Historiography and Urbanization* (Baltimore, Johns Hopkins Press, 1941); Caroline F. Ware, ed., *The Cultural Approach to History* (New York, Columbia University Press, 1940); Henri Pirenne, *Les Villes et les institutions urbaines* (Paris, Alcan, 1939), 2 vols.; W. G. Hoskins, *Local History in England* (London, Longmans, Green, 1959).

among many professional historians performs a distinctly useful service for the sociologist of urban regions.

2. The *demographic*. Since a community or region obviously is dependent on available personnel and their socially relevant physical characteristics, the demographic or population aspect must be given some attention by the sociologist. Population size, density, age and sex distribution, racial and ethnic composition, birth and death patterns, migration, etc., furnish specific clues to the human resources and deficiencies of given areas. Population trends may be viewed as consequences of social and valuational systems and likewise as conditions which affect the stability or variability of these systems.[7]

3. The *ecological*. There is some confusion about the meaning of the ecological approach in social phenomena. Much of the so-called ecological work by sociologists in recent decades seems to aim principally at discerning clear-cut *spatial distributions* of activities and population characteristics. However, while definitions and objectives are always somewhat arbitrary, this orientation seems unduly limited. In view of the history of the term and the special problems of sociology, it might be more useful to consider the ecological approach as generally concerned with the *mechanisms* by which human groups adjust to or modify the physical environment. To the extent that values can be even temporarily ignored in this approach, the human ecologist focuses on three related aspects: (*a*) the spatial distribution of groups and activities; (*b*) the conditions or factors in adjustment to subareas; and (*c*) the nature of the interrelations between and among subareas in an overall sociogeographic division of labor.[8] Since the community and region function with definable geographic bases, the ecological approach is one of the essential preparatory tools used by the urban sociologist.

4. The *cultural-valuational*. The temptation to explain human communities in mechanical, deterministic terms—as expressions of impersonal and irreversible forces—has a long and disastrous history. However, both historical perspective and the contemporary develop-

---

[7] Textbooks in population that emphasize this viewpoint to some degree include: Paul H. Landis and Paul K. Hatt, *Population Problems: A Cultural Interpretation*, 2nd ed. (New York, American Book Company, 1954); Warren S. Thompson, *Population Problems*, 4th ed. (New York, McGraw-Hill, 1953); Harold A. Phelps and David Henderson, *Population in its Human Aspects* (New York, Appleton-Century-Crofts, Inc., 1958); William Petersen, *Population Problems* (New York, Macmillan, 1961).

[8] Quinn, *op. cit.*, Parts I and IV; Hawley, *op. cit.*, Chaps. VI, XII–XIV.

ment of the social sciences furnish overwhelming evidence of human creativity and learning processes—values, ideas, desires, sentiments—in social phenomena. We shall, therefore, give considerable attention to cultural developments in the urban region. In particular, the *economic* aspect of culture—in which are located values of practical rationality, reduction of human efforts in specific enterprises, and standards of use and distribution of desired objects and services—requires appropriate study, without the easy but dangerous shift to economic determinism.[9]

5. The *psychological*. Increasingly, the understanding of complex human productions—especially the modern urban region—is enhanced at crucial points by exploring the *psychological impact* of typical experiences and situations on specific persons. Sociological analysis inevitably needs some psychological supplement, and vice versa. But the urban region is characteristically changeful and therefore always relatively "new" in some respects to its inhabitants. In general, we employ the psychological orientation to provide relevant analyses of variation in personality formation (for convenience, in the form of personality types). These variations may be considered "responses" to unique features of urban living and potentially, at least, as contributing factors in certain urban developments (*e.g.,* the "picture window," the suburban movement, the "do it yourself" fad).[10]

SELECTED REFERENCES

LYNCH, Kevin, *The Image of the City* (Cambridge, Mass., Harvard University Press, 1960).

NELSON, Lowry, RAMSEY, Charles E., and VERNER, Coolie, *Community Structure and Change* (New York, Macmillan, 1960).

SANDERS, Irwin T., *The Community:* An Introduction to a Social System (New York, Ronald Press, 1958), Chaps. I, VIII, XI.

ZIMMERMAN, Carle C., *The Changing Community* (New York, Harper & Brothers, 1938), Chaps. I–IV.

[9] See Robert M. MacIver and Charles H. Page, *Society* (New York, Holt, Rinehart & Winston, 1949), Chaps. XXV, XXVI.

[10] See Gardner Murphy, *Personality* (New York, Harper & Brothers, 1947); S. Kirson Weinberg, *Society and Personality Disorders* (Englewood Cliffs, N.J., Prentice-Hall, 1952), Part I.

CHAPTER 2

The City as
an Emergent Type
of Community

HUMAN SOCIETY has been pre-eminently rural and localized throughout the approximately one million years of its development and
for the larger part of the world's population in the modern era
(1850 to date). Much of this rural experience is forever lost to us
because a concern for posterity through record-keeping (the stuff of
history) is essentially alien to the uncontaminated rural life-style.
Indeed, Spengler insists that rural peoples have no history, that history as we know it is a property of *developing* societies.[1]

But it is clear that some rural communities in antiquity were decidedly unlike their counterparts in other areas of the world; they
were the scene of slowly cumulative cultural changes that eventually
made possible a complex and inherently dynamic context for human
existence: the urban community and its modern offspring, the urban
region. Urbanization, the process of creating and developing urban
communities, can be traced some 6500 years. However, urbanization
until recently has been a relatively *discontinuous* process, with periods
of attenuated growth, rapid and extensive expansion, and eras of stag-
nation and decline. This is a genuinely fascinating story—the tracing
of modern community ancestry—but we are interested primarily in
the basic threads of urbanism and their relevance to modern urban
regions.

[1] Oswald Spengler, *The Decline of the West* (New York, Alfred A. Knopf,
1937), Vol. I, pp. 16–18.

A matter of definition must be first on our agenda. What are the distinctive criteria of urban communities, wherever and whenever we find them?

In general, it will be helpful initially to conceive of a vast rural-urban continuum in terms of three interlocking dimensions: occupational dominance, division of labor, and density of population. The extremes of this continuum are points of reference, rather than reflections of concrete communities (see accompanying figure).

FIGURE 1
Continuum of Community Types in Terms of Social and Cultural Complexity

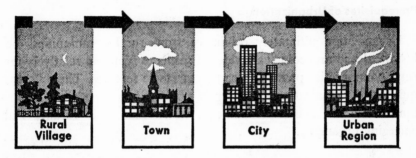

| Rural Village | Town | City | Urban Region |

The urban community may be approached as a general type of community that occupies a roughly delimited portion of this continuum. Thus, it is clear that we may refer to different subtypes or varieties of urban community or, with the aid of the continuum idea, different degrees of "urbanness." In this way, we avoid the temptation of assuming a unitary type of urban community, as well as an unnecessarily sharp distinction between the town and the full-blown city.[2]

The Urban Community Defined

Recalling the definition of community in the previous chapter, we shall define the urban community type as a community (or complex

[2] See discussions of the rural-urban continuum in Richard Dewey, "The Rural-Urban Continuum: Real But Relatively Unimportant," *American Journal of Sociology*, 66 (July, 1960), pp. 60–66; Stuart A. Queen and David B. Carpenter, *The American City* (New York, McGraw-Hill, 1953), Chap. III; Charles P. Loomis and J. Allan Beegle, *Rural Social Systems* (Englewood Cliffs, N.J., Prentice-Hall, 1950), Chap. I; Christen T. Jonassen, "Community Typology," in Marvin B. Sussman, ed., *Community Structure and Analysis* (New York, Thomas Y. Crowell, 1959), Chap. I.

of communities) characterized by a dominance of commercial, industrial, and "service" occupations; an extensive division of labor and its corresponding social complexity; an accompanying and underlying high density of population; and the development of coordination and social controls on a nonkinship basis. Urbanization is therefore a complex of social, ecological, and cultural trends which produce positive developments in any or all of these four aspects. Indeed, our discussions will implicitly combine the *structural* (organizational) with the *dynamic* (process) viewpoints, since the characteristic features of the urban community possess this dual significance.

Prerequisites of Urbanization

Urbanization ultimately originates from rural communities, but historical and archeological evidence seems to focus on relatively few rural communities possessing certain strategic features. These "prerequisites of urbanization" are largely obvious but nonetheless important social and cultural conditions, which link basic rurality with emerging urbanness.

1. Agriculture and domestication of animals

A secure food supply and especially the ability to provide food surpluses are the most fundamental rural contributions to the urban community. It may be assumed that increasing efficiency in food production rests on some combination of favorable geographic conditions and a developed technical competence in raising crops and livestock. Whatever the reasons, food surplus constitutes one of the essential preconditions of the urban community. Surpluses enable a population to establish a *permanent* geographic base, in contrast to many contemporaneous nonliterate peoples, who are compelled to follow a shifting supply of game or to seek alternatives for "worked out" land. In general, over a substantial time period, food surpluses allow for larger population units—either by reducing the death rate or by accommodating the needs of migrants, captives, etc. Extremely significant is the fact that surpluses can either be stored, or present possibilities for trade with other communities. Furthermore, surpluses permit reallocation of time, energy, and skills to other human pursuits and thus may result in greater specialization of roles and an expanded division of social labor. Indeed, increasing specialization (especially *technical* specialization) likewise increases production of articles suitable for trade.[3]

2. Improvements in tools, weapons, and technical methods

Perhaps reciprocally related to surplus food production is the development of more efficient implements for a variety of practical purposes. Pottery-making, weaving, the successive types of plow, the smelting of metals and their fabrication into reliable instruments, the sailboat, etc.—all create additional opportunities for specialization and/or extensions of commerce. Perfection of military weapons is particularly important, since defense of the community (and aggression against neighboring communities) was one of the dominant concerns in early urban experience.[4]

3. Complex social organization

Two of the distinguishing features of genuinely rural communities are the intrusive factors of primary, personal relationships and powerful kinship loyalties. These are, of course, appropriate to rural community life. But urbanization inherently involves somewhat larger social aggregations, the development of minor and major cultural differences within populations, and the problems of coordinating a variety of activities and resolving inevitable disputes and controversies. The dominance of kinship ties perpetuates social fragmentation and a troublesome array of contending factions. Therefore, the urban community becomes an *actuality* (based on the potentialities of urbanization derived from previously discussed conditions) when kin or *gentile* organization is succeeded by *civil* organization.[5]

Civil organization provides for the first time a clear-cut *public,*

[3] V. Gordon Childe, *Man Makes Himself* (New York, New American Library, 1951), Chap. V; Leslie A. White, *The Evolution of Culture* (New York, McGraw-Hill, 1959), Chap. XII; Felix M. Keesing, *Cultural Anthropology* (New York, Holt, Rinehart & Winston, 1958), pp. 94–103.

[4] Childe, *op. cit.,* Chaps. VI, VII.

[5] White, *op. cit.,* pp. 294–314; Lewis H. Morgan, *Ancient Society* (New York, Henry Holt, 1877); Max Weber, *General Economic History* (New York, The Free Press of Glencoe, 1950), pp. 45–46; Werner J. Cahnman, "Religion and Nationality," *American Journal of Sociology,* 49 (May, 1944), pp. 524–529.

community-wide form of coordination and control, in contrast to the narrow, particularized, and private organizations represented by leading clans. In place of status and opportunities associated with specific family connections (or the lack of such connections among newcomers to the community), civil organization is based on *territorial* and *property* criteria. Thus, residence within community boundaries and possession of land, livestock, money, and weapons become relatively rational determinants of *citizenship-community* membership rather than solely *kin* allegiance. Under these conditions, a central, universally applicable and legitimate control system can develop; indeed, this corresponds to the creation of a separate *political institution*. At this point, specialization in the community is accompanied by *class distinctions* (in contrast to previously dominant *lineage distinctions*). Here the *city* and *civilization* become clearly visible on the canvas of history.

Historically, the urban community is the consequence of transformations in a limited number of rural communities, under the conditions we have outlined above. For the greater part of the urbanization process, however, cities have been numerically inferior to villages, and yet politically and economically dominant. The rise of cities, ultimately dependent on rural foundations, seems to have inevitable consequences for the larger and perhaps "vaguer" society in which they appear. In short, cities create civilizations—complex and subtly binding interdependencies among a considerable number of adjacent communities—which possess rather distinctive sociocultural features whenever and wherever they arise. Very briefly, these features are:

1. Cities tend to be few in number, but also tend to cluster near one another.
2. The countryside and its several types of rural community come to be economically dependent on the city.
3. Commerce and exchange become highly developed and diversified.
4. One or more cities attain dominant political positions in extensive geographic areas and often in a politically delimited society.
5. The city (or cities) becomes and remains the *cultural center* of a vast area; in particular, it tends to become the focus of change, innovation, creativity, and deviation in a variety of human pursuits.

URBAN WAVES AND THEIR SIGNIFICANCE

Extensive discussions of these characteristics in modern urban regions will be found in later sections of this work. However, it must be emphasized that any serious attempt to understand the nature of contemporary urbanism and its component parts must recognize the vast *cumulative background* of modern urban living. Indeed, the panorama of world history, when viewed from the special perspective of the urban sociologist, suggests a rough, discontinuous evolution of urban experience—an evolution which is not inevitable but rather a reflection of increasing social complexity that appears to be responsive to specific sociocultural conditions of given historical periods, and, to some extent, to peculiar geographic factors. To organize the rich storehouse of pertinent historical materials, we shall try to analyze it in terms of broad urban phases or "waves," for which we can only hope to fix very approximate dates as boundary lines. More important, we shall try to summarize the unique social and cultural contributions of each "wave" to an evolving urbanization.

The First Urban Wave: 4500 B.C.–500 A.D.

Classical urbanism, which Gordon Childe refers to as the "urban revolution" following the Neolithic Revolution, was developed in a relatively long time span and in an extensive crescent-shaped slice of the Afro-Eurasian land mass.[6] In general, the earliest examples of classical urban centers appeared in the favorable environments of temperate or semitropical river valleys (Tigris, Euphrates, Nile, Ganges, Yangtze), where agricultural surplus was instrumental in transforming peasant villages into recognizable towns and cities. Undoubtedly, such phenomena as wars, migrations, and irregular commerce stimulated cultural contacts between distant urban centers (particularly after 2500 B.C.), which in some degree facilitated or accelerated the crystallization of urban features. However, the attempt to find a central radiation point of urbanization (*e.g.*, the tortured theory of Egyptian diffusion to contemporary urban cultures—the "Heliocentric" theory)[7] contains too many pitfalls to warrant serious

[6] Childe, *op. cit.*, Chap. VII; Ralph Turner, *The Great Cultural Traditions* (New York, McGraw-Hill, 1941), Vol. I.

[7] W. J. Perry, *The Growth of Civilization* (New York, E. P. Dutton, 1923), pp. 32–35, 100–120.

consideration by the sociologist. Let us instead focus on the general character of classical urbanization, without regard for its detailed, ultimate origins.

The most striking feature of this first urban wave is the foundation of cities on the triumvirate of *defense, worship,* and *commerce.* In Mesopotamia, Egypt, India, Crete, and later in Greece and Italy, these three activities were effectively coordinated on a constantly expanding scale. It must be remembered that agricultural surpluses were relatively new and precious, that the pre-existing social fabric was largely a patchy confusion of localisms and errant bands, that newly affluent (in food and supplies) communities or areas were pioneers in a sociocultural wilderness. Consequently, cities were strategically located to draw upon nearby fields and orchards, and to take advantage of natural opportunities (*e.g.,* hills) for defense against jealous marauders. It is not too farfetched to describe the classical city as the "fusion of fortress and market." [8] However, a great deal of evidence seems to underscore the importance of new religious forms in the transition from rural to genuinely urban organization, a topic to which we shall return.

With some variations in time and geography, urban communities in this general period embarked on relatively successful experiments in economic specialization. In addition to the central role of merchants (who were early differentiated but usually were accorded low social status), we can point to the development of such industries as textiles (based in part on advancements in preparation of dyes), pottery, metal-working and the production of alloys such as copper, the crafts of jewel-working, furniture-making, funerary skills, and construction (public buildings and temples). These specialties should be viewed as supplemental to, and perhaps dependent upon, the major technical and scientific innovations of classical cities: irrigation techniques, writing and the alphabet, geometry, astronomy, philosophy, and military science.

Commerce was surely the emerging center of urban interest and the *raison d'être* of many noneconomic innovations. One does not have to be an economic determinist to recognize this insistent pattern of dominance in classical antiquity. Indeed, the problems of disposing of agricultural surpluses could only be dealt with in many cases by some form of intercommunity exchange, since neither long-term stor-

---

[8] Max Weber, *The City,* trans. by Don Martindale and Gertrud Neuwirth (New York, The Free Press of Glencoe, 1958), p. 78.

written down and enforced by figures of authority. Here is the presumed origin of *public law* (criminal and civil types), for which we
have such examples as Hammurabi's Code, the Law of the Twelve
Tables, the constitutions of several Greek cities, and the complex
legal developments of the Roman Empire.

As Max Weber has emphasized, the ancient city (particularly in
the Greco-Roman world) was necessarily a military organization
superimposed on particularistic clan and religious organizations. According to this view, the understanding of military developments is a
prerequisite to analysis of trends in classical urbanization. The essential facts seem to support this position, though it is probably mislead-
ing to explain city development primarily in military terms. Nevertheless, the representative classical cities were marked by a shift from
individual combat to *mass, disciplined formations* (the hoplites, the
phalanxes) for military efficiency. This not only established a firm
basis for defensive operations, but made possible an extensive series
of urban *offensives* and the famous urban *empires* (Egypt, Persia, As-
syria, Athens, Sparta, Rome).[11] However, complex military organization also involved a diffusion of power from leading families to lower
status groups (usually, moderately successful farmers financially able
to equip themselves for battle). As dependence on broader groupings
increased, the dominance of clans was weakened and the internal
policies of the city (*polis*) gradually turned toward prevention of
landlessness. The underlying aim of political leadership and the "reforms" of various tyrants seem to possess this unifying theme. Consequently, the development of classical democracy (which was philosophically and practically different from modern forms) and perhaps
of the first demands for political freedom had their origins in the need
for specialized military organizations.

It is perhaps paradoxical to our contemporaries that democratization in classical cities was accompanied by the emergence of a *class
system,* which we can consider a characteristic feature of urbanization
in general. Pre-urban stratification, as we have already suggested, was
based on lineage and its dominance over economic, political, and
religious spheres. This semicaste structure was inevitably modified by
the significant institutional changes (political, economic, military)
which are inseparable from the processes of urbanization. With considerable variations, the typical urban class system appeared to rest
primarily on such status criteria as *occupation* and *skill,* rather than

11 Weber, *General Economic History*, pp. 322–324.

age nor increased consumption was initially feasibl
must be presumed that successful trade experienc
desired end in itself. Thus, the Sumerians and
bartered or sold wheat, beer, and barley (tempora
pluses in their temples); the Egyptian cities of Hel
and Abydos engaged in extensive trade in grains wit
and the Near East; Cretan-Minoan cities as early as 3
were already leading merchants of figs, barley, and oli
cities such as Athens and Corinth established commerc
the Adriatic and in Italy.[9]

Though the earliest details are not always clear, it
forgotten that many classical cities were in part (at le
of migration, warfare, and conquest. In practice, these
involved increasing attention to the inadequacies of clan
The Greek evidence seems to show initial foundation of
on unions of leading families (*confraternities* or *syno*
mutual defense, rather than for strictly commercial reasons
India, and China, irrigation problems faced by newly devel
resulted in such political characteristics as a developed bu
compulsory labor for dependent groupings, a monopolizatio
tary power by a single ruler, and a related opposition
power. Returning to Greece, the continued predominance o
families (*aristoi*) interfered with commercial developments
aspirations of the urban masses. The famous tyrants of th
through the sixth centuries B.C. (Orthagoras, Cypselus, Pe
Pisistratus, Cleisthenes, Polycrates) seemed to be a favorite m
breaking the aristocratic vise and thereby prepared the transi
civil organization and "the public interest." [10]

As population movements, conquests, and aristocratic declin
ceeded, the classical cities were faced with bothersome gaps in
control. The significance of property was changing; social relat
rights and duties between workers and possessors of surpluses
quired definition; the position of "strangers" and highly mobile
chants likewise needed clarification. Cities therefore constructed
tems or codifications of previously discrete rules, which came to

[9] Michael Rostovtzeff, *A History of the Ancient World* (Oxford, T
Clarendon Press, 1926), Vol. I; Turner, *op. cit.*
[10] Weber, *General Economic History*, pp. 320–331; Weber, *The City*, p
74–93; Karl Wittfogel, *Oriental Despotism* (New Haven, Yale Universit
Press, 1957), Chaps. I, III, VIII.

family and wealth. Normally, the leading groups consisted of the priesthood and military officials, though not without challenge from commercial groupings in the latter part of the classical period. The middle range of status levels (which should not be confused with modern middle classes) was composed of merchants and businessmen, whose position was exceedingly variable according to locality and time period. Finally, there were the lowest strata of peasants, artisans and craftsmen, and slaves (whose social and political status was sometimes greatly inferior to their financial position).[12]

We often forget one of the most important contributions of the first urban wave: *complex, universal religions.* The modern connotation of "urban-ness" is overwhelmingly "secular," "rational," and even "antireligious." However, this is based on a misunderstanding both of the urban community and religion itself, a misconception we hope to remove in Chapter 11. As historical and literary sources rather well demonstrate, pre-urban and early urban communities were marked by a bewildering diversity of local (and sometimes ancestral) religious cults, "mysteries," and rituals.[13] Through the agency of leading clans (especially in Greece), towns and cities arose with a politically dominant "public" cult, supplemented by various tolerated or irrepressible "private " cults. Under these circumstances, leading families supplied both a religious and a political focus (the priest-kings). In general, each city was a "religious island" content in its splendid but limited isolation. The practical logic of urban trends, however, revolutionized religion in a direction from which it has not greatly deviated. While religious and political activities remained intertwined (political leaders were religious leaders and vice versa), the development of urban communities as partially democratized, politically expanding entities provoked persistent movements for national rather than local cults and simplification of the supernatural focus through monotheism.[14]

The Persians had been among the first to achieve religious unification (Zoroastrianism), while Hindu urbanism was exemplified in Brahminism. Under the influence of Ikhnaton, Egypt had likewise ex-

---

[12] Michael Rostovtzeff, *A History of the Ancient World* (Oxford, The Clarendon Press, 1926), Vol. I, pp. 216–223; Turner, *op. cit.,* pp. 454–473.

[13] Fustel de Coulanges, *The Ancient City,* 10th ed. (Boston, Lee and Shepard, 1900), especially Book 3.

[14] See for example E. A. Wallis Budge, *From Fetish to God in Ancient Egypt* (London, Oxford University Press, 1934); H. A. R. Gibb, *Mohammedanism,* 2nd ed. (London, Oxford University Press, 1954).

perimented with monotheism, however briefly. Hebrew monotheism, which was an essential ingredient of Christianity, was itself derived from the military campaigns against religiously diversified urban peoples. Military success and the adoption of urban living solidified a national religion, though frequent reinterpretations by the prophets indicate the Hebrew failure to integrate urbanism and religion. By contrast, the Greek cities continued to nurture local cults and polytheism (backed by the aristocratic families). The Athenian tyrant, Pisistratus, did encourage national cults, especially the cult of Athena and the famous Panathenaic festival, but with only temporary results. The imitative Romans generally followed Greek religious precedent; however, something akin to a national monotheism briefly developed under Augustus, who did more than any succeeding emperor in promoting urbanization in the Empire. Finally, we can only mention the rise of Christianity, at the end of the first urban wave, as essentially urban in derivation and organization (borrowing urban administrative forms from the Empire) and in appeal to new adherents during its infancy.[15]

A final contribution of this first urban wave is the emergence of complex, diversified *arts*—sculpture, architecture, painting and decoration, music, drama, the dance, and literary forms (the dialogue, satire, tragedy, comedy, verse). All the classical civilizations developed competence in at least several of the arts, creating and diffusing relatively distinctive styles over wide areas. Highly significant is the religious origin of the arts, but even more so is their tendency toward autonomous development. It is this typical *artistic independence,* it seems, that explains much of our continued appreciation of classical styles and art objects. The efflorescence of the arts, particularly in their increasingly independent forms, reflects a high point in social specialization, which is one of the hallmarks of genuine urbanization and civilization.

The Second Urban Wave: 1000–1800 A.D.

Two generations of historical investigation have virtually destroyed any basis for viewing the medieval period as a "Dark Age" in which

[15] Lewis R. Farnell, *The Cults of the Greek States* (Oxford, The Clarendon Press, 1896–1907), 4 vols.; Gilbert Murray, *Five Stages of Greek Religion* (New York, Columbia University Press, 1925); Cyril Bailey, *Phases in the Religion of Ancient Rome* (Berkeley, University of California Press, 1932), Chap. V.

civilization was completely arrested and then scattered to the winds. On the contrary, much historical continuity was maintained—in agricultural and military techniques, in commerce, religion, and the major crafts.[16] However, if the barbarians did not embark on wholesale destruction of towns and cities in the fifth century and afterwards, it is certainly clear that urban communities were experiencing strongly regressive trends. As early as the third century A.D., urban areas were losing population, commerce and business enterprise suffered from perennial imperial restrictions, the middle class of officials was taxed to desperation, and the towns became festering sores rather than cases of responsible community life.[17] After the eighth century, rural feudalism, punctuated by short-lived military conquests, was incontrovertibly dominant. By the sixth century, towns were shadows of their former selves, often surviving as ecclesiastical bases for Catholicism. Significantly, *civitas*, which once meant "urban center," came to mean "episcopal city." [18]

A renewal of urbanization under these circumstances required a dramatic stimulus, one which could produce appropriate political and economic underpinnings for a second urban wave. This stimulus was probably the revival of extended commercial opportunities following the Crusades, though some credit must be given to the relative stabilization of political order in Europe (dating from the tenth century) which unwittingly permitted these opportunities to be realized. Thus, from the latter part of the tenth century, itinerant merchants began to cluster in their slack season outside the walls of old fortress-towns —particularly those situated near main travel routes.[19] Originally, these merchant quarters were *suburbs* or *faubourgs*, but gradually

[16] Alfons Dopsch, *The Economic and Social Foundations of European Civilization* (New York, Harcourt, Brace, 1937).

[17] Arthur E. R. Boak, *Manpower Shortage and the Fall of the Roman Empire in the West* (Ann Arbor, Mich., University of Michigan Press, 1955), pp. 93–112; Michael Rostovtzeff, *Social and Economic History of the Roman Empire* (Oxford, The Clarendon Press, 1926), pp. 333, 358; Samuel Dill, *Roman Society in the Last Century of the Western Empire*, 2nd ed. (London, Macmillan, 1933), pp. 253–259.

[18] Henri Pirenne, *Medieval Cities* (Princeton, Princeton University Press, 1925), Chap. III.

[19] Pirenne, *op. cit.*, Chaps. IV and V; Lewis Mumford, *The Culture of Cities* (New York, Harcourt, Brace & World, 1938), pp. 16–18; Henri Hauser, *Les débuts du capitalisme, 1223–1328* (Paris, Armand Colin, 1958), pp. 72–76; Henri Pirenne, *Les Villes et les institutions urbaines* (Paris, Alcan, 1939), 2 vols.; J. Lestocquoy, *Les Villes de Flandre et d'Italie* (Paris, Presses Universitaires de France, 1952); Weber, *The City*, pp. 95–110.

they became the functional foci and then the geographic centers of a revived and vigorous urbanism.

The new city, which was primarily a European phenomenon, was principally organized in terms of six component structures.

1. Economic features

The renewed dominance of commerce was allied to three significant economic developments. First, there was considerable improvement in agricultural methods and utilization of larger acreage for saleable crops (especially after the twelfth century). Second, expanded trade in manufactured goods (cloth, in particular) promoted the development of basic handicraft industries, normally located in the merchants' quarter. Finally, wide-ranging trade inevitably transformed restricted barter economies into money economies, so that a new and universal standard of value infiltrated both the city and the countryside.

2. The rise of the bourgeois

Since merchants were initially strangers and legally unassailable, their economic success was noted, but was also untranslatable into feudal terms. However, their peculiar status prompted the merchants to insure their favorable economic position by demanding (and receiving) political safeguards from feudal authorities (nobles and ecclesiastical lords). By the twelfth and thirteenth centuries, the merchants were becoming a respected and powerful middle class [20] (mediating between the semiskilled worker and the local nobility of the sword or cassock) and the essential unit in the urban social order.

3. Urban legal innovations

The bourgeoisie as a political and social power (as distinct from its economic significance) was intimately connected with the *legitimation* of untrammeled commerce as the central concern of the community. As a result of organized merchant pressures, the city became independent of environing feudal regulations and restrictions. Eventually, freedom from these obligations became the basic *legal status of all in-*

[20] Pirenne, *Medieval Cities*, Chaps. VI and VII; Lestocquoy, *op cit.*, pp. 17–41, 136–169; Sylvia L. Thrupp, *The Merchant Class of Medieval London, 1300–1500* (Chicago, University of Chicago Press, 1948), pp. 12–14, 282–285.

habitants; and residence in such communities for a year and a day guaranteed personal freedom ("Stadtluft macht frei"—city air [residence] extends freedom). From the merchants' standpoint, freedom to engage in trade was fundamental. Therefore, the right to own property and land, and the right to establish urban courts (for settling commercial disputes) was early achieved by the burghers or bourgeoisie. As civic responsibility became a problem, the merchants developed and legalized local police systems, excise and income taxes to pay for community services, and perhaps most important, a city council as the key administrative body armed with extensive powers.[21]

4. The university

Several cities, beginning in the twelfth and thirteenth centuries, unwittingly contributed the minimum essentials of higher, specialized education, which we now call the university. Originally a composite of trade union and fraternal lodge, the university or college was a semiformal organization of persons proficient in or prepared for the scholarly vocations of law, theology, and medicine. In Paris, masters and students banded together; in Bologna, the students developed their own organization and hired masters.[22] Learning was personal, barely dignified, and for many years an extremely mobile business. Ramshackle dwellings, suspicious landlords and neighbors, a few precious manuscripts owned by the masters, a motley assemblage of variously ill-prepared students, and the masters themselves—these were the initial ingredients. Gradually, despite numerous frictions, cities, princes, and the church came to accept (and even to subsidize) universities, whose products satisfied the increasing demand for *civil* professional services (especially law and medicine) in succeeding centuries of urban living.

5. Ecological structure

The fortress-like aspect of cities remained till the late fifteenth century, when gunpowder made ancient walls obsolete. Instead, cities resorted to intensive systems of ringed fortifications, manned by mer-

[21] Pirenne, *Medieval Cities*, Chap. VII.
[22] Mumford, *op. cit.*, pp. 33–35; Nathan Schachner, *The Mediaeval Universities* (New York, Stokes, 1938), pp. 42–49; Hastings Rashdall, *The Universities of Europe in the Middle Ages* (Oxford, The Clarendon Press, 1936), 3 vols.

cenaries, which inevitably limited city expansion. Consequently, population increase was followed by *congestion* and the genuine emergence of urban slums for most strata of urban communities.[23] At the same time, military needs were satisfied by radial, broad avenues, which facilitated deployment of troops at any point in the fortification system. Not till the rise of centralized national governments was this military strait jacket removed from the urban scene.

6. The stratification of art

In general, the arts of the first urban wave were public enterprises in which all or most of the citizens could participate. The arts often developed as expressions of dominant religious activities. Therefore, expansion of urban religions was accompanied by a relative "democratization" of such arts as the drama, sculpture, and architecture. But in the latter part of the second urban wave, the upper classes (the nobility, which had re-established itself in cities, and also some of the long-established mercantile families) assumed a semimonopolistic responsibility for music, dancing, and the theater. The so-called patrons of the arts created private (and sometimes competing) artistic empires through subsidies to writers, musicians, and painters. Under this system, classical music, painting, drama, and literature attained great heights in, for example, Bach, Michelangelo, Shakespeare, and Racine. Yet it established a sharp cleavage between the bulk of the urban population and the cultivated arts ("culture"), which in some respects persists to the present time.[24] In short, the second urban wave emphasized the *creation* of art, rather than the appropriate conditions for its *distribution* and appreciation.

The Third and Current Urban Wave: 1800 to the Present

The economic and political success of urban communities in the sixteenth through the eighteenth centuries led to further economic and social changes that clearly identify the emergence of the modern urban region. Since the remainder of this work focuses on this phase of urbanism, at this point we shall merely outline a number of its most distinctive features as a prelude to the more detailed discussions in later chapters.

[23] Mumford, *op. cit.*, pp. 83–86.
[24] *Ibid.*, pp. 111–113.

1. Expansion and separation of industrial units

The rise of specialized work locations (mills, factories) near efficient sources of power was a response to the optimistic quest for mass production and the consequent invention of ever more complicated machines. Very rapidly, the handicraft and "putting out" systems of production became cumbersome and unprofitable; thus for the urbanite, the job and the home were irrevocably split and the *journey to work* was to take its place in the universal urban pattern.[25]

2. Cooperative capital: the ubiquitous corporation

Expansion of enterprise and the intensification of mining ventures to provide metal for new and more complex machinery required more capital than a few entrepreneurs could muster. The joint stock company and its offspring, the corporation, provided additional capital and then specialized administration for a variety of industrial and maritime ventures. In time, the financier, the banker, and the investment organization played a silent but nonetheless powerful role in urban economic developments, functioning with increasing ease on regional, national, and international levels.

3. The urban-national axis

In the latter part of the second urban wave—and especially with the emergence of modern urban features—the city became the primary center of wealth in the Western world. During the bitter and prolonged struggles between the landed nobility and proponents of centralized government (the king), urban middle classes to a great extent subsidized the creation and maintenance of national states, to which they have been subsequently allied on most major issues. Basically, the city, through its characteristic operations, largely determines the overall functioning of the nation. However, it must be recognized that this "alliance" has been somewhat informal and indirect, especially in the United States. Yet there is growing evidence of closer and more formalized ties between urban areas and the national system (see Part IV). In any case, the city has become an arena of competitive power groups (with internal and external bases) and consequently the new locus of *politics*.

[25] Kate Liepmann, *The Journey to Work* (New York, Oxford University Press, 1944).

4. Ecological complexities

As a consequence of technological and economic developments, the emergence of peculiarly modern urban class structures, and what we might call "urbanized value systems," the urban community has experimentally (and often unconsciously) produced rather marked spatial divisions that reflect the intricate social and cultural specializations of this third urban wave. We shall analyze the nature and consequences of these ecological developments in some detail in Chapters 5 and 6. At this point, it is merely necessary to point to a highly differentiated central commercial-administrative area; the location of numerous retail areas; the relocation of industry in outlying zones; the meticulous diversification and *grading* of residential districts; the special separation of the arts, recreation, education, as well as deviant behavior (prostitution, gambling, crime, drug addiction, etc.,); and finally, the specialization of dependent "urblets" as the urban region expands.

Some Trends in Modern Urbanism

Of course, many more features of modern urban organization might be listed here. As we shall have occasion to note many times, the numerous concrete patterns of the modern urban region are symptomatic reflections and illustrations of these few basic regularities. But it seems to be particularly important that we view modern urbanization as part of an *understandable process* that has been recorded in a series of relatively continuous changes in technique, values and objectives, social organization, achievements, and problems. Indeed, several major trends are more or less explicit in our review of the three urban waves.

First, though various forms of organized religion were inseparable from urban living during the first and second waves, modern urbanism appears to find pre-existing organized religion somewhat incompatible with the other aims of community life. At this point, a widespread error must be corrected. Urbanization, as historical material clearly shows, is *not* basically antireligious. Religion in the formal sense was a basic ingredient in earlier stages of urbanism. It may well be that, for the modern urbanite, new forms of religious expression (not yet achieved or created) are needed to provide necessary spiritual support on his present sociocultural level.

Second, as we move from antiquity to the present, there is in urbanization a growing dominance of economic and technological values (profit, income, efficiency) in organizing and disorganizing clusters of social relationships in the community. However, each wave of urbanism likewise experienced serious challenges to rising economic groups by political and status groups (*i.e.,* landed nobility, barbarian invaders, military cliques). The bourgeoisie of the second urban wave was able to conquer its enemies by encouraging centralized government and then acquiring control of major governmental organs.[26] In the current urban wave, and especially during the last generation or so, the yet dominant economic interests have again faced the necessity of resisting or diverting the resurgence of essentially noneconomic demands. One such demand is extra-urban and derives from the political necessity to be persistently prepared for war.[27] Thus, high taxation, various types of economic controls (price controls, rationing, etc.) and increasing production for a single customer—the government—rather than the market tend to interfere with the free development of economic incentives. The other type of demand is intra-urban; it is variously reflected in the urbanite's desire for security and stable income, for costly but expected public services, for increasing stress on *esthetic* criteria in community developments,[28] and for a widespread sense of civic *responsibility* and *accountability*. Naked economic interest is therefore no longer fashionable, though it may still be pursued if publicity is avoided.

Finally, modern cities (and most obviously, the leading cities) have been increasingly expanding their radii of control over present and future behavior of populations. This is not basically *political* dominance—as in the first urban wave—or the limited economic supremacy of the second wave. The octopal growth of modern cities is instead proceeding on three interrelated levels. (*a*) Most obvious is *geographic expansion* into sprawling superurban units that ignore political and geographic obstacles—the metropolitan or urban region. Modern media of communication and rapid transportation are clearly basic to this growth. (*b*) Concentration of *economic functions*—the provision of jobs, desired services, capital and credit for business and consumption—inevitably attracts mobile individuals and families to aid in producing and/or consuming the fruits of metropolitan eco-

[26] Harold J. Laski, *The Rise of Liberalism* (New York, Harper and Brothers, 1936).

[27] J. Kenneth Galbraith, *The Affluent Society* (Boston, Houghton Mifflin, 1958), Chap. XVIII.

[28] Edward L. Ullman, "Amenities as a Factor in Regional Growth," *The Geographical Review,* 44 (January, 1954), pp. 119–132.

nomic systems. Those who remain outside the geographic orbit find themselves increasingly willing captives in urban economic nets. Consequently, the often quoted desire of Americans to "live in a nice, quiet community—not too far from a big city" is symptomatic of the special "magnetism" of modern urbanism. (c) The spread of urbanism is, finally and most significantly, *cultural*. Urbanization in previous periods was largely reflected in extension of citizenship and legal rights. Modern urbanism is apparently "exporting" tastes, biases, fashions, aspirations, and even abstract values (*e.g.*, education) to society at large.

Urban regions therefore seem to be gigantic *functional empires* in the vague political entities called national societies. Unlike classical empires, they remain more or less dependent on external but legitimate power units (state and/or national governments). As in previous urban waves, modern urban regions contain internal social divisions that are now rarely flagrant and dramatic, but nevertheless persist as latent deterrents to urban consensus and outright urban dominance. The key, sociologically speaking, to modern urbanism is perhaps the *ambivalent status* of urban regions; the political halter tends to limit the extraordinary potentialities for economic and cultural change that are synonymous with urbanism.[29] Cities of the second wave shattered feudal restrictions by supporting the national state. But what forms of alliance are available to modern urban regions?

SELECTED REFERENCES

CHILDE, V. Gordon, *Man Makes Himself* (New York, New American Library, 1951).

MUMFORD, Lewis, *The City in History* (New York, Harcourt, Brace, and World, 1961).

———, *The Culture of Cities* (New York, Harcourt, Brace, and World, 1938).

PIRENNE, Henri, *Medieval Cities* (Princeton, Princeton University Press, 1925).

WEBER, Max, *The City,* trans. by Don Martindale and Gertrud Neuwirth (New York, The Free Press of Glencoe, 1958).

WHITE, Leslie A., *The Evolution of Culture* (New York, McGraw-Hill, 1959).

[29] Gordon Baker, *Rural versus Urban Political Power* (Garden City, N.Y., Doubleday and Company, 1955).

CHAPTER 3

The Problem of Classifying Urban Regions

IF MODERN CITIES—products of the third urban wave all over the world—share a number of distinctive features, it is likewise true that cities possess some uniqueness, divergences, and idiosyncrasies. The resulting variety, which should not be exaggerated, is obvious both to the intelligent traveler and the alert, wide-ranging reader, who thus sets forth on mental pilgrimages to distant urban regions. Therefore, it will be of some use to search for some *order* in this variety, through a *meaningful classification* of urban regions.

It should be stated at the outset that such a classification is quite difficult, and not at all an academic exercise. Basically, our quantitative knowledge of urban regions is highly compartmentalized: population data, occupational distributions, spatial location of various types of activities and functions, housing, traffic surveys, etc. Consequently, with few exceptions, any classification of urban regions according to *one* type of information is likely to be as significant as classifying human beings in terms of hair color.

The essential problem, in line with the sociological viewpoint presented in the first chapter, is to develop and apply a classification or typology that enables us to treat urban regions as relatively coherent systems of component parts, as functional wholes in which specific features (*e.g.,* population facts, zonal developments) can be understood with reference to other components and to the structure of the region itself. This requires, it seems, both detailed cross-sectional information on various aspects of concrete urban regions and a creative, interpretative synthesis of these aspects to provide an intelligible, testable pattern of unity in urban regions. Significantly, though Chicago has been the most completely investigated of American urban regions,[1] we still lack anything resembling a comprehensive sociological picture of the Chicago region as an essential unit, despite the obvious contradictions of competing jurisdictions. Even the sensitive novelist and short-story writer, who are often intuitive but effective sociological interpreters of contemporary life, fail to capture more than isolated fragments of urban regional life (*i.e.*, the slum, Bohemia, and the middle-class suburb). Literature, which is said to be a creative reflection of its social environment, has yet to contribute a sure fictional treatment of the dominant *locale* in modern society—the urban region.

What, then, gives promise of supplying useful criteria for classifying urban regions? The answer must be tentative; it must be alternately cautious and audacious; and it must effectively provide continuity between past accomplishments and emerging ideas of *verifiable intelligibility* in sociological research. Such criteria, which have been chosen for their *synthetic* function (integrating several specific features) and their *cross-cultural* applicability, might well include: factors in the *mature* foundation of urban centers, *relative stage of development* in the urbanization process, and underlying cultural qualities derived from the larger society. Let us first examine these criteria separately, and then in their significant combinations.

1. Mature foundations

Even a rapid survey of cities during the third urban wave indicates that urban centers tend to be distinguishable in terms of the reasons for specific locations and/or later, basic lines of development. One such factor, which is quite important though moderately rare as a dominant consideration, is the *political-administrative type*. Of the major world capitals, very few have appeared in recent years; London, Paris, Moscow, and others achieved recognizable maturity in the second urban wave. Modern examples of this type include Washington, D.C., New Delhi, Tel Aviv, Buenos Aires, and Brasilia.

The *economic* factor is an obvious and perhaps somewhat over-

[1] A sampling of these studies might include: Louis Wirth, *The Ghetto* (Chicago, University of Chicago Press, 1929); Harvey Zorbaugh, *The Gold Coast and the Slum* (Chicago, University of Chicago Press, 1929); Walter C. Reckless, *Vice in Chicago* (Chicago, University of Chicago Press, 1933); Ruth S. Cavan, *Suicide* (Chicago, University of Chicago Press, 1928).

worked criterion of distinction among urban regions. In general, we find three major subvarieties: (*a*) industrial regions, in which "heavy" industrial enterprises and/or "light" manufacturing and processing are significant; (*b*) commercial-financial regions—based on distribution functions, investment and credit activities, and such specialized commercial services as advertising, insurance, and stock exchanges; and (*c*) transportation and communication centers—strategic concentrations of air, rail, trucking, telephone and telegraph, shipping, publishing, radio, and television services. New York City, Chicago, London, and Paris are only a few random examples.

With the enormous economic successes of the past one hundred years, still a third factor is rising toward levels of importance—the matter of *desirable geographic features* ("amenities").[2] The city of consequence that is principally (though not exclusively) attractive because of climate, scenery, and availability of water is largely a phenomenon of the United States. We distinguish here between the *resort* [3] (which tends to be comparatively small, highly seasonal in character, and with few permanent residents) and the *permanent urban playground* (whose development is marked by a steadily increasing, full-time population which seeks to combine economic and recreational pursuits in roughly equal proportions). Atlantic City, Las Vegas, Nice, and Bath are examples of the former, while Los Angeles, St. Petersburg, and Miami best represent the latter type.

However, political, economic, and recreational-geographic factors are rarely independent. Many major urban regions have developed several economic functions, as well as some emphasis on political, recreational, and artistic functions. A clear-cut functional classification of urban regions is therefore somewhat arbitrary, if unaccompanied by other considerations (to be discussed shortly). For example, Grace Kneedler worked out three classifications: one in terms of dominant *economic* activity (manufacturing, industrial, wholesale, retail, and diversified); another on the basis of *occupation* (educational center, governmental center, mining, transportation, amusement-health resort); and a third in terms of *functional status* (independent city, central city, dormitory suburb, balanced suburb, and employing suburb). It should be noted that the third classification

[2] Edward L. Ullman, "Amenities as a Factor in Regional Growth," *The Geographical Review*, 44 (January, 1954), pp. 119–132.

[3] J. Ellis Voss, *Summer Resort: An Ecological Analysis of a Satellite Community* (Philadelphia, University of Pennsylvania Press, 1941).

treats *components* of urban regions, not urban regions as units. Characteristically, most of the large cities (over 500,000 population) were economically diversified, while smaller urban centers showed a *tendency* to be specialized in economic and occupational functions.[4] In the same vein, Paul Gillen classified 1,073 cities (10,000 population and over) by constructing for each a *profile of occupational distribution* and assigning weighted scores for each city.[5] The result is a typology that is quite arbitrary, the categories of which cannot be meaningfully described or labeled (see accompanying table).

TABLE 1

Typology of Cities by Profile of Occupational Distributions, as Expressed in Occupational Scores

BASIC OCCUPATIONAL TYPE OF CITY*	Occupational score range
A	118 +
B	109–117
C	103–108
D	95–102
E	84–94
F	0–83

* Each type is based on predominance of high status, high income, high educational kinds of occupations, with decreasing occupational status from A to F.

SOURCE: Paul G. Gillen, *The Distribution of Occupations as a City Yardstick*, p. 105.

2. Stage of development

If urban regions are to be distinguished in a sociologically useful manner, at least two additional problems must be considered. First, cities and their dependent areas are creative, historical, and constantly developing entities. World cities vary considerably in age, pace of development and growth, and range of community problems. Amsterdam and Cleveland, for example, are not easily comparable because of differing periods and patterns of growth. Indeed, staying within American society, New Orleans was ecologically quite different from

[4] Grace Kneedler, "Functional Types of Cities," in Paul K. Hatt and Albert J. Reiss, Jr., eds., *Reader in Urban Sociology* (New York, The Free Press of Glencoe, 1951), pp. 49–57.

[5] Paul B. Gillen, *The Distribution of Occupations as a City Yardstick* (New York, King's Crown Press, 1951), p. 105.

Cincinnati—until about twenty-five years ago.[6] Consequently, it seems worthwhile to posit *stages* or *phases* in urban development as a means of comparing and differentiating specific urban centers. At least two attempts to discover *processual* stages have been made that deserve some attention.

Griffith Taylor, an urban geographer, focuses on *ecological* developments and changes in land use in the following series of stages:[7]

Infantile: no clear distinction between residential, commercial, and industrial areas.

Juvenile: fairly clear segregation of a commercial district near town or city center, but continuing mixture of shops, offices, and small industries.

Early mature: definite differentiation of residential areas in terms of status, with movement of higher status areas toward the periphery.

Mature: concentration of industrial areas along railways, with major community growth likewise following railway patterns; separation of industrial segment from residential segments.

In cities of over 50,000 population:

1. nearby villages are assimilated by growing city, while satellite villages (at some distance) become separate municipalities.
2. construction of highways, huge viaducts, and bridges to improve traffic between sections of the urban region.
3. satellite communities gradually become formally annexed to the city.
4. regional controls are exercised through zoning laws and their extension, county councils (as in London), metropolitan commissions, regional authorities (such as the Port of New York Authority).

This kind of classification presents a well-ordered succession of changes in the more tangible aspects of urban development. However, it seems to be most directly applicable to industrial regions and to diversified urban regions. Since these types are most frequently found in the Western world, and since the important cities of the East seem to be slowly developing toward these types, Taylor's classification is one valuable guide in urban analysis.

A classification that involves a more *sociocultural* approach to ur-

[6] Harlan W. Gilmore, "The Old New Orleans and the New," *American Sociological Review,* IX (Aug., 1944), pp. 385–394.

[7] Griffith Taylor, *Urban Geography* (New York, E. P. Dutton and Company, 1946), pp. 76–81, 422–423.

ban development has been offered by Patrick Geddes and modified somewhat by Lewis Mumford. As the titles of some of the stages indicate, this classification clearly contains personal judgments (as well as descriptions) of successive phases, which are of course interesting but not sociological. In the following summary of Mumford's stages, we shall ignore these valuations; the reader who wishes a lucid discussion and defense of such judgments is invited to consult Mumford's book.[8]

1. *Eopolis:* the pre-urban village community.
2. *Polis:* the proto-urban community, marked by partial division of labor in the economic sphere, the development of specialized crafts, sciences, and associations; the retention of such rural features as familism and ancestral religious types; a relatively undeveloped ecological organization; and close, interdependent ties with a narrow regional area.
3. *Metropolis:* the rise of a dominant polis, based on strategic location, secure food supply, and attractiveness to migrants; extensive trade with other regions and cultural interchange; development of heterogeneous population; highly developed division of labor and cultural specialization; decline of family influence and rise of individualism; fixation on money as material and symbol; centralized administration, public and private; social divisions into classes and minority groups.
4. *Megalopolis:* emphasis on bigness, expansion of space and scope of construction; the city comes to dominate the region by military or financial-commercial means; standardization, facilitated by money, of most activities (recreation, education, art, architecture, consumption); triumph of complex organization, bureaucratization, and impersonality; smaller cities are drawn into megalopolitan network.
5. *Tyrannopolis:* the city becomes extremely economically-oriented; the budget, taxation, expenditures are dominant mechanisms; politics as a struggle for control of public funds by special interest groups; white collar crime; insufficient revenue prompts appeals for national aid and a consequent lessening of urban autonomy; population exodus to outskirts of the region as an escape from a variety of undesirable living conditions.
6. *Nekropolis:* the final logical (rather than actual) stage of dis-

[8] Lewis Mumford, *The Culture of Cities* (New York, Harcourt, Brace & World, 1938), pp. 285–292.

organization; ghost cities and the resurgence of rural communities.

Mumford's approach to developmental stages has the advantage of emphasizing the broad cultural and organizational character of urban evolution. To a great extent, it complements Taylor's concern with the *ecological* and *physical* evolution of urban centers. But both classifications are couched in terms of *Western* civilization, which limits the present application of these types to the more familiar urban regions of Europe and North America. A distinct contribution of Mumford's basic scheme, however, is its regard for the changing *functional* nature of urban regions—as evolving constellations of interrelated groups, spatial units, and institutionalized activities. Stripped of its value judgments and prophecies, such a classification gives promise of definite sociological utility.

3. The cultural factor

Classifications of urban regions by dominant activities and/or developmental stages tend to assume a universal *rationality* and *freedom of development* in world cities. One finds in many discussions an implicit notion of an "urban dynamic" impelling cities toward economic complexity, physical and organizational expansiveness, and higher levels of functional unity (sometimes judged to be of a detrimental or irresponsible kind).[9] This view is understandably ethnocentric, based on our knowledge and underlying attachment to *American* urban processes. A wider comparative approach would indicate that several types of *cultural differences* help to account for peculiarities of urban regions that are otherwise not explainable. At least three forms of cultural differences may be considered relevant to the problem of classification.

The Culture of Racial Attitudes

As centers of opportunity and varied experiences, urban areas have inevitably attracted or encouraged migration of distinctive racial, religious, and nationality groupings. The process of assimilating these

[9] See Howard W. Odum, *Understanding Society* (New York, Macmillan, 1947), Chaps. XVII, XVIII; Georg Simmel, *The Sociology of Georg Simmel*, trans. by Kurt H. Wolff (New York, The Free Press of Glencoe, 1950), pp. 409–424; John W. Bennett and Melvin M. Tumin, *Social Life* (New York, Alfred A. Knopf, 1948), Chaps. XXI–XXIII.

"minority groups" into urban social and ecological organization is, however, dependent on the values held by the resident majority. In particular, urban regions may be distinguished to some extent in terms of their underlying attitudes toward racial minorities (especially Negroes). These attitudes are reflected in opportunities for freedom in residential selection, occupational mobility to higher status jobs, and participation in the civic affairs of the region. Perhaps three types may be noted here:

1. Formal assimilation

In regions such as metropolitan New York, legal assurance of opportunities for racial groups has expanded the educational, occupational, and political scope of Negroes. Residential restrictions have in recent years been proscribed by law, though informal restrictions continue to operate in the outer edges of the region.

2. Informal segregation

Many Southern urban regions—and Chicago as well—have effectively contained their respective Negro populations within one or two concentrated districts, largely through private restrictions supported by widespread public opinion and the acquiescence of local councils, commissions, officials, and courts. Under these circumstances, the segregated populations constitute relatively complete communities, whose members are linked with the larger community through employment and the provision of public services.

3. Legal segregation

In such urban regions as Durban, South Africa,[10] where "minority groups" are numerically superior, segregation and *apartheid* are key values to the politically dominant European whites. Consequently, these cities are marked in varying degrees by legal restrictions on nonwhites with respect to voting, property-holding, commercial activities, and residential location. In Durban, the situation is complicated by the existence of several nonwhite categories: Africans (Negroes); Coloreds (Negro mixtures); and Hindus. However, under these conditions, the "orthodox" structure of urban regions is greatly altered.

[10] Leo Kuper, *Durban: A Study in Racial Ecology* (London, Jonathan Cape, Ltd., 1958).

For example, in Durban, the high status white population lives principally in a narrow, irregular band around the bay and along the Indian Ocean. Nonwhites, by contrast, are mainly located in a broad, outer crescent to the west.

Political Intervention of the State

We have become accustomed to emphasizing the *functional autonomy* of urban regions—that is, their relative freedom from larger political and administrative units in carrying out typical urban activities. Many cities in the Western world certainly fit this pattern and consequently are able to shape their own development. But some cities—notably Washington, D.C., and Paris—have been cultural wards of a national government; whether by positive consent, resignation, or acquiescence, these cities reflect in their structure and operation historic decisions made by extramunicipal or extraregional authorities. Paris, for example, owes its current physical pattern (common to few major cities) to Napoleon III and his forceful Prefect of the Seine, Baron Haussmann.[11] Washington, D.C., on the other hand, is an urban anomaly in that its resident population is wholly dependent on a Congressional committee, which is not at all answerable to the community it administers.

Traditional and Symbolic-Sentimental Values

If we continue to narrow our attention to American cities—most of which are no more than one hundred years old—the importance of tradition can be easily (and mistakenly) ignored. European and Asiatic cities have long histories as *cities;* often the values of the distant past intrude in contemporary urban centers and effectively restrict the development of "modern" urban features (such as zonal developments and relatively uncontrolled competition for space). Firey has shown,[12] for example, that Boston's deviation from "typical" urban development could be understood by the desire to preserve historic landmarks and high status residential areas and the extended

[11] Good accounts of both the man and his planning activities may be found in Brian Chapman, *The Life and Times of Baron Haussmann* (New York, Macmillan, 1957); David H. Pinckney, *Napoleon III and the Re-Building of Paris* (Princeton, Princeton University Press, 1958).

[12] Walter Firey, *Land Use in Central Boston* (Cambridge, Mass., Harvard University Press, 1947).

refusal of successful immigrant groups (Italians) to leave their fellow
countrymen for the unfamiliar suburbs. Rome, Tokyo, Amsterdam,
Hong Kong, Edinburgh, Vienna, and other cities are still unmistakably
attached to ancient traditions—in housing, street patterns, religion,
etc.—which are difficult to root out, though they are being modified
and, in part, replaced.

A Suggested Classification

How can these major dimensions or considerations be combined
to provide a generally useful classification of urban regions—one
that takes account of urban variety and basic, converging similarities?
The accompanying figure presents a *tentative plan* for incorporating
the crucial features discussed in this chapter. Essentially, it distinguishes urban regions on the basis of ecological organization—which
is analyzed in Part II—and dominant institutional function. Secondary attention is given to the "cultural" factor. Indeed, it may be
useful to conceive of this factor in its various forms as a temporary
deterrent to the development of more "rationalized" urban types. A
great deal of historical material on world cities seems to indicate this
fundamental direction in urban development.[13] Furthermore, this
graphic classification explicitly excludes educational, religious, and
artistic centers, since these are no longer *dominant* functions of modern urban regions.

Since urbanization seems to be concentrating toward the left side
of the figure, most of our discussion in succeeding chapters will reflect
this emphasis. However, it is important to approach the dominant
types in this classification as parts of a larger picture of development.
In the recent past, we have mainly contrasted urban regions with
rural communities to sharpen our understanding of the former. It is
also necessary to make comparisons, wherever possible, between *types*
of urban regions, so that we can discover what is distinctive about urbanization in general, as well as about particular stages or types of urbanization.[14]

[13] William A. Robson, ed., *Great Cities of the World* (London, Allen and
Unwin, 1954); Robert E. Dickinson, *The West European City* (London,
Routledge and Kegan Paul, 1951); Horace Miner, *The Primitive City of
Timbuctoo* (Princeton, Princeton University Press, 1953).

[14] This view is well stated by Gideon Sjoberg, "Comparative Urban Soci-
ology," in Robert K. Merton *et al.*, eds., *Sociology Today* (New York, Basic
Books, 1959), pp. 334–359, and in his *The Pre-Industrial City* (New York,
The Free Press of Glencoe, 1960).

FIGURE 2
Synoptic Classification of Urban Regions

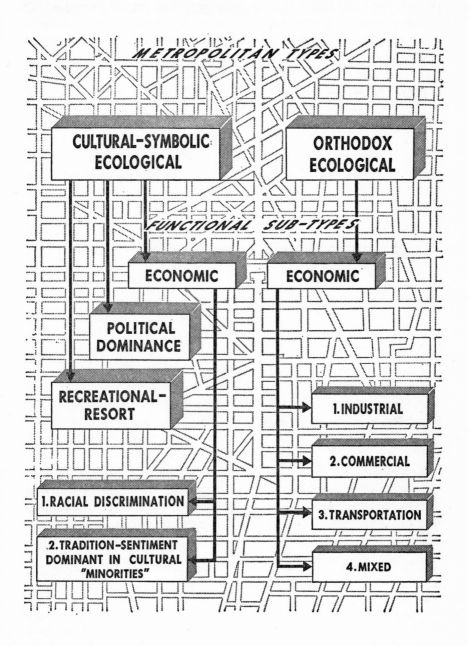

SELECTED REFERENCES

MUMFORD, Lewis, *The Culture of Cities* (New York, Harcourt, Brace, and World, 1938), pp. 283–299.

SJOBERG, Gideon, *The Pre-Industrial City* (New York, The Free Press of Glencoe, 1960).

TAYLOR, Griffith, *Urban Geography* (New York, E. P. Dutton and Company, 1946).

PART II

The Interplay of
Demographic,
Ecological
and Cultural Themes

CHAPTER 4

The Peopling of
Urban Regions:
Basic Population
Characteristics and Trends

UNFORTUNATELY, POPULATION STATISTICS have little attraction for many students and laymen; this kind of information seems to be painfully dull, too often simply confusing, too technical, and only vaguely relevant to the social and cultural interests of the unwary consumer of reports and tables. But to the student of cities and urban regions, population facts provide an indispensable basis for analyzing organization and development. Let us briefly explore the reasons.

It is first important to recognize that population facts supply us with four types of information about a given area:

1. *Size:* the total number of persons in an area at a given time.
2. *Distribution* and *density:* the relative concentration or dispersal of persons within a land area.
3. *Composition:* the distribution of relevant physical and sociocultural characteristics among the members of a population (*e.g.,* sex, age, race, occupation).
4. *Changes* in each of the preceding: the direction and degree of change in an area's population, with clues to the explanation of such changes.

Any *single* variety of population facts (*e.g.* size or density) is admittedly dry and potentially productive of yawns. However, if we consider these four types of population data in terms of their interrelationships, we may then find them extremely useful. Perhaps the attitude we should adopt is that population facts—studied as intertwined sets— serve as *dual indicators* of community and regional organization. Obviously, population statistics—especially those dealing with the composition or make-up of an area's population—give us vital information about the *availability* of persons for the area's functioning, and also its relative *similarity to adjacent or distant areas*. In short, patterns of social interaction and social distance can be clarified by knowledge of the socially pertinent characteristics of an area's population aggregate. In a recent study of Baltimore's population,[1] for example, delinquent behavior was found to be most concentrated in census tracts containing sizeable proportions of whites and nonwhites, rather than in predominantly white or predominantly Negro tracts— holding other population factors constant. The probable explanation for this finding is that areas with mixed population present greater opportunities for frustrating contacts, resultant personal tensions, and motivation for delinquent solutions.

Our major concern in this chapter is to present a simplified review of crucial population features and important trends in modern urban regions. At the present time, truly comparative statistics for the world's urban regions on many important aspects of population are not available. In fact, it is still difficult to obtain reasonably standardized definitions of urbanized population units, and therefore comparable figures on urban population size and composition, for most of the nations reporting. Consequently, we shall concentrate on data for the United States, with some attention to selected portions of world population data where these seem useful.[2]

RECENT GROWTH OF URBAN POPULATION

The revival of the city as an important type of population center can be approximately traced to the beginning of the nineteenth century for the Western nations and late nineteenth or early twentieth century for the rest of the world. In most cases, the development of numerous

[1] Bernard Lander, *Towards an Understanding of Juvenile Delinquency* (New York, Columbia University Press, 1954), pp. 32–34.

[2] See the recent attempt to obtain comparable population figures by Kingsley Davis, *The World's Metropolitan Areas* (Berkeley, University of California Press, 1959).

TABLE 2

Percentage of World's Population Living in Cities, by Regions

AREAS	In cities of 20,000 plus	In cities of 100,000 plus
World	21	13
Oceania	47	41
North America (Canada and U.S.A.)	42	29
Europe (except U.S.S.R.)	35	21
U.S.S.R.	31	18
South America	26	18
Middle America and Caribbean	21	12
Asia (except U.S.S.R.)	13	8
Africa	9	5

SOURCE: Kingsley Davis, "The Origin and Growth of Urbanization in the World," *American Journal of Sociology,* LX (March, 1955), p. 434. Copyright 1955 by the University of Chicago.

TABLE 3

Percentage of Urban Population and Percentage of Population in Cities of 100,000 and Over, for Selected Countries

COUNTRY AND YEAR	Urban	Cities of 100,000 and over
Scotland	82.9	50.7
England and Wales, 1951	80.7	51.9
Israel, 1951	77.5	39.9
Australia, 1947	68.9	51.4
United States, 1950	63.7	43.7
Belgium, 1947	62.7	25.8
Spain, 1950	60.5	23.3
France, 1946	52.9	21.7
Greece, 1940	47.2	19.1
Japan, 1950	37.5	25.6
U.S.S.R., 1939	32.8	17.1
Egypt, 1947	30.1	19.2
Philippines, 1948	24.1	9.3
Korea, 1949	19.6	14.7
India, 1951	17.3	6.8
Ceylon, 1946	15.4	5.4
Haiti, 1950	12.5	4.6

SOURCE: Don J. Bogue, *The Population of the United States* (New York, The Free Press of Glencoe, 1959), p. 34.

urban concentrations has been spurred by industrialization and/or the economic policies of newly created national entities. As Davis and Hertz indicate, the advance of world urbanization has been rapid—

TABLE 4

Percentage Distribution of Urban and Rural Population in the United States by Size of Place, 1790 to 1950

URBAN AND RURAL TERRITORY BY POPULATION OF AREA	1950		1940	1930	1920	1910	1900	1890	1850	1830	1810	1790
	New urban definition	Old urban definition										
United States	*100.0*	*100.0*	*100.0*	*100.0*	*100.0*	*100.0*	*100.0*	*100.0*	*100.0*	*100.0*	*100.0*	*100.0*
Urban territory	*64.0*	*59.0*	*56.5*	*56.2*	*51.2*	*45.7*	*39.7*	*35.1*	*15.3*	*8.8*	*7.3*	*5.1*
Places of 1,000,000 plus	11.5	11.5	12.1	12.3	9.6	9.2	8.5	5.8	—	—	—	—
Places of 500,000 to 1,000,000	6.1	6.1	4.9	4.7	5.9	3.3	2.2	1.3	2.2	—	—	—
Places of 250,000 to 500,000	5.5	5.5	5.9	6.5	4.3	4.3	3.8	3.9	—	—	—	—
Places of 100,000 to 250,000	6.3	6.4	5.9	6.1	6.2	5.3	4.3	4.4	2.8	1.6	2.1	1.6
Places of 50,000 to 100,000	5.9	6.0	5.6	5.3	5.0	4.5	3.6	3.2	1.2	1.7	1.1	1.2
Places of 25,000 to 50,000	5.8	6.3	5.6	5.2	4.8	4.4	3.7	3.6	2.6	.8		
Places of 10,000 to 25,000	7.9	8.3	7.6	7.4	6.7	6.0	5.7	5.5	2.4	1.9	1.5	1.2
Places of 5,000 to 10,000	5.4	5.2	5.1	4.8	4.7	4.6	4.2	3.8	2.6	1.8	1.6	1.2
Places of 2,500 to 5,000	4.3	3.7	3.8	3.8	4.1	4.1	3.8	3.6	1.4	1.0	1.0	1.1
Places under 2,500	.4	—	—									
Unincorporated parts of urbanized areas	4.9											
Rural territory	*36.0*	*41.0*	*43.5*	*43.8*	*48.8*	*54.3*	*60.3*	*64.9*	*84.7*	*91.2*	*92.7*	*94.9*
Places of 1,000 to 2,500	4.3	3.6	3.9	3.9	4.5	4.6	4.3	4.0	—	—	—	—
Places under 1,000	2.7	2.7	3.3	3.6	4.0	4.3	4.0	3.6	—	—	—	—
Other rural territory	29.0	34.7	36.4	36.4	40.3	45.5	52.0	57.3				

SOURCE: Bogue, *op. cit.,* p. 35.

48

particularly since 1900.[3] It is equally clear that urbanites still constitute a minority of world population, though the proportions of urbanites vary considerably by continent and by nation.

Perhaps it is more revealing to investigate the growth of urban populations by focusing on growth patterns for different size categories. This is summarized for the United States for the period 1790 to 1950 in Table 4. Virtually all size categories have increased their proportionate share of a growing national population. However, comparing the situation in 1900 with the present, the largest relative gains can be found in the categories 500,000 and over, followed by the 25,000 to 500,000 set of cities. The evidence therefore indicates not only an increasing concentration of urbanized population groups, but also an increasing proportion of urban population in the larger centers (see Table 5).

Realistically, however, as we shall see in some detail in Chapter 7, the pattern of urban growth is somewhat obscured if we confine our analysis to politically defined cities. Since 1950 the Census Bureau, urban demographers, and many users of population statistics have found it necessary to gather or apply urban population facts in terms of such more comprehensive units as "urbanized areas" and "standard metropolitan areas" (SMA). The latter unit, which is now widely used in the United States, deals mainly with the largest and economically most important urban areas. It is defined as containing one or more (but within 20 miles of one another) central cities of 50,000 or over, plus adjacent counties that exhibit arbitrarily defined "urban" characteristics. These include: either a minimum of 10,000 nonagricultural workers, or areas containing at least 10 per cent of the SMA's nonagricultural worker supply, or at least half of county population living in clusters of 150 or more per square mile. The county's employed labor force must be at least two-thirds in nonagricultural occupations; at least 15 per cent of county workers have employment in the central city; at least 25 per cent of those working in the adjacent county live in the central city (or its county limits), or a monthly average of four or more telephone calls per subscriber from the adjacent county to the central city county.[4] This expanded unit seems to provide more valid measures of urbanization and, with increasing importance, it

[3] Kingsley Davis and Hilda Hertz, "The World Distribution of Urbanization," in Joseph J. Spengler and Otis D. Duncan, eds., *Demographic Analysis* (New York, The Free Press of Glencoe, 1956), p. 324.

[4] See Amos H. Hawley, *The Changing Shape of Metropolitan America* (New York, The Free Press of Glencoe, 1956), pp. 5–6.

TABLE 5

Urban Population Within and Outside Urbanized Areas, by Size of Population, 1950

TYPE OF AREA AND SIZE OF POPULATION	Number of areas	Per cent of total population	Per cent of total
Urban Total	*4,284*	*64.0*	*100.0*
Within Urbanized Areas	—	*46.0*	*71.8*
Central cities, total	172	32.1	50.1
Cities of 1,000,000 or more	5	11.5	18.0
Cities of 500,000 to 1,000,000	13	6.1	9.5
Cities of 250,000 to 500,000	22	5.3	8.3
Cities of 100,000 to 250,000	55	5.5	8.5
Cities of 50,000 to 100,000	68	3.4	5.4
Cities under 50,000	9	0.3	0.4
Urban fringes, total		13.9	21.6
Outside Urbanized Areas	*3,253*	*18.1*	*28.2*
Places of 50,000 or more	21	0.8	1.2
Places of 25,000 to 50,000	172	3.9	6.2
Places of 10,000 to 25,000	547	5.5	8.5
Places of 5,000 to 10,000	908	4.1	6.5
Places of 2,500 to 5,000	1,605	3.7	5.8
Urbanized Areas, Total	*157*	*46.0*	—
Areas of 1,000,000 or more	12	25.1	54.6
Areas of 500,000 to 1,000,000	13	5.8	12.6
Areas of 250,000 to 500,000	24	5.8	12.5
Areas of 100,000 to 250,000	70	7.2	15.7
Areas of 50,000 to 100,000	38	2.1	4.5

SOURCE: Bogue, *op. cit.*, p. 38.

allows for more meaningful comparisons of trends in subareas of urban regions.

Tables 6, 7, and 8 present the essential data for analyzing the nature and degree of urban growth in the United States since 1900. Table 6 demonstrates that urban regions have experienced steady growth, proportionate to total population increase, except for the 1930–1940 period of depression. In general, the SMA's have grown 2–3 and one half times faster than nonmetropolitan areas—again with the exception of the 1930's. Currently, urban regional increase in population accounts for more than 80 per cent of the entire population increase in the United States.

However, as Table 7 shows, the central cities are increasing in population at a decreasing rate. In fifty years, the central city's share

TABLE 6

Growth of Standard Metropolitan Areas, 1900–1950

CENSUS YEAR	NUMBER OF SMA'S	Population (millions) in SMA's	Per cent of U.S. population in SMA's	Rate of growth during preceding decade U.S.	SMA	Non-metrop. areas	Per cent of total U.S. growth claimed by SMA's during preceding decade
All SMA's	162	85.6	56.8	14.5	21.8	6.0	80.6
Principal SMA's							
1950	147	84.3	56.0	14.5	21.8	6.3	79.3
1940	125	67.1	51.1	7.2	8.3	6.2	57.7
1930	115	61.0	49.8	16.1	27.0	7.1	76.2
1920	94	46.1	43.7	14.9	25.2	8.1	67.6
1910	71	34.5	37.6	21.0	32.6	15.0	53.1
1900	52	24.1	31.9	20.7	—	—	—

SOURCE: Bogue, *op. cit.,* p. 47.

in population increased overall by about 50 per cent, while the peripheral areas of SMA's increased their share by over 200 per cent. If we examine growth trends by size of SMA, as in Table 8, we find some interesting variations. The largest SMA's (over one million) have had the largest relative decline in growth rate, with the next largest decline in SMA's of 250,000 to 500,000. Other size categories have had more moderate declines, while a slight *increase* in growth rates is found in those of 500,000 to 1,000,000 population. Perhaps these trends can be understood by examining growth patterns for central cities and ring areas separately. In general, the trend has been toward a declining share of SMA growth contributed by central cities in every size category. But the increase in ring area growth varies considerably. Thus, ring growth has been particularly marked in the 500,000 to 1,000,000 category, which accounts for the continued growth rate of this category (especially during the forties). On the other hand, ring growth has been relatively less in SMA's under 100,000 and in the 250,000 to 500,000 group. In the million and over category, while ring growth is comparatively greater than in 1900, it has not been sufficient to counteract the decline in central city contribution to population increase. At this point, we shall not examine the influence of migration between rural and metropolitan areas, and between segments of metropolitan areas.

TABLE 7

Growth of Standard Metropolitan Areas, by Central Cities and Rings, 1900–1950

CENSUS YEAR	NUMBER OF SMA's	Per cent of U.S. population Central cities	Rings	Rate of growth during preceding decade Metrop. areas	Central cities	Rings	Per cent of total U.S. population growth claimed by SMA's during preceding decade Central cities	Rings
All SMA's, 1950	*162*	*32.8*	*24.0*	*21.8*	*13.9*	*34.7*	*31.6*	*49.0*
Principal SMA's								
1950	147	32.3	23.8	21.8	13.7	34.8	30.7	48.6
1940	125	31.6	19.5	8.3	5.1	13.8	22.8	34.9
1930	115	31.8	18.0	27.0	23.3	34.2	43.3	32.9
1920	94	28.9	14.8	25.2	26.7	22.4	46.8	20.8
1910	71	25.0	12.7	32.6	35.3	27.6	37.4	15.7
1900	52	21.2	10.7	—	—	—	—	—

SOURCE: Bogue, *op. cit.*, p. 49.

TABLE 8

Per Cent Distribution of Population Increase in SMA's by Type of Place and Size of Central City, 1900–1950

POPULATION OF CENTRAL CITY AND TYPE OF PLACE	1940–1950	1930–1940	1920–1930	1910–1920	1900–1910
1,000,000 and over	100.0	100.0	100.0	100.0	100.0
central cities	33.3	46.8	55.6	61.7	68.4
satellite areas	66.7	53.2	44.4	38.3	31.6
500,000–1,000,000					
central cities	23.8	11.9	33.1	57.3	47.9
satellite areas	76.2	88.1	66.9	42.7	52.1
250,000–500,000					
central cities	50.2	50.3	58.0	70.5	62.0
satellite areas	49.8	49.7	42.0	29.5	38.0
100,000–250,000					
central cities	38.4	28.1	61.9	74.1	72.4
satellite areas	61.6	71.9	38.1	25.9	27.6
Under 100,000					
central cities	45.0	40.4	63.8	69.7	67.8
satellite areas	55.0	59.6	36.2	30.3	32.2

SOURCE: Hawley, *The Changing Shape of Metropolitan America*, p. 48.

Of course, much of the recent growth of SMA's is directly traceable to *suburbanization*. While the term "suburb" is not used by the Census Bureau, it is possible to approximate measures of suburban growth by figures on "ring" growth, but especially those designated as "urban rings" or "urban fringe" (within which, according to Duncan and Reiss, 70 per cent live in suburban areas, *i.e.*, incorporated or unincorporated places of 2,500 or more). Suburban movements, of course, have been notable only since the twenties; they seem to be an accompaniment of growth in industrialized urban areas.[5]

Table 9 gives comparative growth rates of suburbs (urban rings) and other segments of SMA's by decade, and also for various size categories. With succeeding decades, suburban growth rates maintain a decided superiority over those of central cities, outer rings in general, and SMA's as a whole. This relation holds for all SMA categories for the fifty-year period as a whole, though not for the 1930–1950 period in comparison to total ring population for most SMA sizes. Consequently, suburban population now accounts for about 24 per cent of the urban region in the U. S.[6]

Another way of approaching suburbanization and peripheral urban growth in general is by comparing growth by concentric zones from the central city (see Table 10). As we would expect, peripheral growth became quite marked in the twenties and thirties for all city sizes. But each size category exhibits its own pattern of increase. Smaller cities had their greatest proportionate increase in the 0–10 mile zone, while medium-sized cities tended to grow somewhat more in the 5–10 mile zone. The larger cities (over 500,000) show a shift in zonal growth. During 1900–1920, their major peripheral growth was in the 0–10 mile zone. However, after the thirties the previous 10–mile limit of substantial population increase was extended to a 20–25 mile radius. In general, then, these zonal trends in growth support the familiar concept of constantly enlarged urban concentrations. But it does not allow us to conclude that urban populations are in process of decentralization or dispersion.[7]

Let us return to this question below in considering urban migration features.

[5] For a summary of suburbanization in Latin America see Kingsley Davis and Ana Casis, "Urbanization in Latin America," in Paul K. Hatt and Albert J. Reiss, Jr., eds. *Reader in Urban Sociology* (New York, The Free Press of Glencoe, 1951), pp. 156–157.

[6] Otis Dudley Duncan and Albert J. Reiss, Jr., *Social Characteristics of Urban and Rural Communities, 1950* (New York, John Wiley and Sons, 1956), pp. 118–119.

[7] This point is discussed by Donald J. Bogue, *The Population of the United States* (New York, The Free Press of Glencoe, 1959), p. 55; and by Svend Riemer, *The Modern City* (Englewood Cliffs, N.J., Prentice-Hall, 1952), pp. 120–121.

TABLE 9

Per Cent Increase in Population of SMA's, Central Cities, and Rings, 1900–1950, Based on 125 SMA's of 1940

PARTS OF SMA'S AND DECADE	Total	Size of SMA in 1940 (thousands)						
		3,000– over	1,000– 2,999	500– 999	350– 499	250– 349	150– 249	100– 149
Number of areas	*125*	*3*	*8*	*13*	*18*	*18*	*34*	*31*
SMA's total								
1940–50	21.3	12.2	25.7	25.3	17.9	28.7	28.2	26.9
1930–40	8.3	5.4	8.5	11.8	6.1	10.6	11.3	10.9
1920–30	27.1	26.8	36.0	23.6	20.0	21.9	29.1	24.1
1910–20	25.5	22.0	32.6	20.8	23.3	32.5	28.0	23.0
1900–10	32.3	33.6	33.9	32.2	29.9	32.9	36.6	22.8
1900–50	177.2	144.4	229.3	176.4	140.6	205.8	221.9	163.8
Central cities								
1940–50	13.0	6.0	13.5	14.6	14.5	21.9	18.3	24.6
1930–40	5.1	3.8	4.5	7.5	3.7	7.3	6.9	6.5
1920–30	23.6	19.9	28.5	20.2	19.1	25.6	34.0	29.3
1910–20	27.4	19.1	34.8	22.4	29.4	44.0	39.0	34.3
1900–10	36.2	32.5	32.6	37.1	40.8	42.1	55.8	37.2
1900–50	214.9	260.4	310.6	231.3	120.1	173.1	182.6	109.8
Rings, urban								
1940–50	28.8	19.3	33.9	40.0	17.0	34.5	42.2	50.6
1930–40	9.1	6.6	10.8	14.4	3.0	10.0	14.3	13.8
1920–30	48.4	58.1	54.8	36.1	33.7	23.5	36.4	36.7
1910–20	38.8	46.2	43.7	23.4	23.2	31.2	64.4	26.4
1900–10	51.3	60.0	53.3	41.5	38.5	50.8	57.7	45.7
1900–50	338.0	370.0	405.9	280.5	174.8	261.8	474.8	331.6
Rings, rural								
1940–50	41.8	44.1	54.1	50.9	27.5	41.3	42.4	27.1
1930–40	19.8	17.2	20.8	28.5	15.9	19.0	19.1	19.8
1920–30	18.9	17.8	30.0	26.0	12.8	13.1	18.6	12.6
1910–20	8.4	4.9	7.1	11.1	9.0	12.9	8.4	6.2
1900–10	10.6	10.4	15.0	7.9	6.2	14.8	14.5	4.7
1900–50	142.1	130.4	198.0	192.9	93.0	146.7	149.7	90.5
Rings, total								
1940–50	34.7	25.7	40.0	45.2	23.0	39.2	42.4	30.5
1930–40	13.8	9.1	13.7	20.7	10.0	16.1	18.1	18.9
1920–30	33.9	46.2	46.9	31.4	21.6	16.4	22.0	15.6
1910–20	22.0	31.0	29.5	17.3	14.6	18.1	15.9	8.4
1900–10	25.8	37.3	35.7	22.6	16.9	23.0	18.8	7.9
1900–50	214.9	260.4	310.6	231.3	120.1	173.1	182.6	109.8

SOURCE: Bogue, *op. cit.*, p. 51.

TABLE 10

Percentage Distribution of Population Increase in Standard Metropolitan Areas, by Size of Central City and Distance Zone, 1900–1950

SIZE OF CENTRAL CITY AND DISTANCE ZONE	1940– 1950	1930– 1940	1920– 1930	1910– 1920	1900– 1910
1,000,000 and over	*100.0*	*100.0*	*100.0*	*100.0*	*100.0*
Central cities	33.3	46.8	55.6	61.7	68.4
0–5 miles	0.4	−0.3	1.1	2.4	2.7
5–10 miles	12.3	10.2	9.9	8.3	6.2
10–15 miles	18.1	11.9	10.7	11.6	9.9
15–20 miles	14.2	13.1	9.0	6.2	4.6
20–25 miles	7.1	8.0	6.9	3.8	3.2
25–30 miles	4.5	4.0	2.9	2.8	2.2
30–35 miles	4.3	3.0	1.5	2.0	1.0
35 miles and over	3.8	3.3	2.4	1.2	1.8
500,000–1,000,000	*100.0*	*100.0*	*100.0*	*100.0*	*100.0*
Central cities	23.8	11.9	33.1	57.3	47.9
0–5 miles	3.0	2.9	6.7	10.5	17.9
5–10 miles	36.6	41.1	36.2	13.9	22.9
10–15 miles	18.3	20.6	11.1	5.2	6.9
15–20 miles	8.9	12.0	7.9	6.5	3.5
20–25 miles	4.9	7.1	2.1	3.5	0.4
25–30 miles	2.3	3.1	2.2	2.6	−0.1
30–35 miles	1.2	0.4	0.2	0.3	0.4
35 miles and over	1.0	0.9	0.5	0.2	0.2
250,000–500,000	*100.0*	*100.0*	*100.0*	*100.0*	*100.0*
Central cities	50.2	50.3	58.0	70.5	62.0
0–5 miles	8.3	6.5	10.6	7.5	4.2
5–10 miles	26.3	26.2	24.5	12.0	17.8
10–15 miles	8.2	12.3	5.8	4.3	4.5
15–20 miles	5.5	2.2	0.8	2.7	4.6
20–25 miles	1.4	2.2	0.3	2.8	3.6
25–30 miles	0.1	0.3	0.0	0.0	2.5
30–35 miles	—	0.0	0.0	0.1	0.7
35 miles and over	—	0.0	—	0.1	0.1
100,000–250,000	*100.0*	*100.0*	*100.0*	*100.0*	*100.0*
Central cities	38.4	28.1	61.9	74.1	72.4
0–5 miles	18.0	20.5	11.9	8.9	9.8
5–10 miles	29.8	33.1	17.3	12.0	12.7
10–15 miles	10.4	8.7	4.6	4.8	5.2
15–20 miles	2.8	8.8	3.0	0.5	0.2
20–25 miles	0.6	0.9	1.3	−0.2	−0.1
25–30 miles	0.3	−0.1	0.0	−0.1	0.0
30–35 miles	0.1	0.1	0.0	0.0	−0.1
35 miles and over	−0.4	−0.1	0.0	0.0	−0.1

SOURCE: Hawley, *op. cit.*, p. 49.

TABLE 11

Age Composition of the United States Population, by Urban and Rural Residence, in Terms of the Life Cycle, 1950

STAGE IN LIFE CYCLE	AGE GROUP	Urban	Rural non-farm	Rural farm	Per cent-point change, 1940–1950			
					Total	Urban	Rural non-farm	Rural farm
All ages		*100.0*	*100.0*	*100.0*	—	—	—	—
Childhood	*0–8*	*16.7*	*20.5*	*20.4*	*3.6*	*4.6*	*3.9*	*2.1*
Infancy	0–1	2.0	2.3	2.1	0.6	0.7	0.5	0.3
Early childhood	1–5	9.8	11.9	11.6	2.4	3.1	2.5	1.4
Late childhood	6–8	4.9	6.2	6.8	0.6	0.9	0.8	0.5
Youth	*9–17*	*11.4*	*14.6*	*19.0*	*-2.9*	*-3.0*	*-2.0*	*-1.1*
Preadolescence	9–11	4.0	5.2	6.4	-0.5	-0.5	-0.3	—
Early adolescence	12–14	3.8	4.9	6.5	-1.1	-1.1	-0.7	-0.4
Late adolescence	15–17	3.6	4.5	6.1	-1.4	-1.5	-1.0	-0.7
Adulthood	*18–64*	*63.8*	*56.3*	*53.0*	*-2.0*	*-2.9*	*-3.3*	*-2.0*
Early maturity	18–24	10.8	10.6	9.3	-2.1	-1.9	-1.7	-3.3
Maturity	25–44	31.7	28.3	24.5	-0.2	-1.1	-1.2	0.4
Middle age	45–64	21.3	17.4	19.3	0.4	-0.1	-0.5	1.0
Old age	*65–over*	*8.2*	*8.6*	*7.6*	*1.4*	*1.4*	*1.3*	*1.0*
Early old age	65–74	5.6	5.7	4.8	0.8	0.8	0.7	0.6
Advanced old age	75–over	2.5	2.9	2.3	0.6	0.5	0.6	0.4

SOURCE: Bogue, *op. cit.*, p. 101.

POPULATION COMPOSITION IN URBAN REGIONS

If urban patterns of growth are reasonably clear, the *composition* of urban populations presents several problems of analysis and understanding. Viewing the diversity of world urban areas, and also the changes in given cities over several generations, it is difficult to distinguish temporary or "accidental" trends from fundamental and characteristic population traits. The relative age of cities, their economic bases and broad cultural functions, geographic location, and the nature of specific urban historical events (*e.g.*, diversion of railroad lines to other areas)—all of these subtly combine to create some diversity in population features. Essentially, urban populations are confluences of migration waves over several generations. Therefore, conditions both in cities and nations at large affect urban characteristics through the complex media of migration and social mobility. Let us try to be faithful to urban diversity and yet search for the most probable ingredients in the urban make-up. We may find that several widespread notions about cities require basic alteration, and even discard.

Age Distribution

Virtually all the available data for various nations, and for a period as long as 70 years, indicate that urban populations are relatively younger than rural categories. The materials for such a comparison are presented for the United States in Tables 11 and 12, for Japan in Table 13, and for India in Figure 3. As we shall see later in more detail, this differential in age distribution is primarily a result of young urbanward migration from rural and small town areas; (*b*) ruralward migration of older urban dwellers; and for the United States, the vast numbers of young European immigrants up to 1920. However, urban-rural age differences show some tendency to decrease, principally in the 0–4, 20–29, 45–64, and 65 and over categories.

Nevertheless, the apparently typical concentration of urban populations in the productive age groups (20–44), compared with rural areas, exists in the United States in all major geographic regions. (See Table 14). There is some tendency for Southern urban areas to show a lower median age—28–30 years—as compared with 32–33 years for most of the other regions. This is perhaps due to the survival of rural population patterns in Southern cities, *e.g.*, a comparatively

FIGURE 3

Age Distribution in the Largest Cities of India as a Percentage of the All-India Distribution, 1931

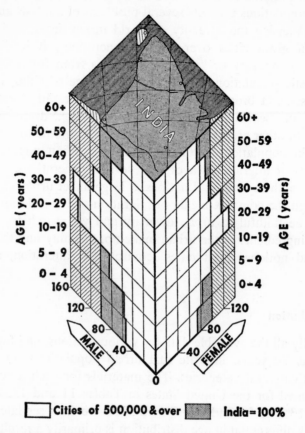

☐ Cities of 500,000 & over   ▨ India = 100%

SOURCE: Kingsley Davis, *The Population of India and Pakistan* (Princeton, Princeton University Press, 1951), p. 141.

higher proportion in the 9–19 age group and a relatively lower proportion in the over 65 category.

In suburban or ring areas, the age composition differs somewhat from that of central cities. As an area typically settled by young families with children, suburban areas consequently have a lower median age than central cities.[8] There is, understandably, a substantially greater proportion in the 0–13 suburban group, a slightly higher proportion in the 14–19 and 25–44 groups, and somewhat less in the 20–24 and 45 and over groups. Whether this reflects the attractiveness

[8] Duncan and Reiss, *op. cit.*, pp. 120–121.

TABLE 12

Age Composition of Urban and Rural Areas: 1890 to 1950

AREA AND YEAR	MEDIAN AGE	Total	Per cent distribution by age 0–4	5–19	20–29	30–44	45–64	65– over
Urban (new definition)								
1950	31.6	100.0	10.1	20.5	16.7	23.0	21.4	8.2
1940	31.0	100.0	6.7	23.4	18.1	23.7	21.2	6.9
1930	28.4	100.0	8.2	26.3	18.3	24.0	18.2	5.1
1920	27.4	100.0	9.7	26.1	19.2	23.5	17.0	4.2
1910	26.3	100.0	9.9	26.8	20.9	23.1	15.2	4.0
1890	24.6	100.0	10.7	29.1	22.1	21.7	13.4	3.0
Rural nonfarm								
1950	27.9	100.0	12.1	25.7	15.5	20.5	17.5	8.6
1940	27.7	100.0	9.3	27.6	17.1	21.0	17.9	7.3
1930	25.8	100.0	10.5	29.8	16.3	20.1	16.7	6.5
1920	25.1	100.0	11.6	29.8	16.6	20.1	15.9	6.0
Rural farm								
1950	26.3	100.0	11.4	30.9	12.0	18.6	19.4	7.5
1940	24.4	100.0	10.0	32.7	15.2	17.3	18.2	6.6
1930	21.6	100.0	11.1	36.2	14.2	16.9	16.4	5.1
1920	20.7	100.0	12.7	36.2	14.7	17.2	14.7	4.4

SOURCE: Bogue, *op. cit.*, p. 103.

TABLE 13

Age Distribution in Japan, by Size of Commune, 1930 and 1950

AGE GROUP	All Japan	100,000 & over	50,000– 99,999	10,000– 49,999	5,000– 9,999	Under 5,000
	1930					
0–5	16.5	14.4	15.8	16.8	17.3	17.1
6–14	20.1	16.4	18.2	20.0	21.3	21.4
15–19	10.2	13.1	12.3	10.8	9.5	8.5
20–64	48.5	53.4	50.7	48.5	46.8	46.9
65 & over	4.7	2.7	3.0	3.8	5.1	6.1
	1950					
0–4	13.5	13.0	13.5	14.0	13.7	13.3
5–14	21.9	19.7	21.2	22.5	23.1	22.9
15–19	10.3	10.3	10.5	10.4	10.4	10.0
20–64	49.4	53.4	50.6	48.5	47.3	47.4
65 & over	4.9	3.6	4.1	4.6	5.5	6.4

SOURCE: Irene B. Taeuber, *The Population of Japan* (Princeton, Princeton University Press, 1958), p. 77.

TABLE 14

Age Composition of Geographic Divisions, by Urban and Rural Residence, 1950

GEOGRAPHIC DIVISION	Total	Per cent distribution by age					65 & over
		0–4	5–19	20–29	30–44	45–64	
U.S. Total	*100.0*	*10.7*	*23.2*	*15.7*	*21.9*	*20.3*	*8.2*
U.S. Urban	*100.0*	*10.1*	*20.5*	*16.7*	*23.0*	*21.4*	*8.2*
New England	100.0	9.5	20.4	15.8	22.0	22.7	9.7
Middle Atlantic	100.0	9.1	19.5	16.0	23.8	23.3	8.2
East North Central	100.0	10.2	20.3	16.6	22.9	22.0	8.1
West North Central	100.0	10.2	20.4	16.7	21.2	21.8	9.5
South Atlantic	100.0	10.6	21.4	18.3	24.0	19.0	6.8
East South Central	100.0	11.1	22.6	18.1	22.7	18.5	7.0
West South Central	100.0	11.6	22.9	18.1	22.5	18.2	6.6
Mountain	100.0	11.7	23.2	16.8	21.9	18.8	7.7
Pacific	100.0	10.3	19.1	16.2	24.0	21.6	8.9
U.S. Rural Nonfarm	*100.0*	*12.1*	*25.7*	*15.5*	*20.5*	*17.5*	*8.6*
New England	100.0	11.2	23.1	14.6	21.5	19.7	9.9
Middle Atlantic	100.0	10.9	23.5	15.0	21.6	19.7	9.3
East North Central	100.0	11.8	24.2	14.8	20.5	18.5	10.0
West North Central	100.0	10.7	23.0	13.2	18.7	20.9	13.5
South Atlantic	100.0	13.2	28.0	17.5	20.5	14.7	6.0
East South Central	100.0	13.4	28.3	16.5	19.5	14.8	7.2
West South Central	100.0	12.4	27.7	14.8	19.7	17.0	8.3
Mountain	100.0	13.3	28.2	15.3	20.3	16.2	6.6
Pacific	100.0	11.9	24.6	16.0	21.9	18.1	7.5
U.S. Rural Farm	*100.0*	*11.4*	*31.0*	*12.0*	*18.6*	*19.4*	*7.6*
New England	100.0	9.7	26.6	11.9	18.6	22.1	10.9
Middle Atlantic	100.0	10.2	27.4	12.9	18.8	21.4	9.4
East North Central	100.0	10.3	27.9	11.6	19.1	21.9	9.0
West North Central	100.0	11.2	28.5	12.2	19.9	20.9	7.3
South Atlantic	100.0	12.1	34.5	12.4	17.5	16.6	6.8
East South Central	100.0	12.2	34.0	11.9	17.6	17.1	7.3
West South Central	100.0	11.5	32.2	11.3	18.7	19.3	7.1
Mountain	100.0	12.3	31.4	12.8	19.5	18.4	5.6
Pacific	100.0	10.0	26.9	11.5	20.8	23.4	7.6

SOURCE: Bogue, *op. cit.*, p. 109.

of the suburb for families with children or the encouragement of fertility among settled suburban families is not clear. In any case, the age distribution of suburban areas is a product of selective migration of families with high "urban" birth rates.

It may be instructive to examine the effect of urban size on age distribution, particularly since the number of larger urban areas is increasing from decade to decade (see Table 15). In general, the

TABLE 15

Age Composition of the United States Population, by Area and Population, 1950

AREA AND POPULATION	All ages	Age Groups by percentage 0–4	5–19	20–34	35–44	45–64	65 & over
Total United States	*100.0*	*10.7*	*23.2*	*23.3*	*14.3*	*20.3*	*8.2*
Urbanized areas							
3,000,000 or more	100.0	9.2	18.8	24.2	16.3	23.6	7.8
1,000,000 to 3,000,000	100.0	10.0	20.0	25.2	15.3	21.9	7.6
250,000 to 1,000,000	100.0	10.5	20.1	25.4	14.8	21.3	7.8
Less than 250,000	100.0	10.6	21.3	25.0	14.6	20.5	8.0
Outside urbanized areas							
25,000 or more	100.0	10.5	21.8	25.4	13.8	20.2	8.4
10,000 to 25,000	100.0	10.5	22.3	24.7	14.0	19.7	8.8
2,500 to 10,000	100.0	11.0	23.4	23.5	13.6	19.2	9.2
1,000 to 2,500	100.0	11.0	24.3	21.8	13.3	19.4	10.3
Incorporated places less than 1,000	100.0	10.3	24.3	19.0	12.4	20.7	13.5
Other rural	*100.0*	*12.2*	*29.1*	*20.8*	*12.8*	*17.9*	*7.4*
Nonfarm	100.0	12.9	26.8	23.8	12.9	16.3	7.2
Farm	100.0	11.5	31.2	17.9	12.6	19.3	7.5

SOURCE: Bogue, *op. cit.*, p. 117.

larger urban regions have smaller proportions of younger people (0–19) and larger proportions of those in the 20–64 categories. Undoubtedly, these differences are largely a result of fertility differences among the size categories, as summarized in Table 16, and perhaps

TABLE 16

Fertility Ratio* of the U.S. Population, for Central Cities and Suburbs of Urbanized Areas, by Size of Area, 1950

POPULATION OF AREA	Total area	Central cities	Suburbs and urban fringe
Average of all urbanized areas	476	452	534
3,000,000 or more	433	404	495
1,000,000 to 3,000,000	478	444	531
250,000 to 1,000,000	503	480	569
Under 250,000	510	490	586

* Children under 5 years of age/1000 women aged 20–44.
SOURCE: Otis D. Duncan and Albert J. Reiss, *Social Characteristics of Urban and Rural Communities, 1950* (New York, John Wiley, 1956), p. 121.

also a consequence of differences in age distribution of migrants to each size category.

Sex Ratio

The sex ratio (the number of males per 100 females) is one of the most sensitive aspects of population composition, since it records the effects of selective migration. (Differential death rates also affect sex ratios, of course.) However, there has been a tendency to inflate the *significance* of *general* sex ratios, particularly when ratios diverge from a presumably desirable standard of equality. From the urban sociologist's standpoint, sex ratios not only reflect family structure and problems, but also economic conditions, and the nature of available services in different parts of the community.

Urban sex ratios appear to be extremely varied, if we examine different societies, different types and sizes of urban regions, specific segments of urban regions, and different age categories.

TABLE 17

Sex Ratio of Urban and Rural Areas, by Color and Nativity, 1910–1950

		White			Nonwhite		
AREA AND YEAR	ALL CLASSES	*Total*	*Native*	*Foreign born*	*Total*	*Negro*	*Other races*
Urban							
1950							
(*new definition*)	94.6	94.9	94.3	100.5	91.6	90.0	151.8
1940	95.5	96.1	94.5	106.8	90.2	88.1	191.4
1930	98.1	98.5	96.0	111.2	94.2	91.3	216.0
1920	100.4	100.5	96.9	115.9	98.6	95.4	276.9
1910	101.7	102.2	97.3	118.9	95.9	90.8	571.6
Rural Nonfarm							
1950							
(*new definition*)	103.6	103.6	103.1	116.3	102.7	101.7	115.0
1940	103.7	103.9	102.8	124.4	100.9	99.8	118.6
1930	105.0	105.0	102.9	132.6	104.5	102.8	133.0
1920	106.5	106.6	102.7	146.2	105.4	103.7	134.7
Rural Farm							
1950							
(*new definition*)	110.1	111.4	110.8	136.5	102.7	101.7	121.1
1940	111.7	113.1	112.2	140.3	104.1	103.1	122.4
1930	111.0	113.0	111.6	139.3	102.2	101.2	123.4
1920	109.1	110.8	109.5	136.2	100.9	100.3	121.9

SOURCE: Bogue, *op. cit.*, p. 159.

Focusing on the United States, we find that urban areas tend to have consistently lower sex ratios than rural areas. Indeed, the urban sex ratio has declined in successive decades (see Table 17). If on the other hand, non-Western urban regions are examined, the situation is quite different. In India, urban sex ratios are higher than rural ratios, and also show a progressive *increase* from 1890 to 1940. Similarly, in Japan, urban sex ratios show a surplus of males, but this seems to be declining. Nevertheless, Japanese cities also maintain a higher sex ratio than that of rural areas. We must conclude, then, that specific urban sex ratios reflect the larger society rather than a typical demographic pattern for urban communities.

TABLE 18

Sex Ratio of Urban and Rural Population: India, 1891–1941

DATE	Urban	Rural
1891	112.2	103.7
1901	111.9	103.0
1911	116.9	103.7
1921	120.9	104.3
1931	121.9	104.6
1941	122.8	104.8

SOURCE: Kingsley Davis, *The Population of India and Pakistan* (Princeton, Princeton University Press, 1951), p. 139.

Within the same society, urban sex ratios likewise fall into several types. Industrial cities and "military" cities, such as Norfolk, San Diego, Detroit, and San Francisco, have relatively high sex ratios. On the other extreme, commercial and administrative centers tend to have rather low sex ratios (between 80 and 90 males per 100 females). In general, the highest urban sex ratios can be found in the largest urban regions, perhaps because these cities furnish more balanced employment opportunities for both sexes. Smaller cities, on the other hand, seem to develop a wider range of sex ratios than other size categories; both rather high and rather low ratios are primarily found in this group.[9] It is likely that, since smaller cities are more specialized occupationally, they tend to be especially attractive to male rather than female migrants, or vice versa.

Since the urban region is a complex of communities, we would expect some variation in sex ratios in its different segments. White

[9] *Ibid.*, p. 44; Joseph H. Greenberg, *Numerical Sex Disproportion* (Boulder, Colo., University of Colorado Press, 1950), pp. 21–23.

TABLE 19

Sex Ratios in Japan, by Types of Area, 1920–1955

TYPE OF AREA AND AGE GROUP	Males per 1,000 Females				
	1920	1930	1940	1950	1955
Metropolitan, total	*1,103*	*1,107*	*1,061*	*1,001*	*1,022*
0–4	1,016	1,023	1,027	1,048	1,060
5–14	1,063	1,048	1,042	1,031	1,039
15–19	1,239	1,191	1,194	1,073	1,179
20–34	1,189	1,189	1,040	952	1,052
35–49	1,142	1,197	1,171	1,005	911
50–64	1,006	998	1,004	1,072	1,044
65 and over	674	666	662	685	720
Other industrial, total	*1,032*	*1,025*	*1,024*	*966*	*974*
0–4	1,014	1,017	1,028	1,043	1,064
5–14	1,018	1,012	1,019	1,025	1,218
15–19	1,043	997	1,052	988	961
20–34	1,105	1,084	1,041	901	972
35–49	1,068	1,102	1,114	973	907
50–64	995	982	976	1,000	999
65 and over	764	736	717	726	722
Intermediate,* total	*1,015*	*1,020*	*1,005*	*950*	*944*
0–4	1,018	1,019	1,029	1,052	1,036
5–14	1,030	1,024	1,020	1,019	1,019
15–19	1,067	1,052	1,022	1,000	982
20–34	1,081	1,101	1,041	883	911
35–49	996	1,037	1,051	925	862
50–64	980	952	950	976	981
65 and over	795	775	744	723	771

* Areas with 40–49% of gainfully employed in agricultural work.
SOURCE: Taeuber, *op. cit.*, p. 79.

sex ratios are lowest in central cities and adjacent urbanized areas; they show an approximately equal proportion of the sexes in suburban and urban fringe areas; and are similar to the high sex ratios of the farm population in the outer or rural fringe of the urban region. Incidentally, all segments of American urban regions are developing lower sex ratios, which may be partially attributed to the decline in the foreign-born, and the increasing proportion of nonwhites (who tend to have comparatively lower sex ratios; see Table 17).

Another internal comparison deals with sex ratios by differentiated cultural areas of the central city. Adequate comparative material on this point is not available, but intensive studies of such cities as Chicago, Cincinnati, and Los Angeles enable us to discern rather sharp differences. In the innermost zones of Chicago and Cincinnati, the

TABLE 20

Males Per 100 Females in the Civilian Population, by Type of Residence, April, 1959 and 1950

RESIDENCE	1959	1950
Total	*95.2*	*97.3*
Standard metropolitan		
statistical areas	*93.5*	*94.9*
Urban	91.5	93.6
Rural nonfarm	100.7	102.1
Rural farm	106.4	109.3
Other territory	*97.6*	*100.4*
Urban	91.8	93.3
Rural nonfarm	97.8	100.6
Rural farm	105.7	108.2

SOURCE: *Civilian Population of the United States, by Type of Residence, April, 1959 and 1950*. Bureau of the Census, Current Population Reports, Series P–20 (Washington, D.C., Feb. 25, 1960), p. 3.

sex ratio is high, with an understandable preponderance of males in rooming-house districts near the central business area (a ratio of 900 or more). With increasing distance from the center, sex ratios tend to decline—first sharply from 800–900 to just over 100, then more gradually to the 90–95 range.[10] This rough gradient in urban sex ratios, however, is difficult to establish in many cities that do not approximate the concentric pattern of growth found in Chicago. Shevky and Williams have been able to distinguish for Los Angeles levels of sex ratios related to cultural areas, regardless of their *geographic* location in the city.[11] These areas are categorized by *degree of urbanization* and *level of social rank* (based on occupation, education, and income). In general, sex ratios are low in areas of high social rank and highest degree of urbanization (as indicated by low fertility, low proportion of women working, and high proportion of multifamily dwellings). The highest sex ratios are in low social rank and high urbanization areas. From a geographic standpoint, Los Angeles' highest sex ratios are near the downtown area and in Long Beach, while the low sex ratios are in the inner ring of older, fashionable residential areas (Wilshire, Hollywood, and Westlake).

Finally, urban sex ratios may be analyzed for various age groups

[10] Hatt and Reiss, *op. cit.*, p. 288; James A. Quinn, *Human Ecology* (Englewood Cliffs, N.J., Prentice-Hall, 1950), pp. 438–445.

[11] Eshref Shevky and Marilyn Williams, *The Social Areas of Los Angeles* (Berkeley, University of California Press, 1949), map facing p. 70, and p. 77.

in the population. In the United States, high or moderate sex ratios occur in categories under 14 years of age, after which ratios decline progressively in the productive, mature, and old age groups—for all sizes of urban regions. This pattern is a consequence of young female migration to cities, and also of differential mortality rates. Incidentally, urban Negroes show a rise in sex ratio in the 40–60 age group, which may be an indication that the more stable families (with husband present) are clustered among Negroes in the over 40 age group.[12] By contrast, Japan's urban sex ratios favor males at most age groups. The highest ratios have been the 15–19 category for at least forty years, while the lowest (91) is currently in the 35–49 age group.[13]

Marital Status and Household Characteristics

The demographic character of urban families is especially confusing to the layman, and therefore open to many misconceptions and, sometimes, to forebodings about the "instability" of urban family life. What, then, are the special features of urban families, and what is the direction of their development?

TABLE 21

Estimated Median Age at First Marriage by Color and Sex, Urban and Rural, 1950

AREA	Male Total	White	Nonwhite	Female Total	White	Nonwhite
United States	*22.9*	*22.9*	*22.6*	*20.2*	*20.2*	*19.8*
Urban	23.1	23.1	22.5	20.6	20.6	19.9
Rural nonfarm	22.4	22.3	22.8	19.3	19.3	19.5
Rural farm	23.2	23.3	22.5	19.7	19.6	19.8

SOURCE: Duncan and Reiss, *op. cit.,* p. 68. By permission of the publisher.

1. Age at marriage

The overall age for first marriages has been declining since 1940. However, urban whites tend to marry at about the same age as rural whites (probably for different reasons), while rural nonfarm whites (in fringe and suburban areas) show a somewhat lower age at marriage. Urban Negroes marry on the average about eight months earlier than

[12] Duncan and Reiss, *op. cit.,* p. 54; Bogue, *op. cit.,* p. 160.
[13] Irene B. Taeuber, *The Population of Japan* (Princeton, Princeton University Press, 1958), p. 79.

urban whites. Furthermore, according to a recent study by the Office of Vital Statistics, urbanites marry persons closer to their own age than do rural people. This is particularly true for urban whites, who show a median age difference of 2.8 years between husband and wife. Urban Negroes seem to resemble the rural pattern, with a median age difference of 3.7 years. Incidentally, the typical urban age differential is found most frequently among high school graduates, followed by those with some high school, and then by urbanites with one or more years of college (see Table 22).

TABLE 22

Median Years Difference in Age Between Mates, for First Marriages or Remarriages of Husband Between January 1947 and June 1954, by Color, Residence, and Education

| | Median years husband older than wife | |
CATEGORY OF PERSONS	First marriage	Remarriage
Total	3.0	6.1
White	3.0	6.0
Nonwhite	3.6	7.4
Urban-Rural Residence		
Urban	2.9	6.1
White	2.8	5.8
Nonwhite	3.7	—
Rural nonfarm	3.3	5.5
Rural farm	3.8	—
Years of School Completed		
Elementary: less than 8 years	4.0	8.4
8 years	3.7	6.3
High School: 1–3 years	2.9	5.3
4 years	2.8	5.5
College: 1 year or more	3.0	5.7

SOURCE: *Socioeconomic Characteristics of Persons Who Married Between January 1947 and June 1954: United States,* U.S. Public Health Service, Vital Statistics, Vol. 45, No. 12 (Washington, D.C., Sept. 9, 1957), p. 291.

2. Family-building

Perhaps the most controversial aspect of urban population composition is marital opportunities and marital status. In general, rural-urban differences are less marked than many suppose. For white males, the differences are slight, with a rate higher among urbanites. Nonwhite urban males seem to show marriage rates intermediate between those in farm and fringe areas. Among females, however, urban areas show somewhat lower rates than farm and fringe areas for whites, and more comparable rates for nonwhites. Indeed, 91–95 per cent of the urban population (over 14 years of age) has been married at one time or another, compared with 91.8–97 per cent of rural or fringe populations.

Yet the "currently single" present a problem. Apparently, urban males over 14 years of age are also more often single than urban

TABLE 23

Per Cent Ever Married in the United States Population, by Color and Residence, 1950

RESIDENCE	Females		Males	
	White	Nonwhite	White	Nonwhite
Urban	91.0	95.6	91.8	93.6
Rural nonfarm	93.4	95.2	90.6	91.8
Rural farm	95.4	97.1	91.7	96.1

SOURCE: Bogue, *op. cit.*, p. 227.

TABLE 24

Per Cent Distribution of United States Population Over 14 by Marital Status, Sex, and Residence, 1950

MARITAL STATUS AND SEX	Urban	Rural Nonfarm	Farm
Single			
Male	25.0	27.0	31.2
Female	20.6	17.7	20.5
Married (spouse present)			
Male	64.9	62.7	62.1
Female	60.0	65.7	68.9
Separated			
Male	1.8	1.4	1.0
Female	2.4	1.5	1.1
Widowed			
Male	4.1	4.4	3.8
Female	12.7	11.4	7.9
Divorced			
Male	2.2	1.9	1.0
Female	2.9	1.7	0.8

SOURCE: *Census of Population; U.S. Summary, 1950,* Bureau of the Census (Washington, D.C., 1953), pp. 182–188.

TABLE 25

Per Cent of Employed Civilian Population Ever Married, by Major Occupation Group, Sex, and Age, United States, 1957 and 1940

	March 1957			April 1940		
	25–34	35–44	45 & over	25–34	35–44	45 & over
MAJOR OCCUPATION GROUP						
Male, all classes	*83.8*	*92.8*	*93.8*	*74.3*	*88.4*	*91.9*
Professional, technical, and kindred	78.4	91.8	92.3	68.9	87.9	91.7
Farmers and farm managers	84.2	86.1	92.6	84.2	90.9	93.4
Managers, officials, proprietors	89.2	96.9	96.6	81.6	92.9	95.2
Clerical and kindred	77.8	89.1	89.8	67.2	87.1	91.3
Sales workers	86.6	96.5	96.8	71.7	88.8	92.7
Craftsmen, foremen, and kindred	88.8	95.6	96.2	80.2	91.6	94.3
Operatives and kindred	85.1	93.6	93.1	76.7	89.5	92.3
Service workers	81.5	89.8	92.5	70.4	78.3	84.1
Farm laborers and foremen	66.7	76.9	80.9	52.8	66.4	73.2
Laborers, except farm and mine	79.1	86.8	91.3	72.4	84.7	88.4
Females, all classes	*78.6*	*87.5*	*86.6*	*54.4*	*70.8*	*73.8*
Professional, technical, and kindred	63.1	76.8	72.4	33.4	44.5	43.1
Farmers and farm managers	100.0	89.5	97.2	77.4	87.0	89.9
Managers, officials, proprietors	84.7	92.3	90.1	69.2	82.1	83.7
Clerical and kindred	74.6	82.1	80.5	43.7	54.7	51.8
Sales workers	83.9	94.9	93.2	58.2	80.0	79.3
Craftsmen, foremen, and kindred	76.1	83.1	89.5	61.2	77.6	77.3
Operatives and kindred	86.0	87.1	89.5	66.9	82.8	81.3
Service workers	85.3	94.3	90.9	62.7	80.5	82.2
Farm laborers and foremen	90.4	94.9	96.1	73.2	87.8	93.0
Laborers, except farm and mine	89.7	83.8	83.3	65.9	84.2	86.8

SOURCE: *Statistical Bulletin*, Metropolitan Life Insurance Company, Vol. 39 (New York, Jan., 1958), p. 7.

females, but have a smaller proportion of currently unmarried than in farm or fringe communities. Single urban females are proportionately similar to farm areas, but are more concentrated than those in fringe or suburban areas.[14] It is likely that the surplus of single urban females and males is a condition found in the largest metropolitan areas, perhaps a consequence of unfavorable age distributions. However, it is probably necessary to know the importance of educational, occupational, and religious contacts before we can understand these variations in single males and females for urban regions.

Another way of approaching the marital make-up of urban regions is somewhat more detailed and yet indirect. If we analyze marital

[14] Duncan and Reiss, *op. cit.*, pp. 69–71.

status by occupation, several significant differences and trends can be located (see Table 25).

There is considerable difference among occupational marriage rates, part of which does not correspond to rural-urban differences. In 1957, the largest disparity in rates was between farm laborers on the one hand, and skilled workers, sales personnel, and managers and proprietors on the other—in short, a rural-urban differential, but in favor of *urban* occupations. However, among typically urban occupations, the marriage rate for males was lowest among clerical, professionals, operatives, and service workers; and highest among such middle status occupations as craftsmen, sales personnel, and managers. It is therefore unrealistic to speak of "urban marriage rates" without specifying subgroups. As Table 25 suggests, all but two occupational groups show increases in rates for males, but all but one (laborers) show increases for females. Among distinctively urban populations only male clerical workers have had a decrease in marriage rates since 1940. It appears that urban marriage rates are rising, especially in those categories that are most identified with urban prosperity and urban regional expansion.

As a final demographic clue to family-building, let us explore the comparative distributions of types of "family units." The Census Bureau distinguishes: *primary families*—related persons with a family head; *secondary families*—related persons without a recognized head of the household; and *subfamilies*—married couples (with or without children) living with in-laws. Further tabulations are available for family units containing one parent and children (*parent-child groups*) and *unattached individuals* who are either family heads or not (*primary* or *secondary* sub-types). The distributions are summarized in Table 26.

Unfortunately, these distributions are not further broken down by such important categories as race and nationality, or occupation. However, it is clear that cities have somewhat smaller proportions of normal family units (with male heads, and only spouses and children present), larger proportions of families with female heads, as compared to farm and fringe areas.[15] This is undoubtedly due to the higher concentration in urban areas of groups with unconventional family structures (*e.g.,* Negroes and certain foreign-born groups). Secondary families—those without a genuine household head—are

[15] Bogue, *op. cit.,* pp. 281–282.

TABLE 26

Households, Families, and Subfamilies in the United States, by Residence, March, 1960

HOUSEHOLD AND FAMILY TYPES	United States	Per cent distribution Urban & rural nonfarm			
		Total	Urban	Rural nonfarm	Rural farm
Households	*100.0*	*100.0*	*100.0*	*100.0*	*100.0*
Head with no relatives in household	14.7	15.4	17.9	9.8	7.1
Head with relatives	85.3	84.6	82.1	90.2	92.9
Husband-wife households	74.6	73.8	70.2	81.8	85.0
Other households with male head	2.3	2.1	2.3	1.7	3.5
Households with female head	8.4	8.7	9.6	6.7	4.4
Families	*100.0*	*100.0*	*100.0*	*100.0*	*100.0*
Husband-wife families	87.3	86.9	85.2	90.5	91.4
Other families with male head	2.7	2.6	2.9	2.0	3.9
Families with female head	10.0	10.5	11.9	7.5	4.7
Primary families	*100.0*	*100.0*	*100.0*	*100.0*	*100.0*
Husband-wife families	87.6	87.2	85.5	90.7	91.5
Other families with male head	2.6	2.5	2.8	1.9	3.8
Families with female head	9.8	10.3	11.7	7.4	4.7
Secondary families	*100.0*	*100.0*	*100.0*	*100.0*	*100.0*
Husband-wife families	36.4	34.9	38.2	—	—
Other families with male head	22.3	21.4	19.7	—	—
Families with female head	41.3	43.7	42.1	—	—
Subfamilies	*100.0*	*100.0*	*100.0*	*100.0*	*100.0*
Husband-wife subfamilies	57.6	57.4	55.9	60.0	59.0
Other subfamilies with male head	7.5	7.8	7.9	7.8	4.9
Subfamilies with female head	34.9	34.8	36.2	32.2	36.1

SOURCE: *Household and Family Characteristics: March, 1960,* Bureau of the Census, Current Population Reports, Series P–20, No. 106 (January 9, 1961), p. 12.

principally an urban phenomenon, and a substantial part of this group seems to contain unmarried couples or wives without currently available spouses. Finally, subfamilies (families lodging with in-laws) seem to be proportionately similar for urban and rural areas, though the incidence of married couples living with in-laws is greater in farm and fringe areas. It may be concluded, therefore, that urban families are less likely to be conventionally constituted, but are more likely to achieve independent household status.

TABLE 27

Level of School Completed by Persons 25 Years and Over, for the United States Civilian Population, by Area and Size of Place, March 1959

AREA AND POPULATION SIZE	Per cent by level of school completed			
	Less than 5 years of elementary school	4 years of high school or more	4 or more years of college	Median school years completed
United States	8.0	42.9	7.9	11.0
Urban	7.0	45.3	8.8	11.4
In urbanized areas	6.9	45.5	8.9	11.5
Areas of 3,000,000 or more	7.1	46.3	10.3	11.6
Areas of 1,000,000 to 3,000,000	6.0	46.3	8.9	11.6
Areas of 250,000 to 1,000,000	6.7	45.1	8.7	11.5
Areas of less than 250,000	7.8	43.7	7.0	11.2
Not in urbanized areas	7.2	44.8	8.5	11.3
Places of 25,000 or more	5.7	47.3	9.9	11.7
Places of 10,000 to 25,000	7.7	44.3	8.7	11.2
Places of 2,500 to 10,000	7.9	43.6	7.5	11.1
Rural nonfarm	8.2	44.2	7.9	11.1
Rural farm	13.5	26.5	3.1	8.7

SOURCE: *Literacy and Educational Attainment; March, 1959,* Bureau of the Census, Current Population Reports, Series P–20, No. 99 (Feb. 4, 1960), p. 5.

3. Educational Distribution

The increasingly widespread emphasis on more formal education for more young people (and for senior citizens as well) is still an *urban* value, as Table 27 demonstrates for the passing generations in the United States. The sharpest difference, in median school years completed, is almost 3 years of schooling as between the farm population and residents of the largest urban areas. In the past generation or so, urban youth have been two to three times more likely to complete college (and some graduate work) than farm youth. As recently as 1958, greater proportions of urban, as compared to farm and fringe youngsters, were enrolled in school, in every age group from 5 to 19 years. And while proportions in school decline with age, for all residence categories, the proportion in school drops most precipitately for farm youth after the age of 15.

Currently, we have the apparent paradox of higher proportionate enrollments at the elementary and high school levels, among males 16 to 24 years of age, in farm and fringe areas. The same pattern of differences is found for females (see Table 28). However, the major remaining difference in favor of urban youth is at the college level. Indeed, the same sort of difference extends to plans for attending college among present high school seniors. For males, the urban-rural differential is as much as 20 per cent. For females, the small number of farm youth sampled does not allow reasonable comparison. Fringe area seniors seem to anticipate a college career in slightly greater degree than their urban counterparts (see Table 29).

TABLE 28

Educational Status of Persons 16 to 24 Years Old, by Residence and Sex, October, 1959 (Civilian Noninstitutional Population)

EDUCATIONAL STATUS	*Total*		*Urban*		*Rural nonfarm*		*Rural farm*	
	Male	Female	Male	Female	Male	Female	Male	Female
Total	*100.0*	*100.0*	*100.0*	*100.0*	*100.0*	*100.0*	*100.0*	*100.0*
Enrolled in								
Regular school	44.4	30.9	45.4	30.1	44.7	31.0	39.6	35.7
Special school	3.0	3.0	3.8	3.6	2.2	2.2	1.2	1.2
Not enrolled in regular or special school	52.6	66.1	50.8	66.2	53.1	66.8	59.2	63.2
Enrolled in regular school	*100.0*	*100.0*	*100.0*	*100.0*	*100.0*	*100.0*	*100.0*	*100.0*
Elementary school	1.3	0.9	0.9	0.4	1.6	0.7	2.7	3.0
High school, 1st to 3rd year	35.2	37.7	31.3	35.3	40.0	42.0	44.4	40.0
High school, 4th year	24.7	30.4	23.7	30.6	24.1	29.1	31.2	32.6
College	38.7	31.0	44.0	33.7	34.3	28.2	21.6	24.7

Per cent distribution

SOURCE: *Educational Status and School Plans of Farm and Nonfarm Youth, October, 1959*, Bureau of the Census, Series Census-AMS P–27, No. 27 (April 29, 1960), p. 6.

4. Occupational distribution

Since urban regions are principally organized about economic activities, the degree and types of participation in economic functions provide important clues about urbanites. In general, urban areas have a somewhat smaller proportion of their male residents in the labor force, either working or looking for some job. The reverse is true for females. In line with our expectations, labor force participation tends to rise as we turn from the larger to the smaller urban areas. This is probably due to the longer period of formal education found in larger

TABLE 29

Plans to Attend College for High School Seniors, by Residence and Sex: Civilian Noninstitutional Population, October 1959

| | | Per cent by plans to attend college | | |
| | | Plan to | Do not plan | |
RESIDENCE AND SEX	Total	attend	to attend	Undecided
Total	*100.0*	*47.1*	*33.0*	*19.9*
Urban	100.0	50.8	31.0	18.2
Rural nonfarm	100.0	47.0	33.0	20.0
Rural farm	100.0	32.0	41.2	26.8
Male	*100.0*	*49.1*	*28.7*	*22.2*
Urban	100.0	55.0	24.9	20.1
Rural nonfarm	100.0	44.4	31.5	24.1
Rural farm	100.0	34.4	38.8	26.9
Female	*100.0*	*45.2*	*37.3*	*17.5*
Urban	100.0	46.6	37.1	16.3
Rural nonfarm	100.0	49.5	34.5	16.0
Rural farm	—	—	—	—

SOURCE: *Educational Status and School Plans of Farm and Nonfarm Youth, October, 1959,* Bureau of the Census, Series Census-AMS P–27, No. 27 (April 29, 1960), p. 1.

TABLE 30

Labor Force Participation Rates of United States Population Classified by Size of Place, Sex, and Color: 1950

| | White | Nonwhite | White | Nonwhite |
AREA AND POPULATION SIZE	Male		Female	
U.S. total	79.2	76.6	28.1	37.1
Urban areas	79.8	77.0	32.2	42.8
In urbanized areas	80.7	77.8	32.7	42.5
Places of 100,000 or more	80.3	77.9	34.4	42.5
Places of 50,000 or more	80.0	77.5	33.7	44.9
Places of 25,000 or more	81.7	80.1	30.6	42.9
Places of 2,500 to 25,000	81.8	78.5	28.0	41.7
Other urban	81.9	75.0	27.0	38.5
Not in urbanized areas	77.5	74.3	30.9	43.8
Places of 25,000 or more	77.8	75.4	32.9	44.9
Places of less than 25,000	77.4	73.9	30.2	43.4
Rural nonfarm	74.7	67.6	22.2	29.4
Places of 1,000 to 2,500	75.7	72.3	25.2	36.4
Other rural nonfarm	74.2	66.3	20.5	26.8
Rural farm	82.9	83.3	15.1	22.1
Places of 1,000 to 2,500	79.3	81.2	19.5	31.7
Other rural farm	83.0	83.3	15.1	22.0

SOURCE: Bogue, *op. cit.,* p. 444.

TABLE 31

Labor Force Participation Rates for Civilian Population, by Residence, Age, Sex, and Color, 1950

	White			Nonwhite		
AGE AND SEX	Urban	Rural nonfarm	Rural farm	Urban	Rural nonfarm	Rural farm
Males, 14 years						
and over	79.8	74.7	82.9	76.9	67.6	83.4
14–19 years	35.5	38.8	47.6	33.7	42.1	59.8
20–24 years	78.8	85.8	92.6	78.5	75.5	91.3
25–29 years	90.5	90.4	95.4	84.9	75.3	93.7
30–34 years	94.7	92.6	96.6	88.7	79.3	95.5
35–39 years	95.4	92.9	97.0	90.7	82.6	96.7
40–44 years	95.1	91.8	96.8	90.8	83.8	96.3
45–49 years	94.0	89.8	96.2	89.9	82.1	95.9
50–54 years	91.8	85.4	94.2	86.7	78.6	94.7
55–59 years	87.9	79.4	91.8	82.2	73.2	92.7
60–64 years	80.5	70.1	87.3	73.9	66.8	89.1
65–69 years	59.2	48.8	76.4	52.1	47.6	79.6
70–74 years	36.0	29.8	61.0	32.4	30.0	64.9
Females, 14 years						
and over	32.2	22.2	*15.1*	42.8	29.4	22.0
14–19 years	28.1	18.0	13.2	19.1	16.6	17.3
20–24 years	50.2	31.1	24.3	45.2	30.8	25.8
25–29 years	36.0	22.6	17.0	48.3	33.5	24.6
30–34 years	32.9	23.2	16.7	52.5	36.7	24.2
35–39 years	36.1	27.4	17.8	54.9	40.5	25.9
40–44 years	39.3	29.9	18.4	54.5	40.1	26.5
45–49 years	37.9	29.2	17.2	50.9	39.1	26.2
50–54 years	33.8	25.5	14.8	45.7	36.1	25.6
55–59 years	28.7	21.0	12.5	38.8	31.4	23.7
60–64 years	22.9	16.1	10.0	30.5	25.4	19.2
65–69 years	14.2	9.6	7.3	17.6	14.9	14.0
70–74 years	7.3	4.9	5.1	8.7	7.7	8.3

SOURCE: Bogue, *op. cit.*, pp. 427, 430.

cities. Furthermore, suburban and fringe areas tend to have the lowest proportion of gainfully employed persons, as a consequence of greater proportions under 14 years of age (see Table 31). If we compare population types, excluding youngsters, we find that suburban and fringe areas still have lower proportions of males in the labor force, but intermediate proportions (lower than urban, higher than farm) of females. This differential may be due to a concentration of retired males in suburban and fringe areas, and to greater employment opportunities for suburban females, as compared with rural females.

The typical pattern of urban occupations can be approached either in terms of major occupational or skill groups, or by broad types of economic activities (see Table 32). It is clear from this table that urban areas are distinguishable by higher proportions in "urban" skill groups: professional, managerial, clerical, sales, and service workers. Craftsmen and skilled laborers form about equal proportions of urban and suburban categories, both of which are considerably higher than

TABLE 32

Composition of the Employed Labor Force, by Major Occupational Group, Major Industry Group, and Residence, 1950

MAJOR OCCUPATION AND INDUSTRY GROUP	Per cent distribution 1950			Estimated per cent change, 1940–1950		
	Urban	Rural non-farm	Rural farm	Urban	Rural non-farm	Rural farm
Occupation group, total	*100.0*	*100.0*	*100.0*	*27.6*	*49.6*	*=19.8*
Professional, technical, & kindred workers	9.3	6.1	1.2	44.9	35.5	0.5
Farmers & farm managers	0.4	3.0	56.3	—	—	−19.6
Managers, officials, & proprietors	13.0	10.7	2.0	35.9	33.0	−0.9
Clerical & kindred workers	8.4	4.3	1.0	21.7	45.4	28.1
Sales workers	8.2	5.1	1.1	6.1	40.0	5.3
Craftsmen, foremen & kindred	21.2	21.6	5.5	42.7	74.6	31.3
Operatives & kindred workers	21.8	25.0	7.8	28.5	52.4	33.5
Private household workers	0.2	0.2	0.1	—	—	—
Service workers except private household	7.6	4.3	0.8	13.6	38.7	5.4
Farm laborers and foremen	0.6	6.5	19.1	—	56.0	−44.9
Laborers, except farm & mine	8.2	11.8	4.0	8.2	28.2	−15.3
Industry group, total	*100.0*	*100.0*	*100.0*	—	—	—
Agriculture	1.1	9.1	71.0	—	72.7	−25.1
Mining	0.9	4.9	1.3	—	19.5	—
Construction	6.0	8.9	3.1	63.3	89.6	28.7
Manufacturing	29.4	25.6	9.4	31.4	57.1	30.0
Transportation	9.0	7.4	2.1	35.5	54.5	24.9
Trade	21.9	18.0	4.3	33.7	57.3	23.6
Finance	4.4	1.9	0.5	22.8	—	—
Business services	2.7	3.1	0.8	55.1	74.8	—
Personal services	7.2	5.9	1.7	−15.5	6.3	—
Entertainment services	1.2	0.8	0.1	—	—	—
Professional services	9.5	8.4	2.7	44.8	47.8	−12.0
Public administration	5.2	4.0	1.2	74.8	81.4	—

SOURCES: Bogue, *op. cit.*, p. 519; Bogue, "Urbanism in the United States, 1950," *American Journal of Sociology*, Vol. LX (1955), p. 483.

those in farm areas. Incidentally, the greatest percentage increase in urban occupations is in professional, managerial, and skilled worker categories, whereas suburban and fringe communities seem to be growing most noticeably in skilled workers and farm laborers.

A more simplified and perhaps more conspicuous picture can be found in a comparison of major types of work. Not surprisingly, urban areas are particularly concentrated in manufacturing and trade, while farm areas have less than 15 per cent of their labor force in these activities. Urban areas also have higher concentrations in transportation, finance, personal services, entertainment, professional services, and public service. In many of these categories, suburban and fringe populations show considerable similarity to urban areas; likewise, rates of growth in these categories are highest for suburban and fringe areas—evidence that the latter are increasingly "urban" in character.[16]

5. Income distribution

An interest in urban income patterns may have some mercenary implications to some, but the urban sociologist is primarily concerned with the *cultural* and *organizational* consequences of income distributions. For example, comparative income distributions inevitably reflect occupational differences. In addition, income statistics provide measures of comparative *community resources* (for taxation, private welfare funds, etc.) and clues to changing motives or habits in consumption of available goods and services.

As Table 33 demonstrates, urban populations have smaller proportionate shares of low income brackets (under $4000) and larger shares of higher incomes ($10,000 and over), compared to farm and suburban or fringe populations. The differential is greatest between urban and farm populations, as we would expect. Furthermore, the comparative rates of increase (from 1947 to 1959) indicate that suburban areas are narrowing their moderate differential, increasing by 94 per cent while cities increased by 72 per cent. Farm areas show only a 57 per cent rise in median income.

Table 33 also indicates that median income is positively related to size of urban community. Suburban and fringe areas seem to be most similar to cities under 250,000 population, and to densely populated areas (25,000 and over) that are not included in "urbanized areas" as defined by the Census. An interesting income pattern is also

[16] Duncan and Reiss, *op. cit.,* pp. 96, 129, 175.

TABLE 33

Per Cent Distribution of Income Among Families in the United States, 1959, by Area and Size of Place

TOTAL MONEY INCOME FOR FAMILIES	Total	Urbanized areas				Places not in urbanized areas		Rural nonfarm	Rural farm
		Total	1,000,000 and over	250,000 to 1,000,000	Under 250,000	25,000 & over	Under 25,000		
Under $500	1.6	1.5	1.3	1.4	2.2	1.9	1.7	2.3	8.3
$500 to $999	1.7	1.5	1.0	1.8	2.2	2.0	2.6	3.0	8.7
$1,000 to $1,499	3.0	2.8	2.3	3.3	3.4	3.4	3.8	4.0	10.1
$1,500 to $1,999	3.7	3.5	3.0	4.0	4.0	3.6	4.7	4.2	8.9
$2,000 to $2,499	4.1	3.6	3.1	4.6	3.6	4.7	5.5	4.1	9.8
$2,500 to $2,999	4.4	3.9	3.0	4.9	4.9	6.0	5.4	4.6	7.0
$3,000 to $3,499	4.9	4.5	3.8	4.6	6.0	5.8	6.2	5.2	7.9
$3,500 to $3,999	4.6	4.2	3.6	4.2	5.7	5.2	5.7	5.1	5.9
$4,000 to $4,499	5.8	5.7	5.8	5.3	5.9	6.6	5.9	6.1	6.0
$4,500 to $4,999	5.8	5.8	5.5	5.0	7.3	6.7	5.7	6.3	3.9
$5,000 to $5,999	13.6	13.6	13.0	14.9	14.0	12.2	14.0	14.2	6.6
$6,000 to $6,999	11.9	11.8	12.0	11.5	11.8	12.9	11.7	10.9	5.1
$7,000 to $7,999	8.8	9.1	9.2	9.3	8.4	8.2	8.3	9.2	3.2
$8,000 to $9,999	11.9	12.7	13.8	12.1	10.6	11.4	9.3	10.1	3.4
$10,000 to $14,999	10.6	11.8	14.3	19.6	7.8	8.4	7.3	8.0	3.3
$15,000 to $24,999	2.7	3.2	4.0	2.5	1.9	0.9	1.7	2.1	1.6
$25,000 and over	0.8	1.0	1.1	1.1	0.5	0.3	0.6	0.6	0.2
Median income	$5,755	$5,956	$6,366	$5,732	$5,350	$5,348	$5,211	$5,361	$2,800

SOURCE: *Income of Families and Persons in the United States: 1959,* Bureau of the Census, Current Population Reports, Series P-60, No. 35 (Washington, D.C., Jan. 5, 1961), p. 23.

apparent when comparing incomes by age of family heads. The highest median income for farm heads occurs in the 25–34 age group. Suburban and fringe median incomes are highest in the 35–44 group, while the highest median for urban heads is in the 45–54 age group.

Two additional aspects of income distribution have generally been neglected, though they are of some interest. All three population categories attain their highest median incomes in families composed

TABLE 34

Median Family Income by Age of Head and Residence, 1959

TOTAL MONEY INCOME	Age of head					
	14–24	25–34	35–44	45–54	55–64	65 & over
Urban	$4,075	$5,580	$6,366	$6,729	$6,150	$3,335
Rural nonfarm	$3,760	$5,664	$6,347	$5,802	$4,683	$2,195
Rural farm	—	$3,250	$3,196	$3,107	$2,356	$2,176

SOURCE: *Income of Families and Persons in the United States: 1959,* Bureau of the Census, Current Population Reports, Series P–60, No. 35 (Jan. 5, 1961), p. 25.

TABLE 35

Median Family Income by Size of Family and Residence, 1959

TOTAL MONEY INCOME BY RESIDENCE	Families having specified number of persons						
	Total	2	3	4	5	6	7 or more
Urban	$5,755	$4,701	$5,963	$6,355	$6,439	$6,036	$5,945
Rural nonfarm	$5,361	$4,105	$5,136	$5,980	$6,042	$5,951	$5,173
Rural farm	$2,800	$2,049	$2,976	$3,329	$3,750	$3,514	$2,473

SOURCE: *Ibid.,* p. 26.

TABLE 36

Median Family Income by Number of Earners and Residence, 1959

MEDIAN INCOME AND RESIDENCE	Families having specified number of earners				
	Total	None	1	2	3 or more
Urban	$5,755	$1,773	$5,208	$6,676	$8,823
Rural nonfarm	$5,361	$1,476	$5,145	$5,960	$7,160
Rural farm	$2,800	—	$2,397	$3,459	$3,271

SOURCE: *Ibid.,* p. 27.

of five persons (*i.e.,* three children), even though the median size of family differs to some extent between farm and city populations. This may mean that these populations or community types are approaching convergence in desirable family size among the more successful families. A second point of interest concerns the consequences of multiple family earners for median income. In all three population categories, two or more earners are quite prominent. Indeed, for all three categories, families with only one earner show less than median incomes for their respective groups. Only with an additional earner do family incomes surpass the population medians. However, one sharp difference emerges from the statistics. Farm families with three or more earners have median incomes lower than those of farm families with two earners. City and suburban fringe families, on the other hand, show vastly increased median incomes when three or more earners are involved. It may well be that farm families with multiple earners are in the lowest income categories occupationally, while the individual incomes of multiple earner city families are reflections of higher educational and occupational status.

Apparently, there is some significance not only in urban-rural income distributions, but in variations among urban regions. Duncan and Reiss compared high and low income categories of urban population units on a number of demographic and economic items. In general, they found high income areas tended to have more formal education, lower proportions of nonwhites, higher sex ratios, higher proportions in the productive age groups, and higher proportions in professional, managerial, and manufacturing categories.[17]

6. Color, nationality, and religion

It is likely that the widest variation in urban population composition in the world today is in racial, religious, and nationality make-up. These factors are responsive to other features of urban regional operation (economic and political), but are more often reflections of policies in the larger society, opportunities for international migration, and historical idiosyncrasies of individual nations. In cities of India and Pakistan, for example, about two-thirds of the population is Hindu, almost 30 per cent is Muslim, about 3 per cent is Christian.[18] By

[17] *Ibid.,* pp. 351–365.
[18] Kingsley Davis, *The Population of India and Pakistan* (Princeton, Princeton University Press, 1951), p. 142.

TABLE 37

Color, Nativity, and Race Composition of the United States Population, by Area and Population Size, 1950

AREA AND POPULATION SIZE	White			Nonwhite		
	Total white	Native	Foreign born	Total non-white	Negro	Other
United States, total	89.5	82.8	6.7	10.5	10.0	0.5
Urbanized areas						
3,000,000 or more	91.1	74.7	16.4	8.9	8.4	0.5
1,000,000 to 3,000,000	87.6	76.9	10.7	12.4	12.0	0.5
250,000 to 1,000,000	88.6	82.4	6.3	11.4	11.1	0.2
Less than 250,000	90.0	83.5	6.6	10.0	9.7	0.2
Outside urbanized areas						
25,000 or more	90.8	85.7	5.1	9.2	9.0	0.2
10,000 to 25,000	91.2	86.7	4.5	8.8	8.6	0.2
2,500 to 10,000	91.5	87.5	3.9	8.5	8.3	0.2
1,000 to 2,500	92.7	88.9	3.8	7.3	7.0	0.3
Incorporated places less than 1,000	94.5	91.6	3.0	5.5	5.2	0.2
Other rural	87.7	84.8	2.9	12.3	11.5	0.8
Nonfarm	90.2	86.6	3.6	9.8	8.9	0.9
Farm	85.4	83.1	2.3	14.6	13.8	0.8

SOURCE: Bogue, *op. cit.*, p. 138.

contrast, cities in the United States are predominantly Christian, with few Muslims and perhaps 5 per cent who are Jews. Similarly, racial and religious distributions in African and South American cities are clearly different from those in North America and the Far East.[19]

In view of this diversity, we can only make the generalization that urban regions tend to have more diversified mixtures of racial, religious, and nationality categories than rural areas. Let us focus on each of these three separately for the United States.

1. *Color.* The concentration of nonwhites, most of whom are Negroes, is generally greater in urban regions than in small towns and rural areas (except for the South). *Within* urban regions, on the other hand, central cities have higher proportions of nonwhites than do suburban and fringe areas.

2. *Nationality.* Foreign-born persons constitute a larger portion

[19] See Leo Kuper, *Durban: A Study in Racial Ecology* (London, Jonathan Cape, Ltd., 1958); Richard Morse, *From Community to Metropolis* (Gainesville, Fla., University of Florida Press, 1958); Horace Miner, *The Primitive City of Timbuctoo* (Princeton, Princeton University Press, 1953).

of urban populations than of farm or small town categories. However, immigration restrictions since 1920 help to explain a decreasing proportion of the foreign-born in all urban size categories. As in the case of nonwhites, the foreign-born are primarily located in central cities, rather than in suburban or peripheral areas of urban regions. Yet Table 37 also shows considerable variation in proportions of the foreign-born (and of nonwhites) among central city categories and among suburban rings. Geographic location of cities and differentials in job opportunities in previous generations may account for these differences.

TABLE 38

Per Cent Distribution of the United States Population by Race and Nativity for Central Cities and Suburbs of Urbanized Areas, 1950

RACE AND NATIVITY	Total Urbanized Areas	Central cities	Suburbs and urban fringe
Native white	78.9	75.9	86.2
Foreign-born white	10.5	11.1	9.1
Negro	10.2	12.6	4.5
Other races	0.4	0.4	0.2

SOURCE: Duncan and Reiss, *op. cit.,* p. 122.

3. *Religion.* Statistics on religion are notoriously limited in accuracy and often well out-of-date. However, a sample survey taken by the Census Bureau in 1957 is summarized in Table 39. Urban areas tend to have smaller than national, farm, or suburban-fringe proportions of Protestants, higher proportions of Catholics, and considerably higher proportions of Jews.

NATURAL INCREASE

A good deal of apprehension about the urban region's ability to survive demographically was current in the thirties, when urban growth was primarily based on rural-urban migration and high birth rates of recent immigrant families. Clearly, urban birth rates in the United States and most parts of the world have for a long time been lower than rural birth rates. But what does this mean when a greater range of relevant population statistics is examined? How can we reasonably characterize "urban vitality?"

TABLE 39

Per Cent Distribution of Religious Affiliations in the United States Civilian Population, by Residence, March 1957

RELIGIOUS AFFILIATION	Total	Urbanized areas of 250,000 or more	Other urban	Rural nonfarm	Rural farm
Per cent by religion (14 years old and over)					
Protestant	58.6	49.1	71.3	77.8	83.2
White	49.5	38.4	64.4	70.8	72.3
Nonwhite	9.1	10.7	6.9	7.0	10.9
Roman Catholic	31.7	37.8	23.4	16.6	11.9
Jewish	4.9	7.7	1.0	0.5	0.1
Other religion	1.6	1.9	1.2	0.8	0.9
No religion	2.3	2.2	2.4	3.4	3.3
Religion not reported	1.0	1.3	0.6	0.9	0.7
Per cent by residence (14 years old and over)					
Protestant	56.6	27.2	29.5	28.7	14.7
White	55.2	24.5	30.7	30.1	14.7
Nonwhite	66.1	44.6	21.6	19.3	14.5
Roman Catholic	78.8	53.9	24.9	15.8	5.4
Jewish	96.1	87.4	8.7	3.6	0.2
Other religion	77.4	52.9	24.5	14.9	7.7
No religion	54.2	29.5	24.7	31.3	14.5
Religion not reported	68.2	49.5	18.7	23.4	8.4

SOURCE: *Religion Reported by the Civilian Population of the United States: March, 1957,* Bureau of the Census, Current Population Reports, Series P–20, No. 79 (Washington, D.C., Feb. 2, 1958), p. 7.

First, and still the outstanding generalization, is a prevailing difference between urban and rural fertility rates. In the United States, as well as in Japan and India, fertility ratios (the number of children under 5 years of age per 1000 women in childbearing age groups) are lowest in the largest cities and generally increase in smaller population centers.

Second, it is sometimes forgotten that in non-Western cities, and more recently, in the highly industrialized urban regions of the West, urban fertility has been high enough to insure population replacement without migration. Evidence for this is of three sorts. Gross reproduction rates, which measure the supply of females for the next generation of childbearing, tend to be above normal replacement in Japanese

TABLE 40

Child-Woman Ratios in India, by Population of City, 1931–1941

POPULATION OF CITIES	Average child-woman ratio,* 1931	Average child-woman ratio,* 1941
500,000 and over	523	545
100,000 to 500,000	666	621
50,000 to 100,000	649	665
Below 50,000	701	621
Rest of India	770	714

* Obtained by dividing all the children in each class of cities by the number of women aged 15–39 and multiplying by 1,000.
SOURCE: Davis, *The Population of India and Pakistan*, p. 71.

TABLE 41

Number of Children Ever Born per 1,000 Women in Japan, by Age of Women and Area, 1950

AGE OF WOMEN	All Japan	Metrop. areas	Other industrial	Inter-mediate	Agri-cultural
15 and over	*2,634*	*2,085*	*2,455*	*2,689*	*2,825*
15–19	17	14	15	20	17
20–24	416	296	389	452	443
25–29	1,423	1,170	1,329	1,466	1,490
30–34	2,588	2,134	2,468	2,589	2,746
35–39	3,641	2,960	3,374	3,630	3,949
40–44	4,388	3,411	4,044	4,336	4,857
45 and over	4,632	3,864	4,355	4,563	4,928

SOURCE: Taeuber, *op. cit.*, p. 245.

cities, though the figures for 1955 indicate the first descent below replacement. In the United States, India, and other nations, urban areas likewise now show rates above normal replacement.

Another trend that is extremely important is the relative course of urban mortality rates since 1900. For Japan, crude mortality rates have been lower for cities than for rural areas, though both show sharp declines during the last 15 years. In fact, urban mortality rates for females are lower than rural rates, for the younger age groups (10–34 years), while urban mortality rates for males are higher than rural rates only in the 10–14 year group. Turning to the United States, while urban mortality is higher than rural rates, urban rates have dropped to a differential of about 1.5 deaths per thousand population.

TABLE 42

Fertility Ratios of the United States Population, by Size of Place, for Central Cities and Suburbs of Urbanized Areas, 1950

SIZE OF PLACE	Total	Central cities	Suburbs & urban fringe
All urbanized areas	*476*	*452*	*534*
3,000,000 or more	433	404	495
1,000,000 to 3,000,000	478	444	531
250,000 to 1,000,000	503	480	569
Under 250,000	510	490	586
Places outside urbanized areas			
25,000 or more	522	—	—
10,000 to 25,000	525	—	—
2,500 to 10,000	570	—	—
1,000 to 2,500	609	—	—
Under 1,000 (incorporated)	629	—	—
Other rural			
Nonfarm	717	—	—
Farm	766	—	—

SOURCE: Duncan and Reiss, *op. cit.,* pp. 50, 121.

TABLE 43

Gross Reproduction * Rates in Japan, 1925–1955, by Area

AREAS	1925	1930	1947	1950	1955
All Japan	2.6	2.4	2.2	1.8	1.2
Metropolitan	2.1	1.9	1.8	1.5	0.9
Other industrial	2.4	2.1	2.0	1.7	1.0
Intermediate	2.6	2.4	2.2	1.8	1.2
Agricultural	2.8	2.7	2.3	2.0	1.4

* Net reproduction rate equals number of daughters born per 1000 women in child-bearing age groups, less the deaths among women expected under the assumption of persistent death rates for that category.

SOURCE: Taeuber, *op. cit.,* p. 246.

A substantial part of this decline in mortality is found among non-whites in urban areas, somewhat less in rural areas.[20]

The composite effects of fertility and mortality on natural increase can be gauged most directly by *net reproduction rates,* which take account of the supply of new females as adjusted by their probable reduction through mortality. This replacement rate is difficult to obtain for distinct urban and rural components for most nations, but such a

[20] Bogue, *op. cit.,* p. 195.

TABLE 44

Death Rates per 100,000 Population in Japan, by Sex, Age, and Area, 1920–1941

AGE GROUP AND AREA	1920–1921	1925–1926	1930–1931	1935–1936	1940–1941
Females					
10–14					
Six cities	4,437	2.715	2,462	2,290	1,878
Outside	2,559	1,937	1,800	1,711	1,539
15–19					
Six cities	6,394	4,259	3,990	3,637	3,546
Outside	5,927	4,724	4,312	4,394	4,095
20–24					
Six cities	7,059	4,307	4,365	3,835	3,279
Outside	7,130	5,172	5,187	5,049	4,844
25–29					
Six cities	7,293	4,647	4,312	3,903	3,313
Outside	6,802	4,623	4,461	4,365	4,317
30–34					
Six cities	7,031	4,676	4,561	3,850	3,517
Outside	6,323	4,528	4,345	4,028	3,937
Males					
10–14					
Six cities	2,540	1,829	1,746	1,603	1,317
Outside	1,765	1,396	1,317	1,282	1,228
15–19					
Six cities	5,044	3,541	3,459	3,265	3,153
Outside	4,714	3,734	3,734	3,806	4,192
20–24					
Six cities	5,034	3,430	3,758	3,579	3,579
Outside	6,210	4,643	4,987	5,320	4,982
25–29					
Six cities	4,877	3,216	3,367	3,420	2,998
Outside	5,666	3,999	4,115	4,537	4,590
30–34					
Six cities	5,330	3,434	3,676	3,308	3,177
Outside	5,486	3,681	3,671	3,816	4,033

SOURCE: Taeuber, *op. cit.*, pp. 300, 304.

breakdown has been computed for the United States (see Table 47). Clearly, the historic trend in the United States toward low urban replacement rates has been reversed. At present, therefore, American urban regions are more in line with the growth patterns of the less industrialized cities. Furthermore, a careful analysis by Bogue shows that about 70 per cent of the increase in urban population during the forties (and by implication, the fifties as well) can be attributed to

TABLE 45

Crude Mortality Rates for Japan, 1947–1955, by Area

AREA	Deaths per 1,000 total population			
	1947	1950	1952	1955
All Japan	*14.6*	*10.9*	*8.9*	*7.8*
Metropolitan	12.8	8.6	7.0	6.0
Other industrial	14.1	9.9	8.2	7.2
Intermediate	15.1	11.3	9.3	8.3
Agricultural	15.0	11.9	9.8	8.5

SOURCE: Taeuber, *op. cit.*, p. 295.

TABLE 46

Age-Adjusted Mortality Rates, by Color and Residence, United States, 1940 and 1950

RESIDENCE AND COLOR	Deaths Per 1,000 Population	
	1940	*1950*
Urban	11.4	8.9
Rural	9.8	7.4
White urban	10.8	8.5
Nonwhite urban	18.1	13.1
White rural	9.3	7.1
Nonwhite rural	14.4	10.9

SOURCE: C. Horace Hamilton, "A Study of Ecological and Social Factors in Mortality Variation," unpublished paper delivered to the American Sociological Society, 1955.

natural increase—the difference between birth and death rates—while only about 30 per cent of the increase derives from rural-urban migration.[21]

MIGRATION

As much of the preceding discussion in this chapter indicates, migration patterns affect virtually every sort of population statistics. In addition, migration provides an excellent source of information on the inherently dynamic nature of urban regions. Unfortunately, despite their incalculable importance, migration data of a widely comparable and detailed sort are not available for urban analysis. Only in recent years, in fact, have demographers in the United States been able to acquire reasonably adequate *direct* information on migration, and to

[21] *Ibid.*, pp. 39. 55.

TABLE 47

Net Reproduction Rates * for the United States, by Residence, 1942–1947 and 1935–1940

	1942– 1947	1935– 1940	Per cent increase
Urban	1.085	.726	49
Rural nonfarm	1.465	1.150	27
Rural farm	1.859	1.661	12

* Net reproduction rate equals number of daughters born per 1000 women in child-bearing age groups, less the deaths among women expected under the assumption of persistent death rates for that category.

SOURCE: Cited by Noel P. Gist and L. A. Halbert, *Urban Society* 4th ed. (New York, Crowell, 1956), p. 237.

discover recognizable (rather than probable or guessed) patterns in population movements related to the urban region.[22]

One genuinely useful discovery is the fact that several streams of migration coexist in modern urban regions, instead of the oversimplified notion of "rural-urban" migration. These are:

1. *Intra-city migration:* changes of residence within municipal limits in a given time period.
2. *Intra-metropolitan migration:* changes of residence from central city to suburb and fringe areas, or vice versa.
3. *Inter-urban migration:* migration between central cities.
4. *Inter-metropolitan migration:* movements between suburban and fringe areas of different urban regions.
5. *Rural-urban migration:* movements from farms to central cities.
6. *Rural-metropolitan migration:* movements from farms to urban fringes or suburbs.

Urban regional migration, therefore, consists of two aspects: the population characteristics of *incoming* migrant categories; and the character of migrant patterns among *existing* urban populations. In short, migration and mobility are distinguishable into *urban-building* and *urban-dispersion* types. But urban mobility is itself responsive to the particular nature of various urban (or urbanizing) nations. Such

[22] In the past, migration has been estimated by comparing an actual age distribution with one predicted on the basis of mortality rates for each age group. The difference between actual and predicted figures was then taken as a measure of migration.

factors as the current proportions of rural and urban populations, the type and pace of economic growth, the amount and variety of demand for labor, the relative development of large, competitive urban centers —these and others help to account for a substantial diversity in urban migration throughout the world. However, several conclusions about urban migration seem tenable.

In early stages of urban growth, rural-urban migration is most important. This type of migration seems to attract relatively young, single (or married but migrating without family) persons—white and nonwhite—with limited skills and formal education. Sex ratios among migrants are variable, but tend to be selective of more males.[23] In general, long-distance migration to cities is higher among males, shorter distances among females. In addition, migrants in this "stage" tend to settle first in central cities and in the informally designated "migrant zones" (the zone of transition in Western cities, suburban slums in African and some Far Eastern cities). Some interurban migration occurs during this period, it is true; this usually consists of family units with young children.[24]

A later stage in urban migration patterns is reached when economic and residential opportunities have combined to convert the central city into the nucleus of an urban or metropolitan region. Since this has attained its most advanced stage in the United States, let us try to outline the composite of major ingredients of American urban migration and residential mobility as a potential direction for trends in other urban regions.

1. The suburban movement, which has a long history in American cities, began to assume a new level of importance by the late thirties. But the *continuing* migration to suburbs has changed both in character and in its demographic impact on central cities. During the forties—and presumably also in the fifties—suburban migrants came from two "mobile" sources, according to the calculations of Bogue. One source was a category of relatively long-term city residents, which

[23] Taeuber, *op. cit.*, pp. 133, 156–159; Davis, *The Population of India and Pakistan*, pp. 134–136. See also Michael Banton, *White and Coloured* (London, Jonathon Cape, 1959); Sydney Collins, *Coloured Minorities in Britain* (London, Lutterworth Press, 1957); I. Schapera, *Migrant Labour and Tribal Life* (London, Oxford University Press, 1947); E. P. Hutchinson, *Immigrants and their Children, 1850 to 1950* (New York, John Wiley and Sons, 1956).

[24] Ronald Freedman, *Recent Migration to Chicago* (Chicago, University of Chicago Press, 1949), Chap. IV; Taeuber, *op. cit.*, p. 161.

accounts for only about 10 per cent of net suburban population increase. Even this "loss" by the cities was counterbalanced by *urban* migration from nonmetropolitan areas. The other source was migration from farms and population centers outside the SMA's.[25]

2. Suburban and similar peripheral movements were increasingly selective of higher status occupational and racial groups, though there is evidence of surprisingly high Negro migration to urban rings in two Southern areas.

TABLE 48

Sources of Migration to Suburbs in the United States, by Age of Migrant, 1940–1950

AGE	From central cities (net)	From non-metropolitan areas (net)
0–9	40.7	5.9
10–14	5.8	8.0
15–19	—	10.2
20–24	—	12.0
25–29	—	21.2
30–34	7.9	16.9
35–39	9.7	10.0
40–44	7.8	6.8
45–49	5.9	4.4
50–54	4.8	3.1
55–59	4.7	1.3
60–64	3.8	0.8
65–69	2.9	0.4
70–74	3.0	−0.8
75 & over	3.1	−0.2

Per cent distribution of white migrants

SOURCE: Bogue, *op. cit.,* p .407.

3. Age groups among migrants to suburban areas tended to differ by racial group and by community of origin. Migrants from central cities were mainly children under 9 years of age (40.7 per cent); also city migrants were more concentrated in the 40 and over age category than those from nonmetropolitan areas. White migrants from nonmetropolitan areas were somewhat more likely to be older and married than their predecessors a few decades ago, or than nonwhite migrants from nonmetropolitan areas.

[25] Bogue, *op. cit.,* pp. 406–410.

4. Though there have been occasional intimations of this tendency for some years, it is now quite clear that interurban (and to some extent intermetropolitan) migration is even more pronounced than rural-urban or other types. As early as the thirties, rural-urban migration accounted for only about 19 per cent of total migration, while interurban and intermetropolitan types constituted almost half of the migration during 1935–1940.[26] If we focus on the migration of males during 1949, the results are equally striking.[27] This general pattern

TABLE 49

Migration Patterns Among Males in the U.S., 1949, by Community of Origin and Destination

MIGRATION CATEGORY	Per cent
Nonfarm to nonfarm	73.7
Farm to nonfarm	7.2
Farm to farm	7.8
Nonfarm to farm	4.5
Origin not known, to nonfarm	6.3
Origin not known, to farm	.5
Total	*100.0*

SOURCE: Beyer, *Housing,* p. 29.

was previously suggested by a study of migration to Stockholm and in a careful analysis of migration to Chicago in the period 1935–1940. Apparently, most migrants to urban regions come from other urban areas (cities or urban fringe), or in stages of migration from farm to "urban" to metropolitan areas.[28]

5. If we compare rates of migration to any destination *from* cities with those from rural areas, we find that the former are somewhat lower. This means that urban populations tend to be proportionately less *mobile* than ruralites or suburbanites. Furthermore, as Bogue has demonstrated, the *velocity* of migration (*i.e.,* the number of migrants in a given stream as a proportion of its "home" population, multiplied by the population in the specific destination area as a proportion of the population of all potential areas of destination) is lowest for urban to rural migration, rural to urban, and suburban to

[26] *Ibid.,* p. 410.
[27] Glenn H. Beyer, *Housing: A Factual Analysis* (New York, Macmillan, 1958), p. 29.
[28] Freedman, *loc. cit.;* Jane Moore, *Cityward Migration* (Chicago, University of Chicago Press, 1938).

rural types. The highest velocity seems to be found among rural to rural and suburban to suburban streams. In short, urbanites are more "stable" than our folklore suggests, while the greatest proportionate movement is really among the suburbanites and ruralites.

TABLE 50

Streams of Internal Migration Among Urban and Rural Areas in the United States, 1935–1940

ORIGINS AND DESTINATIONS	Per cent distribution (adjusted)	Migration rate (adjusted)	Stream velocity
Total internal migration	*100.0*	*13.0*	*13.0*
In-migration to urban	52.3	11.9	11.9
In-migration to rural nonfarm	28.4	18.2	18.2
In-migration to rural farm	19.3	11.2	11.2
Out-migration from urban	50.9	11.5	11.5
To urban	32.5	7.4	12.9
To rural nonfarm	14.0	3.2	15.8
To rural farm	4.5	1.0	4.4
Out-migration from rural nonfarm	25.0	16.0	16.0
To urban	13.1	8.4	14.7
To rural nonfarm	9.1	5.9	29.2
To rural farm	2.8	1.8	8.0
Out-migration from rural farm	24.1	13.9	13.9
To urban	6.8	3.9	6.8
To rural nonfarm	5.3	3.1	15.3
To rural farm	12.0	6.9	30.7

SOURCE: Bogue, *op. cit.*, p. 410.

6. Since 1940, however, rural-metropolitan migration has increased, probably as a result of World War II and postwar economic opportunities. Likewise, there is some evidence that an increasing part of urbanward migration comes from small towns and villages, rather than farm areas.[29]

Before we attempt to summarize and interpret the specific materials on urban populations that have been presented in this chapter, several limitations must be recognized. First and most important, population data for urban areas of the world are not comparable in definition of units, in accuracy of compilation, and in attention to statistical breakdowns useful for the urban sociologist. Consequently, our discussion

[29] Bogue, *op. cit.*, p. 413.

has been confined to nations with the best record-keeping, and particularly, the United States.

Second, it is difficult to make more than tentative generalizations from population data of the past few decades, since population phenomena seem to show numerous short-term variations, in response to the rapid cultural and social changes of our times. For example, birth rates have been a constant source of difficulty to those who try to make population predictions or to explain rather sharp changes in fertility.

Finally, and this is related to the previous point, population data are products of an infinite number of events and decisions. But these events and the social actions associated with them are the meaningful core of processes that are largely removed from the simplified end-figures (e.g., birth rates). Therefore, analysis of population statistics requires persistent recourse to facets of social organization and attitudinal trends, some of which have not yet been adequately investigated (e.g., the relation of perceived status to fertility). With these limitations in mind, we may draw several plausible implications from urban population trends.

1. Urban population growth has been comparatively high for several generations in the Western world, for 20–50 years in Asia, Africa, and the Pacific region. Statistics show a continually high level of growth, not primarily in central cities, but in regional patterns. Consequently, the old fear of urban decline is at least demographically unfounded.

2. Urban populations consistently show the fundamental urban attribute of heterogeneity. However, the nature of heterogeneity can and does undergo recognizable changes. In American urban regions, internal variations in *nationality, occupation,* and *education* have been reduced, but, on the other hand, there has been a notable increase in the proportion of nonwhites and a continuing broad range of income categories. In other urban regions of the world, particularly where nonwhites are relatively numerous, racial heterogeneity either remains a dominant feature, or is replaced in significance by occupational heterogeneity—when legal and social restrictions are loosened. Throughout the world, urban heterogeneity is patterned through *specialization of function* (occupation, education, income) and through the development of distinctive areas or segments in the urban region ("natural areas," suburbs, *etc.*).

3. Population composition in urban regions seems to be moving

toward the more "normal" patterns of older communities. For example, the initially high proportion of young adults is being replaced by a somewhat "older" concentration in the more advanced urban regions. This is explained by such trends as reduced mortality rates, the decline in immigration, and the shift in economic opportunities toward persons with greater formal education.

Furthermore, the unusual sex ratios of early urban growth are no longer typical of regions that have advanced beyond the pioneer stage of demand for huge pools of unskilled labor. A rough sequence of stages may be posited. In the first phase, industrial needs attract high proportions of male migrants, though mill towns constitute a clear exception. The second phase involves a commercial and clerical functions as supplements to, or competitors of, the industrial focus. Females are consequently attracted in this phase. A third phase accompanies a more balanced economic base and increased opportunities for family life in the city and in an expanding suburban fringe. At this point, sex ratios tend to move from the 80–90 range to the upper 90's—the continuing "excess" of females reflecting differential mortality rather than differential migration.

Another aspect of increasing normality is related to the growing proportion of married persons in urban regions. This is found both in resident groups and in recent migrant streams. Furthermore, the proportion of "complete" families (both mates present), of primary families, and of families with two or more children has recently increased in American urban regions.

4. A surprising trend in urban population is an apparent reversal in the role of natural increase in population growth. It is sometimes forgotten that early migrants to cities have moderately high fertility (though less than rural populations) and therefore contribute substantially to urban growth, quite apart from subsequent rural-urban migration. During the twenties and thirties, at least in the United States and Western Europe, any net increases in urban population were primarily contributed by migration. In the thirties for example, urban net reproduction rates in the United States were about 76 per cent, an indication that urban population would decline by 24 per cent without the counterbalancing effect of migration. Since the mid-forties, however, American urban regions have become self-sufficient in population growth. We can only guess about the continuation of currently high urban birth rates, but it seems likely that they will persist throughout the sixties and early seventies.

5. Despite a good deal of grumbling and literary denunciation of urbanism, urban population statistics tend to support the conclusions that urban regions are here to stay (if humans are not obliterated by their own destructive abilities) and that people are increasingly satisfied with the urban regional life-style. Several kinds of evidence bear on this point. Throughout the world, wherever substantial rural populations exist, urbanward migration continues at a high rate. In highly urbanized societies, and in particular the United States in recent decades, urbanites show little tendency to move to farms or small towns; they move instead within cities, to suburban outposts, or to other cities. Urbanites with greater exposure to life in urban regions seem to be better adjusted to urban complexity than their predecessors (the rural-urban migrants in the nineties to the thirties), though there is some room for improvement in the mental health of contemporary urbanites. They seem to be giving more attention to family formation, to planning for *larger* families than the previous generation of urbanites.

A comparison of urban population statistics for various nations of the world, and for different time periods since 1870 or so, seems to lend support to the idea of "stages" in urban development, as we have suggested in this chapter in terms of demographic data, and in Chapters 2 and 3. In this sense, population data reflect the state of human resources as "inputs" into the community. These very same facts also represent the *products* of social and cultural organization and change in the urban region.

In particular, we can analyze urban population data for basic clues about specific facets of urban life. In Chapter 2, it was suggested that the distinctive characteristics of urbanism include: (*a*) extensive division of labor; (*b*) dominance of commercial, industrial, and "service" occupations; (*c*) high density of population; and (*d*) dominance of social control mechanisms on a nonkinship basis. The necessary evidence for (*a*) and (*b*) is provided by data on occupational and income distributions, educational levels, etc., while census enumerations of population size by well-defined census tracts enable us to measure (*c*). Only in the case of (*d*) do we find population data to be of limited utility.

But other important aspects of urbanism can be directly or indirectly analyzed through adequate population statistics. For example, the extent of social and cultural heterogeneity is largely found in such data as religious and racial distributions, nationality backgrounds, occupational distributions, and also by comparing subareas of the urban region on any population dimension of interest (*e.g.*, sex ratio, non-whites, median age). Likewise, the relative stability or change of urban regions can be measured and understood in some degree by analyzing data for trends in births, deaths, migration, and age distributions. In addition, the urbanite's opportunity (as distinct from motivation) for informal and formal associations with other residents can be estimated from analyses of the present chapter (see pp. 72–82). Perhaps most of our prevalent notions about urban life derive from information and experiences in the earlier and more chaotic phases of urbanism. It is therefore specially important to take account of the latest data and investigations, wherever possible, for clues to continued trends or significant shifts in composition and distribution of urban populations.

This chapter has generally concentrated on population composition and its changes, with only secondary attention to patterns of *distribution*. In the next three chapters, we shall give primary emphasis to (*a*) the typical ways in which urban populations and their dominant activities are arranged in urban areas; (*b*) the interrelations between these urban segments; and (*c*) *changes* in these patterns.

SELECTED REFERENCES

BOGUE, Donald J., *The Population of the United States* (New York, The Free Press of Glencoe, 1959).

DAVIS, Kingsley, *The Population of India and Pakistan* (Princeton, Princeton University Press, 1951).

———, *The World's Metropolitan Areas* (Berkeley, University of California Press, 1959).

DUNCAN, Otis D. and REISS, Albert J. Jr., *Social Characteristics of Urban and Rural Communities* (New York, John Wiley and Sons, 1956).

FREEDMAN, Ronald, *Recent Migration to Chicago* (Chicago, University of Chicago Press, 1949).

GOLDSTEIN, Sidney, *Patterns of Mobility 1910–1950* (Philadelphia, University of Pennsylvania Press, 1958).

HAWLEY, Amos H., *The Changing Shape of Metropolitan America* (New York, The Free Press of Glencoe, 1956).

TAEUBER, Irene B., *The Population of Japan* (Princeton, Princeton University Press, 1958).

CHAPTER 5

Ecological Organization: Understanding the Socio-Geographic Differentiation of Urban Communities

AS WE HAVE SEEN in the preceding chapter, the nature of a given population (size, composition, growth pattern) furnishes valuable clues to the potentialities of community organization and functioning. In all communities, and particularly in urban communities, the population seems to distribute itself in recognizable patterns within the land area occupied by an identifiable community. These patterns may be conceived as reflecting a differentiation of land usage, as well as a division of social labor. In other words, it is possible to view the community as consisting of patterns of allocating population and human activities to subunits of a specific land area. However, it is extremely important to recognize that allocation and distribution are accompanied by some coordination and implicit or explicit regulation. Taken together, these patterns constitute the *ecological organization* of human communities, which we may define as the organization of population and land units, through processes of social interaction and the pursuit of values, into definable entities. It should be noted that ecological organization is not equivalent to community organization, but is rather a *level* or *aspect* of community organization.

Ecological organization may be profitably studied in two ways: (*a*) as a system or structure in its own right, whose component parts and processes require investigation; and (*b*) as a special component of the community, regarded as a system or structure. In this chapter and the next, emphasis will be given to the first type of analysis, while later chapters (notably Chapters 7 and 14) will be more concerned with ecological organization as a functional subsystem of the community. There are several compelling reasons for the sociologist's continued interest in the ecological organization of urban communities and urban regions.

1. To begin with, the sheer complexity of urban activities and social organizations demands orderly attempts to simplify this overwhelming mass of facts by the obvious expedient of classifying them in terms of their objective—*e.g.,* economic, familial, etc. and spatial location. In this manner, the tendency to view social behavior too abstractly, in terms of implicit *values* and somewhat intangible regularities called *social relations* and *social groups* is corrected (but not replaced) by a recognition of the material setting in which human groups necessarily operate.

2. In addition, ecological analysis of urban communities provides a realistic approach to universal human problems of devising creative accommodations between a variety of social-cultural needs and a more or less differentiated physical environment. This is particularly evident in ecological studies of regularities in *spacing* and *timing* the cumulative stream of urban activities so that maximum use of limited units of land by dense populations can be successively approached.

3. Ecological analysis likewise depicts in graphic form an extensive division of labor among groups in complex communities, which supplements and perhaps deepens our understanding of the nature and functioning of numerous specialized groups. There has been a noticeable tendency in sociology toward studying social groups apart from larger social settings and the direct or indirect influences of "competing" groups. For example, we may mention the investigations of small groups, industrial organizations, modern families, and religious groups.[1] One of the contributions of ecological analysis is a

[1] See such compilations or summaries of these fields in Dorwin Cartwright and Alvin Zander, *Group Dynamics* (Evanston, Row, Peterson and Company, 1953); Michael S. Olmsted, *The Small Group* (New York, Random House, 1959); Allan W. Eister, "Basic Continuities in the Study of Small Groups," in Howard Becker and Alvin Boskoff, eds., *Modern Sociological Theory* (New York, Dryden Press, 1957), Chap. X; Delbert C. Miller and William H. Form, *Industry, Labor, and Community* (New York, Harper and Brothers, 1960); Marvin B. Sussman, ed., *Sourcebook in Marriage and the Family* (Boston, Houghton Mifflin, 1955).

necessary consideration of specific groups and activities in their role as *segments* of larger, more complex enterprises—communities. Indeed, one of the special features of the ecological approach is the search for patterns of organization that create and sustain some coordination above and beyond the more obvious facts of division and separation.

4. Finally, and perhaps most important, ecological analysis supplies clues to the nature and problems of social organization in the community. If ecological organization is a human product, imperceptibly constructed from antecedent social processes, it is also a set of conditions that affect in some manner the daily decisions of individuals and groups in the routines of community functioning. Thus, knowledge of ecological organization provides an essential link among past, present and probable future developments in the community. However, since communities are inherently dynamic and subject to external influences, complete consistency in community organization is ordinarily lacking. Ecological analysis therefore can indicate the points at which the community exhibits discontinuities or gaps in its organization, both as an explanation of current problems and as an omen of potential difficulties.

The ecological approach, in short, stresses the importance of relative *location* of groups and activities with respect to one another and to the units of land they respectively occupy. As Mukerjee has wisely suggested,[2] relative location or position in the ecological order is comparable (and perhaps somewhat equivalent) to relative *status* (*i.e.,* differential opportunities, responsibilities, and rewards) in the social order. But it is unprofitable to ask which order has priority, or which "causes" the other. We may only conclude that ecological organization and social organization are related aspects of human communities.

Location of Urban Communities [3]

Obviously, ecological organization is in part dependent on the character of the urban *site*. For over one hundred years, economists,

---

[2] Radhakamal Mukerjee, *Social Ecology* (London, Longmans, Green, 1945).
[3] For the most useful summary of theories and studies, see Harold M. Mayer and Clyde F. Kohn, eds., *Readings in Urban Geography* (Chicago, University of Chicago Press, 1959), Part VII; Edward L. Ullman, "A Theory of Location for Cities," *American Journal of Sociology,* 46 (May, 1941), pp. 853–864.

historians and urban sociologists have analyzed the factors presumed to be basic in the location of cities. We have already discussed this problem for cities of the first and second waves (Chapter 2). At this point, we are concerned only with understanding modern cities. At least two cautions must be observed in our discussion.

1. The search for ultimate origins of urban location is inevitably a matter of considerable inference from fragmentary facts. Under these circumstances, it is easy to substitute *our hindsight* for the foresight of urban pioneers. We should always be wary of imputing "modern" motives and needs to our predecessors. Often we have only three sets of facts to work with: the geographic base (extent, topography, natural resources, etc.); the number and social characteristics of the initial population; and the recorded activities of this population.

2. In addition, we must recognize a distinction between *initial location* of a *potential* city and the location of a clearly realized urban community. In other words, the factors and motives connected with the earliest choice of a site may be quite irrelevant to some subsequent change in the significance of that site for genuinely urban development. As we have already suggested in Chapter 3, the city may be properly conceived as a "stage" in community development, which requires careful analysis of cultural factors. For example, it is erroneous to explain the extraordinary development of Chicago as an illustration of its "favorable" location (at the base of Lake Michigan). This location was certainly not favorable in the 1840's and 1850's, when Chicago was merely a name for well-scattered clusters of shacks. Intensive political activity (which diverted the transcontinental railroads to Chicago), the favorable economic gains derived from the Civil War, an aggressive group of businessmen, and the massive financial support of bankers in New York City enabled Chicago to convert mere potentiality into well-defined actuality in a scant generation.[4] Communities within a 100-mile radius of Chicago (mostly south of Lake Michigan) were, from a purely geographic standpoint, as favorably located as Chicago. But they have become essentially minor cities, such as Rockford, Beloit, and Kankakee. With these cautions in mind, we may now consider the most useful attempts to explain urban location.

[4] Bessie L. Pierce, *A History of Chicago* (New York, Alfred A. Knopf, 1937–1957), 3 vols.; Homer Hoyt, *One Hundred Years of Land Values in Chicago* (Chicago, University of Chicago Press, 1933); Wyatt W. Belcher, *The Economic Rivalry Between St. Louis and Chicago 1850–1880* (New York, Columbia University Press, 1947), pp. 114–116, 185.

1. The theory of central place

In general, proponents of this theory seem to focus on those cities that may be called "regional service centers." The urban community is viewed as a response to the economic needs of a fairly definite agricultural region: middleman services in buying and disposing of agricultural production; provision of technical and financial services; and availability of products from other regions. Consequently, the location of these cities tends to be at the most accessible (*i.e.,* central) position in the service region. A corollary of this theory is the plausible hypothesis that the larger the service region (both in population and extent), the larger and more complex the central city.[5]

Several limitations seem to be generally recognized in this theory. First, it is primarily applicable to agricultural rather than highly industrialized areas. Second, its predicted patterns of urban location are quite distorted by developments in transportation, which change patterns of accessibility. Third, variations in fertility of soil, type of cultivation, and local administrative patterns tend to interfere with theoretically "central" locations.

2. The "break in transportation" theory

Urban location, according to this theory, is likewise understandable in terms of accessibility. However, instead of accessibility to a service area, we now shift our attention to the problem of accessibility with respect to *differing but converging forms of transportation.* The problem of storing and transferring commodities from one type of transportation to another is crucial in a commercial-industrial society. Therefore, cities tend to develop at these transfer points (or "breaks") to coordinate needed transfers, maintain records of changes in ownership and responsibility, and to provide the normal range of services for the necessary personnel. The most frequent breaks in transportation are between: water traffic (lake, river, and ocean) and railroads; railroad and truck; airplane and railroad; and intersecting railroad routes. Indeed, many of the most important world cities—often called *entrepôts* or *gateway cities*—can be basically understood as illustrations of this theory.[6] New York City, London, Chicago, Boston,

[5] Ullman, *op. cit.;* James A. Quinn, *Human Ecology* (Englewood Cliffs, N.J., Prentice-Hall, 1950), pp. 86–96, 286–289.

[6] Mayer and Kohn, *op. cit.,* Sect. 12; Charles H. Cooley, "The Theory of Transportation," in *Sociological Theory and Social Research,* ed. by R. C. Angell (New York, Holt, Rinehart & Winston, 1930), pp. 75–83.

Philadelphia, Stockholm, Amsterdam, and Calcutta are outstanding instances.

3. The theory of historical accidents

Both of the preceding explanations reflect the operation of rational motives in urban location, particularly with respect to facilitating economic processes (production, distribution). A few cities, however, seem to have been located as a result of such nonrational "historic accidents" as personal whims of powerful leaders and political "deals." Washington, D.C., for example, was clearly a consequence of a power struggle between contending factions in the Constitutional Convention. St. Petersburg (now Leningrad) was located in part for military reasons, in part to satisfy the egotism of Peter the Great. Even Paris, the city of light, which was almost a forgotten, out-of-the-way village for centuries, was transformed into a major city when the Capetians assumed the French throne and willfully moved the capital from Aachen.[7]

These theories of urban location, which seem to be complementary rather than contradictory, aid in understanding several aspects of basic urban ecology. However, it is increasingly clear that these theories *by themselves* in many instances do not adequately explain the location of specific cities. Essentially, it is unwise to analyze the origins and development of cities without consideration of *regional* and sometimes *national* conditions. Indeed, the location of particular cities is often affected by the number and relative distance of pre-existing cities. Furthermore, changes in transportation, technological advances, and political vicissitudes undoubtedly function to alter the desirability of given sites for urban development.

We should not underestimate the great *diversity* of urban locations —near oceans, rivers, lakes; on plains, plateaus, on mountainsides as well as below sea level; in agricultural and industrial areas; as far as several hundred miles from other major cities or as close as thirty miles (*e.g.*, Dallas and Fort Worth); in extremely dry to rather humid climates. Perhaps it is more fruitful to stress the distinctive ways in which cities generally make use of their diversified locations in performing urban functions. Locational factors, in other words,

[7] See William A. Robson, ed., *Great Cities of the World* (London, Allen and Unwin, 1954), especially Chaps. VI, X, XII.

provide a base for the development of subsequent ecological organization.

Urban Ecological Units

Accurate and useful description of urban ecological organization—the distribution and functional coordination of population, organized activities, and material culture—ultimately rests on the way in which ecological parts or units are selected. Ideally, these units should be both geographically limited and socioculturally homogeneous. In other words, they should be easy to identify on a map (for convenience) and should represent relatively distinctive population features and cultural and social organization (as functional units). In practice, however, this dual aim is difficult to achieve because the actual distributions reflect considerable mixture of activities and populations; and processes of mobility and social change alter the significance of previously useful units. Urban sociologists must therefore seek compromises which produce simplified but sociologically important analyses of urban communities. Before we turn to an extended discussion of basic ecological patterns, let us briefly review the *types* of ecological units that have received most use.

1. Natural areas

One of the earliest concepts of urban ecology is the natural area, an unplanned segment of urban development marked by definable physical features (topography, and boundaries supplied by hills, rivers, railroad tracks, streets and highways) and a high degree of cultural uniformity among the resident or functioning population.[8] Because of these features, the natural area usually has a pointedly descriptive name, which does not correspond to administrative designations (*i.e.,* 2nd ward, 10th Assembly district, etc.). Some natural areas possess distinctive connotations, not only to the sociologist, but to the layman as well. Consider, for example: the Gold Coast, Skid Row, the Black Belt, Wall Street, the Bottoms, Little Sicily, Bohemia, and Downtown

[8] Robert E. Park, *Human Communities* (New York, The Free Press of Glencoe, 1952), Chaps. I, II, XIV; Paul K. Hatt, "The Concept of Natural Area," *American Sociological Review,* 11 (August, 1946), pp. 423–428; Harvey W. Zorbaugh, *The Gold Coast and the Slum* (Chicago, University of Chicago Press, 1929).

or the Loop. With some local modifications, these areas can be identified in many urban communities, which lends great weight to their usefulness. However, natural areas are rather large and sometimes difficult to delimit sharply. Furthermore, a considerable portion of the urban community fails to "fit into" any of the more clearly identifiable natural areas; the resultant "islands" provide a picture of urban discontinuity that perhaps overestimates the genuine "gaps" in the urban fabric.

2. Concentric zones

The division of the urban community into circular zones radiating from the central business district is a classic device first used extensively by Burgess and others at the University of Chicago. Basically, the zonal unit may be variable in width, but most often it has been arbitrarily (and conveniently) conceived in terms of one or two-mile bands. In general, zones have been used to detect *gradients* (patterns of increase or decrease) in such community phenomena as crime and delinquency, divorce, mental disorders, land values, etc.[9] It is assumed that urban development is relatively uniform in all directions from the center, though topographical features (rivers, lakes, hills) are recognized as distorting factors. On the whole, the zonal approach must be considered a useful *orientation* to ecological organization, rather than a source of functional ecological parts.

3. Sectors

As a realistic supplement to, and modification of, zonal units, Homer Hoyt's analysis of radial sectors is of great value.[10] Using rental figures and surveys of housing quality, Hoyt found that urban growth could be substantially described as a series of residential "fingers" expanding in radial fashion around major transportation routes

[9] The classic reference is Ernest W. Burgess, "The Growth of the City," in Robert E. Park *et al.*, eds., *The City* (Chicago, University of Chicago Press, 1925), pp. 47–62. A good discussion and bibliography may be found in Quinn, *op. cit.*, Chap. VI.

[10] Homer Hoyt, *The Structure and Growth of Residential Neighborhoods in American Cities* (Washington, Federal Housing Administration, 1939), pp. 74–78; Arthur M. Weimer and Homer Hoyt, *Principles of Urban Real Estate* (New York, Ronald Press, 1939), pp. 61–68.

toward the outskirts of the city. Each sector tends to reflect segregation of population groupings according to income and social status and thus helps to account for some of the deviations from expected zonal patterns. In a sense, sectors correspond to elongated natural areas, with relatively homogeneous physical, cultural, and social character-istics in each type of sector. Since more than a third of the city's land area is devoted to residential usage, sector patterns furnish helpful clues to fundamental ecological organization.

4. Nuclei

Zones and sectors perhaps simplify urban ecological patterns with-out sufficient regard for deviations and irregularity of urban devel-opment. Many cities seem to develop typical clusterings of population and activities that defy their easy inclusion in zones or sectors. These clusters, which have been called urban nuclei,[11] appear to arise in portions of the urban landscape that are peculiar to *specific types* of nuclei (as we shall see later). Some obvious examples are the central business district (and its specialized subareas), the wholesale district, distinctly high status and low status residential areas, dormitory sub-urbs, and heavy industrial concentrations. Urban nuclei likewise seem to be a form of natural area, though the influence of rational planning is often considerably stronger in the former.

5. Census tracts

In the last thirty years, the emphasis on convenient ecological units has resulted in widespread use of census tracts. The popularity of this approach is indicated by the fact that 136 cities (of 50,000 popula-tion or over) in the United States had been officially divided into census tracts, while 37 urban regions (Standard Metropolitan Areas) had been completely tracted by early 1955.[12] The census tract is a relatively small, clearly defined area of the city (or its dependent area) which is designed to encompass a resident population that is

[11] Chauncy D. Harris and Edward L. Ullman, "The Nature of Cities," in Hatt and Reiss, *op. cit.*, pp. 229–232.

[12] Calvin F. Schmid, "Research Techniques in Human Ecology," in Pauline V. Young, *Scientific Social Surveys and Research,* 3rd ed., (Englewood Cliffs, N.J., Prentice-Hall, 1956), p. 418.

demographically and culturally homogeneous and limited in size to a few thousand persons. Since tract boundaries remain officially fixed, various types of information (income, sex and age distributions, etc.) for any and all tracts can be studied for possible changes or trends over a period of years or decades.[13] However, several criticisms of tracts as ecological units has appeared, to which no adequate reply has yet been made. (*a*) Tracts tend to be too numerous—60 to 150 tracts seems to be the range for most cities—to aid in supplying a *comprehensible* picture of relevant conditions in the community. Consequently, census tracts are often supplemented by some *grouping* method (*e.g.,* zones) to retrieve some recognizable pattern from a puzzling mosaic of small units. (*b*) Census tracts tend to be *arbitrary* units, separately constructed without serious consideration of their relation to the larger entity. (*c*) Closely related, finally, is the recent discovery (long suspected, however) that individual census tracts contain measurable and perhaps significant *internal* variations in demographic and social characteristics.[14] It is not clear at this point that this variability can be interpreted as a *recent* development or a defect in the original tracting.

6. Social areas

The most recent attempt to combine convenience and sociological distinctiveness in ecological units is called *social area analysis*. Based on the initial use of census tracts, this method classifies tracts according to three sets of significant characteristics—*social rank* (in terms of occupational distribution, formal education, and rent), *urbanization* (measures of fertility, housing types, and proportion of women in the labor force), and *segregation* (derived from figures on racial composition). In its first application to Los Angeles, the tracted area was divided into nine types of areas, representing different combinations of urbanization and social rank scores (see figure). Each of these nine areas was further distinguished into high and low areas of segregation, giving in all, eighteen types of units. In this way, a city map could graphically present clusters of census tracts having similar characteristics, as well as the spatial distribution of different types of

[13] *Ibid.,* pp. 418–423.
[14] John H. Mabry, "Census Tract Variations in Urban Research," *American Sociological Review,* 23 (April, 1958), pp. 193–196.

FIGURE 4

Typology of Social Areas in Cities, by Social Rank and Degree of Urbanization

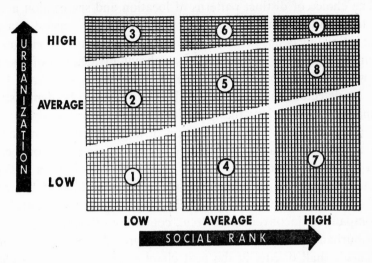

SOURCE: Shevky and Williams, *The Social Areas of Los Angeles*, p. 64.

social areas. Thus far, social area analysis has been mainly descriptive; we shall have to await its application to problems of explanation and understanding.[15]

Before we can decide which type of ecological unit (or units) is most helpful, one basic fact about urban ecology should be noted. Whether we explore urban space on foot, by auto, or from a low-flying plane, or carefully study zoning and land use maps, we are uniformly confronted with an overall *segregation of major activities and functions*. Most commonly, residential, commercial, industrial, and civic functions tend to be sharply separated from one another in a spatial division of labor that is possible only in increasingly extensive territories. The general pattern (or patterns) of this segregation, however, often defies simplified description. To obtain reasonable order from this complexity, therefore, we shall approach urban ecological organization as a product of relative emphases on two major social motivations: *status* and *rational-functional needs*.

[15] Eshref Shevky and Marilyn Williams, *The Social Areas of Los Angeles* (Berkeley, University of California Press, 1949); Eshref Shevky and Wendell Bell, *Social Area Analysis* (Stanford, Stanford University Press, 1955). See the critical evaluation of Amos Hawley and Otis D. Duncan, "Social Area Analysis: A Critical Appraisal," *Land Economics*, 33 (November, 1957), pp. 337–345.

Status and Ecological Organization

The choice of distinct patterns of location and segregation according to definite criteria of status is well known. In general, status is most intimately connected with *residential* location and development,[16] though status considerations are not absent in location of specialty shops and professional establishments. Essentially, the status factor may be detected whenever any of the following can be demonstrated as motives for location: the quest for "amenities"—desirable scenery and an impressive view, the selection of an elevated or commanding site, an emphasis on "space" for the sake of space alone, or location at a "comfortable distance" from "nuisance" activities; a desire to locate or remain close to persons and groups of similar status; and a desire to locate in areas of established high reputation, regardless of accompanying inconveniences (*e.g.,* commuting time).

Suburban developments and the recent growth of "Exurban" areas, which we shall discuss in the next chapter, are obvious examples of the status factor in location. Likewise, the presence of a "Gold Coast" in many major American cities—despite their proximity to slum areas—is at least partly understandable when we consider that they often contain tall buildings with magnificent views of a lake, river, or impressive bridges—all of these being particularly attractive on clear evenings. We have, furthermore, the evidence of such otherwise disparate communities as Boston, Massachusetts and Bangalore, India, in each of which high status groups (and the newly rich) have chosen to remain in old, familiar residential areas rather than relocate in roomier suburbs.[17] Indeed, the status motive is so persistent that families may distinguish sharply between street designations *in the same neighborhood.* In Norfolk, Virginia, the *named* streets in the upper West Side have more attraction for status-conscious families

[16] Harold A. Gibbard, "The Status Factor in Residential Succession," *American Journal of Sociology,* 46 (May, 1941), pp. 835–842; Peter Collison, "Occupation, Education, and Housing in an English City," *ibid.,* 65 (May, 1960), pp. 588–597; Otis D. Duncan and Beverly Duncan, "Residential Distribution and Occupational Stratification," *ibid.,* 60 (March, 1955), pp. 493–503; Arnold S. Feldman and Charles Tilly, "The Interaction of Social and Physical Space," *American Sociological Review,* 25 (December, 1960), pp. 877–884.

[17] See Walter Firey, *Land Use in Central Boston* (Cambridge, Harvard University Press, 1947); Noel P. Gist, "The Ecology of Bangalore, India: An East-West Comparison," *Social Forces,* 35 (May, 1957), pp. 356–365.

than the *numbered* streets. Therefore, the former often contain houses of lower market value, despite comparable accommodations.

Functional Needs and Ecological Organization

Urban activities, by their very nature, exhibit a characteristic emphasis on rational, economic motives. Location of specific activities and organizations is consequently guided by more or less practical attempts to link *tangible objectives* and *available facilities*. Indeed, the most obvious criterion of rational-functional location is expressed in the choice of sites that give access to personnel, materials, or services considered vital for the operation of a given group or organization. This is clearly indicated in such instances as: the location of industries in spacious, peripheral areas, close to railway spurs or trucking routes; the tendency for families to consider homes and apartments in terms of their proximity to schools, shopping facilities, and transportation lines; and the development of shopping centers at presumed points of greatest convenience to their respective clienteles. The rational factor is also prominent in the "clustering" of *competitive* firms (to keep an eye on competitors) and in the calculated settlement of dissimilar but complementary activities in adjacent locations (*e.g.,* a variety of "service" establishments near college campuses, restaurants near the theater district).

The Principle of Median Location

To the extent that urban groups and organizations pursue rational standards of functioning, given the opportunity to locate themselves without restrictions, the patterns of actual distribution tend to confirm Quinn's *hypothesis of median location*.[18] Simply stated, this generalization asserts that various kinds of urban activities assume patterns of location at points which minimize effort and cost in use of necessary services and/or furnishing services to clients, customers, or adherents. This, of course, assumes equal availability of these central locations and accurate knowledge of costs for alternative locations so that rational decisions can be made. Significantly, the hypothesis of median location provides a common foundation for the apparently divergent development of zones, sectors, and nuclei. All three rest to some degree on rational-functional motives, but each reflects different eco-

[18] Quinn, *op. cit.,* pp. 86–94, 105–106, 279–289.

logical consequences because each uniquely ignores or takes account of additional factors (*e.g.*, the sector pattern stresses radial transportation routes and facilities).

Ecological patterns for concrete cities are consequently products of *differential emphasis* on status and rational-functional criteria of segregation. Since the actual combinations are quite numerous, we can only hope to identify here a few basic types of urban ecological structure.

1. The orthodox type

In general, the more recently established cities of the Western world —and particularly those in politically stable societies—tend to stress functional standards of ecological distribution. The "orthodox" type, which has been diligently studied by sociologists at the University of Chicago since the early twenties, consists of rough zonal divisions corresponding to successive time periods—the outer zones being more recently developed, as modified by geographic obstacles, the complementary growth of two or more residential sectors, and the concomitant rise of commercial and industrial nuclei. Status factors are by no means absent, but operate in *intermittent patterns*. For example, the early development of intermediate and outer zones stems from the migration of high status families to more spacious areas. This permits commercial expansion from the central business district and a consequent need for connective transportation facilities. Status factors in part intrude again in the growth of residential sectors and in suburban residential nuclei located in a peripheral zone. Within this basic pattern, deviations from the functional emphasis tend to be minor, since a competitive advantage normally lies with the financially superior rational-functional organizations (business corporations of various types). Only with the advent of community-wide planning is the orthodox pattern potentially subject to significant change.

2. The symbolic type

By comparison with the "orthodox" ecological pattern, the symbolic type appears to be without perceptible organization. Zones and sectors are especially difficult to identify. However, we might properly characterize the symbolic type as a continuation of early ecological patterns or a reflection of organized resistance to the liberation of

FIGURE 5
The Orthodox Ecological Structure of Cities

1.Central business district 2. Low class residential
3.Middle class residential 4.Higher class residential
■■■■■■■■■■■■■5. Manufacturing (light or heavy)

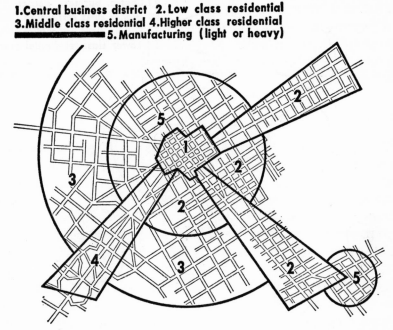

rational, competitive motives in allocation of land. In place of zonal and sector developments, the symbolic type is compounded of a series of nuclei, which are maintained in roughly their traditional form by the stubborn immobility of high status families. Under these circumstances, residential nuclei (both high and low status types) are evaluated *symbolically*, in terms of past associations, not as areas to be manipulated for future development or exploitation. At this point, it is not necessary to distinguish the operation of *private* and *public* (governmental) organizations in applying symbolic evaluations to urban subareas.

Several features are distinctive of the symbolic type, as presented in rather simplified form in Figure 6. (*a*) There is a tendency for the core business district to be somewhat large and not well differentiated internally. Business establishments appear to be only vaguely separated according to type; and complementary (symbiotic) activities fail to achieve adjacent locations. In Bangalore, for example, banking facilities are highly dispersed, as are the finer hotels, which also are quite distant from the major shopping areas and the railway terminal. (*b*)

FIGURE 6
The Symbolic Ecological Structure of Cities

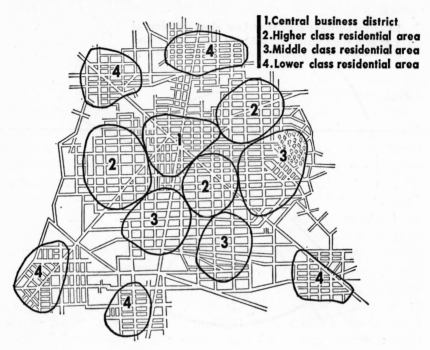

1. Central business district
2. Higher class residential area
3. Middle class residential area
4. Lower class residential area

High status families prefer to reside in a series of attractive nuclei close to the central business area. There is, consequently, no clear inner "zone of transition" in this type. (*c*) Middle and low status families tend to locate in scattered residential nuclei *beyond* high status areas. Low status areas are generally "outer slums," leftover areas that often possess otherwise desirable but undeveloped geographic features (hills, scenery).[19]

New Orleans: An Example of Symbolic Ecology[20]

While New Orleans deviates to a considerable extent from some of the previously listed features, it has been one of the best American

[19] Gist, *loc. cit.*; Leo Kuper, *Durban: A Study in Racial Ecology* (London, Jonathan Cape, Ltd., 1958); G. Balandier, "Urbanism in West and Central Africa," in *Social Implications of Industrialization and Urbanization in Africa South of the Sahara,* International African Institute (Paris, UNESCO, 1956), pp. 496ff.

[20] Harlan W. Gilmore, "The Old New Orleans and the New: A Case for Ecology," *American Sociological Review,* 9 (August, 1944), pp. 385–394.

instances of urban symbolic ecology. It is likewise particularly interesting as a unique blend of topological and cultural factors in the development of a distinctive ecological structure. Situated between a bend in the Mississippi River and Lake Pontchartrain, New Orleans is marked by low-lying land that is separated by two major ridges. One ridge, running east and west, is about midway between river and lake; the other, running north and south, extends to the river near the French Quarter.

By 1900 or so, New Orleans had developed primarily as a gateway city. For over one hundred years, a succession of rather distinctive population groupings had been incorporated into the growing community by informal but highly patterned residential segregation (see accompanying figure). The earliest and most persistent residents, the Creoles (French) possessed—or claimed to possess—high status and an attachment to the convenient "French Quarter." Despite increasingly crowded conditions, many families remained in this district, though others moved steadily northward into the "new Creole" district. The American businessmen, who were considered culturally inferior by the Creoles, first settled in substantial numbers immediately west of the business district and then moved farther westward (but still at a convenient distance from the business district) to the so-called Garden District. Irish immigrants, imported to allay a labor shortage, gradually moved into the area vacated by business families, which came to be known as the Irish Channel. Meanwhile, other nationality groups—notably Germans—took up truck-farming and residence in the spacious, neglected area east of the Creole sector. New Orleans therefore developed a noticeable "T" pattern, which stemmed from the special sentiments and cultural conflicts of its component nationalities.

Urban ecology should therefore be approached as a relatively *dynamic patterning* of spatial allocation and coordination. At any point in time, the ecological structure of a given community represents a temporary equilibrium (or compromise) of rational and status factors, which constitutes a limiting framework for subsequent ecological developments. But, in varying degrees, urban areas of the world have tended to emphasize the rational factor, with unanticipated nonrational consequences. In the following chapter, and at various points in the remainder of this book, we shall try to analyze and explain ecological dynamics as a significant aspect of urban community organization. In particular, we shall be concerned with those factors

FIGURE 7
The Symbolic Ecology of New Orleans

SOURCE: Adapted from Harlan W. Gilmore, "The Old New Orleans and the New," *American Sociological Review,* 9 (Aug., 1944).

that *sustain* given ecological patterns as well as those that help to account for substantial *variations* in structure.

SELECTED REFERENCES

ALIHAN, Milla A., *Social Ecology* (New York, Columbia University Press, 1938).

BARTHOLOMEW, Harland, *Land Use in American Cities,* 2nd ed. (Cambridge, Mass., Harvard University Press, 1955).

FIREY, Walter, *Land Use in Central Boston* (Cambridge, Harvard University Press, 1947).

HAWLEY, Amos H., *Human Ecology* (New York, Ronald Press, 1950).

MAYER, Harold M. and KOHN, Clyde F., eds., *Readings in Urban Geography* (Chicago, University of Chicago Press, 1959).

PARK, Robert E., *Human Communities* (New York, The Free Press of Glencoe, 1952).

QUINN, James A., *Human Ecology* (Englewood Cliffs, N.J., Prentice-Hall, 1950).

RATCLIFF, Richard U., *Urban Land Economics* (New York, McGraw-Hill, 1949).

THEODORSON, George A., ed., *Studies in Human Ecology* (Evanston, Row, Peterson and Company, 1961).

CHAPTER 6

The Dynamics of
Urban Ecological Patterns

FROM THE URBAN sociologist's standpoint, *the nature of ecological facts* is crucial to the understanding of significant *changes* in ecological organization. Following the distinctions suggested by MacIver, we may best describe ecological patterns as resultants of *conjunctural social phenomena.*[1] Essentially, conjunctural phenomena derive from a host of individual attitudes and activities of subtly interdependent persons and social groups. The overall consequences of these actions are largely unpremeditated but nevertheless important structures or patterns, which usually represent some division of rewards, facilities, opportunities, and responsibilities among the implicated persons and groups. In many instances, the development of a national economic system, patterns of social disorganization, and systems of social stratification seem to be primarily comprehensible in these terms.

Two aspects of conjunctural phenomena must be emphasized in analyzing ecological patterns. First, the location and movement of persons, groups, or activities always rests on more or less perceived social and cultural motivations. "Availability," "access," and "opportunity" have no meaning unless persons and groups recognize "availability," etc.—and proceed to act on that recognition. Second, individual and group decisions about settlement or relocation inevitably produce—simultaneously—*restrictions* on the decisions of other

[1] See the important discussion of distributive, collective, and conjunctural phenomena in the social sciences by Robert M. MacIver, "Social Causation and Change," in Georges Gurvitch and Wilbert E. Moore, eds., *Twentieth Century Sociology* (New York, Philosophical Library, 1945), pp. 121–125; and Robert M. MacIver, *Social Causation* (Boston, Ginn and Company, 1942).

groups by occupying desired areas; and *opportunities* for occupancy in vacated areas. These are inevitable consequences because expansion of densely settled urban areas is limited by time-cost factors in transportation and provision of public utilities and services, and the buildings and facilities of vacated areas are relatively permanent investments. Under these circumstances, ecological patterns can best be understood as somewhat temporary resultants of facilitating and restrictive factors influencing the separate but interdependent actions of subgroups in the urban community. Ecological changes, therefore, assume meaning only when considered as deviations from pre-existing patterns or trends. But these deviations or changes must be examined from two aspects: (*a*) what accounts for alterations in facilitating and restrictive factors that make possible *initial* variations in a given ecological pattern; and (*b*) how do these initial variations affect the motivations and opportunities for decision of other groups in the evolving ecological structure?

Ecological Processes

The traditional approach to these general problems has been a *descriptive* account of the basic ecological processes.[2] These processes, however, are rarely investigated as *processes* in the strict sense of the term, *i.e,* as a succession of understandable changes through a given period of time. It is extremely difficult and costly to pursue a genuinely processual study. Consequently, urban ecologists normally assemble and analyze the *products* of ecological redistribution. The availability of comparable data, however, is generally limited to (*a*) population figures—with respect to size and distribution; and (*b*) urbanized types of activity, in the form of economic statistics, religious data, deviant behavior, etc.

Ecological change consists of several facets or problems, for which specific ecological processes provide some clarification and understanding. One aspect of change is the relative *size* of the urban community. A second type of ecological dynamics concerns changes in the *interrelations* among component areas in the community or region. Finally, and perhaps most fundamental, is the focus on changes in the *geographic position* of individuals, groups, and their material equipment (*e.g.,* factories, stores, homes).

[2] James A. Quinn, *Human Ecology* (Englewood Cliffs, N.J., Prentice-Hall, 1950), Part III.

1. Processes related to relative size

Aggregation refers to the increase in population units (and their property) within a defined area over a specific time period. This is reflected in changing density of population and is related to the process of *expansion,* which involves the growth of useable, populated areas beyond previously defined limits.

2. Processes related to interrelation of subareas

Bridging processes of the previous type and the present category, *concentration* reflects the relatively higher rates of aggregation for specific subareas, as compared with other subareas in the community. Thus, in the early stages of urban development, inner areas were the focus of concentration processes. More recently, outer zones have been more clearly marked by processes of concentration.

Centralization, which is sometimes confused with concentration, is the process of *accumulating* important functions and services in one (or a limited number of) strategic subareas. The result is an increasing dependence on these highly specialized areas on the part of the remaining areal units in the community. An obvious example is the development of the central business district.

While both concentration and centralization emphasize positive processes of interrelations, *segregation* as an ecological process describes the conscious or unconscious development of separable and specialized areas in the community. In this process, particular population categories and types of activities assume identifiable concentration in specific areas. The segregation of racial and nationality groupings in given neighborhoods is merely a dramatic instance of a pervasive and inevitable process in urban communities. Segregation also occurs, for example, in the distinction between residential, industrial, and commercial areas, in the differentiation of low, medium and high status residential areas, and in the emergence of such specialized areas as "Skid Row," the red light district, and the civic center.

3. Processes related to changes in relations between subareas

The last ecological processes to be mentioned here are normally dependent on prior processes of segregation, centralization, and concentration, which serve to establish a referential ecological structure.

Invasion refers to a visible shift in population or function from one area to another (often adjacent areas) in a community. This "encroachment" is illustrated in the expansion of commercial activities into surrounding residential areas, and of course the emotion-charged movement of previously segregated racial and/or nationality groupings into informally forbidden areas. Invasion is followed by *succession* (and perhaps subsequent processes of invasion) when the invading function or population grouping becomes dominant, and concomitantly motivates the withdrawal of previously dominant groups or functions.[3]

Underlying all ecological processes is the crucial process of *migration,* which also provides an important link between demographic and ecological aspects of community organization. Migration simply refers to the physical movement of individuals and groups from one location to another. The *effects* of such movements, however, rather than the movements themselves, are of particular interest to the urban sociologist. One such effect, often called the process of *ecological mobility,* involves the rate of redistribution of population and functions within a given area—or between areas. Mobility in this sense is not necessarily equivalent to *social mobility,* which refers to changes in social relationships—quite apart from changes in spatial position.

These ecological processes, as previously suggested, provide descriptions of changes in ecological patterns; they are important but *preliminary* devices for studying these changes. Essentially, an analytic approach to ecological dynamics must seek to *explain* both maintenance and change in ecological organization of urban communities. Ecological organization is a complex product of ecological processes, but these in turn are reflections of social, cultural, and psychological variables. Perhaps we can suggest the basic interconnection of these variables by approaching ecological dynamics as a reflection of *community organization* and of the social and cultural changes that challenge existing modes of organization. Since this broader set of

[3] Invasion and succession are well analyzed in the works of Robert E. Park and his disciples. See Robert E. Park, "Succession, An Ecological Concept," *American Sociological Review,* 1 (April, 1936), pp. 171–179; R. D. McKenzie, "Ecological Succession in the Puget Sound Region," *Publications of the American Sociological Society,* 23 (1929), pp. 60–80; Paul Cressey, "Population Succession in Chicago," *American Journal of Sociology,* 44 (July, 1938), pp. 59–69; Otis D. Duncan and Beverly Duncan, *The Negro Population of Chicago: A Study of Residential Succession* (Chicago, University of Chicago Press, 1957).

processes is quite intricate, we shall try to select a few illustrative aspects of ecological dynamics in the urban community, with particular attention to the sociocultural context in which ecological changes occur.

CHANGES IN INDUSTRIAL LOCATION

The industrial function of cities during the nineteenth century was largely performed in or near central areas. Several reasons for this early pattern are clear. In that period, with limited transportation facilities, a central location provided maximum accessibility to labor supply, transport, and source of power. Before the expansion of housing and other land-competitive activities, the central area was not yet inflated in value, nor was considerable space required for most industrial operations. Then, too—and this must not be ignored—there was little or no attempt to challenge (let alone *restrict*) patterns of industrial location.

Since World War II, with varying degrees of clarity, the ecological niche of urban industries has been progressively shifted toward outer areas [4]—both in the relocation of existing plants and in the selection of sites for new plants. In general, light industries (involving limited equipment and a small labor force) have remained near the central business district, though a Detroit study indicates that some light industries seek the convenience of one-story plants in suburban areas. Heavy industry, on the other hand, has rather consistently tended to find peripheral locations more desirable than those in inner zones. This is especially evident in the largest urban centers, and for those industries that produce durable goods (appliances, machinery, etc.). Some outstanding examples of this trend are the huge Fairless Plant of United States Steel in the Philadelphia area, and General Electric's Appliance Park near Louisville.[5]

This new pattern of location is a direct consequence of several changes in urban life and in the character of modern society. Most

[4] Leo G. Reeder, "Industrial Location Trends in Chicago in Comparison to Population Growth," *Land Economics,* 30 (May, 1954), pp. 177–182; Evelyn M. Kitigawa and Donald J. Bogue, *Suburbanization of Manufacturing Activity Within Standard Metropolitan Areas* (Oxford, Ohio, Scripps Foundation for Research in Population Problems, 1955).

[5] *The New York Times,* March 15, 1953; Detroit Planning Commission study, cited by Noel P. Gist and L. A. Halbert, *Urban Society,* 4th ed. (New York, Thomas Y. Crowell, 1956), p. 110.

obviously, industrial location is motivated by rational-functional needs (more plant space, lower land values and tax rates, and less traffic congestion). But increasingly, industrial corporations are discovering that efficiency is also dependent on concern for their workers and the technical and professional staff. The suburban trek of residences for a widening range of status groupings is a highly important factor in problems of hiring competent personnel. Furthermore, an increasing demand for highly trained professional persons necessarily involves attention by the corporation to the normal residential and community aspirations of this segment of the labor force. Their desire for the amenities (space, modern homes, scenery, etc.) and for adequate and convenient schools, churches, and shopping areas is an increasingly powerful argument for peripheral location. We must not forget the impact of the city and regional planning movement, sponsored by a variety of public and private organizations, which has diligently encouraged the newer locational trends for industry.[6] Often, attractive tax benefits are offered by county, township, or state units with the hope of improving the economic base of predominantly residential areas.

CHANGES IN RESIDENTIAL PATTERNS

It is by now well known that changes in residential patterns have been in the form of zonal and sector developments, and also in outer, nucleated locations. Much of this trend reflects the *successive relocations* of urban residents, who try to match occupational and financial success with higher status residential location. But, as we have seen in Chapter 4, the character of *rural-urban migration* is related to residential patterns. Several important changes in migration trends are particularly relevant here.

1. Most obviously, the immigration restrictions of 1920 and 1924 (with minor modifications since 1950) have sharply reduced the stream of foreign-born, rural immigrants, who had traditionally settled in the zones of transition of American cities.[7] The lone, dramatic exception to this restrictive trend is the Puerto Rican influx of the past ten years. As a result, inner zones of cities are generally losing population—proportionately and often absolutely.

[6] See Part IV.
[7] Donald J. Bogue, *The Population of the United States* (New York, The Free Press of Glencoe, 1959), Chap. VII.

2. In the United States there is some evidence—for Chicago at least—that migrants to cities have tended to shift their *initial location* from the cheap rent, transitional zone to broader and more varied residential areas. During the period 1935–1940, migrants to Chicago were disproportionately concentrated in a long, narrow band along Lake Michigan. Significantly, foreign migrants were also attracted to this extensive "migrant zone," a large part of which consisted of high rent areas. Various types of comparisons indicate that native migrants to Chicago in this period tended to locate in those portions of the "migrant zone" that were most similar to the social characteristics of the migrants. Thus, migrants from other cities (who were generally in service and middle-class occupational categories) settled in the high rent areas of the narrow band. Migrants from rural communities (mainly from the South) tended to locate in or near the zone of transition.[8]

While supporting data for other cities is lacking, this provisionally noted shift in migrants' location is understandable. In view of the changing character of American industry and the urban occupational structure (which is discussed more fully in Chapter 11), we can expect relatively more migrants with higher educational and occupational status, more persons migrating in family units; and more migrants with previous experience in other urban or suburban communities. Indeed, with the major exception of Southern Negro migrants, the reservoir of distinctively *rural* migrants is rapidly diminishing, since the farm population continues to decrease as a result of past rural-urban migrations. From the standpoint of urban residential patterns, these demographic trends are accompanied by value systems and financial resources that impel migrants to seek locations that are both convenient and physically desirable.

Minority Residential Patterns

Perhaps the most instructive aspect of changes in residential patterns is the dynamics of residential segregation of minority groups [9]—

[8] Ronald Freedman, *Recent Migration to Chicago* (Chicago, University of Chicago Press, 1949).

[9] For a summary of trends among Chinese in the U.S. see Rose Hum Lee, "The Decline of Chinatowns in the United States," *American Journal of Sociology,* 54 (March, 1949), pp. 422–432; and her *The Chinese in the United States of America* (New York, Oxford University Press, 1960).

especially Negroes. But an overall picture of trends in residential segregation is not yet available. One study of 23 cities, using census tracts as units of measurement, found a slight tendency toward decentralization (desegregation) of nonwhites from 1940 to 1950. By contrast, a study based on analysis of *block statistics* for 185 cities— for the same period—seems to demonstrate some increase in residential segregation on nonwhites.[10] In view of these inconsistent findings, it is probably too early to draw conclusions of a general nature. However, the processual aspect of residential segregation may be clarified by focusing briefly on a few representative instances.

1. Chicago

Several studies agree in demonstrating an increase in Negro segregation in Chicago during the 1940–1950 decade.[11] An overwhelming proportion of Chicago's Negro population is concentrated in the so-called Black Belt, which is a well-defined, deteriorated rectangle on the South Side. Unlike Philadelphia, which has a number of minor Negro areas, Chicago has retained and intensified racial segregation. But what explains this *persistence* of ecological pattern? Prejudice and discrimination are undoubtedly factors—but not adequate answers. Several conditions must be kept in mind. One, the major Negro district was originally located in an area that was vacated by whites and relatively accessible to firms requiring unskilled labor, *i.e.,* the Loop and the stockyards.[12] Two, as the Negro population expanded through migration following World War I, opportunities for residential movement were limited by Lake Michigan on the east and stockyards on the west. Three, Negro migration continued at high levels, since the depression and the mechanization of Southern agriculture intensified the already precarious economic position of many Negroes. Four,

[10] Richard W. Redick, "Population Growth and Distribution in Central Cities, 1940–1950," *American Sociological Review,* 21 (February, 1956), pp. 38–43; Donald O. Cowgill, "Trends in Residential Segregation of Nonwhites in American Cities, 1940–1950," *ibid.,* pp. 43–47.

[11] Redick, *loc. cit.;* Cowgill, *loc. cit.* A more detailed study may be found in Otis D. Duncan and Beverly Duncan, *The Negro Population of Chicago* (Chicago, University of Chicago Press, 1957). A contrasting trend in Washington is analyzed in George D. Nesbitt, "Dispersion of Nonwhite Residence in Washington, D.C.: Some of its Implications," *Land Economics,* 32 (August, 1956), pp. 201–212.

[12] Homer Hoyt, *One Hundred Years of Land Values in Chicago* (Chicago, University of Chicago Press, 1933), pp. 97, 215–216, 315.

various attempts by Negro families to settle in white areas have been met by informal but effective rebuffs, or the use of violence. Ecological change in Negro residential patterns has, in short, been blocked by social and geographical obstacles.

2. New Orleans

A good example of a major shift in Negro residential patterns may be found in several Southern cities. However, the process is especially clear in New Orleans (see the earlier discussion, pp. 112–113).[13] During the early part of the nineteenth century, each of the major residential areas had Negro slaves living on the premises, as well as a fringe of Negro residences. This general dispersion of Negroes was temporarily challenged by the settlement of Americans, who wished to live near their ethnic rivals, the Creoles, and apparently were not concerned about proximity to Negro areas. However, since the turn of the century, two community developments were followed by a significant change in Negro location. Drainage of former swamp areas north of the older residential districts greatly expanded the area available for residences. During the same period, the use of the electric street car facilitated transportation to various parts of the city. Consequently, Negroes increasingly moved from their former "residential fringes" to a voluntarily concentrated area north of the business district, from which they could conveniently reach their jobs.

3. Durban, South Africa [14]

The residential distribution of nonwhites (Indians and native Africans) in Durban has for a long time been quite divergent from urban patterns in the United States. In general, Durban's nonwhite population has been concentrated in several dispersed districts, with a considerable degree of residential intermingling in Durban's approximation to the familiar "zone of transition." The accompanying table summarizes patterns of segregation by distinctive sociographic zones, which are also approximately scaled in terms of desirability and status. Essentially, the nonwhite population is located in middle or

[13] Harlan W. Gilmore, "The Old New Orleans and the New: A Case for Ecology," *American Sociological Review*, 9 (August, 1944), pp. 385–394.
[14] Leo Kuper, *Durban: A Study of Racial Ecology* (London, Jonathan Cape, Ltd., 1958).

outer zones—away from the refreshing ocean breezes and the major commercial district.

TABLE 51

Percentage of Ethnic Distribution of Population in Durban According to Socio-graphic Zones, 1951

SOCIO-GRAPHIC ZONES	Europeans	Coloreds	Indians	Africans	All Non-Europeans
Alluvial flats	4.81	4.81	56.59	33.79	95.19
Peripheral	12.48	2.75	39.70	45.07	87.52
Inland transitional	23.18	7.16	57.66	12.00	76.82
Seaward transitional	65.91	7.18	17.22	9.69	34.09
Sea front	67.43	0.62	5.83	26.12	32.57
Central Berea Ridge	88.59	0.43	1.78	9.20	11.41
Total	*32.75*	*4.01*	*36.28*	*26.96*	*67.25*

SOURCE: Leo Kuper *et al., Durban: A Study in Racial Ecology,* p. 110.

Since 1950 the City Council, representing the Europeans, has been developing plans for a more sharply segregated system of residential location. The underlying idea is to establish well-defined "group areas" (*i.e.,* racially distinct areas), with the desirable inner areas reserved for Europeans, and a rough band of outer areas north and south of the central area for Africans and Indians. Such a program would require extensive resettlement of non-Europeans, but in addition many Europeans would face the annoyance of relocation. As a result, some resistance from Europeans—on grounds of expediency rather than "humanitarianism"—has caused review and modification of these plans. In view of the prevailing political climate in South Africa, some drastic resettlement along racial lines will undoubtedly be attempted. At present, the nonwhites seem to be more interested in expanding economic opportunities and health services than in stability or change in residential patterns per se.

CHANGES IN COMMERCIAL LOCATION AND FUNCTION

Since 1945, the mammoth suburban or semisuburban shopping center has become a familiar accompaniment to the rapid growth of

suburban residential areas. Until a few years ago, these new commercial nuclei primarily catered to the daily and weekly needs of their
customers—drugs, groceries, laundry and dry cleaning, etc. Consequently, the significance of these centers was limited to competition
with commercial clusters in older neighborhoods.[15] With the increasing
location of department store branches in suburban centers, however,
a genuine ecological revolution is at hand, a reversal of the multiform
commercial dominance of the central business district.

The clearest and most advanced case of this revolution can be
found in the New York City region. Macy's, Gimbel's, Lord and
Taylor, and others have invested heavily in suburban branches in New
York, New Jersey, and Connecticut. Lord and Taylor, a moderate-
sized enterprise for many years, furnishes an interesting example of
expansion. Founded in 1820 on Fifth Avenue, the first suburban
branch was opened in Manhasset, Long Island in 1941. A West-
chester branch opened its doors in 1948, soon to be followed by
others in West Hartford (1953), Bala-Cynwyd (1955), and Garden
City (1956).

Federal Reserve figures for the New York region convincingly show
that suburban department store sales rose dramatically in the early
fifties—as compared with a very modest rise for the downtown stores.
Currently, it is not clear that these suburban increases have been
achieved at the expense of the parent stores. It has been suggested
that suburban branches have instead invaded the previous commercial
monopoly of smaller, local competitors.[16] In any case, the convenience
and variety now available to suburban families in peripheral centers
(in 15-30 minutes driving time) undoubtedly signifies a commercial
decentralization that presents vexing problems for downtown merchants.

A dramatic aspect of this general trend—at least for New York
City—is the closing of several large department stores in downtown

[15] See Harold M. Mayer, "Patterns and Recent Trends of Chicago's Outlying
Business Centers," *Journal of Land and Public Utility Economics,* 18 (Febru-
ary, 1942), pp. 4–16; Homer Hoyt, "Classification and Significant Character-
istics of Shopping Centers," in Harold M. Mayer and Clyde F. Kohn, eds.,
Readings in Urban Geograpy (Chicago, University of Chicago Press, 1959),
pp. 454–461; Mabel Walker, *Business Enterprise and the City* (Princeton, Tax
Institute, Inc., 1959), pp. 108–144; J. Ross McKeever, *Shopping Centers Re-
Studied: Part 2, Practical Experiences,* Urban Land Institute, Technical Bulletin
No. 30, (Washington, D.C., 1957).

[16] Walker, *op. cit.,* p. 110; *The New York Times,* February 5, 1956.

areas.[17] Since 1952, eight such establishments have gone out of business in Manhattan and Brooklyn. The reasons are obvious to merchandisers. These stores failed to provide a modernized, attractive setting for a new generation of shoppers; the traditional, hard core of steady customers, who had received personal attention from favorite sales personnel, who once cared little for superficial physical improvements in the store, are virtually gone—because of death, removal to other cities, and even the competition of the more modern stores. The young, middle-class homemakers (the heaviest spenders in department stores) have moved to the suburbs and require extraordinary methods of enticement to shop downtown. Some stores, notably McCrory's, had emphasized a narrow range of merchandise—e.g., linens and materials by the yard—which is too restricted for the newer style of living. It is interesting to note that, with one exception, none of these stores had previously established suburban branches. Only one of the newly closed stores, Lewis and Conger (specializing in a stimulating variety of house-wares), has as yet moved to a suburban location.

Somewhat less sensational but also symptomatic of ecological changes is the growing crisis of business offices in downtown districts. Since World War II, there has been a shortage of competent secretarial and clerical employees. A partial explanation lies in the recent development of new business offices in suburban areas. To this must be added the familiar fact that many potential typists and secretaries are suburban residents and refuse to bear the expense and inconvenience of commuting. Furthermore, a growing proportion of young women (suburban or urban) is college-trained, and therefore desires more creative positions than switchboard operator, typist, or stenographer. In desperation, several New York offices have migrated to the suburbs. But they have been confronted with a rebellion of their "urban" employees, who miss the opportunity of downtown shopping during the lunch hour.[18]

ECOLOGICAL DYNAMICS: A SUMMARY

Significant changes in urban ecological patterns normally develop over a span of decades, since most of the unit decisions in this process are made without extensive knowledge and evaluation of other decisions. Despite the popular fiction of the *calculating urbanite*, consid-

[17] *The New York Times*, February 17, 1957.
[18] *Ibid.*, February 24, 1952.

erable time often elapses before the opportunities for change are noted and acted upon. Ecological patterns are therefore of varying clarity to the urban sociologist, and at the same time apparently are rarely of conscious significance to most residents.

Nevertheless, we may conclude that the key to urban ecological dynamics is the *social and cultural structure* of given regions—at least after the initial location and settlement have been achieved. Essentially, as our previous discussion has illustrated, a major change in land use, population distribution, and the interrelations between subareas derives from changes in valuation or changes in the techniques of applying existing values. As examples of the first type, we may mention industry's recent concern for more space and for more desirable living conditions for its employees, the increasing emphasis on *visible* signs of status ascent, and a persistent change in taste in emulation of the traditional "leisure class." On the other hand, changes in techniques of realizing values—particularly accessibility and convenience —can be seen in a variety of transportation improvements (automobile, bus, street car, modern highway system) and in the use of numerous electrical appliances (*e.g.*, the recent "Dogomatic," which grills six frankfurters). Ultimately, then, ecological change depends on valuational change and the technical and financial ability to translate values into action. The latter condition, in turn, is related to specific institutional structures of the region and society—which will be discussed in Part III.

Altered valuations and technical resources may be considered *facilitating* factors in ecological change. *Resistance* to ecological change—whether conscious or unconscious—rests on adherence to traditional values that are immune to competition, or on outmoded facilities that defy change except through drastic methods. For example, Tokyo has a heavy industrial concentration in three inner areas, which are linked with outer residential areas by a comparatively small number of very narrow streets, which were haphazardly laid out to follow ancient goat paths. The resultant traffic congestion could be reduced by either relocating Tokyo's industrial establishments or widening a limited number of key streets, and opening the Imperial Palace area to public transportation. But neither approach has yet been seriously considered. Financial problems are of course involved, though tradition seems to be the major obstacle.[19]

[19] *Ibid.,* April 26, 1959.

Ecological Change and Planning

It seems likely that the era of uncoordinated operation of facilitating and restrictive factors in ecological change is coming to a close, though not without opposition. City and regional planning bodies, the focus of Part IV, constitute a new aspect of urban social organization. They seek—with varying success—to guide ecological changes with conscious concern for reducing undesirable by-products of change for the region as a whole. But the essential factors in ecological dynamics remain. Planning merely introduces the possibility of new combinations and more responsible attention to varied community and regional needs.

SELECTED REFERENCES

HAWLEY, Amos H., *Human Ecology* (New York, Ronald Press, 1950), Part IV.

HOYT, Homer, *One Hundred Years of Land Values in Chicago* (Chicago, University of Chicago Press, 1933).

QUINN, James A., *Human Ecology* (Englewood Cliffs, N.J., Prentice-Hall, 1950), Part III.

THEODORSON, George A., ed., *Studies in Human Ecology* (Evanston, Ill., Row, Peterson, 1961), Part II, Section C.

CHAPTER 7

Emergence and Structure
of the Urban Region:
Suburb, Satellite, and Fringe

THE URBAN REGION, which is a continuously evolving entity, is slowly gaining serious recognition as the most important and strategic unit in modern society. However, the identification of urban regions requires some major alterations in our patterns of thought and our evaluation of public and private affairs. In general, the development of the urban region reflects a continuing tension between traditional political organization and boundary-lines, on the one hand, and rapidly changing radii of personal and institutional relations in pursuing needs and providing services, on the other hand. The urbanite unconsciously faces this problem almost every day in referring to his area, and particularly so when talking to visitors or chance acquaintances. If he lives in a well-defined suburban area, the *name* of the locality certainly has meaning, but this is normally accompanied by the frequent reminders of metropolitan mass media that he is a resident of "Chicagoland," the Los Angeles area, etc. Indeed, as I sit here several miles from the city limits of Atlanta, in a densely populated, unincorporated suburban belt, I cannot help realize that many necessary services are supplied by organizations located in downtown Atlanta. Specifically, the provision of police and fire protection, education, and water for this area largely rests on taxes derived from incomes earned in the central city.

Under these conditions, the name of the central city has constantly enlarged applications and reference points. Perhaps this phenomenon is most clearly illustrated by the London Region, which consists of ten official and approximately concentric zones—all of which possess in their special fashion the "London" label: [1]

1. *The City of London:* about one square mile, containing the financial and economic heart of the region.

2. *The County of London:* approximately 116 square miles, including a 5-mile radius around the City.

3. *Drainage London:* virtually coextensive with London County.

4. *"Water" London:* the area served by the Metropolitan Water Board; this is larger than Drainage London and contained about seven and one-half millions in 1939.

5. *Greater London:* the area involving a 15-mile radius from Charing Cross Station.

6. *Police London:* almost 700 square miles, with a population of eight and two-thirds millions (1939); contains 101 local government units.

7. *Electricity London:* 25-mile radius from Charing Cross.

8. *Transport London:* 30-mile radius from Charing Cross; population of almost ten million (1939).

9. *Traffic London:* 40-mile radius from Charing Cross.

10. *Planning London:* area under the jurisdiction of the Greater London Regional Planning Committee.

The London region and its various "functional" zones exemplify the basic nature of urban regions: a cumulative system of more or less segregated functions or services whose performance establishes networks of dependence between (*a*) service centers and their clients, customers, or adherents; and (*b*) service areas—made up of service organizations and clients—and the central city. Indeed, the emergence and growth of urban regions is essentially a process of exporting specific functions (or clusters of functions) to peripheral areas, supplemented by the process of "encroachment" on existent areas and functions which lie in the path of regional expansion.[2]

[1] Albert Lepawsky, "The London Region: A Metropolitan Community in Crisis," *American Journal of Sociology,* 46 (May, 1941), pp. 826–834. See also J. B. Cullingworth, *Housing Needs and Planning Policy* (London, Routledge and Kegan Paul, 1960), Chap. VIII.

[2] R. D. McKenzie, *The Metropolitan Community* (New York, McGraw-Hill Book Company, 1933), pp. 70–76, 313.

In the processes of exporting and encroaching, a series of new (or newly significant) areas have become familiar supplements to the central city. Each "part" or "specialized area" in the urban region has acquired distinctive characteristics that seem to reflect its peculiar position and function in the region. As the accompanying figure shows in a highly simplified form, these parts are typically arrayed in an intelligible though mainly unplanned manner, which in essence constitutes the *ecological pattern* of modern urban regions. The major tasks of this chapter, therefore, consist of analyzing the emergence, features, and functioning of suburbs, the urban fringe, the satellite city, and the exurban area, and then reviewing and assessing the evidence for their interdependent operation as *regional entities*.

FIGURE 8

A Simplified Ecological Diagram of the Urban Region

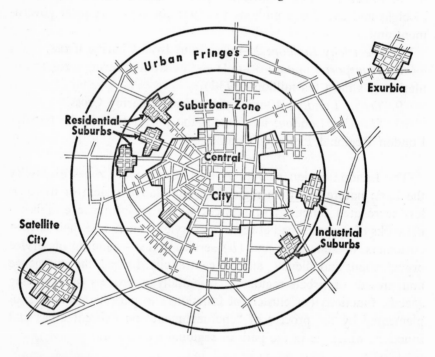

THE SUBURB

Though the suburb is an ancient phenomenon in human communities—for example, the suburbs of the Greek *polis* and the merchants' quarter of the late medieval town—it is only with the flowering of the modern metropolis (*ca.* 1870 in the United States; *ca.* 1800-1850 in Europe) that the suburb has increased in number and importance. The modern suburb is at the same time a creature of, and a reaction to, the complex development of the central city. Essentially, suburban growth has been made possible by successful expansion of a variety of commercial and industrial enterprises and the consequent creation of a rising middle class, improvements in communication and transportation, and the perceptive investments of real estate subdividers and builders, who have produced residential facilities and a tantalizing concept of "gracious living," formerly limited to a favored minority.[3] To these opportunities have been added the necessary *motivations* of urbanites: the desire for space, scenery, home ownership, proximity to social equals, and a communal identity distinct from the visible controls of the big city.[4] The ubiquitous result is *suburbia,* particularly in its residential form.

But how may we distinguish suburbs from other "parts" in the outer portions of modern urban regions? As a beginning, we may define suburbs as those *urbanized nuclei* located outside (but within accessible range) of central cities that are politically independent but economically and psychologically linked with services and facilities provided by the metropolis. By "urbanized nuclei" we mean those areas outside the central city that have relatively substantial population densities, a preponderance of nonrural occupations, and distinctly urban forms of recreation, family life, and education.[5] In addition, the economic and social structure of urbanized nuclei can be shown to reflect continuing bonds of dependence on the opportunities, selected services, and essential values of the central city. It should be pointed out that most of the territorial expansion of the central city

[3] Chauncey Harris, "Suburbs," *American Journal of Sociology,* 49 (July, 1943), pp. 1–13; Leo F. Schnore, "The Growth of Metropolitan Suburbs," *American Sociological Review,* 22 (April, 1957), pp. 165–173; C. Wright Mills, *White Collar* (New York, Oxford University Press, 1950), pp. 251–258; H. Paul Douglas, *The Suburban Trend* (New York, Appleton-Century-Crofts, Inc., 1925); Carl Von Rhode, "The Suburban Mind," *Harper's Magazine,* 192 (April, 1946), pp. 289–299.

[4] This is the theme of Robert C. Wood, *Suburbia: Its People and Their Politics* (Boston, Houghton Mifflin, 1959).

[5] Otis D. Duncan and Albert J. Reiss, Jr., *Social Characteristics of Urban and Rural Communities* (New York, John Wiley and Sons, 1956), pp. 117–119; Nathan L. Whetten, "Suburbanization as a Field for Sociological Research," *Rural Sociology,* 16 (December, 1951), pp. 319–328; Robert C. Schmitt, "Suburbanization: Statistical Fallacy?" *Land Economics,* 32 (February, 1956), pp. 85–87.

since 1890 has been accomplished by political annexation of existing or potential suburban areas.

With this initial characterization as a guide, we may turn to a more detailed review of suburban features. However, there is a popular view of "suburbia," which is a caricature of suburban areas, because it fails to take account of important types of suburban developments. The first distinction to be made is based on variation in suburban functions. Thus, there are predominantly *industrial suburbs, residential suburbs,* and *recreational* or *resort suburbs.* In the residential type, however, it may also be helpful to classify areas with respect to relative age, social class structure, and migration patterns. With some oversimplification, then, we may identify three subtypes of residential suburb:

1. Traditional upper-class suburb

This type, so ably dissected by Cleveland Amory,[6] is numerically small and increasingly untypical of recent trends in suburban development. Essentially, this type is marked by: a preponderance of long established, high status families; comparatively little turnover in population; location near towns or villages that have extensive, independent histories; and an understandable concentration in the Northeast (*e.g.,* near Boston, New York City, and Philadelphia).

2. The stable middle-class suburb

More recent in origin than the previous type, this suburban form is perhaps the most representative of modern suburbia. It attracts families from the middle income and status range, who seek relatively permanent residence in newly developed segments of the urban fringe. In general, the occupations of this group are concentrated in such professions as medicine, law, teaching, in medium-level proprietors, and the more stable executive positions in commercial and industrial organizations.[7]

[6] Cleveland Amory, *The Proper Bostonians* (New York, E. P. Dutton and Company, 1947).

[7] Good examples of this type are discussed in John R. Seely *et al., Crestwood Heights:* A Study of the Culture of Suburban Life (New York, Basic Books, 1956); and Alvin H. Scaff, "The Effect of Commuting on Participation in Community Organizations," *American Sociological Review,* 17 (April, 1952), pp. 215–220.

3. The "packaged" suburb

This is the most obtrusive and controversial type of residential suburb—the recent object of much fiction and impressionistic diagnosis. In contrast to the other types, it is quickly and uniformly carved out of apparent nothingness deep in the urban fringe. Occasionally, it is referred to as the "mass produced suburb," which indicates that most or all dwelling units are faithful replicas of one or two simplified designs and that the area is fully developed "at birth" rather than a gradual accumulation of physical facilities, housing styles, and population. The packaged suburb reflects an insistent need for respectable but moderate-priced housing, which the stable middle class suburb cannot satisfy. Most of the residents seem to be highly mobile (geographically and socially), comparatively young, and in the junior executive category of national corporations.[8]

The Industrial Suburb

It is quite apparent that the industrial or "employing" suburb has been relatively ignored in recent years as an object of urban studies, in favor of the residential or "dormitory" type. Perhaps two features of the industrial suburb, however, can be considered well established. (a) Understandably, the occupational and social class distributions of industrial suburbs are weighted toward the skilled and semiskilled categories, and likewise toward lower and lower middle status groups. (b) In recent years, the relative population growth of industrial suburbs has been significantly smaller than that of residential suburbs. This is true for all sections of the nation, for all sizes of central city and suburb, and for all distances from the central city. Perhaps these comparative trends reflect an approximation to "saturation" in growth of industrial suburbs, particularly of the *larger* and *older* suburbs. The rate of growth is lowest, for example, in the Northeast and

[8] Studies of this suburban type include: Harold Wattell, "Levittown: A Suburban Community," in William Dobriner, ed., *The Suburban Community* (New York, G. P. Putnam's Sons, 1958), pp. 287–313; William H. Whyte, Jr., "The Transients," in Llewellyn Miller, ed., *Prize Articles 1954* (New York, Ballantine Books, 1954), pp. 39–112 [These originally appeared in Fortune Magazine during 1953.]; William H. Whyte, Jr., *The Organization Man* (Garden City, N.Y., Doubleday and Company, 1956), Part VII. A readable and broad-ranging critique of the packaged suburb is John Keats, *The Crack in the Picture Window* (New York, Ballantine Books, 1956).

highest in the newer industrial suburbs of the West and South.[9] Suburban growth in general seems to depend on expansion of residential areas, rather than on employment opportunities in industrial suburbs.

The Residential Suburb: Basic Features

Since the residential suburb in its various forms—rather than the industrial type—is increasingly representative of suburban segments in the urban region, its basic characteristics are important in locating its identity and in understanding the generalized suburban function in the urban regional complex. Unfortunately, we do not have adequate comparative data for all the residential subtypes. In the absence of such information, we are only able to offer several tentative conclusions about suburban population features in terms of comparisons with the central city.

1. Suburban areas, particularly residential types, have experienced the highest rate of population increase of any urban component in the last twenty years. By 1950, suburban areas contained 21.2 per cent of the total population in the nation's urban regions (the Urbanized Areas of the United States Census Bureau figures).[10]

2. The sex ratio of suburbs is generally slightly higher than that of central cities,[11] though we do not know the differential in sex ratio between residential and industrial types. This suggests a more "balanced" population in the suburbs, which may be related to the following feature.

3. A higher proportion of married males and females is found in suburbs, as compared with central cities.[12]

4. The median age of suburban populations is almost two years below that of central cities. Comparatively greater concentrations in the lower and middle age groups (0–19 and 25–44 years) and higher fertility ratios for suburban areas also support the image of suburban youthfulness.[13]

5. The proportion of nonwhites is significantly smaller in the suburbs. Foreign-born whites likewise are somewhat less concentrated

[9] Leo F. Schnore, "The Growth of Metropolitan Suburbs," op. cit., pp. 29–34. A recent study of an industrial suburb in California is Bennett M. Berger, Working-Class Suburb (Berkeley, University of California Press, 1960).

[10] Duncan and Reiss, op. cit., p. 119.

[11] Ibid., p. 120.

[12] Ibid., p. 123.

[13] Ibid., pp. 120–121.

in suburbs,[14] though it is likely that most of the foreign-born suburban population resides in the industrial suburb.

6. Suburban residents show a somewhat higher amount of formal education, as measured by median school years completed by persons 25 years of age and over, than do city people. For suburban non-whites, however, this difference is reversed, perhaps indicating a selection of nonwhites from lower occupational categories to industrial suburbs.[15]

7. Despite the somewhat incompatible mixture of data from residential and industrial suburbs, suburban areas show rather clear-cut differences in occupational distribution from that found in central cities (and satellite cities). Greater concentrations of professional, managerial, business proprietors, and skilled craftsmen live in suburbs, compared to the central city, while the city contains somewhat higher proportions of service workers and unskilled laborers.[16]

8. In the larger suburbs at least, population increase seems to be differentially explained in industrial and residential types. The residential suburb has grown in population during 1940–1950 more as a consequence of migration than of natural increase. In industrial suburbs, natural increase is a considerably stronger factor than migration. Outstanding exceptions to these patterns have been found for Los Angeles and Chicago suburban areas, though no adequate explanation for these deviations is at hand.[17]

The Roles of the Suburb

The suburb is a specialized outpost of the large city. It is not, nor can it be, a community in the full sense of the term. Instead, it represents a selection of urban "fragments" or functions that seem to operate more efficiently (or more satisfactorily) when segregated from the immediate heterogeneity of the central city. In the case of the in-

[14] *Ibid.,* p. 122. See also the analysis of 1960 trends in *The New York Times,* May 7, 1961.

[15] Duncan and Reiss, *op. cit.,* pp. 127–128.

[16] *Ibid.,* pp. 174–177.

[17] Leo F. Schnore, "Components of Population Change in Large Metropolitan Suburbs," *American Sociological Review,* 23 (October, 1958), pp. 570–573. See also the analyses of Leo F. Schnore, "Satellites and Suburbs," *Social Forces,* 36 (December, 1957), pp. 121–129; and Donald J. Bogue and Emerson Seim, "Components of Population Change in Suburban and Central City Populations of Standard Metropolitan Areas: 1940 to 1950," *Rural Sociology,* 21 (1956), pp. 267–275.

dustrial suburb, the reciprocal advantages of specialization are fairly clear. From the standpoint of the central city, industrial relocation reduces inner congestion and physical annoyance, while furnishing a continuing demand for labor and a flow of desired commodities. The industrial suburb, on the other hand, enjoys the advantages of ample space, reduced production costs, a generally shorter "journey to work," the relative promiximity to needed urban services, and often a local market for its products.

What, then, is the functional significance of the residential suburb in the urban region—since it produces nothing more tangible than babies? The immense popularity and expansion of these suburbs in recent years is neither accidental nor temporary. Suburbs may be regarded as symptoms or perhaps symbols of a solution to the persistent problem: how to make the best of two worlds. While it would be difficult to estimate the success of the "suburban solution," its ingredients and some of their effects on both city and suburb can be tentatively analyzed.

1. With some variation, residential suburbs probably provide the best available conditions (both physical and psychological) for family living and child rearing in the urban region. The emphasis on the home as an end in itself, relatively undisturbed by the competition of commercial, semi-industrial, and other closely situated family groups, is difficult to sustain in most parts of the central city. For the increasing number of suburban families, a cardinal motivation is the opportunity for more "gracious living," more comfort and relaxation for all family members. Suburbia is not Utopia by any means, but it does represent in part a "resurgence" of satisfying family life for many reared in the frustrations of the Great Depression. The suburban birth rate, which is somewhat higher than the urban average,[18] may be interpreted as a psychological response to the suburban "atmosphere."

2. The physical and social segregation of residential suburbs also facilitates the development and expansion of middle class segments in the urban region. It has been suggested, with some justification, that the urban way of life rests on the support and allegiance of the middle classes. And yet, paradoxically, urban developments of the past two generations have been uncongenial to middle class ideals—within the inner zones of the central city. The residential suburb, therefore, provides a haven for the middle class pursuit of status, for each member of the family.

[18] See chapter 4, pp. 85, 88.

3. As a direct result of the preceding function, the residential suburb is becoming a major source in motivating, educating, and supplying the professional, managerial, and technical personnel required in the economic and political functions of the central city.

4. Both interview and questionnaire data and the pattern of suburban social participation (see pp. 134–136) suggest that the residential suburb serves as a kind of "frontier" for portions of the urbanized population. The suburbanite indicates in many ways a desire for greater *independence* and *self-expression,* which, he feels, are inevitably restricted by the established bureaucratic structures (in government and politics, welfare, etc.) in the city.[19] This "escape" from the "urban treadmill" may be detected in the continuous search for new and relatively active organizations (the PTA, the League of Women Voters, local units of major political parties, taxpayers' associations, etc.), in the "do it yourself" movement, and in the apparently perverse self-denial of such desired services as public education and improved roads (which is not so much a reflection of "conservatism" as of the opportunity to assert one's veto power).

5. From the city's standpoint, the residential suburb is a mixed blessing. Suburban growth adds to the urbanized population, particularly in terms of the new census unit—the SMA. But this growth is not immediately expressed in tangible advantages to the city. Until the suburb is absorbed by annexation or is economically linked by the municipal income tax, the central city discovers that suburbia cuts deeply into municipal revenues [20]—principally in personal and real property taxes, sales tax returns, and in business taxes. In addition, Community Chest campaigns inevitably suffer from suburban movements, unless regional agreements encompassing suburban areas are reached.

6. Yet, in another sense, the residential suburb is highly significant for the urban region. In a planless but nonetheless effective manner, suburban developments serve to relieve somewhat the population congestion of cities caused by continuous urbanward migration and the relative scarcity of adequate housing. By reducing the insistent

[19] Wood, *op. cit.,* pp. 153–166; Richard Dewey, "Peripheral Expansion in Milwaukee County," *American Journal of Sociology,* 54 (September, 1948), pp. 118–125.

[20] One study of large cities in 1940 demonstrated a connection between suburban growth and tax burdens on city residents. See Amos H. Hawley, "Metropolitan Population and Municipal Government Expenditures in Central Cities," *Journal of Social Issues,* 7, Nos. 1 and 2 (1951), pp. 101–108.

pressure for residential space in the "middle zones" of the city, the suburbs in effect provide a safety valve and an opportunity for alert cities to replace slum areas and substandard housing, to accelerate the movement by city residents to more desirable, existing housing facilities, and thus eventually to diminish the financial and social loss connected with rapid suburbanization. However, these opportunities must be recognized and acted upon by intelligent and concerted leadership in the city, if they are to be translated into achievements.

THE URBAN FRINGE

It is to be expected that the nature of the urban region becomes increasingly difficult to identify and analyze as one moves from the city proper to the region's periphery. At the present time, the urban fringe (and closely related labels for this type of area) is therefore understandably vague, or so variably defined that its characteristics do not form a coherent whole. But there is enough valid information to conclude that the fringe is not chaotic, but a meaningful entity in the urban regional complex.

If we recall the imputed nature of the urban region as a "system" in continuous operation, involving the basic processes of growth, differentiation, and coordination, then the fringe can be initially approached as that part of the region *most immediately relevant* to regional expansion and therefore least subject to the process of regional coordination. From a purely geographic standpoint, most of the fringe area thus defined is peripheral. But, as many urban land inventories have shown, there are "fringe areas" or "islands" in the suburban zone, and even within the city limits.[21]

Since suburban areas develop from previously "fringe" territories, it is clearly necessary to distinguish these two regional "parts" from one another. The fringe possesses several identifying features:

1. Its general location is beyond the suburban zone or cluster, but normally near main highways or watercourses.

2. The land use pattern of the fringe is a crescive, uncoordinated accumulation of residential, commercial, manufacturing, and special

[21] See Richard B. Andrews, "Elements in the Urban Fringe Pattern," *Journal of Land and Public Utility Economics*, 18 (May, 1942), pp. 169–183; George S. Wehrwein, "The Rural-Urban Fringe," *Urban Geography*, 18 (July, 1942), pp. 217–228; Walter Firey, "Ecological Considerations in Planning for Urban Fringes," *American Sociological Review*, 11 (August, 1946), pp. 411–421.

service (private hospitals, cemeteries, etc.) types, with considerable amounts of vacant land.

3. The residential facilities of the fringe *tend* toward lower levels of attractiveness and physical repair (*e.g.,* tourist cabins, trailer homes).

4. The employed population tends to be drawn from lower status categories than are found in the residential suburb.

5. Since the fringe as an urban appendage is relatively new, or in early stages of development, it normally lacks both urban services (*e.g.,* pressurized gas for cooking and heating, adequate water systems, paved streets, etc.) and local social organization, such as its own government, school system, police and fire protection, and churches. Firey and Wehrwein have therefore called the fringe "an institutional desert." [22]

6. The "outer rim" of the fringe, also called the "extended fringe," is adjacent to, or intermixed with, more or less active agricultural areas.

7. Because of the encroachment of more settled suburban areas, the fringe is in constant change with respect to boundary lines. In general, however, fringe areas and fringe population are declining.

The Role of the Fringe

The importance of the fringe is considerable, though comparatively little definitive data are available. Essentially, the urban fringe has been a major source of urban expansion, from which have eventually emerged the residential and industrial suburbs. In addition, the fringe provides an interesting but still unexplored locus of social and cultural contacts between urban and rural families, since population movements to the fringe involve families from farms and villages, as well as from the central city.[23] On the other hand, the absence of effective social controls (either from the city, county, or local area) tends to make the fringe attractive to irresponsible land developers, criminals, gamblers, and nuisance activities (roadhouses, dumping areas)—all of which may interfere with the orderly expansion of the

[22] Wehrwein, *op. cit.*, p. 223; Walter Firey, *Social Aspects of Land Use Planning in the Country-City Fringe* (East Lansing, Michigan State College Agricultural Experiment Station, June, 1946).

[23] Myles W. Rodehaver, "Fringe Settlement as a Two-Dimensional Movement," *Rural Sociology*, 12 (March, 1947), pp. 49–57.

urban region and with the search for adequate residential accommodations.

SATELLITE CITIES

At the outer edge of the fringe, but often in a segment of the fringe of the largest cities, are located one or more *satellite* communities whose status and functional importance to the urban region are somewhat unique. Known variously as independent cities (*i.e.,* not within census-defined regions), employing satellites, hinterland cities, and subdominant communities, the satellite city is in some respects a miniature version of the central city.[24] However, the satellite should be distinguished both from the central city and the industrial suburb (with which it has sometimes been confused). For simplicity, it may be helpful to classify satellite cities into two categories—*large:* 100,000 population or over; and *small:* 10,000 to 100,000 population, thus enabling us to note gross variations in characteristics related to size whenever the data permit.

In general, satellite cities appear to have their origin prior to and therefore independent of the rise of central cities. Many satellites once had pretensions to urban grandeur, but newer and more favorably situated cities (both geographically and politically) have come to overshadow their older, less fortunate competitors. Thus, the satellite, as the name implies, operates in a functionally restricted manner in the regional complex. This is substantially true for both size categories.

Unlike most suburbs but in line with central cities, satellite cities are politically independent, formally organized communities. They generally supply their residents with the normal range of community services—often with distinct quality in the larger satellites—but are rarely able to afford such urban accomplishments as art museums, symphony orchestras, etc.

The relative location of smaller satellite cities is normally beyond the fringe and frequently at points roughly intermediate to contiguous urban regions. Consequently, the satellite tends to have an "exposed" or marginal location, in contrast to the relatively shorter distance between the suburb and central city. In some instances (*i.e.,* the larger satellites), the satellite is almost adjacent to its central city—across

[24] Donald J. Bogue, *Population Growth in Standard Metropolitan Areas 1900–1950* (Washington, Housing and Home Finance Agency, December, 1953), pp. 40–45.

a river or bay (*e.g.,* Council Bluffs, Iowa and Omaha, Nebraska; Jersey City and New York City; Camden, N. J. and Philadelphia).

By comparison with either residential or industrial suburbs, the satellite tends to have a larger average population size. This results from the greater life span of the satellite, but more significantly from the greater range of activities and services.

The satellite city, unlike the residential but somewhat similar to the industrial suburb and the central city, is a predominantly *employing area* of the urban region, as measured by the proportion of residents who work in the community as against those who commute to the central city for employment. Recent studies indicate that satellites specialize both in manufacturing and various types of retail trade, with a preponderance of manufacturing in northern and midwestern satellites, and diversified retail trade in the south. As Schnore points out, satellites provide few employment opportunities in transportation, resort and recreational functions, or wholesale activities.[25] Consequently, while the satellite resembles the central city as a source of jobs, it functions as a supplement, rather than a competitor, to the metropolitan center.

There is some evidence that satellite communities possess distinctive population characteristics, which seem to be intermediate to those of the central city and suburban areas. On the basis of incomplete data, the satellites seem to lie between the city and suburb on such features as: percent of nonwhites, sex ratio, proportion of married males, and proportion of younger persons. Other studies point to the comparatively lower status levels of satellite populations, as measured by median rentals and property values.[26]

In general, satellite communities show an average population increase considerably below that of suburbs, though comparable to or higher than that of central cities. The relative stability of satellites probably indicates a continuing specialization in a few economic functions, with a consequent de-emphasis on *residential* expansion (which is currently the greatest source of population increase).

[25] Schnore, "Satellites and Suburbs," *loc cit.;* Grace M. Kneedler, "Functional Types of Cities," in Paul K. Hatt and Albert J. Reiss, Jr., eds., *Reader in Urban Sociology* (New York, The Free Press of Glencoe, 1951), pp. 49–53; Clarence F. Ridley *et al.,* eds., *The Municipal Year Book 1953* (Chicago, International City Managers Association, 1953), pp. 54–56.
[26] Duncan and Reiss, *op. cit.,* pp. 171–175; Schnore, "Satellites and Suburbs." *loc. cit.*

The role of the satellite city in urban regions has been well described as "subdominant." [27] It is important as a specialized though unofficial agent of the central city which aids in furnishing services and organization to the distant subareas of the region. This function is neither planned nor voluntary, but is probably the major basis for survival of satellite communities. The unintended result is a strengthening of the invisible bonds which maintain a regional identity. Not only does the satellite flourish under this division of labor, but the central city is thereby relieved of some of its staggering responsibilities in providing facilities for urbanites beyond municipal limits. It should be recalled that a substantial proportion of the population in the urban fringe (as defined by the Census Bureau)—20 per cent—resides in incorporated areas each having 2,500 population or over.[28]
These areas are often what we have referred to as "satellite communities."

EXURBIA [29]

The farthest thrust of the urban region is both relatively recent and somewhat rare. Only the very largest cities—New York City, Chicago, and Los Angeles—seem to develop one or more *exurban outposts,* which are located well beyond the fringe in what were originally rural or village communities. The exurban area may or may not be geographically continuous with the more familiar segments of the urban region. But it is nevertheless closely linked with the central city.

Exurbia is generically similar to suburbia, although the exurbanite often refuses to consider himself in the same universe with the suburbanite. Both types represent a basic ambivalence toward the big city; both wish to escape—but not too far (either physically or psychologically) from the cultural magnetism of the metropolis. Exurbia and suburbia differ, however, in their *opportunities* to express this ambivalence and in the *means* used to implement it.

The exurbanite, by virtue of his occupation, has superior opportunities for escape. He (or she) is typically in the "creative" branches of the vast urban communications industry—advertising, commercial

---

[27] Donald J. Bogue, *The Structure of the Metropolitan Community* (Ann Arbor, Mich., Horace H. Rackham School of Graduate Studies, University of Michigan, 1949), pp. 18–20, 61–62.

[28] Bogue, *Population Growth in Standard Metropolitan Areas,* p. 43.

[29] The following discussion is primarily based on A. C. Spectorsky, *The Exurbanites* (Philadelphia, J. B. Lippincott, 1955).

art, radio, television, films, magazines, and playwriting. From an ecological standpoint, given the desire to escape, these occupations are significant in that they do *not* require daily attendance at a downtown office or studio. In addition, they yield comparatively large salaries—$20,000 and up, with an average probably around $30,000. Consequently, the exurbanite can easily arrange to live at a considerable distance from the central city, unlike the typical suburbanite.

If exurbia is therefore both residence and workshop, how are specific locations selected? Escape involves physical distance, of course, but also physical *contrast* with the city and some link with previous marks of successful escape. These conditions are satisfied by rural and semirural areas where artists and writers of the recent past lived and worked—*e.g.*, Bucks County, Pennsylvania and Fairfield County, Connecticut.[30] Exurbia is therefore a specialized, modernized, financially successful version of the artists' colony, located 40-50 miles from the commercial center with which it maintains a sustained symbiotic relationship.

It is difficult to appraise the role of exurbia in the urban region. However, some relevant inferences can be made from the fragmentary information now available. Exurbanites, far out of proportion to their numbers, control (or at least significantly channel) the tastes and underlying ideals of urbanites in general. This is inherent in their occupational role, though many exurbanites would rather be "artistic" than merely expert tools of persuasion and amusement. In addition, as a special status group (based on their "glamorous" occupation, high income, and semibohemian living), exurbanites are among the pacesetters of urban fashion. The foreign car as a status item (rather than a more economical form of transportation), for example, was first adopted by exurbanites. Finally, exurban populations seem to be unwitting agents of a *restrictive* urban regionalism, while trying to retain the low density and high social status of "snob zoning" (such as requiring a minimum of four acres and $30,000 homes).[31]

THE URBAN REGION AS A FUNCTIONAL ENTITY

Throughout the preceding analyses of specialized parts in the urban region, it was difficult to ignore linkages *between* parts, and also the

[30] Boston seems to have acquired an exurban area in Hillsborough and Rockingham Counties of New Hampshire. See *The New York Times*, February 5, 1961.

[31] *The New York Times*, November 11 and December 16, 1956.

interrelations between specific parts and the central city. Indeed, the development and special character of each type of regional part could only be understood as a cumulative set of adjustments to some aspect (or aspects) of the central city. However, urban sociologists regard the central city as the dominant unit, not only with respect to influence on any one type of subdominant community, but as the subtle integrator of interrelations in the entire regional complex. In other words, the urban region is approached as a functional unity based on a territorial-social division of labor more or less influenced by the operation of the central city; and on recognizable patterns of coordination among the parts, which are directly or indirectly imposed by ongoing processes (social, cultural, and ecological) within the central city. Since this coordination and regional organization are highly complex, at present we can only try to indicate their essential character through research evidence that is illustrative and inferential, rather than conclusive.

Dominant Ecological Patterns

With some variations by region and size of central city, the basic dominance of the metropolis is most clearly evident in the familiar constellation of specialized zones or rings around the central city. (See Figure 8). This remarkably consistent pattern of differentiation is usually interpreted as a consequence of attempts (conscious or unintended) to accommodate to the centralized economic and political influence of the metropolis.

It has been suggested, furthermore, that specialized zones closest to the central city should therefore show greater *internal specialization* (*i.e.,* sharper differences between community units) than that of more distant zones. This is based on the theory that the power of an organizing center decreases with distance, and that its power over dependent units is reflected in varying *degrees* of specialization (which is viewed as an adjustive mechanism) within such units. Recently, some evidence has been presented which supports this theory for a sample of 24 SMA's.[32] Suburban communities closest to the central city were found to exhibit greater variations among themselves than were discovered in "outer" suburban areas in such relevant factors as occupational distribution (particularly in per cent of professionals and

[32] Leslie Kish, "Differentiation in Metropolitan Areas," *American Sociological Review,* 19 (August, 1954), pp. 388–398.

operatives), average monthly rental and physical condition of dwellings, concentration of nonwhites, and voting behavior. Perhaps these
differences can be explained as a consequence of the urban emphasis
on *status distinctions,* which presumably diminishes as urbanization
decreases.

Patterns of Population Distribution

Theoretically, metropolitan dominance should be indirectly expressed in the overall pattern of population density and distribution
in the urban region. More specifically, the various areal parts of the
region should exhibit predictably different population features as a
consequence of their respective relations with the central city. For
example, we would expect the urban fringe to have a lower density
of population than the residential and industrial suburbs and a greater
prevalence of "urban" population features in areas most accessible to
the central city.

In general, these expectations have been fairly well substantiated by
Bogue in studies of 67 of the largest urban regions of the U. S.[33] Not
only does population density tend to decrease with distance from the
metropolis, but the larger the metropolis (and therefore the greater
the presumed influence) the greater the relative density. As expected,
Bogue also demonstrates a relative concentration of persons with
"urban" features in areas closest to central cities. A special analysis
of sectors radiating from the metropolis to the regional periphery
further shows that population density is considerably higher in sectors
containing *highways to other major cities* and in those marked by the
presence of *satellite cities* than in sectors which had neither feature.
Central cities, therefore, seem to operate as latent regulators of regional population patterns, a situation that perhaps facilitates the
economic dominance of the metropolis.

Economic Dominance

A growing fund of investigations concerned with metropolitan dominance emphasizes the direct and indirect economic dependence of
the so-called hinterland on the central city. The pioneer formulations
of this approach were made by Gras, McKenzie, and several urban
geographers, but it is only recently that economic control has been

[33] Bogue, *The Structure of the Metropolitan Community,* pp. 31–54.

verified by Bogue and others.[34] In the decade 1940–1950, central cities tended to provide disproportionately higher amounts of wholesale, retail, and diversified services (*e.g.,* repairs, warehousing facilities) than other components of the urban region. Bogue found that population groupings within a 35-mile radius of the metropolis were specially dependent on the latter for retail commodities and diversified services, while dependence on wholesale services was even more marked for a 65-mile radius from the city. Beyond a 65-mile radius, in sectors containing either intermetropolitan highways or satellite cities, this dependence of the hinterland gradually declined. As summarized by McKenzie and Bogue, these economic patterns indicate that satellite cities, suburbs, and the fringe specialize in activities which do not directly compete with the superior resources of the metropolis.

Metropolitan dominance is not maintained without cost to the city population, however. Based on information for 76 cities of 100,000 population or over in 1940, it was discovered that per capita cost of city governmental services increases somewhat with increases in the proportion of regional population residing in the hinterland.[35] It would be interesting to know whether or not this situation persists, as well as the comparative changes in governmental costs for central cities and for hinterland communities since 1940.

Miscellaneous Facets of Metropolitan Dominance

Several indirect measures of metropolitan influence should also be noted. The effective range of significant contact with the central city has been fairly well established by studies of: relative frequency of telephone calls to or from the city; origin and destination surveys of automobiles, and other traffic surveys; and analysis of daily and Sunday newspaper circulation.[36]

Let us briefly examine newspaper circulation. Following the pattern

[34] N. S. B. Gras, *An Introduction to Economic History* (New York, Harper and Brothers, 1922), Chaps. V, VI; McKenzie, *op. cit.,* pp. 70–84, 313; Eugene Van Cleef, *Trade Centers and Trade Routes* (New York, Appleton-Century-Crofts, Inc., 1937); Harold M. Mayer and Clyde F. Kohn, eds., *Readings in Urban Geography* (Chicago, University of Chicago Press, 1959), Sections 7, 10; Bogue, *The Structure of the Metropolitan Community,* pp. 38–40, 54–60; Melvin E. DeFleur and John Crosby, "Analyzing Metropolitan Dominance," *Social Forces,* 35 (October, 1956), pp. 68–75.

[35] Hawley, *loc. cit.*

[36] James A. Quinn, *Human Ecology* (Englewood Cliffs, N.J., Prentice-Hall, 1950), Chap. VIII.

of earlier studies by Park and McKenzie, recent research indicates that a declining rate of readership of metropolitan newspapers accompanies increasing distance from the central city.[37] By itself, newspaper circulation does not provide clear-cut "limits" to the urban region; but circulation rates seem to be closely related to degrees of dominance in retail trade. Since advertising policy (*e.g.*, the space given to local merchants and regional branches of metropolitan firms) affects circulation patterns, this relationship is understandable. But it remains to be established that either advertising policy or special features in metropolitan dailies (syndicated columns, fuller news coverage, etc.) are more attractive to hinterland residents. Another consideration is the rapid rise of local community and neighborhood papers,[38] which corresponds to the recent development of peripheral population movements and new outlying business centers. It is too early to estimate the degree of competition these local papers offer, but it may be symptomatic that in North Hollywood, California, about 65 per cent of the readers of the Valley *Times* (circulation of 50,000) read no Los Angeles paper at all.[39]

SELECTED REFERENCES

BOGUE, Donald J., *The Structure of the Metropolitan Community* (Ann Arbor, Mich., Horace Rackham Graduate School, University of Michigan, 1949).

DICKINSON, Robert E., *City, Region and Regionalism* (London, Kegan Paul, Trench and Trubner, 1947).

DOBRINER, William, ed., *The Suburban Community* (New York, G. P. Putnam's Sons, 1958).

DUNCAN, Otis D. *et al., Metropolis and Region* (Baltimore, Johns Hopkins University Press, 1960).

GEDDES, Patrick, *Cities in Evolution,* new and enlarged ed. (New York, Oxford University Press, 1950).

HOOVER, Edgar H. and VERNON, Raymond, *Anatomy of a Metropolis* (Cambridge, Mass., Harvard University Press, 1959).

[37] Robert E. Park, "Urbanization and Newspaper Circulation," *American Journal of Sociology,* 35 (July, 1929), pp. 60–79; McKenzie, *op. cit.,* Chap. VIII; Noel P. Gist and L. A. Halbert, *Urban Society,* 4th ed. (New York, Thomas Y. Crowell, 1956), pp. 223–224.

[38] Morris Janowitz, *The Community Press in an Urban Setting* (New York, The Free Press of Glencoe, 1951).

[39] *Newsweek,* April 1, 1957.

MARTIN, Walter T., *The Rural-Urban Fringe* (Eugene, Ore., University of Oregon Press, 1953).

MCKENZIE, R. D., *The Metropolitan Community* (New York, McGraw-Hill, 1933).

PICKARD, Jerome P., *Metropolitanization of the United States*, Urban Land Institute, Research Monograph No. 2 (Washington, D.C., 1959).

SWEENEY, Stephen B., ed., *Metropolitan Analysis* (Philadelphia, University of Pennsylvania Press, 1958).

VANCE, Rupert B. and DEMERATH, Nicholas J., eds., *The Urban South* (Chapel Hill, N.C., University of North Carolina Press, 1954).

PART III

Social Organization and Cultural Foci of the Urban Region

CHAPTER 8

Primary Groups

As we have seen in Part II, the urban region exhibits a rather complex underlying structure, which we call its *ecological organization*. But ecological organization is not an independent or autonomous aspect of the urban regional system; we have already mentioned several typical instances in which specific group interests and general value systems clearly affect, and even alter, ecological organization (see pp. 110–113). Indeed, one of the themes of this book is the continual interplay between the basic ecological structure of the urban region and its distinctive social and cultural patterns.

As a backdrop to the discussion of urban social organization, let us briefly review the general nature of urban regions. First, the urban region encompasses a large, densely populated, irregularly shaped area. Partly as a consequence of its extent and population size, but very closely tied to its variety of services, is the development of highly specialized and increasingly segregated patterns of population location and activities. This division of regional labor—into subareas of the city and also in the form of specialized communities—often gives an impression of isolation, parochialism, and a defensive impersonality. A third feature is the impressive dominance of the central city over the region and, at the same time, a restless resistance to such dominance in the form of peripheral settlement and the frequent reluctance to support annexation. Finally, the basic organization of the urban region reflects a strong emphasis on rationality and efficiency, and a resultant pressure for expansion and change. The overall picture, then, is one that highlights a desired complexity, greater levels of performance, conscious or semiconscious forms of competition or emulation, and a strain toward coordination.

The present chapter and succeeding chapters in Part III will examine major segments of modern social and cultural organization in the urban region in terms of a few recurrent questions. How has the basic character of urban regions influenced the structure and operation of pre-existing types of social organization, especially those found in the rural community? What new types of social groups and cultural forms have been developed in the urban region? Can these new forms be better understood as adjustments to the special character of the urban region? And finally, what are the consequences of these socio-cultural innovations for urban ecological organization and the life-style of the urbanite?

The primary group is an extremely essential form of social organization in any community. It is normally marked by relatively few members, personal relationships, the concern for a variety of its members' needs and interests, informal and often unstated controls over individual behavior, an emphasis on personal qualities rather than performance, and the provision of emotional security.[1] Obviously, these features are in essential contradiction to the underlying patterns of the urban region. Consequently, we would expect rather substantial changes in urban primary groups. Yet we might also anticipate that the great psychological and social importance of the primary group would tend to limit or retard dramatic changes. Since the focal primary group relationships are in the family, the clique, the gang, and the various forms of association related to the practice of "youth culture," each of these will be analyzed for distinctive clues to the understanding of primary groups in urban regions.

FAMILY RELATIONS IN URBAN REGIONS

After a generation of analyzing and discussing modern urban families, there is little doubt in most people's minds that the urban family has changed considerably since World War I, and that it greatly deviates from the traditional rural family.[2] While this general impres-

---

[1] See Charles H. Cooley, *Social Organization* (New York, Charles Scribner's Sons, 1909); William F. Whyte, *Street Corner Society* (Chicago, University of Chicago Press, 1943); George C. Homans, *The Human Group* (New York, Harcourt, Brace and World, 1951).

[2] Well-known texts that discuss these changes include: Ernest W. Burgess and Harvey Locke, *The Family,* 2nd ed., (New York, American Book Company, 1960); Clifford Kirkpatrick, *The Family: As Process and Institution* (New York, Ronald Press, 1955); Joseph K. Folsom, *The Family and Democratic Society,* 3rd printing (New York, John Wiley and Sons, 1945).

sion is substantially correct, several warning signals should be raised to avoid the dangers of oversimplification.

First, we should recognize that much of our knowledge about urban families concerns relatively superficial aspects (*e.g.,* purchasing patterns) and family interaction in crisis situations (wartime separation, unemployment).[3] Second, a good deal of information is gathered from children and students, rather than the parents themselves. Third, it is very difficult to generalize about "the urban family"—since there are some important variations in family life related to social class level and location in the urban region.[4] Fourth, family life in the urban milieu is influenced by fashion and fad; consequently, there are cycles of change which sometimes appear to represent little change, if the intermediate phases are ignored. Finally, it is important to distinguish among the identifiable changes in family life those which are significant for understanding urban social organization from those which are merely incidental (*e.g.,* the television furor of the past ten or twelve years).

Urban families have in general developed three fundamental patterns that are by now obvious and crucial to any serious analysis of family relations. First, virtually all urban occupations are pursued away from the home and family members. This separation of work and domestic relations, which is contrary to the typical rural pattern, is both physical and cultural. In effect, it isolates the breadwinner from his family; specifically, it hampers meaningful communication between these two worlds of experience. The father-husband who lacks sympathy with minor household crises and the numerous details of child-rearing is not a brute, but a partial outsider. This is often matched by the family's ignorance of the skills and frustrations connected with the husband's job or career. A further consequence of this separation, however, is that the time patterns of the job (and the

[3] Mirra Komarovsky, *The Unemployed Man and his Family* (New York, Dryden Press, 1940); Robert C. Angell, *The Family Encounters the Depression* (New York, Charles Scribner's Sons, 1936); Ruth S. Cavan and Katherine H. Rank, *The Family and the Depression* (Chicago, University of Chicago Press, 1938); Reuben Hill, *Families Under Stress* (New York, Harper and Brothers, 1949); Samuel A. Stouffer and Paul Lazarsfeld, *Research Memorandum on the Family in the Depression,* Social Science Research Council, Bulletin 29 (New York, 1937).

[4] See Ruth S. Cavan, *The American Family* (New York, Thomas Y. Crowell, 1953), Part II; *American Journal of Sociology,* 53 (May, 1948), entire issue.

necessary "journey to work") [5] inevitably influence the scheduling and co-ordination of home activities. It may not be too extreme to suggest that one of the most important material inventions for urban families is the multi-bathroom home or apartment.

A second general pattern in urban families is their voluntary abdication of responsibility for many functions formerly identified with the home. Religion, formalized education, recreation, design and manufacture of clothing, baking (and sometimes cooking) are largely provided by specialized organizations beyond the influence of the individual family. As many students of family life have indicated,[6] this stripping of disposable functions allows for (but does not insure) greater stress on child care and affectional relationships in the home.

Third, the urban family tends to be "streamlined" in size and in range of routine family relationships. In contrast to the traditional rural family, with its normal complement of three (or more) generations and numerous "close" relatives—resembling the *clan* or *gens* of the anthropologist—urban families have become essentially independent *conjugal units,* made up of husband, wife, and offspring. This conjugal or nuclear form of family is *relatively* isolated from other relatives; with some exceptions, it is the principal unit of child care, of consumption, and of social status in the urban region.

In general, these features are most evident in middle income and status families. Both lower and upper status families have tended to retain traditional family organization and values, though several changes in the lower status levels will be noted later. Inherent in the urban regional complex, however, is the central importance of middle class groupings—their aspirations, values, and problems—despite the fact that they account for little more than a third of the urban population. Consequently, we shall largely restrict our analysis of urban family adjustments to this category. In addition, we shall give special attention to middle status families living in the "outer ring"

[5] Kate Liepmann, *The Journey to Work* (New York, Oxford University Press, 1944); George P. Stevens, Jr., "Sample Study of Residential Distribution of Industrial Workers in an Urban Community," *Land Economics,* 28 (August, 1952), pp. 278–283.

[6] Cavan, *op. cit.,* Chap. IV; Burgess and Locke, *op. cit.,* Chaps. I, II; William F. Ogburn and Meyer F. Nimkoff, *Technology and the Changing Family* (Boston, Houghton Mifflin, 1955); John Sirjamaki, *The American Family in the Twentieth Century* (Cambridge, Mass., Harvard University Press, 1953).

(suburbs and fringe) of the region, since these families are becoming increasingly representative of life in the urban region.

Roles of the Wife-Mother

One of the most widely noted changes in the urban middle class family is the growing variety (and often contradiction) of social roles assumed by the wife-mother.[7] She is typically adding to her responsibilities, either voluntarily or under pressure from social peers and superiors:

1. *The Glamor Girl Role,* in which she must keep in step with fashion in clothes and cosmetics, and when on public display give the impression of eternal, vivacious, assured youthful attractiveness. Much of the advertising industry seems to be dedicated to reminding her—incessantly—of her responsibilities in maintaining a gracious appearance, not to her family but to social equals.

2. *The Civic Role,* in which she has the obligation to devote part of her spare time to one or more worthy causes in the community—religion, education, welfare, fine arts, political activity, etc.

3. *The Co-Pilot or Companion Role.* This involves a persistent and intelligent interest in the husband's quest for occupational advancement. Essentially, the wife is expected to provide informal, understanding attention to his occupational problems. Ideally, she should appreciate the special demands which the job makes on her husband and be willing to endure minor or major sacrifices in scheduling her time, entertaining, and sharing her husband with his business or professional associates. It is well known that several large corporations are as interested in the wife's readiness to assume this role as in the husband's own qualifications for executive responsibility.

4. *The Career Role.* With the social and cultural emancipation of the female has come the opportunity to follow a career in business or one of the professions, even after the wedding ceremony, and often after the birth of one or more children. Recent reports from the Census Bureau indicate that working wives in career roles are mainly concentrated in middle class families.[8] This probably reflects greater

[7] See Talcott Parsons, *Essays in Sociological Theory Pure and Applied* (New York, The Free Press of Glencoe, 1949), Chap. XI.

[8] Bureau of the Census, Current Population Reports, *Family Characteristics of Working Wives: March 1957* (Washington, D.C., U.S. Government Printing Office, March, 1958), pp. 2–3.

educational opportunities and achievement, higher motivation for self-expression, and greater facility in re-assigning household duties.

5. *The Economic Supplement Role.* The working wife in her career role works for challenging experiences and to display or sharpen personal skills—not for income. On the other hand, many wives have taken jobs, either full-time or part-time, to supplement the husband's salary. This role seems to be found in families where the husband is unemployed; and it is somewhat more prevalent in cases of low family income.[9]

It is not yet possible to evaluate the impact of this variety in role demands on the urban wife. Many laymen believe, however, that the rather vague definition of the "good wife" in the urban region inevitably produces family irritations and instability. Indeed, one study of divorced couples in Chillicothe, Ohio, suggests that the major underlying condition of marital difficulties is continuing disagreement about *proper* roles of both wife and husband.[10] Yet in an investigation of working wives and family relations in Michigan, the expected role conflicts did not materialize. It was discovered instead that the wife's job tended to develop more equalitarian attitudes toward authority in the home, among wives and husbands. Furthermore, a significant adjustment to the wife's employment role was the fact that husbands in these families assumed greater responsibility for housework.[11] The key to the Michigan findings is perhaps the type of family studied. About 90 per cent were on the middle class level. More than 50 per cent had completed a year or more of college. Finally, 96 per cent of the working wives were employed as teachers or in white collar jobs, indicating that the career role was at least partially involved in this sample. The tentative conclusion can be drawn that middle class families have tended to accommodate themselves to the urban milieu with some success.

This conclusion is partially corroborated by recent statistics on divorce in urban regions. Contrary to popular notions, divorce rates are substantially higher among lower class families. The lowest rates

[9] *Ibid.,* p. 1.

[10] Alvin H. Jacobson, "Conflict of Attitudes Toward the Roles of the Husband and Wife in Marriage," *American Sociological Review,* 17 (April, 1952), pp. 146–150.

[11] Robert O. Blood, Jr. and Robert L. Hamblin, "The Effects of the Wife's Employment on the Family Power Structure," *Social Forces,* 36 (May, 1958), pp. 347–352.

are found among professionals, proprietors, and white collar workers.[12] If we also consider the rather high desertion rates among lower class families, the impression of relatively successful adjustment among urban middle class families is even further strengthened.

Urban Parent-Child Relationships

Because of our widespread sensitivity to the family as an emotional milieu for the child, and also as a consequence of the comparatively small size of urban families, much attention has been given to parent-child relationships and child-rearing practices in the urban region. However, a considerable folklore, perhaps once true, has been woven about this essential and somewhat intangible aspect of urban family life. We often hear about child neglect in the lower class, maternal overprotection in the middle class, neurotic tendencies in middle class children, etc.[13] But what does a review of the available evidence suggest?

Studies in Detroit, Chicago, New Haven, San Francisco, and Washington during the past fifteen years fail to provide a sharply etched picture of parent-child relationships. Havighurst's study of southside Chicago families in the early forties seemed to point to substantial differences between lower and middle class rearing of children. The major conclusion was that middle class parents were more demanding, more restrictive, with their children, while lower class parents were more permissive.[14] Recently, a careful analysis of family practices in two New England suburbs also uncovered significant differences between lower and middle class parents, but a perplexing finding was that the *lower class* mothers were more demanding than middle class mothers.[15] Perhaps a decade or more had produced new motivations

[12] William J. Goode, "Economic Factors and Marital Stability," *American Sociological Review,* 16 (December, 1951), pp. 802–812; J. A. Livingston, "Divorce Totals Upset Notion That Workers Live on Love," Norfolk *Virginian-Pilot,* February 19, 1956 (summarizes studies of Thomas P. Monahan and William M. Kephart).

[13] David Levy, *Maternal Overprotection* (New York, Columbia University Press, 1943); Arnold W. Green, "The Middle Class Male Child and Neurosis," *American Sociological Review,* 11 (February, 1946), pp. 31–41.

[14] Robert J. Havighurst and Allison Davis, "A Comparison of the Chicago and Harvard Studies of Social Class Differences in Child Rearing," *American Sociological Review,* 20 (August, 1955), pp. 438–442.

[15] Robert R. Sears, Eleanor E. Maccoby, and Harry Leven, *Patterns of Child Rearing* (Evanston, Ill., Row, Peterson and Company, 1957) pp. 426–446.

among urban families. On the other hand, perhaps relative location in the urban region (central city *vs.* suburb) accounts for differential child-rearing practices within the same class level. Still a third possible explanation of these incompatible findings is the unwitting neglect of social and attitudinal differences among families on the same status level in the same urban setting.

A tentative path through the wilderness has been laid out by an ingenious set of interviews with mothers in the urban region of Detroit.[16] Although middle and lower class families remain the focus, the *social orientation* of the family also receives special attention in analyzing child-rearing practices. Thus, on each class level an *entre-preneurial* type is contrasted with a *bureaucratic* orientation toward social experience. In the former, parents engage in risk-taking, small economic ventures (*e.g.,* small proprietors), or recently come from farm areas where a similar economic ideology prevails. The bureau-cratic type, on the other hand, places relatively more emphasis on adjustment to large, complex organizations, on security, group morale, and "togetherness."

What is the effect of social orientation on child-rearing? Within the middle class families, entrepreneurial mothers are somewhat more demanding with youngsters than are bureaucratic mothers; they put greater emphasis on feeding babies on a regular schedule; they begin toilet training earlier (normally before eleven months); they use sym-bolic punishment (stressing self-control, guilt, and shame) more than direct, material rewards or punishments. However, there is little differ-ence in weaning practices. Among lower class mothers in this sample, such differences are much less marked between bureaucratic and entrepreneurial types, although once more the bureaucratic type seems more permissive. In a comparison of bureaucratic middle class and bureaucratic lower class families, similarities in child-training greatly outweigh differences. The net result is a surprisingly marked con-vergence in parent-child relations among bureaucratic middles, and bureaucratic and entrepreneurial lowers—all of which have apparently geared their child-training to the modern tone of the urban region. In contrast, the entrepreneurial middle type clings to an earlier urban ideal of inner direction, personal responsibility, and initiative.

As Martha Wolfenstein has shown in her illuminating review of suc-

[16] Daniel R. Miller and Guy E. Swanson, *The Changing American Parent* (New York, John Wiley and Sons, 1958), pp. 97–153.

cessive editions of "Infant Care," there have been definite changes in the recommended styles of child care.[17] We do not have much information on the practical application of these recommendations—particularly of reactions to revised recommendations—though the widespread sale of this bulletin in its editions of 1914 through 1951 probably indicates considerable attention to its views. It seems likely that urban families have experimented with various techniques and that there is now a trend toward the bureaucratic orientation. While this represents a shift from the traditional rural family and its relatively entrepreneurial emphasis, the middle class urban family has also reverted (or perhaps retained) several "rural" features which support the growing impression of a new, composite type of family organization in the urban region.

Contrary to prevailing urban folklore, there is some evidence that "neighboring" and informal visiting are quite common among urbanites. Studies in Detroit and Los Angeles, for example, report very substantial degrees of home visiting *on all status levels* with friends, relatives, neighbors, and co-workers. In general, the amount of visiting with neighbors, etc., tends to be greater in higher status families, but these differences are not very sharp.[18]

Familism

In middle class families—and especially in suburban and fringe areas—an urban variety of *familism* is being discovered piecemeal by urban sociologists. A New Haven study casts some doubt on the "isolation" of the nuclear family. Among white, Protestant middle class, and probably semibureaucratic families, strong affectional and economic ties were found between middle-aged parents and their married children. The former provided moderate economic assistance to the latter in the form of gifts, loans, and baby-sitting. In addition, as a moral and financial obligation, 120 of 195 married couples exchanged nursing care with their parents—mainly during illness and

[17] Martha Wolfenstein, "Fun Morality: An Analysis of Recent American Child-Training Literature," in Margaret Mead and Martha Wolfenstein, eds., *Childhood in Contemporary Cultures* (Chicago, University of Chicago Press, 1955), Chap. X.

[18] Scott Greer, "Urbanism Reconsidered: A Comparative Study of Local Areas in a Metropolis," *American Sociological Review,* 21 (February, 1956), pp. 19–25; Morris Axelrod, "Urban Structure and Social Participation," *ibid.,* pp. 13–18.

childbirth. On the other hand, sons were given opportunities in family businesses in only 18 of 90 cases.[19]

As mentioned above, several studies point to the prevalence of visiting patterns among urban families. In particular, extensive visiting with relatives—at least once a week—was found in all social class levels, with the most frequent family contacts reported in middle status urban families. Indeed, on almost all status levels, visits to relatives substantially exceeded visits to friends or neighbors.[20] This in itself is fairly good evidence of the resurgence (or merely *continuation*) of urban familism.

Since World War II, birth patterns in urban regions seem to suggest a revival of familism. For example, the overall increase in birth rates for urban regions is less significant for present purposes than the increase in third and fourth births among middle class groups from 1942 to date. Since contraception is widely practiced, these added births probably reflect a desire for larger families, a crucial element in familism.[21]

Closely connected to the preceding feature is the increasing emphasis on the home and family-related activities. The former is illustrated by rising rates of home ownership in central cities and suburban zones and in increasing sales of household furnishings. As for family-related activities, it is uncertain whether urban families show greater participation as a unit in home-centered occasions—meals, entertainment, etc. But among middle class families, there is widespread involvement of parents in activities related to the status and welfare of their children. Some common instances are: membership in Parent-Teacher Associations; baby-sitting pools, cooperative nurseries; private music lessons; Boy Scout and Girl Scout organizations; and Sunday Schools.

FRIENDSHIP AND CLIQUE GROUPS

Apart from rather superficial information on frequency of visits, surprisingly little is known about the patterns of friendship in modern urban regions. However, the stereotype of the cold, unfriendly, and socially isolated urban resident is increasingly remarkable for its

[19] Marvin B. Sussman, "The Help Pattern in the Middle Class Family," *American Sociological Review,* 18 (February, 1953), pp. 22–28.

[20] Axelrod, *loc. cit.;* Greer, *loc. cit.*

[21] Ronald Freedman, P. J. Whelpton, and Arthur A. Campbell, *Family Planning, Sterility, and Population Growth* (New York, McGraw-Hill, 1959), Chaps. IX–XI.

persistence, despite its disregard of many personal observations to the contrary. Perhaps also the stereotype survives because urban sociology has not extensively examined the nature of urban friendship. Yet a few available studies enable us to suggest that friendship and clique formations constitute an important source of primary group relations in the urban region.

Turning first to friendship groups, it is becoming apparent that the urban region, as compared to rural and small town areas, provides a wider *range* of friendship-producing situations. Unlike the traditional ruralite, the urbanite is not bound by the *proximity* factor in choosing friends. In general, the greater mobility of the urbanite permits any or all of four major sources of close friendship or more than casual acquaintance.

1. In childhood and young manhood, school and college are frequent "gardens of friendship," even though some educational systems are called "educational wastelands." Compulsory public education, or an equivalent form of private education, is a process of almost inevitable social mixing and common experiences. Friendships thus formed seem to be based on similarities in social class, ethnic background, and religion [22]—not on accessibility of residence or personality type. School chums are often memorable for one reason or another, but it is not known what proportion of these friendships survive graduation. It may be reasonably suspected that the mobility of urbanites severely restricts the number of one's friends who *first* became congenial in a school setting.

2. Church affiliation, particularly among middle status urbanites and in the suburban ring, is a consistent factor in stimulating close personal ties for young people, and to some extent for adults. Indeed, most congregations encourage their young members to participate in a variety of "social" events—Sunday School, discussion groups, dances, bazaars, parties, musical activities, etc.

3. For the urban adult, office, shop, and factory are not only economic locations, but also excellent opportunities for informal contacts with fellow workers. Considerable research in industrial plants demonstrates an almost inevitable formation of workers' cliques, the members of which come from the same crew, department or section. In offices and commercial establishments, coffee breaks, lunch hours, and normal work routines provide numerous opportunities for per-

[22] George A. Lundberg and Lenore Dickson, "Selective Association Among Ethnic Groups in a High School Population," *American Sociological Review,* 17 (February, 1952), pp. 23–35.

sonal chatter and closer acquaintanceship.[23] According to the Detroit study mentioned above, visiting with co-workers (off the job) is a substantial part of the informal associations of urbanites. In fact, about one-third of the Detroit sample spent part of its leisure time with fellow workers *at least once a month*.[24] It would be useful to know if informal contacts with co-workers are greatly affected by proximity of residence, to which we shall now turn.

4. Several recent studies—mainly in the newer areas of the urban region and among medium status families—strongly suggest that urban friendships with close neighbors and with families within a limited radius of blocks are more numerous than had been expected.[25] This is clearly shown in postwar housing projects and in newer suburban areas, where intimacy of contact seems to be related to proximity of residence, the availability and choice of playmates among children, and similarity in socioeconomic status. Whyte's widely discussed picture of friendship patterns in Park Forest, a suburb of Chicago, offers a sympathetic and yet objective account of the "web of friendship" among junior executives' families, which can be understood in terms of such "accidental" causes as juxtaposition of apartment units, location of play areas, and placement of driveways and lawns.[26] In a study of Lansing, Michigan, friends appeared to be chosen almost equally between neighbors and nonneighbors. But it was found that close neighborhood friendships were more prevalent in higher socioeconomic groupings and areas.[27] The apparent explanation is that the greater average length of residence in an area for middle and upper status families permits more intimate friendships than those for the relatively more mobile lower status families.

[23] F. J. Roethlisberger and W. J. Dickson, *Management and the Worker* (Cambridge, Mass., Harvard University Press, 1939); Delbert Miller and William H. Form, *Industrial Sociology* (New York, Harper and Brothers, 1951); William F. Whyte, *Human Relations in the Restaurant Industry* (New York, McGraw-Hill, 1948).

[24] Axelrod, *op. cit.*, p. 16.

[25] William H. Whyte, Jr. "The Transients," in Llewellyn Miller, ed., *Prize Articles, 1954* (New York, Ballantine Books, 1954), pp. 39–112. This appeared in four installments in *Fortune* (1953). See also William H. Whyte, Jr., *The Organization Man* (Garden City, N.Y., Doubleday and Company, 1956), Part VII; Sylvia F. Fava, "Suburbanism as a Way of Life," *American Sociological Review*, 21 (February, 1956), pp. 34–37.

[26] Whyte, "The Transients," pp. 81–95.

[27] Joel Smith, William H. Form, and Gregory P. Stone, "Local Intimacy in a Middle-Sized City," *American Journal of Sociology*, 60 (November, 1954), pp. 276–284.

Cliques as Quasi-Primary Groups

It is sometimes difficult in specific instances to distinguish between informally organized friendship groups or "circles" and the somewhat more specialized, quasi-primary groups known as *cliques*. Both types of group possess little formal organization; both types are normally composed of persons from the same status level; both types, finally, emphasize personal relations among members.

On the other hand, the clique is unique in several respects by comparison with other primary groups. Unlike the family or friendship group, the clique relationship is limited to a fairly specific set of activities; there are cliques in professional circles, in commercial and industrial organizations, in amusement and recreation, in politics and public administration, in private community services, and in the specialized realm of status per se. A second distinctive trait of the clique is its tendency toward *exclusiveness*, often perhaps a rekindled consciousness of its distinctiveness to assure desirable social segregation from "outsiders." Consequently, cliques possess rather sharp though informal criteria of recruitment. Generally, entrance into cliques depends more on an individual's *status* than on personal qualities or achievements. Thirdly, the clique normally forms as an unanticipated component of a larger, more formal organization. Indeed, it may be suggested that modern cliques operate either to circumvent or promote the efficiency of complex social organizations (*e.g.,* factories, universities, government agencies) or abstract collectivities (social classes, communities).

The adult clique is a venerable form of social organization, which is found both in rural and urban communities. In rural areas and small cities, cliques tend to supplement and even strengthen the existing social order. This conservative function of cliques rests on the fact that many are formed among upper status persons, who regard the clique as an effective and desirable form of social control. This is the case, for example, in such otherwise varied communities as Middletown, Yankee City, Plainville, Elmtown, and Old City (southern town).[28]

[28] Robert S. Lynd and Helen M. Lynd, *Middletown in Transition* (New York, Harcourt, Brace, and World, 1939); W. Lloyd Warner and Paul S. Lunt, *The Social Life of a Modern Community* (New Haven, Yale University Press, 1941); James West, *Plainville, U.S.A.* (New York, Columbia University Press, 1945); Allison Davis, Burleigh B. Gardner, and Mary Gardner, *Deep South* (Chicago, University of Chicago Press, 1941).

But what is the nature of cliques in larger urban settings? From the limited number of available investigations, it is possible to identify some urban cliques as essentially "rural survivals," as far as their function is concerned. Baltzell's study of the Philadelphia elite, Amory's delightful scrutiny of the "Proper Bostonians," and Hunter's demarcation of Atlanta's informal leadership are surprisingly similar in demonstrating the basic conservatism of the most "visible" cliques.[29] They are "rural survivals" in their respective attachments to earlier, "sacred" periods of community organization, but also in their common attempt to bypass or nullify such modern urban features as mass media and mass tastes, complex and impersonal bureaucracies (particularly in government), and the free play of romantic love.

While many urban cliques are found among adults and on upper status levels, the clique type of organization is also a favorite device among adolescents in the middle and lower status categories. However, these cliques seem to have an entirely different significance for their members. In general, they function not as supplements to existing social order, but as contrived reactions to *deficiencies* in social order, as "radical" innovations in the interstices of the evolving urban sociocultural complex. For this reason, we shall call such cliques "counter-cliques," the major forms of which are represented by urban gangs.

The gang is unfortunately a much misunderstood phenomenon in modern society and one which has been studied more often by journalists than by social scientists.[30] Since there are at least two types of gangs—a fact that is often overlooked—a preliminary definition of gangs in general is certainly desirable at this point. The gang is a form of clique organization which emphasizes fairly regular social contacts among its members, attracts members who are remarkably similar on such items as sex, age, social class level, and often, nationality, and perhaps most significantly, functions as a potential or actual competitor to the prevailing social order of adults. There is considerable variation among gangs in degree of organization, yet most urban

[29] E. Digby Baltzell, *Philadelphia Gentlemen* (New York, The Free Press of Glencoe, 1958); Cleveland Amory, *The Proper Bostonians* (New York, E. P. Dutton, 1947); Floyd Hunter, *Community Power Structure* (Chapel Hill, University of North Carolina Press, 1953).

[30] The journalists are well represented by Dale Kramer and Madeline Karr, *Teen Age Gangs* (New York, Holt, Rinehart, and Winston, 1953); Harrison E. Salisbury, *The Shook-Up Generation* (New York, Harper and Brothers, 1959); and Herbert Asbury, *The Gangs of New York* (New York, Alfred A. Knopf, 1928).

gangs reflect in their individual operation an overarching set of organizing values, which has been accurately called "youth culture."

Gangs and youth culture are predominantly urban, though rural areas have had both gangs and the partial intrusion of youth culture in recent years. Youth culture consists of a series of innovations in values and activities which enable adolescents to achieve status and a measure of independence from the adult world of responsibility, impersonal organization, and deferred gratification. In the process of creating and sustaining the technical specialization that marks urban organization, the adolescent has been a "forgotten man," a "marginal" person, no longer a child, but not yet an adult. The urban family has been largely unable to provide adequate links to future experience; it is itself typically isolated. The same limitation of specialization is evident in the school, the church, and in economic groups.

The paradox of urban youth culture is that it is simultaneously impersonal and generalized, and the basis for the proliferation of specific quasi-primary organizations among adolescents (counter-cliques). Essentially, youth culture reflects the transitional, problematical status of urban adolescents. Its major values are the intrinsic importance of fun, amusement, recreation; withdrawal from "responsible" activities and concerns, as defined by adults; an emphasis on physical skills—such as complex dancing steps, sports, driving and dismantling automobiles; a love of constant minor novelties in dress, jargon, amusements; the acceptance of *conformity* to peer group standards; and the emphasis on gregariousness, on direct personal interaction with one's peers, accompanied by an apparent fear of isolation or extended privacy.[31]

Youth culture, which is largely the property of youth groups that resemble the previous definition of cliques, is practiced by two general types of gang. The first and less obvious type may be called—more for simplicity than accuracy—the *normal* or *approved* gang.[32] While many would hesitate to call these groups "gangs," it is becoming increasingly clear that many noncriminal organizations of adolescents share with their unapproved contemporaries in many values of the youth culture, basic social organization features—*e.g.,* leadership, and meeting similar social and psychological needs of their members. The normal gang is found among lower and middle class adolescents, and

[31] See Talcott Parsons, *Essays in Sociological Theory*, pp. 220–222.
[32] One of the few recent studies of this type is Herbert Bloch and Arthur Niederhoffer, *The Gang*, (New York, Philosophical Library, 1958).

appears to be an essential part of the adolescent's transition to adult status.

Among middle class urban youngsters, the normal gang sometimes arises within specific neighborhoods (in the form of athletic groups), but more often the high school or college provides the opportunities for social contacts that culminate in this type of gang. Such groups are commonly referred to as "crowds," "circles," "cliques," or "the bunch." From the admittedly scanty information available, the middle class "normal gang" appears to have a loose but recognizable organization as a clique or counter-clique, with three kinds of focal activities.

One type may be called the "sports gang," since it involves habitual association of like-minded boys either for playing one or more sports (but not necessarily as an organized team) or for attending sports events as a nucleus of spectators. The sports gang probably has a relatively brief history and a minimum of clique-like features.

A second type of middle class normal gang operates at the *borders* of social approval. Its focus is semiuninhibited diversion, adolescent hilarity, and boisterousness as ends in themselves. Boys in these gangs meet in public establishments (such as drive-ins, ice cream parlors, drug stores—often near school grounds) to the mixed amusement and annoyance of other customers. Occasionally, these gangs erupt into minor roughhouse behavior, with some damage to crockery, windows, and clothing, but this is unplanned and regretted by most members.

Finally, and perhaps most significantly among middle class normal gangs, there is the "dating gang," an urban innovation which has enormous implications for family organization, the amusement industry, and advertising. Dating, as distinct from courtship, is a characteristic expression of youth culture. But it is erroneous to consider dating as the mere pairing of youngsters for fun and amusement. Typically, dating occurs within circumscribed reservoirs of desirable males and females; dates are exchanged, succeeded, and resumed largely in well-defined "crowds" whose members more or less accept common standards of exclusion and inclusion. These standards are explicit and easily verbalized. Most dating gangs—and in particular those developed on college campuses and in high schools—reflect common concern for status (social level of parents, academic and social status on campus), up-to-date dancing skills, as well as consensus on proper attire and physical attractiveness. In such circumstances, clique members view the date both in terms of personal enjoyment and in comparison with the dating experiences of other members. The latter concern is the source of Willard Waller's graphic designation, "the rating and dating complex," for such groups and activities.[33] Parenthetically, dating gangs have generally looked with disfavor at the current epidemic of "going steady," perhaps because these "personal monopolies" signify independence from, and therefore a challenge to, the adolescent clique.

Gangs among middle class youngsters are generally *mild* counter-cliques, functioning as acceptable and temporary protests against the restraints of family and formal education. These gangs are conventional, expedient, and dispensable to their members, who soon exchange their brief period of rebellion for higher degrees in conformity. But lower class adolescents likewise develop many approved gangs, usually the sports and seminuisance type, though these rarely receive the publicity reserved for delinquent associations.

The classic sociological account of approved gangs is that of the "Corner Boys" in a lower class neighborhood of Somerville, near Boston.[34] The "Corner Boys" are especially interesting to those who want a balanced picture of the urban gang. For one thing, the "Corner Boys" are essentially a normal, law-abiding form of primary association in an immigrant area that lacked legitimate social organization beyond the family and the settlement house. In a sense, then, the gangs served to counterbalance neighborhood inadequacies. Indeed, the gangs were so necessary to their members that they spent most of their time in gang "hangouts" and—significantly—remained as members well beyond adolescence. Finally, unlike delinquent groups, the "Corner Boys" were largely concerned with sports activities and approved forms of entertainment (one exception: betting on numbers).

The second type of urban gang, the *delinquent* or *criminal gang*, seems to be a lower class urban phenomenon. In general, as Thrasher demonstrated in his classic study of about 1300 Chicago gangs in the twenties, these gangs arise in zones of transition, in areas of mixed racial and nationality groupings. The distinguishing features of these gangs are extreme sensitivity to status frustration and a consequent repudiation of middle-class values. In practice, then, the gang as a

[33] Willard Waller, "The Rating and Dating Complex," *American Sociological Review,* 2 (October, 1937), pp. 727–737; E. W. Burgess and Paul Wallin, *Engagement and Marriage* (Philadelphia, J. B. Lippincott, 1953). Chap. III.

[34] William F. Whyte, *Street Corner Society* (Chicago, University of Chicago Press, 1943), especially pp. 115–118.

primary group is geared for and thrives on conflict with the symbols and vehicles of respectability, and also with rival, similarly irritable gangs. As Cohen, and more recently, Cloward and Ohlin have suggested, delinquent gangs are both creators and creatures of "delinquent subcultures," whose major themes are violence, malice, impulse, and "face." But even delinquent gangs exhibit specialization in objectives and techniques. The *criminal gang* seeks economic success through organized theft. By contrast, the *conflict gang* is more idealistic; it wages organized warfare with other gangs for morale and "honor." Finally, the *retreatist variety* seeks the substitute satisfaction of narcotics, as a desperate alternative to failure in both "normal" and delinquent pursuits.[35]

SUMMARY AND INTERPRETATION

Perhaps two generalizations may be drawn from the preceding discussions of urban primary groups. First, it is quite evident that primary group relationships are difficult to sustain as isolated segments of experience; complex organizations and impersonal social processes inevitably intrude on pre-existing primary forms, such as the family and the traditional neighborhood. Consequently, urban primary groups have been faced with the need for re-formation, for adjustment to the special circumstances of urban regional life. Changes in family structures, and the personal and social problems that accompany these changes, are dramatic illustrations of such adjustment. In addition, relatively new kinds of primary groups—adult and adolescent cliques, and counter-cliques—may also be interpreted as organizational adjustments to gaps or deficiencies in the complex but loose structure of the urban region.

Second, although the "problem" aspect of urban primary groups was not specially emphasized (this will be discussed in Chapter 15), it is becoming clear that urbanites implicitly recognize that primary groups are unequal to the task of satisfying numerous, specialized needs. The underlying quest for more conscious, more formal organization of urban activities therefore constitutes one of the dominant themes in the urban order. In succeeding chapters, we shall examine

[35] Frederic Thrasher, *The Gang* (Chicago, University of Chicago Press, 1927); Albert K. Cohen, *Delinquent Boys* (New York, The Free Press of Glencoe, 1955); Richard Cloward and Lloyd Ohlin, *Delinquency and Opportunity* (New York, The Free Press of Glencoe, 1960), pp. 20–27.

several important variations of this theme, beginning with the so-called *voluntary associations*.

SELECTED REFERENCES

BOTT, Elizabeth, *Family and Social Network* (London, Tavistock Publications, Ltd., 1957).

CLOWARD, Richard and OHLIN, Lloyd E., *Delinquency and Opportunity* (New York, The Free Press of Glencoe, 1960).

COHEN, Albert K., *Delinquent Boys* (New York, The Free Press of Glencoe, 1955).

FESTINGER, Leon *et al., Social Pressures in Informal Groups* (New York, Harper and Brothers, 1950).

MILLER, Daniel R. and SWANSON, Guy E., *The Changing American Parent* (New York, John Wiley and Sons, 1958).

RIESMAN, David, *The Lonely Crowd* (Garden City, N.Y., Doubleday and Company, 1953).

SEARS, Robert R. *et al., Patterns of Child-Rearing* (Evanston, Row, Peterson and Company, 1957).

THRASHER, Frederic, *The Gang* (Chicago, University of Chicago Press, 1927).

WHYTE, William F., *Street Corner Society* (Chicago, University of Chicago Press, 1943).

WHYTE, William H., Jr., *The Organization Man* (Garden City, N.Y., Doubleday and Company, 1956).

CHAPTER 9

Voluntary Groups
and Formal Associations

FOR MANY PERSONS, the calendar and the date book have become indispensable items in the routine of urbanized living. This is not a result of faulty memory or a compulsive desire for order, but merely a consequence of the increasing load of *organizational activities* to which the urbanite is committed. In the urban region, these activities are largely separate from the direct pursuit of one's occupation, and therefore are channeled through specially created groups called *voluntary groups* or *formal associations*. The urban *milieu* is liberally sprinkled with such groups; indeed, they seem to be proliferating at such a rate and constitute such a firm, semiobligatory part of urban living, that some students occasionally question the designation "voluntary." Whatever the proper label, these associations are increasingly significant components of urban organization.

In its essential form, the formal association is a highly specialized, explicitly organized group composed of persons with a common interest (though not necessarily common *degrees* of interest) that cannot be satisfactorily pursued individually, or by pre-existing forms of social interaction. For example, John Smith may have some interest in reading and gaining appreciation of the "classics" or "Great Books." Yet he may feel unable to spare the necessary time; he may even doubt his ability to accomplish much on an independent basis. At the same time, he may also be reluctant to enroll in one or more courses at a local college. If the interest persists despite these obstacles, he is a likely prospect for a Great Books Reading Group, a very popular variety of voluntary association in urban regions. The variety of voluntary or formal associations is so great that several central features must be given special attention.

CHARACTERISTICS OF VOLUNTARY AND FORMAL ASSOCIATIONS

It may be useful to approach voluntary organizations as an *intermediate* type of social organization, somewhere between primary groups on the one hand and firmly established, highly bureaucratized groups on the other. Unlike primary groups, voluntary associations tend to function with limited sets of definite objectives or interests, and exhibit rather visible attempts at formalized organization. However, as in the case of most primary groups, membership is normally voluntary; entrance and withdrawal are dependent on personal decisions of high interest or of frustrating disaffection with the specific aims or methods of a given organization. Yet if voluntary associations resemble highly formalized and well-established groups—in such respects as specialization, formal structure, and general impersonality—two important distinctions nevertheless recur. Understandably, the highly institutionalized groups are often older, more conservative, and perhaps defensive, more fully legitimated, and therefore exercise a more encompassing control over one's experience. As a result, these groups tend to inhibit deviant opinions and values among members, either by providing no regularly approved channels for creativity or disagreement, or by specifically penalizing unapproved variations (*e.g.,* dismissal for insubordination on the job, excommunication for heretical beliefs, fines and imprisonment for disobeying current but unpalatable laws). Voluntary associations, by contrast, emphasize (or try to) some degree of freedom for change, deviation, creativeness, or merely variation from routine responsibilities.

This intermediate position of voluntary associations (or as Voltaire called them, "private associations") is probably a consequence of the fact that they arise and function to *supplement*—not supplant—both existent primary groups and highly institutionalized groups. While the latter forms of social organization are certainly indispensable—their absence would be unthinkable and impractical to the highest degree —they have apparently been judged inadequate by themselves to provide the range and quality of organization deemed necessary for coping with the desired complexities of urban living. Therefore, voluntary associations fill a gap in urban organization, by experimental blends of primary group and institutionalized group traits.

Voluntary associations may be simply classified into two major types, according to dominant objectives or functions perceived by their members.[1] One important type, called *expressive associations* by Rose, provides regular opportunities for self-expression, creativity, and perhaps innocent deviation. In this type, the members merely desire to exchange ideas and experiences in some limited field of interest. Garden clubs, literary societies, hobby groups, fraternal lodges, many veterans' organizations, and book clubs are fundamentally constructed in terms of this general set of goals.

Many expressive associations seem, upon close examination by outsiders, to pursue their stated interests in a somewhat haphazard way. This leads to the suspicion that these associations are more important as facilitators of social interaction, of expression, and even of sociability than for the *content* of expression and interaction. Where this suspicion is well founded, it probably indicates that expressive associations are essentially supplements to one's stock of primary group experiences—perhaps even substitutes for inadequate or frustrating primary group relations.

A second type of voluntary association—possibly the more dominant variety—is organized to initiate or encourage desired changes in local, national, or international institutional organization. Instead of providing a forum for mutual expression of opinions, ideas, and information, this type attempts to influence persons and organizations beyond the particular association to accept and implement proposed changes. Obviously, politics is marked by innumerable *social action* or *influence* associations (taxpayers' groups, independent voters' leagues, and various lobbying groups). But these are also found in education, religion, intergroup relations, welfare, medicine, industry, agriculture, and even the issue of possible calendar reform. If expressive associations supplement primary groups, social action associations try to repair or improve the major institutional arrangements. However, social action associations inevitably develop *counterassociations,* when threats to established patterns become increasingly difficult to ignore. As social action associations achieve some success and momentum, they become the foci of social movements [2] and thus

[1] Arnold Rose, *Theory and Method in the Social Sciences* (Minneapolis, University of Minnesota Press, 1953), pp. 55–66. See also his *Sociology* (New York, Alfred A. Knopf, 1956), Chap. X.
[2] Ralph Turner and Lewis Killian, eds., *Collective Behavior* (Englewood Cliffs, N.J., Prentice-Hall, 1957), Part IV; Rudolph Heberle, *Social Move-*

constitute one of the most important levers of social and cultural change in modern society.

As both Robin Williams and Arnold Rose have perceptively remarked, voluntary associations in the urban region arise and persist in a social environment of diffuse power.[3] However, it is doubtful that this "permissive power situation" is inherent in urban regions in general. In France, for example, Rose found considerably less diversity of, and participation in, such organizations than in American cities. The apparent explanation is that the cultural dominance of the Catholic Church—and perhaps the vastly greater authority of the national government in French cities—either makes these organizations unnecessary, or implicitly discourages the emergence of competing groups and loyalties. [4] On the other hand, in American cities, the government has not tended to be greatly concerned with private affairs (despite the general enlargement of government functions); and many of the established religious organizations have not been able to match the pervasive influence of the Catholic Church over its adherents. The result is vast opportunities for new, specialized organizations.

Under these facilitating conditions, voluntary associations have developed and attracted members for a variety of reasons. Indeed, an important characteristic of such organizations is the fact that both collectively and individually, they may satisfy a diversity of motives.[5] Some urbanites join voluntary associations because of a consuming interest in literature, lower taxes, or improved public education. Others are attracted to these groups because they bolster or enhance personal status. Still others feel a personal obligation, a sense of social responsibility or "service" toward civic groups and "action" organizations. We must recognize that some persons desire additional opportunities for social contacts—often of a quasi-personal character— and perhaps as antidotes to unsatisfactory primary group relations. Thus, as in other forms of social organization, voluntary associations

ments (New York, Appleton-Century-Crofts, Inc., 1952); Kurt Lang and Gladys E. Lang, Collective Dynamics (New York, Thomas Y. Crowell, 1961), Chaps. XVI, XVII.

[3] Robin M. Williams, Jr., American Society, 2nd ed. (New York, Alfred A. Knopf, 1960), pp. 497–500; Rose, Theory and Method in the Social Sciences, pp. 58–61.

[4] Rose, Theory and Method in the Social Sciences, Chap. IV.

[5] Williams, op. cit., pp. 499–501; Ronald Freedman et al., Principles of Sociology, rev. ed. (New York, Holt, Rinehart and Winston, 1956), pp. 450–452.

serve both rational and nonrational purposes. Despite these variations in organizational aims and individual motives for membership, the urban voluntary association has developed a characteristic structure that dovetails with the general features of urban living.

1. In many cases, the voluntary association exhibits a semibureaucratic form—official positions, definite responsibilities, records, minutes, and often parliamentary procedures at formal meetings. Yet this surface formality of structure is often accompanied by personal interaction among members (in the organizational framework as well as in other social contexts) through use of first names, exchange of family information, pooling of transportation to meetings, and in consideration of members' other responsibilities in allocating duties in the association. Thus, the voluntary association implicitly permits the pursuit of a specific interest without the annoyance of unrelenting pressure to subordinate personality and personal problems to organizational demands.

2. The scheduling of regular meetings—once a week or once a month—is perhaps a small detail, but an important one. In the vague competition of activities and responsibilities that marks urban living, specification of definite meeting times *well in advance* performs at least two functions for members. First, it supplies or strengthens a feeling of *continuity* despite the time-consuming attention to routine responsibilities (the job, household chores, etc.). Primary groups (*e.g.,* friendships) generally operate more haphazardly, since their underlying assumption is that members should interact spontaneously, rather than by design. Perhaps, in the urban setting, many friendships "expire" or "drift away" for lack of minimum "design," rather than through conflicts or divergent interests. It appears that voluntary associations avoid some of the limitations of primary groups by recognizing that interest must be supplemented somewhat by an appropriate routine.

A second function of regularly scheduled meetings is the opportunity to plan for participation in other activities and the discharge of other obligations. Few things are more productive of annoyance to the urbanite than unexpected, hastily called meetings, whatever the justification. The necessary rearrangements may involve a chain reaction of irritation among family members, plus several strategic telephone calls. Indeed, relatively infrequent meetings (once a month, or less often) have the latent consequence of allowing many persons active affiliation with several associations concurrently, thus permitting a small core of interlocking memberships in a given community.[6]

3. It is a current truism that a few persons do most of the work in most organizations. This is often true in bureaucratic groups. But perhaps the relatively clear-cut division of responsibility and authority in such groups accounts for differences in genuine participation. On the other hand, voluntary associations also tend to have a core of active participants ("live wires") and a large proportion of "peripheral," semiapathetic members. An adequate explanation of this feature is not yet available. However, it seems probable that the "voluntary" nature of the association implicitly tolerates great variations in participation. Though information is lacking, experience suggests that lower levels of participation are often found among new members and that greater turnover in membership tends to inhibit active participation. A final consideration: since personal motives for joining vary a good deal, we might reasonably expect corresponding differences in *involvement* in associational functions. The pressure to conform is more likely to reveal itself in *superficial* matters for most members—paying dues and attending meetings. Perhaps the lack of genuine emphasis on intensive participation is unconsciously attractive to many urbanites, whose primary identification is with the family or the job.

4. *Committees and Programs.* To fulfill its basic function, either as a forum for various creations of its members or as a pressure group working for some "cause," the voluntary association normally requires two closely related patterns—committees and programs. The formation of committees, their deliberations, and reports are symbols of the need for efficiency and the eager recourse to internal specialization. These committees have received their share of ridicule from cartoonists, whimsical social scientists, and intellectuals in general.[7] But these critics have principally evaluated committees from the standpoint of *tangible results* (in which case the consequences are often trivial), not from the standpoint of *latent* contributions.

In view of the necessary infrequency of regular meetings, the voluntary association achieves much of its continuity and part of its ability to compete with other social obligations of its members through

[6] W. Lloyd Warner and Paul S. Lunt, *The Social Life of a Modern Community* (New Haven, Yale University Press, 1941), Chap. XVI.

[7] One of the best critiques is C. Northcote Parkinson, *Parkinson's Law* (Boston, Houghton Mifflin, 1957).

a succession of committees. Membership on committees gives urbanites an opportunity for limited responsibility without the necessity of crucial achievement. To many persons, this is a pleasant contrast to the routine, imposed responsibilities of home and office. Not to be ignored is the fact that participation in committees also furnishes opportunities for more personal relations with members of the larger organization, for converting mere similarities of interest into subtle patterns of acquaintance and friendship. Of course, involvement in committee work does not reach an overwhelming proportion of the membership; the distinction between the dedicated and the apathetic "hanger on" in voluntary associations as a whole applies with particular force at this point as well. Nevertheless, the trend in all but the most hidebound or personally dominated associations is toward encouraging wider participation through committee assignments, and through performance in one or more *programs*.

Since meetings of many associations are typically infrequent but yet regularly spaced, each formal meeting assumes great importance for the vitality of the association. Purely routine meetings—concerning business matters, election of officers, etc.—tend to clash with the ultimate aims of the organization and with one or more personal motives for joining. Consequently, a key feature is the avowed necessity for several "programs" during the organizations's yearly round. A program is essentially a dramatic deviation from routine, an opportunity for display and temporarily heightened activity. The pattern is simple and often effective. An outside dignitary is invited to give a provocative talk. Sometimes one or more members are plucked from the fringes of participation to discuss a crucial issue, to recount their achievements, or to display some skill. This is followed by open discussion, appreciation and criticism, and often by refreshments. When properly planned and executed, the program stimulates or maintains interest, provides sanctioned freedom for self-expression, and lends a personal flavor to the formalized aspects of organization.

5. A great many voluntary associations are affiliated with their counterparts in other communities in regional, national, or international federations. Whether a local association boasts an independent origin or was founded by the efforts of some parent organization is for present purposes a minor issue, a matter of historical detail. More important, it seems, is the sense of linkage with a wider world of experience and the occasional feeling of vicarious power that is a tonic to further participation.

Voluntary associations in urban regions are to a large extent attuned to the special traits of urban social organization. But how do they collectively operate in urbanized society? Direct information on this problem is, unfortunately, meager. However, we can profit from such indirect evidence as the extent of participation in voluntary associations and the concentration of membership in specific social categories of the urban region.

Several recent investigations indicate that relatively small proportions of urban males belong to no voluntary associations at all. In the Detroit area, 37 per cent were nonmembers, while in the San Francisco region, only 23 per cent were in that category.[8] An often cited study by Komarovsky in New York City during the depths of the depression, on the other hand, found that between 50 per cent and 60 per cent of the males (and between 63 per cent and 88 per cent of the females) questioned had no formal group affiliation apart from church membership. Similarly, a national sample survey of the National Opinion Research Center (in 1953) provided the incidental finding that 64 per cent of the respondents belonged to no voluntary association, excluding unions.[9]

These striking differences can be largely discounted, if a few basic points are considered. The Komarovsky study was mainly confined to the *central city* and was carried out in a depression period, when motivation for voluntary association was understandably low. In addition, though this study was one of the first of its kind, it did not attempt to draw a representative sample of adults—as Wright and Hyman have remarked. As for the NORC study, we do not know with any assurance that the sample adequately represents urban regions in the United States. Indeed, a special tabulation of respondents from metropolitan counties and rural counties furnishes results that diverge significantly from the overall findings. As the accompanying table shows, associational membership is considerably less marked in the rural counties and in rural farm segments of metropolitan

[8] Morris Axelrod, "Urban Structure and Social Participation," *American Sociological Review,* 21 (February, 1956), p. 15; Wendell Bell and Maryanne T. Force, "Urban Neighborhood Types and Participation in Formal Associations," *ibid.,* pp. 27–28.

[9] Mirra Komarovsky, "The Voluntary Associations of Urban Dwellers," *American Sociological Review,* 11 (December, 1946), pp. 686–698; Charles R. Wright and Herbert H. Hyman, "Voluntary Association Memberships of American Adults: Evidence from National Sample Surveys," *ibid.,* 23 (June, 1958), p. 287.

counties. Consequently, it seems likely that—in the contemporary urban region—participation in at least one voluntary group is widely distributed, perhaps accounting for 60 to 70 per cent of adult males.

TABLE 52

Differential Membership in Formal Organizations, by Residential Category and Population Type, 1953

PER CENT OF FAMILIES WHOSE MEMBERS BELONG TO:	Metrop. counties (with city of 500,000 or more)			Other urbanized counties (with city of 10–50,000)			Primarily rural counties (no town of 10,000)		
	Urban	Rural nonfarm	Rural farm	Urban	RNF	RF	Urban	RNF	RF
No organization	42	40	67	46	46	53	54	52	70
One organization	33	37	21	36	34	28	27	24	21
Two or more organizations	25	23	12	18	20	19	19	24	9
Total	100	100	100	100	100	100	100	100	100

SOURCE: Charles R. Wright and Herbert H. Hyman, "Voluntary Association Memberships of American Adults: Evidence From National Sample Surveys," *American Sociological Review*, Vol. 23 (June, 1958), p. 290.

Despite this rather broad involvement in urban voluntary groups, the various social categories of the urban region do not seem to be equally represented. With virtually no exceptions, studies on this point indicate that status level (measured in several ways) is highly correlated with participation. In particular, the middle and upper status groupings have a significantly greater involvement in the range of available associations than lower status categories. This pattern has been identified in such widely dispersed areas as New York City, Detroit, Spokane, Los Angeles, San Francisco, Columbus (Ohio), Evanston, Denver, and Columbia (South Carolina).[10]

As the accompanying table shows, these differences in participation

[10] Komarovsky, *loc. cit.;* Morris Axelrod, "Urban Structure and Social Participation," *American Sociological Review*, 21 (February, 1956), pp. 13–18; Scott Greer, "Urbanism Reconsidered: A Comparative Study of Local Areas in a Metropolis," *ibid.*, pp. 19–25; Wendell Bell and Maryanne T. Force, "Urban Neighborhood Types and Participation in Formal Associations," *ibid.*, pp. 25–35; Alfred C. Clarke, "The Use of Leisure and its Relation to Levels of Occupational Prestige," *ibid.*, 21 (June, 1956), pp. 301–307; Howard E. Freeman, Edwin Novak, and Leo G. Reeder, "Correlates of Membership in Voluntary Associations," *ibid.*, 22 (October, 1957), pp. 528–533; Leonard Reissman, "Class, Leisure, and Social Participation," *ibid.*, 19 (February, 1954), pp. 76–84; James H. Williams, "Close Friendship Relations of Housewives Residing in an Urban Community," *Social Forces*, 36 (May, 1958), pp. 358–362.

TABLE 53

Differences of Formal Group Participation for Selected Status Characteristics in the Detroit Area

STATUS FACTOR	Per cent who are members	Per cent who are very active
Family income		
Under $3,000	42	8
$3,000–3,999	66	9
$4,000–4,999	67	14
$5,000–5,999	62	12
$6,000–6,999	65	12
$7,000 and over	81	21
Education		
0–6 years	52	2
7–8 years	60	9
9–12 years	63	14
Some college	78	19
Occupation of family head		
Service worker or laborer	50	19
Operative	40	9
Craftsmen, foremen, etc.	40	11
Clerical, sales, etc.	62	21
Professional, managers, and proprietors	61	11

SOURCE: Morris Axelrod, "Urban Structure and Social Participation," *American Sociological Review,* Vol. 21 (February, 1956), p. 15.

persist regardless of the specific measure of status levels—family income, occupation, formal education, and type of neighborhood. Obviously, too, these measures do not reveal equally sharp distinctions in participation (compare lines 3 and 4). Income seems to be one of the more useful indicators of differential participation, in addition to occupation. This casual conclusion is corroborated by a careful analysis for Spokane. In addition to demonstrating that class level is correlated with membership, Freeman and his associates found that salary was more intimately related to membership than such status measures as the Index of Status Characteristics, rent, or subjective identification.[11]

Many studies of the membership of voluntary groups also find that people in middle and upper status categories tend to belong to a greater number of such associations than do lower status persons. It

[11] Freeman *et al., op. cit.,* p. 531.

is not yet clear that sheer *number of memberships* is a significant fact. Therefore, important clues may well be sought in the *types* of associations selected by persons in each status level, on the assumption that identifiable and meaningful differences exist between status levels. In Komarovsky's investigation, carried out in 1934–1935, several such differences were sufficiently clear to permit the following "class profiles" of membership to be identified: [12]

Economic (occupational) Level	Associational Pattern
1. Unskilled	Only 32 per cent belong to any group; social and athletic club; fraternal lodges.
2. Skilled	44 per cent belong to one or more groups; labor unions and fraternal lodges.
3. White collar	47 per cent belong to one or more groups; lodges, social clubs, religious groups; secondarily, Masons, fraternities, military groups, unions.
4. Business	67 per cent belong to one or more groups; fraternal groups, Masons, economic groups, civic and "cultural" associations.
5. Professional	68–98 per cent (depending on salary) belong to one or more groups; professional groups, cultural and civic types, Greek letter societies.

More recently, Bell and Force have searched for possible relations between broad types of organization (according to focus of interest) and status level of members.[13] Voluntary organizations were classified into three types: (*a*) general interest—devoted to the public good rather than a particular segment of the community (*e.g.*, Rotary, Kiwanis); (*b*) special stratum interest—devoted to particular status groups, such as veterans groups, labor unions, the Parent-Teacher

[12] Komarovsky, *loc. cit.*
[13] Wendell Bell and Maryanne T. Force, "Social Structure and Participation in Different Types of Formal Associations," *Social Forces,* 34 (May, 1956), pp. 345–350.

Associations, business groups; (c) special, individualized interest—involving either a nonstatus interest of members (such as hobby groups) or aiding a specific grouping not represented within the membership (e.g., charitable organizations for underprivileged boys, for the crippled, the aged, etc.).

Several suggestive patterns were found in comparing four neighborhoods in San Francisco, as summarized in Table 54. General interest and specially individualized interest associations were not greatly represented in either high or low status areas. However, general interest associations were somewhat more popular with high status males, while special stratum interest associations were more often found among low status males. In general, then, high status persons seem to show a greater diversity of associational interests, as well as greater inclination to participate in community-conscious groups. It is interesting to note also that apartment dwellers in high status areas have the highest proportionate participation in charitable groups. Whether these patterns reflect conscious motives (either of an altruistic or selfish nature) or imitation of one's peers has not been investigated.

TABLE 54

Participation in Formal Associations by Type of Neighborhood and Type of Interest, San Francisco, 1953

	Neighborhood Type			
	Low family Low economic status	Low family High economic status	High family Low economic status	High family High economic status
TYPE OF INTEREST				
General Interest*	20.6	29.3	22.4	27.9
Special-stratum interest†	67.7	40.3	65.3	56.1
Special-individual interest‡	10.5	24.3	11.4	12.7
Other§	1.2	6.1	0.9	3.3

* Church connected groups, fraternal organizations, and civic groups.

† Labor unions, patriotic organizations, PTA's, nationality associations, professional groups, political organizations, and business organizations.

‡ Recreational groups, hobby clubs, welfare and charitable groups.

§ Mainly neighborhood clubs or community centers.

SOURCE: Wendell Bell and Maryanne T. Force, "Social Structure and Participation in Different Types of Formal Associations," Social Forces, Vol. 34 (May, 1956), p. 348. By permission of the editors of Social Forces.

Intra-Regional Variations in Membership

Since the urban region is composed of several interrelated areas, as discussed in Chapter 7, we might reasonably expect participation in voluntary groups to vary among central city, suburb, and fringe areas. Only two studies provide information on this matter, however. Zimmer and Hawley discovered that residents of Flint, Michigan's fringe area had fewer associational memberships than the residents of Flint.[14] Very probably, Flint's population size and economic structure are not representative of American urban areas. It is also likely that its fringe and suburban populations do not correspond to the general features of comparable areas throughout the nation. As a result, it is unwise at this point to draw any conclusions about intraregional patterns of membership.

On the other hand, in the previously cited study by Wright and Hyman, special tabulations of associational membership by size of county and type of residence within counties contain very suggestive and possibly meaningful patterns of difference. In general, smaller urban centers have higher proportions of families *without* associational membership, as compared with cities of 50,000 or more population. Conversely, larger cities have higher proportions of families with two or more memberships. Furthermore, within two of the three size categories of county sampled, the sharpest difference is between farm residents, and urban and rural-nonfarm (suburban) areas. Perhaps the most significant finding—one that contradicts our plausible hypothesis—is that patterns of membership are quite similar in urban and rural-nonfarm areas, particularly so in the metropolitan counties studied.[15]

Migration and Membership

Some attention has been given to the possible impact of mobility on associational membership, since migration and commuting are widespread processes in the urban region. Survey data for Denver, analyzed by Wright and Hyman, show comparatively small differences between migrants and long-term residents. Furthermore, roughly similar degrees of participation were found in the various commuting zones.

---

[14] Basil Zimmer and Amos H. Hawley, "The Significance of Membership in Associations," *American Journal of Sociology*, 65 (September, 1959), pp. 196–201.

[15] Wright and Hyman, *op. cit.*, p. 292.

The largest difference was between a nearby zone (less than 25 minutes travel time) and a 35–44 minute zone—with the latter showing the higher participation rate. Yet Scaff's study of Claremont, a suburb of Los Angeles, indicates that length of residence is closely related to associational membership. Relative newcomers to the community (an average of 7.6 years residence) participate less in various organizations than the more established residents (average residence of 13 years). A specially interesting fact is that newcomers to the area are very likely to be commuters to other cities and suburbs of the Los Angeles region, thus combining two important facets of urban mobility. Consequently, the commuter category is on the average less involved in voluntary groups than noncommuters. And in contrast to the Denver study, among commuter families, rate of participation in organizations *declines* sharply as commuting distance increases.[16]

It may very well be that these studies fail to take account of important subgroups in the migrant or commuting category. Freedman's analysis of migrants to Chicago in 1935–1940, for example, demonstrated that important differences in migrants could be related to regional variations and type of community background.[17] This approach has been applied to an analysis of associational memberships in a Midwestern community of about 20,000 population. In general, it was found that membership increases with length of residence, and that younger migrants (those under 40) attain higher rates somewhat more rapidly than older migrants. But participation is also dependent on the types of migrants involved. Migrants from farm areas had decisively lower rates of participation during the first two years of residence, as compared with those from urban and rural-nonfarm areas. Furthermore, migrants from the latter areas tended to increase participation more rapidly than did rural migrants. Even after twenty years' residence, rural migrants still showed less participation than the urban category. These differences in participation probably are closely related to educational and occupational differences among migrants, and possibly to the difference in availability of voluntary associations for each migrant category.[18]

[16] Alvin H. Scaff, "The Effect of Commuting on Participation in Community Organizations," *American Sociological Review*, 17 (April, 1952), pp. 215–220.

[17] Ronald Freedman, *Recent Migration to Chicago* (Chicago, University of Chicago Press, 1949), Chaps. IV, V.

[18] Basil Zimmer, "Participation of Migrants in Urban Structures," *American Sociological Review*, 20 (April, 1955), pp. 218–224.

Social Attitudes and Social Participation

While all the preceding differences in participation seem plausible and coherent with respect to one another, there is a continuing lack of information on the *attitudinal* and *motivational* factors that may make these patterns more meaningful. A few clues are available that deserve further investigation. In a sample of Protestants from Columbus, Ohio, Dynes discovered that membership in voluntary groups was significantly related to basic religious attitudes. Persons with *sectarian* attitudes (characterized by relatively complete integration of religion and social life, and illustrated by "emotionalism," evangelism, and other-worldliness) belonged to fewer nonchurch organizations than those with "Church-institutional" attitudes toward religion (*i.e.*, separation of religion from other major facets of social life). Dynes suggests that the sectarian feels comparatively little need for formal organizational membership, since he is more likely than the nonsectarian to establish friendships within his religious group, and also participates in more organizations *within* his religious group. In fact, Dynes found that sectarians derived considerably greater satisfaction from their religious affiliation than did the nonsectarian.[19] Unfortunately, this study did not attempt to relate participation and religious attitudes to status differences.

Another motivational clue may be found in the previously cited study of Spokane by Freeman and associates. While social class differences were most closely related to patterns of participation in voluntary groups—as expected, *attitudes toward the community* also seemed to be moderately significant in distinguishing gross differences in participation. In particular, those who indicated general satisfaction with the size and operation of the community, as well as optimistic attitudes about the community's future, were somewhat more likely to belong to two or more voluntary associations. It is likely that these attitudes have some basis in the class position of the persons studied, as Freeman suggests, but at this point a clear picture of the basic factors in community attitudes is not available.[20]

---

[19] Russell R. Dynes, "The Consequences of Sectarianism for Social Participation," *Social Forces*, 35 (May, 1957), pp. 331–334.

[20] Freeman *et al.*, *loc. cit.*; Reissman, *op. cit.*, pp. 81–83. See also Dorothy L. Meier and Wendell Bell, "Anomia and Differential Access to the Achievement of Life Goals," *American Sociological Review*, 24 (April, 1959), pp. 189–201.

THE PLACE OF VOLUNTARY GROUPS IN URBAN REGIONS

The rise and multiplication of voluntary associations provide fairly good illustrations of "latent consequences" in human behavior—those largely unplanned, unpremeditated patterns of values, activities, and organizations that nevertheless satisfy one or more important needs of individuals and of their social organizations. If any single voluntary association seems to reflect conscious planning, awareness of purpose, and recruitment of membership, these facts should not obscure the underlying similarities, the implicit common features, that have been analyzed in this chapter. Let us briefly review these features.

1. A fundamental feature of most voluntary groups is their generally effective *compromise* between formal and personal relationships. Since the dominant tendency of urbanization has been a separation of primary and secondary relationships, of private and public spheres, the voluntary association may be interpreted as an organizational invention that aids in the continual transitional process of urbanization by *combining complementary social experiences*.

2. As previous discussion has suggested, though voluntary associations are well distributed throughout the urban region, there is increasing evidence that voluntary associations have not been equally attractive to various subgroupings (class, religious, residence status, etc.). If the voluntary group is fundamentally a means of adjusting to the special nature of the urban region, it surely follows that membership will be most meaningful and desirable to those who are most motivated by uniquely "urban" goals. Mere *residence* in the urban region does not insure urban *culture*.[21] Essentially, voluntary groups are supported by middle class persons who share a *basic social stability* (reflected in respectable or responsible occupations, moderately long residence in the community, and in general, optimism about community prospects), plus an accompanying emphasis on *personal and community "progress"* (reflected in concern for education and upward mobility, a secularized religion that does not resist the necessity for change, and a somewhat greater involvement in broader, "service" organizations).

By contrast, other social categories—recent migrants (especially from rural areas), lower status persons, adherents of sectarian religious forms—seem to have a more limited identification with urban

[21] Adolph S. Tomars, "Rural Survivals in American Life," *Rural Sociology*, 8 (December, 1943), pp. 378–386.

values, and therefore—on the average—less need for and appreciation of voluntary associations as a normal part of their experience.
Perhaps the essential difference between associational members and
nonmembers lies in understandable variations in frustration, pes-
simism, and uncertainty in achieving success—what has been called
anomia. Meier and Bell, for example, found several striking differences in participation patterns related to anomia. Taking males of
low socioeconomic status, they discovered higher proportions of
anomia among those who identified themselves as "lower or working
class" rather than "middle class." Anomia tended to be higher among
older males, regardless of class identification, but more important to
our discussion is the finding that anomia was somewhat more pronounced among lower status persons who did not belong to voluntary
groups. For persons in middle and high status categories, the difference in anomia was even sharper between participants and non-
participants.[22]

TABLE 55

**Percentage of Males With High Anomia Scores, by Socioeconomic Status, Class
Identification, Age, and Social Participation, for San Francisco, 1953**

	Socioeconomic status of participants in formal groups			
			Middle and high	
CLASS IDENTIFICATION	*Young*	*Old*	*Young*	*Old*
Lower and working class	48	56	24	24
Middle and upper class	43	44	8	21
	Socioeconomic status of isolates			
Lower and working class	23	63	37	43
Middle and working class	40	39	17	16

SOURCE: Dorothy L. Meier and Wendell Bell, "Anomia and Differential Access
to the Achievement of Life Goals," *American Sociological Review,* Vol. 24
(April, 1959), p. 195.

3. In short, voluntary associations as a whole appear to serve a
generalized function of more enduring value than the explicit purposes of any single association. Paradoxically, they provide a continuing source of *morale* for the supposedly heartless, impersonal, and
fragmented urban region. To be more exact, voluntary associations
bolster the social and psychological stability of an otherwise precarious urban middle class. This is accomplished, without plan, in two

[22] Meier and Bell, *op. cit.,* p. 195.

ways. Positively, the associational contacts of middle class families inspire and sustain a sense of responsibility and purpose, of movement and "progress," which are so closely related to the middle class *ethos*. But voluntary associations have an important negative function as well, as Robin Williams has noted. There is a very popular variety of *expressive association* (*e.g.,* the fraternal order or "service" organization) that is particularly congenial to middle class persons because they provide a refreshing contrast to the *competitive* routine of the dominant business and professional pursuits in the middle classes.[23] Thus, to the extent that the urban region relies on its middle classes for leadership and stability, the voluntary association is an unheralded but indispensable component of urban social organization.

SELECTED REFERENCES

BANTON, Michael, *West African City: A Study of Tribal Life in Freetown* (London, Oxford University Press, 1957).

LANG, Kurt and LANG, Gladys E., *Collective Dynamics* (New York, Thomas Y. Crowell, 1961), Chaps. XVI, XVII.

ROSE, Arnold, *Theory and Method in the Social Sciences* (Minneapolis, University of Minnesota Press, 1953), Chaps. III, IV.

STACEY, Margaret, *Tradition and Change: A Study of Banbury* (Oxford, Oxford University Press, 1960), Chap. V.

[23] Williams, *op. cit.,* p. 499.

CHAPTER 10

Social Class Divisions
in Urban Regions

AT MANY POINTS in previous chapters we have noted the importance of *status* and *status differences* in the operation of the urban region. Perhaps without using the proper technical terms, many of us have also impressionistically encountered differences in status as we walk or drive from one neighborhood to another, observe obvious differences in housing quality, scan the covers and inside pages of prominently displayed magazines, examine the variety of work space and facilities for employees in a large office or bank, or simply compare the clothing of people on major urban thoroughfares. In this chapter, the realm of status and social class as a focal component of urban social organization receives special attention.

"Status" and "class" are *relative* terms; they refer first to different degrees of importance or value assigned to specific persons and categories of persons in a community or society. Thus, we may rightly speak of parental status as distinct from child status, managerial status and employee status, faculty status and student status, married status and single status. In practice, status differences mean differences in responsibility, opportunities for social contacts, and material rewards. Consequently, there is, secondly, a tendency for persons of similar status to recognize their similarities—more or less consciously—and to be aware of their cultural and social separation from persons on other status levels.

In simpler types of communities, types of status distinction are relatively few in number—age, sex, skill, physical prowess, and family are the most frequent. More important, in such communities, specific distinctions do not normally coincide with one another. Thus, a person who is noted for physical prowess may come from a family of low repute. Social classes arise and become "visible" when people are evaluated, and judge themselves, in terms of a commonly used complex of status distinctions, which is applied to persons regardless of their sex or age. When these distinctions are formalized in law and sanctioned by a dominant religion, one's social position is permanently fixed in a social *caste* system, or an approximation to a caste system. However, throughout the past three centuries and in widening portions of the world, caste systems have been diluted and eventually replaced by more flexible types of social positions—social classes.[1] In the modern urban community, social classes constitute the key to its characteristic maze of status distinctions.

If class and caste are more adequately conceived in comparison with single status distinctions, urban classes are perhaps more meaningful in contrast to rural and small town classes. In Plainville, a village-centered community in Missouri, the residents recognized a basic division into two classes that were separated by differences in family background, wealth, morality, and, most visibly, by *manners*. More recently, a study of Gosforth, an English village, also found a basic division into two social classes. However, the upper and lower classes were further separated by a buffer category of persons of indeterminate position (called "intermediate" by the researcher). Furthermore, each major class seemed to possess subdivisions or secondary distinctions, which suggest that rural residents in recent years do not fit the stereotype of bucolic equalitarianism.[2] The same general picture emerges from the frequently cited study of Prairie Town, which found a fairly distinct set of three class strata.[3] Essentially, people in Prairie Town evaluated one another in terms of *stability of residence* in the community, *permanence* of occupation, and economic

[1] Useful discussions of status and class systems may be found in Bernard Barber, *Social Stratification* (New York, Harcourt, Brace, and World, 1957), Chaps. I–IV; Joseph A. Kahl, *The American Class Structure* (New York, Holt, Rinehart, and Winston, 1957), Chaps. I, II; E. T. Hiller, *Social Relations and Structures* (New York, Harper and Brothers, 1947), Part VI; Gunnar Landtman, *The Origin of the Inequality of Social Classes* (Chicago, University of Chicago Press, 1938).

[2] James West, *Plainville, U.S.A.* (New York, Columbia University Press, 1945); W. W. Williams, *Gosforth: The Sociology of an English Village* (New York, The Free Press of Glencoe, 1956), Chap. V.

[3] John Useem, Pierre Tangent, and Ruth Useem, "Stratification in a Prairie Town," *American Sociological Review*, 7 (June, 1942), pp. 331–342.

independence. Thus, the highest social stratum consisted of large land-holders and successful businessmen. A middle category contained small shopkeepers, retired farmers, independent craftsmen, and a few professional persons. At the bottom rank, consequently, were unskilled workers, ex-farmers, and former farm hands.

How, then, may we characterize in general terms a typical rural or small town class structure? Despite the obvious variations just noted, several features seem specially distinctive.

First, the limited size of the community gives residents rather intimate knowledge of the rest of the population. Consequently, judgments of relative status tend to be sharp and inclusive of all residents.

Second, most rural studies have discovered only two or three broad strata, with little or no development of finer distinctions within a major social division. This relative simplicity is partly explained by the size of the community, but more probably by the high degree of cultural and occupational homogeneity of the population.

A third feature is especially noteworthy: in genuinely rural communities, status lines are drawn with an implied finality and permanence. To the ruralite, initial position is not viewed as subject to much change by effort, striving, or imitation. Indeed, except for outmigration, the opportunity for changing social position is obviously limited.

Fourth, because of its small size, relative homogeneity and stability, there seems to be a higher degree of consensus about the standards of differential evaluation and social position.

Finally, rural and small town standards of evaluation tend to emphasize the more "personal" and "subjective" aspects—family background, length of residence, morality—in short, items that are difficult to "measure" but are nevertheless easily available to the judgment of most community participants.

Urban class systems cannot be expected to possess the relative simplicity or consensus of their rural counterparts. Basically, the heterogeneity and dynamic nature of the urban region have not produced a clear-cut system of social strata, but rather a series of shifting fragments that recurrently appear to represent a hierarchical complex of responsibilities, rewards, opportunities, and power. Most of our earlier investigations of urban social strata have failed to consider these issues because they were made in comparatively small, slowly changing urban areas. Yankee City (Massachusetts) and

Elmtown-Jonesville (Illinois), which are frequently cited as illustrations of urban class systems, each had a population of 10,000 (or less) when studied.[4] Only Middletown (Muncie, Indiana) approaches a more typical phase of urban development. When the Lynds restudied Middletown in 1935–1936, it had grown to almost 50,000 population. But more important, Middletown was a relatively new city in the midst of vast economic and social changes derived from the general industrialization following World War I and the crisis of the Great Depression.[5]

The Distinctiveness of Urban Stratification

What, then, are the distinctive traits of urban stratification, which we can consider as meaningful reflections of the modern urban region?

Probably the most important is the increasing trend toward *spatial segregation* between families of different statuses. As we have already seen in Chapter 5, the urban region is becoming a mosaic of class-linked areas and neighborhoods, the suburb perhaps being the purest form of recent segregation by class level. Consequently, apart from fleeting contacts in offices and plants, in retail outlets and in provision of services to the home, urbanites are increasingly insulated from direct and sustained knowledge of persons on other social levels.[6] A generation ago, it was considered proper among comfortably situated families to ask "how the other half lives." More recently, *personal knowledge* of other class levels has become not so much a matter of distaste or impropriety as one of *disinterest*. The overall result is that urbanites tend to be more conscious of their own position and opportunities (or frustrations) than of a *system* of graded positions. This is a form of "class consciousness" that Marx and his followers simply could not comprehend.

[4] W. Lloyd Warner and Paul S. Lunt, *The Social Life of a Modern Community* (New Haven, Yale University Press, 1941); A. B. Hollingshead, *Elmtown's Youth* (New York, John Wiley and Sons, 1949); W. Lloyd Warner, ed., *Democracy in Jonesville* (New York, Harper and Brothers, 1949).

[5] Robert S. Lynd and Helen M. Lynd, *Middletown* (New York, Harcourt, Brace, 1929); and *Middletown in Transition* (New York, Harcourt, Brace, 1937).

[6] A good discussion of the "excluding" nature of class divisions is Carl E. Ortmeyer, "Social Interaction and Social Stratification," *Rural Sociology*, 17 (September, 1952), pp. 253–260.

Closely related to this spatial segregation of status categories is a general inability to evaluate the position or status of more than a small fraction of residents in the urban region. Not only does segregation restrict interaction between status levels; it also tends to blur otherwise meaningful connections between the community or region as a unit and the activities of numerous specific persons and families. To the urbanite, beyond a limited circle of neighbors, relatives, friends, and associates, other urbanites are paradoxically familiar strangers who are accepted as "givens" in the urban context. Just as the urbanite is notoriously (and understandably) poor in giving street directions, so is he basically uncertain about the social standing of anyone who cannot be easily identified with either extreme of the social scale.

Nevertheless, urban custom and experience demand that evaluation of status be made for all who enter a field of potential interaction, no matter how tenuous or impersonal. Therefore, the urbanite necessarily acquires standards of evaluation that are simple, quick, "objective," and easily applicable to large numbers of persons. In short, urban status criteria are characteristically *material,* rather than behavioral or motivational, since the latter are only feasible in situations of prolonged contact and intimacy. As Simmel and others have shown, the simplest, most objective measure in the urban community is *money* (whether inherited, earned, or borrowed).[7] Yet income or wealth is not directly visible. Consequently, a number of indirect but normally visible (external) standards have become part of the urbanite's evaluation apparatus: occupation, material possessions, residential area and type of housing, formal education, travel, and membership in formal associations.[8]

This urban emphasis on a *variety* of status criteria inevitably yields some discrepancies between one's ratings on the above mentioned standards. It is becoming increasingly difficult to discover close connections, for specific persons, between such criteria as income, formal education, type of housing, and material possessions. Unfortunately, we do not know the extent of this inconsistency of statuses (what Lenski calls "low status crystallization"). Yet several studies have

[7] Georg Simmel, "The Metropolis and Mental Life," in Kurt H. Wolff, ed., *The Sociology of Georg Simmel* (New York, The Free Press of Glencoe, 1950), pp. 409–424; Talcott Parsons, *Essays in Sociological Theory Pure and Applied* (New York, The Free Press of Glencoe, 1949), pp. 178–180.

[8] Barber, *op. cit.,* Chap. VIII; Kahl, *op. cit.,* Chaps. III, IV.

shown that evidence of inconsistency exists on all "traditional" class levels.[9] The significance of this aspect of urban stratification should not be misconstrued, though it is specially tempting to do so. The facts of status inconsistency do not allow us to dismiss social classes as out-moded or purely imaginary conceptions. There is, for example, con-siderable evidence of status *consistency* (which will be discussed be-low). Perhaps two useful cautions can be derived from this brief discussion. First and foremost is the recognition that urban stratifica-tion systems tend to be more complex, more fluid than those found in older, more tradition-bound communities. Secondly, the use of "judges" or "raters" of family status in specific urban areas is in-evitably of limited value unless some means of compensating for status inconsistencies is devised—in which case the raters are unnecessary.

Quite characteristic of urban "open class" systems is the rather general finding that urbanites on all status levels tend to share similar valuations about the nature and personnel of the highest and lowest status positions, but disagree on the criteria of distinction for a broad, intermediate range of statuses.[10] This vagueness about a fluid "middle status range" results from the varied criteria of status, limited social experience with other strata, and a more or less constant *cultural emphasis* on the desirability of *movement,* progress, and opportunity for those assumed to be at middle status levels. Urbanites are some-what disturbed and gratified by this fluidity of definition. In fluidity there is hope of social ascent. Perhaps the increasing residential segregation by status reflects in part a search for status consistency in reaction to vagueness and fluidity. A few studies indicate that people tend to overestimate the size of the status level with which they identify.[11] This, too, may represent a desire to extend the boundaries of familiar status into the no man's land of the muddled middle.

[9] Gerhard Lenski, "Status Crystallization: A Non-Vertical Dimension of Social Status," *American Sociological Review,* 19 (August, 1954), pp. 405–413; Gerhard Lenski, "Social Participation and Social Status," *ibid.,* 21 (August, 1956), pp. 458–464. See the earlier discussion of this problem by Emile Benoit-Smullyan, "Status Types and Status Interrelations," *ibid.,* 9 (April, 1944), pp. 151–161.
[10] Gregory P. Stone and William H. Form, "Instabilities in Status: The Problem of Hierarchy in the Community Study of Status Arrangements," *American Sociological Review,* 18 (April, 1953), pp. 149–162; O. A. Oeser and S. B. Hammond, eds., *Social Structure and Personality in a City* (New York, Macmillan, 1954), Chap. XXII; Allison Davis, Burleigh B. Gardner, and Mary Gardner, *Deep South* (Chicago, University of Chicago Press, 1941).
[11] Oeser and Hammond, *op. cit.,* p. 281.

In view of all the preceding features, a rather unique aspect of urban stratification should be quite understandable. With some oversimplification, it appears that the urban open class structure stimulates (or permits) upward social mobility, but principally by providing opportunities for *imitating* higher status levels, rather than techniques for achieving *validated entrance* into higher strata. This is at first glance a surprising conclusion, perhaps because we are still accustomed to thinking of classes in the European or the American small town setting. Yet the nature of the modern urban region—its complexity and heterogeneity, extensiveness, stress on segregation of activities and groups, and the importance of mass media of communication—tends to remove the process of social mobility from a personal to an impersonal plane. With the decreasing opportunity for contacts between clear-cut social levels, with the development of superficial, tangible criteria of status, with the incessant promptings of merchandisers and advertisers—status movement (the "status game") inevitably becomes depersonalized, a competition for *symbols* of position rather than the positions themselves.[12]

Indeed, the imitative, impersonal nature of urban social mobility has become so marked in American urban regions that *personal* competition for higher status is largely muted. "Keeping up with the Joneses" is a wearisome game of matching possessions within a circle of neighbors; it is of no status value to its participants beyond that circle. One of the striking findings in recent years is the discovery of a "keeping *down* to the Joneses" attitude,[13] a fear among neighboring families of similar social status of creating local jealousies by converting outwardly invisible status increments into visible form too quickly.

It is, of course, a moot question whether or not mobility by imitation is mobility at all. If it appears dubious to an observer, urbanites place great faith in its potential, as evidenced in their persistent resort to two channels of status imitation (which may be considered by-products of distinctively urbanized forms of stratification). There is

---

[12] This is brought out in several ways by C. Wright Mills, *White Collar* (New York, Oxford University Press, 1951), especially Chap. XI; Vance Packard, *The Status Seekers* (New York, David McKay, 1959); Lucy Kavaler, *The Private World of High Society* (New York, David McKay, 1960); Pierre Bleton, *Les Hommes des temps qui viennent: essai sur les classes moyennes* (Paris, Editions Ouvrières, 1956).

[13] William H. Whyte, Jr., *The Organization Man* (Garden City, N.Y., Doubleday and Company, 1956), Chap. XXIV.

the obvious and ubiquitous process of *imitation by status objects*. This simply involves acquisition of those objects, appliances, and gadgets that are most closely identified with higher status positions (expensive cars—until recently, foreign cars—large homes, clothing, etc.). During the early years of commercial television, it was not uncommon to find, in cities of the northeastern United States, rows of roof-adorned television aerials, unaccompanied by television receivers in the apartments below. Advertising and installment buying assume special significance as technical foundations for this form of status imitation.

But an impressively growing form—and perhaps ultimately the more successful form—has been *imitation by formal education*. From the urbanite's standpoint, an inherent limitation of imitation by status objects is that it is both an endless process and difficult to convert into opportunities for higher status contacts. Formal education, on the other hand, can often provide both entrance into higher occupational levels and opportunities for vocational and social contacts with higher status persons. As far as mobility is concerned, urban education therefore consists of two essential acquisitions: vocational or technical skills; and the broader, "cultural" skills appropriate to each major occupational level. Many people cynically declare the second more important than the first for mobility. This has not yet been investigated, however. Yet the cultural skills (which are part of "style of life," to be discussed later) are more difficult to acquire in the typical educational setting—or almost anywhere beyond the family. Hence the importance of the college and university. On the other hand, formal education as a means of imitation is dependent on an expanding economy. In Calcutta, thousands of university students are discovering that limited job opportunities are rapidly making a mockery of the "status value" of formal education.[14] The same situation in the Germany of the twenties was a source of great social instability.

For our purposes, a final aspect of urban classes concerns the dominant type of relations between persons on different class levels. As analyzed by Ortmeyer, these interrelations may take some combination of three forms: (*a*) The "circumscribing or excluding" type emphasizes social distance, segregation of classes. (*b*) The "manipulating" type is marked by exploitation of one class by another. (*c*) In the "nurturing" form, currently found in several South American

[14] *The New York Times,* December 27, 1959.

FIGURE 9
A Schematic Version of the Structure of Urban Life-Styles

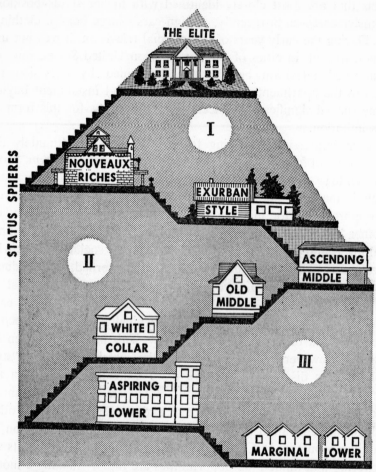

communities, one class feels obligated to provide protection and aid to members of a subordinate class.[15] While all three kinds of relationships can be found in modern urban regions, in the more complex regions of Western Europe and North America the opportunity (and perhaps the motivation) for pursuing the manipulatory and nurturing types is being gradually but surely reduced. Political ethics, education, the growth of private organizations, and the institutionalization of welfare activities largely explain this trend.[16] Much of the evolving urban

[15] Ortmeyer, *loc. cit.;* Melvin M. Tumin, *Caste in a Peasant Society* (Princeton, N.J., Princeton University Press, 1952), pp. 127–129.

[16] See a fictional treatment in Edwin O'Connor, *The Last Hurrah* (Boston, Little, Brown, 1956).

class system—which is a system by courtesy—as reflected in behavior and verbalized aspirations, seems to be focusing around the issue of *impersonal but informal exclusion.* Those on higher status levels wish to promote or protect minimal social distance, for various reasons. We find this in typical forms of segregation—racial, residential, educational, and in formal associations. On the other hand, in view of the fluid aspects of urban stratification, those on comparatively lower status levels seek to contract social distance by using genuine channels of mobility (such as education). Those who cannot do so successfully become resigned to, or oblivious of, social distance, and instead content themselves with imitation by status objects.

DISTINCTIVE STYLES OF LIFE AND SOCIAL STRATA

The nature of urban stratification, as summarized in the last few pages, does not permit the identification of a well-ordered hierarchy of social classes in the urban region—such as may be found in smaller cities and in European and many non-Western cities. The main tendency is instead toward the demarcation of three roughly defined *status spheres,* in each of which subspheres have appeared with fluid boundaries. It is often difficult to determine the relation between subspheres; in some instances, they are more coordinate than hierarchically related. In any case, these status spheres and subspheres (or social classes) rarely exhibit the organization or "class consciousness" that are found in more static stratification systems. Urban classes, to the extent that they can be reliably identified at all, are primarily expressed through a series of distinctive *life-styles,* which are rather difficult to copy and therefore constitute a useful means of conceptualizing "class differences." [17] The accompanying diagram is intended as a simplified summary of the urban class system in these terms.

An analysis of urban classes through the medium of "style of life"

[17] For valuable discussions of differences in "life styles" see Hans H. Gerth and C. Wright Mills, eds., *From Max Weber: Essays in Sociology* (New York, Oxford University Press, 1946), pp. 187–191; Warner and Lunt, *op. cit.;* Cleveland Amory, *The Proper Bostonians* (New York, E. P. Dutton, 1947); E. Digby Baltzell, *Philadelphia Gentlemen* (New York, The Free Press of Glencoe, 1958); Thorstein Veblen, *The Theory of the Leisure Class* (New York, Modern Library, 1934), Chaps. II–VII; William H. Whyte, Jr., "Budgetism: Opiate of the Middle Class," *Fortune,* 53 (May, 1956), pp. 133–137, 164–172; Herbert Hyman, "The Value Systems of Different Classes," in Reinhard Bendix and Seymour M. Lipset, eds., *Class, Status, and Power* (New York, The Free Press of Glencoe, 1953), pp. 426–442.

requires some definition and justification. Style of life refers to the basic values, aspirations, and responsibilities that can be attributed to a segment or stratum of a population. It concerns not only the *possession* of desirable objects and experiences, but also the opportunity of acquiring possessions and the characteristic *motivations* concerning their use. A style of life is a meaningful *composite* of values, activities, possessions, and motives; it cannot be imitated piecemeal without some embarrassment to the imitator and scorn from those being imitated. In general, a distinctive style of life takes years to develop—and years to unlearn—and therefore is an important source of stability in the flux of urban stratification. Indeed, it is very likely that traditional class labels and self-identification with a given stratum are less useful than analysis of life-styles in capturing the fundamentals of urban stratification.

Thus far, urban studies have identified six (and possibly seven) styles of life. In the following "status portraits" some simplification is inevitable, since we are searching for similarities among urban areas, principally in Western societies.

The Social Elite; Traditional Upper Class [18]

This stratum is perhaps least representative, both numerically and culturally, of the modern urban region. The way of life of the social elite is in many respects reminiscent of an earlier urbanism, partly medieval and partly the rarified urbanism of royal capitals. Perhaps this special cultural ancestry helps to explain both the immense social distance from other contemporary urban strata and the social and cultural attachment to social elites in more static societies (*e.g.*, England, France, pre-Nazi Germany, nonfascist Italy).

Style of life is ultimately dependent on the happy accident of inherited wealth, and on the assurance and unimpeachable position normally guaranteed by this form of wealth. Striving and social climbing, therefore, are not only conveniently relegated to the past, but any evidence of current social striving is viewed as improper and in poor taste. Inherited wealth, with some exceptions, leads to the underlying viewpoint that stability is preferable to potentially disruptive innovations; conservatism, not reactionary ideals, is visible in a variety of fields—including politics.

[18] Warner and Lunt, *op. cit.*, pp. 422–430; Baltzell, *op. cit.*, Chaps. X, XII, XIII; Kahl, *op. cit.*, pp. 187–193.

Conservatism to the social elite means a deep respect for the past, but in particular that portion of the past that is most significant to the elite. Almost all evidence points to the family line and family tradition as the primary focus; it is the acknowledged source of support, position, facilities, and continuity. The family name is perhaps the major object of worship, though the elite is prominent in the more public forms of religion. Emphasis on family background normally restricts choice of mates to families of equivalent status, though a dearth of proper candidates may be remedied by permitting marriages with members of the next highest stratum. Stratum *endogamy* among the so-called "Proper Bostonians" is clearly revealed by the "royal family" spate of intermarriages among the Cabots, Amorys, Saltonstalls, and Lodges. And a careful analysis of "society" marriages would indicate a similar process of marital segregation.

Members of the urban elite should not be confused with the "leisure class" as acidly described by Veblen more than sixty years ago. Upper-upper class persons tend to follow a modern version of the "Protestant Ethic," which demands industriousness and serious attention to some sphere of business enterprise. The "playboy" is an exception, a deviant case, in contemporary elite circles. With all the assured financial resources of inheritance and devotion to enterprise, the elite—particularly the elder members—refuse to engage in *conspicuous consumption* and material display. They tend to be parsimonious in routine family expenditures, though few probably equal the attitude of the "Proper Bostonian" who seriously complained about the price of batteries for his hearing-aid.[19] This parsimonious attitude also extends to the question of publicity, for the members of the elite generally maintain pride in privacy and do not seek frequent inclusion in society columns of metropolitan newspapers. However, their names invariably appear in the Social Register (or its local equivalent) and often in *Who's Who*. This is considered a proper and expected form of publicity.

Another aspect of the elite style of life concerns a special sense of social responsibility, *noblesse oblige,* toward the community and region, and often the nation. This is expressed in several ways: as consistent patrons of the expensive arts (museums, symphony orchestras, opera, etc.); as major contributors to various welfare activities; and as members of long-established formal organizations. This responsibility is rarely reflected in the pursuit of political office unless

[19] Amory, *op. cit.,* p. 206.

there is a family tradition of this sort, as in the case of the Lodges or Saltonstalls of Boston.

Finally, there is a predominant yet simple focus on "gracious living," not as a sought after antidote to the routine of career and upward mobility (as in the middle strata), but as the basis and justification of "success." Comfort, assurance, continuity, balance in interests as ends in themselves, rather than as means of display or rivalry—these are the components of gracious living that are not only desired, but are readily available. Travel, for example, means a renewal of contact with acquaintances, places, and objects. It is a normal, necessary part of the elite round of life, an experience worthy in itself—not a symbol of "success" or as a useful conversation piece.

Nouveaux Riches; the Lower-Upper Life-Style [20]

This stratum is one of the most representative of urban stratification processes and one which probably has had the greatest changes in membership during the last twenty years. The quality of *dynamism* is perhaps the basic theme in a wearing style of life that eventually produces opportunities to enter the elite, or psychological casualties for those who cannot do so.

Lower-upper persons acquire a distinctive life-style when success in a business or professional career reaches (or gives promise of reaching) well beyond the average expectation of income, responsibility, and power. The desire to convert worldly success into acceptance by the elite becomes the fundamental ideal, though they are often mistakenly and superficially criticized as *materialistic*. The ideal is pursued by various routes and with a special cluster of guiding attitudes. Most prominent is the emphasis on a definite career, with intense striving and competitiveness as indispensable personal traits. Formal education is principally viewed as preparation for a career and upward social mobility, not as a link with the experience of past generations or as a means of developing a rounded personality.

This life-style is hopefully viewed as transitional or preparatory, a kind of implicit social probation. Consequently, the lower-upper category strives to give evidence of current "achievement." One avenue is active participation in voluntary associations, principally those in the public eye. Another is the necessity of being among the first to follow

[20] Few studies of this stratum are available. See Warner and Lunt, *op. cit.*, pp. 430–434; Kavaler, *op. cit.;* Aline Saarinen, *The Proud Possessors* (New York, Random House, 1958); S. N. Behrman, *Duveen* (New York, Random House, 1952).

new fashions in clothes, housing, appliances and gadgets, and leisure. For whatever is achieved or purchased, adequate publicity and display are particularly important. Thus, at the height of this life-style, considerable emphasis is given to collecting (and advertising) valuable and notable art objects—often acquired through the services of a knowledgeable agent who is necessarily given carte blanche. (Several of the leading art galleries and private museums had their origins in this process.)

The recently rich and successful do not yet assume the elite's devotion to lineage and family name. Instead, as an accompaniment of striving, they foster a belief in individual talent and initiative, and the value of optimism. Increasingly since World War II, the individualistic emphasis has been modified by the recognition of large organizational contexts (corporations, political parties, institutes and foundations), but this is a *strategic move* that does not blunt the acuteness of striving.

Perhaps the growing corps of rising junior executives, so well depicted by William Whyte, provides a social reservoir from which new adherents to the lower-upper ideal will be recruited. It is interesting to note that this category is in many instances still too young, too undecided about open striving and conspicuous consumption, too limited in income and achievement, to adopt more than fragments of another style of life. But the "organization man" does place considerable emphasis on career and an uncomfortable degree of striving, which is reflected in his willingness to move or be transferred (upward, of course) and even in his moderately numerous shifts to other organizations. In view of the distinctive nature of modern urban economic systems, it is reasonable to expect that a sizeable portion of lower-uppers will necessarily come from the ranks of properly motivated "organization men."

The Exurban Life-Style [21]

A relatively new stratum and style of life has appeared at the edge of the urban region, almost as an exile from the status whirl of the city and suburb. Because it is so new, it is difficult to locate on the urban scale of status. Yet the exurbanite seems to be *just within* the upper status sphere, distinct from and yet not completely unrelated to the recently rich.

The exurban style of life is based on a compound of artistic aspira-

[21] A. C. Spectorsky, *The Exurbanites* (Philadelphia, J. B. Lippincott, 1955).

tions and employment in the vast and expanding communications industries of modern urban regions. Since these elements are ultimately incompatible, an immediate compromise is necessary—the exurban life-style. Closely dependent on city affairs, the exurbanite settles in semirural retreats and pursues a superficially bucolic way of life by owning split-rail fences, quaint lanterns, hitchingposts near the driveway, and coffee tables made from cobbler's benches.

Exurbanites are also "recently rich." Their incomes range from $20,000 to over $100,000, with a median income probably above $30,000. This wealth is principally used for display among other exurbanites—in the "rural" articles previously mentioned, in week-end parties with substantial liquor bills, and foreign cars. But exurbanites think of themselves as frustrated artists and writers; they want to compose "great" works, rather than "saleable" ones. Their exurban residence presumably provides the conditions for creativity (time, space, quiet, and very infrequent commuting to the job), yet the wish is often unequal to these conditions (or to creative abilities). As a result, exurbanites are also strivers, but mainly for esthetic ideals, not social reputation, power, or entrance into the elite.

The Middle-Class Ethos and Variations

Since the middle segments of the class structure are difficult to pinpoint by the usual criteria of occupation and income, we can also expect style of life to possess equally fluid or vague features. Perhaps the key to this broad category is the fact of marked status inconsistencies. For example, occupational prestige and educational achievement are frequently out of line with income—among teachers, some sales personnel, and many bank employees. In addition, there is an underlying fear of being identified with lower status categories and life-styles, compounded with a modified attempt to raise status for the next generation. Thus, the major goals involve some combination of security, respectability, and mobility.

1. The new middle class

Generally denied more than token opportunities for increased social responsibility, the new middle class stresses respectability and morality, as well as security.[22] Several items point to this central set of themes. There is a serious adherence to organized religion and parti-

[22] Kahl, *op. cit.*, pp. 202–205; Mills, *op. cit.*, Chaps. X–XII.

cipation in church-related activities, particularly in fringe areas of the larger metropolitan regions. Formal education—increasingly college —is highly valued, not only for related occupational opportunities, but as a mark of "culture." In the same way, home ownership assumes intrinsic value, despite the financial sacrifices that often accompany purchase of a house. Perhaps, the addiction to membership in various voluntary groups, book clubs, and the like can be interpreted as another aspect of the quest for respectability.

Mills has discovered among some white collar workers a special ideology of security through regular contacts with higher status persons—the "reflected glory" theme. For example, sales personnel in medium-sized cities appeared to borrow (however tenuously) the prestige of their prestigeful patrons, and also derived a feeling of momentary power in influencing their patrons' selection of articles.[23]

2. The organizational men

The life-style of the rising junior executive and salaried professional, on the other hand, seems to stress the somewhat contradictory goals of security and mobility. Their income level is peculiarly marginal: it provides enough for *current* security, but frequently offers only limited possibilities of status increase (through possessions, memberships, etc.). The striving for upward mobility, however, is partly satisfied by the knowledge that in many cases mobility in the corporation or bureaucracy is moderately well assured. Perhaps these twin goals explain a deepening involvement—almost a fanatical dependence on—continuous installment buying and a dethronement of the traditional virtues of thrift and savings. With the recent creation of "revolving credit" by department stores and the giant mail order houses, mortgaging of the future has become even easier.[24] In fact, revolving credit is available to a fairly wide category of families, which may thereby imitate important aspects of this life-style.

3. The old middle class

The so-called "old" middle class category of small, independent proprietors and independent professionals seems to be gradually losing its identity in the American middle status sphere, probably as a

---

[23] C. Wright Mills, "Middle Classes in Middle-Sized Cities," *American Sociological Review,* 11 (October, 1946), pp. 520–529.

[24] William H. Whyte, "Budgetism: Opiate of the Middle Class," *loc. cit.*

result of the centralization and bureaucratization of business and industry. However, the few available studies of this stratum in recent years indicate that its distinctive life-style is focused on mobility and respectability. While the income level is often comparatively high (on a par with upper ranges of white collar and lower ranges of the *nouveaux riches*), thus providing economic security, the social origins of many small proprietors seem to be in the lower strata. Proprietorship signifies a rise in independence and income, but not necessarily in life-style. Consequently, this stratum tends to develop two related themes. There is, first, the rejection of lower status memories through converting income into higher status possessions (home, auto, appliances) and by intermarriage with girls from more substantial middle class families. Second, there is a tendency to view economic trends and community issues from the standpoint of the elite and the *nouveaux riches*.[25] This identification with the higher status businessman and entrepreneur may be interpreted as an unconscious quest for vicarious respectability, by emulating their opinions, even if the heights of influence and acceptability remain unattainable.

The Solid or Aspiring Lower Group

Realistically, the dominant situation of the unskilled, the poorly educated, and the marginal wage worker is the comparatively low probability of upward mobility. But it is the reaction to this situation that is crucial in distinguishing a general working class style of life, and *variations* in the basic style. The solid or stable working class family clearly recognizes its position, but either accepts it philosophically or makes limited gestures toward preparing for a son's occupational ascent.[26]

Adjustment to immobility normally entails a meaningful cluster of values, activities, and avoidances. A frequent source of comfort—perhaps of harmless fantasy—is a vaguely defined possibility of owning a small business, "working for myself." This tends to lose psychological value with increasing age, but even such a modest hope has important consequences. Inclinations toward thrift, for example, though difficult to implement, may be traced to the hope of some independence. Likewise, this level of aspiration generally prevents the

[25] Mills, "Middle Classes in Middle-Sized Cities," *loc. cit.*

[26] Kahl, *op. cit.*, pp. 205–210, 287–288; James S. Coleman, "The Adolescent Subculture and Academic Achievement," *American Journal of Sociology*, 65 (January, 1960), pp. 337–347.

development of more ambitious but unrealistic strivings (great wealth, extensive power, or social acceptance by the elite). Thus, this life-style reflects realism, undramatic dignity, and an unconscious quest for respectability.

A major facet of this style of life is reluctance to participate in community affairs, politics, and in more than one or two voluntary associations. Instead, there is considerable emphasis on maintaining the nuclear family and on retaining close family ties. Since 1940, at least in the United States, home ownership has come to be both an aspiration and a reality. Several studies have also shown a marked inclination toward hobbies involving either the home or friends.[27]

The Marginal Life-Style [28]

In urban regions, the lowest status (by every index or standard known to social scientists) is held by those who are unwilling or unable to adjust to relative social immobility. Families—and often unattached persons—in this situation are plagued by intermittent employment. They view a job as an eternal evil, an interlude of no intrinsic value, as the "price" of getting a little money. Typically, there is no longing for a cherished past, no hope for a brighter future; only the immediate present has meaning. Such a life-style derides "respectability" and "deferred gratification." The strongest tendency is—to the outsider—physical and moral vagrancy. In the informal world of stratification, this lowest status is equivalent to *no* status. Only the formal network of courts, police, and social agencies recognize the marginal life-style by assigning to its practitioners the negative statuses of criminal, hopeless alcoholic, hardened delinquent, and "hard core" families.

Apparently, the marginal status occurs most often among those migrants to urban regions who lack proper cultural preparation for urban living and its system of regularized striving. Probably, a dis-

---

[27] See Chapter 9 for references on voluntary associations. For evidence of an emphasis on hobbies and home ownership see John M. Mogey, *Family and Neighbourhood* (New York, Oxford University Press, 1956); Michael Young and Peter Willmott, *Family and Kinship in East London* (London, Routledge and Kegan Paul, 1957); T. Cauter and J. S. Downham, *The Communication of Ideas* (London, Chatto and Windus, 1954); Bennett M. Berger, *Working-Class Suburb* (Berkeley, University of California Press, 1960); Glenn H. Beyer, *Housing: A Factual Analysis* (New York, Macmillan, 1958), pp. 151–168.

[28] Kahl, *op. cit.*, pp. 210–215.

proportionate number in this category come from the ranks of rural Negroes, Southern rural whites, Puerto Rican migrants, and Southern European immigrants.[29] However, many persons in these "vulnerable" migrant streams manage to rise above marginality and become indistinguishable from older participants in other urban styles of life.

THE SIGNIFICANCE OF URBAN STRATIFICATION

The foregoing outline of status levels and styles of life is largely descriptive and static, though some attention to relations between status levels has also been given. However, the pursuit of these life-styles and the direct or indirect interdependence of the three status spheres may be regarded as an implicit "operating" part of urban social organization. Many sociologists interpret class stratification as an inevitable, necessary development in complex communities.[30] Many laymen, on the other hand, prefer to think in terms of ideals of social equality, equal opportunity, and the widespread distribution of power and responsibility. The existence of class differences therefore seems an uncomfortable deviation from the "American Way." What, then, is the "contribution" of social divisions to the urban community? Does the unique system of stratification found in urban regions produce contradictory or compatible consequences?

Unfortunately, very few studies furnish direct answers to these questions. Indeed, sociological research on this problem has been virtually confined to rather small urban centers. In Elmtown, where the class structure was more rigid than that of metropolitan regions, stratification was found to have a decisive influence on the public school system and the behavior patterns of adolescents (e.g., performance in school, choice of friends, extracurricular activities, and dating). By implication, Elmtown's class system bolstered the general conservatism of a fledgling city, discouraging competition, change, and

[29] C. Wright Mills et al., The Puerto Rican Journey (New York, Harper and Brothers, 1950); Elena Padilla, Up From Puerto Rico (New York, Columbia University Press, 1958); Oscar Handlin, The Newcomers: Negroes and Puerto Ricans in a Changing Metropolis (Cambridge, Mass., Harvard University Press, 1959).

[30] For example, Kingsley Davis, Human Society (New York, Macmillan, 1949), Chap. XIV; Barber, op. cit., Chap. I; A. B. Hollingshead and Fritz Redlich, Social Class and Mental Illness (New York, John Wiley and Sons, 1958), Chap. I.

mobility. The Lynds' study of Middletown interprets the class system as an arena of conflict between workers and businessmen in responding to the crisis of the Great Depression. In effect, Middletown's experience suggests that urban communities are hindered by class divisions in periods of rapid and dramatic change—a conclusion drawn many years ago by Cooley and MacIver. Finally, in an unusually perceptive study of Burlington, Vermont, Elin Anderson concludes that social divisions in terms of occupation, religion, and ethnic background were accompanied by two consequences: (a) security for the individual and a consequent stability for the community; and (b) inertia and a limitation on creativity, leadership, and change.[31]

From a variety of investigations of larger urban communities, several themes recur that suggest that urban stratification has somewhat more complex consequences for urban regions than had been suspected. Most of these consequences rest on trends that have been formulated from scattered clues, and must therefore be continually checked against newer sources of relevant information. Furthermore, many of these consequences are not at all apparent to urbanites; they are *latent effects* of routine behavior, ideas, and aspirations and therefore are difficult to demonstrate in the usual direct sequence of situation, introduced "cause," facilitating or inhibiting role of aspects of the situation, and "effect."

1. Opportunities for social mobility

Urban class systems combine sharply defined "upper" and "lower" status segments with somewhat vaguely delimited "middle" positions. But this juxtaposition of clarity and blur is characteristically accompanied by an invitation to progress, achievement, and status ascendancy. Consequently, there are created both motivation and opportunity for social mobility. If the essence of social mobility is acquisition and practice of a "higher" style of life—and acceptance by those already conversant with that style of life—then the urban class system in practice must provide the *mechanisms* for mobility. Essentially, the key mechanism is *upward occupational mobility,* with obvious supplementary aid from either educational or marital mobility.

[31] Hollingshead, *Elmtown's Youth;* Lynd and Lynd, *Middletown in Transition;* Charles H. Cooley, *Social Organization* (New York, Scribner, 1909), pp. 209–239; Robert M. MacIver, *Community* (London, Macmillan, 1917), pp. 72, 270; Elin Anderson, *We Americans: A Study of Cleavage in an American City* (Cambridge, Mass., Harvard University Press, 1938).

Studies on three continents indicate that considerable occupational mobility is typical of urban centers and that the overall degree of such mobility has not been lessening. However, it is reasonably clear that the greatest focus of mobility is in the amorphous middle occupational status sphere.[32] This dominant pattern of mobility very probably reflects an underlying process of "controlled" mobility, which operates by three interrelated means.

1. Mobility aspirations, achievement motives, and deferred gratification patterns tend to be less stressed in lower status and occupational categories, as reported by several sociologists.[33] This tendency is visible in student achievement (grades) in primary and secondary schools, and in verbalized plans for further education and future jobs. In most cases, family status and values—rather than abilities or perceived opportunities—are the bases for the individual's decision "to strive or not to strive."

2. The formal educational system tends to be specifically geared to students with aspirations for mobility, or those from families that can afford the expense of a continued education. Lipset and Bendix discovered that appropriate academic counseling and vocational advice —from school and other sources—are more often given to students from middle status families than from lower status families. The resultant drop-out rate is, therefore, consistently higher for the latter category of student.[34] However, a college education seems to be a necessary element in opportunities for middle class occupations for sons of manual workers. As the accompanying tables show, college entrance and graduation largely remain the prerogative of middle and upper status categories.

[32] Seymour M. Lipset and Reinhard Bendix, *Social Mobility in Industrial Society* (Berkeley, University of California Press, 1960), Chaps. II, IV; Natalie Rogoff, *Recent Trends in Occupational Mobility* (New York, The Free Press of Glencoe, 1953); D. V. Glass, ed., *Social Mobility in Britain* (London, Routledge and Kegan Paul, 1954). For an exceptional case see A. B. Hollingshead, "Trends in Social Stratification: A Case Study," *American Sociological Review,* 17 (December, 1952), pp. 697–686.

[33] Bernard C. Rosen, "The Achievement Syndrome: A Psychocultural Dimension of Stratification," *American Sociological Review,* 21 (April, 1956), pp. 203–211; Russell R. Dynes *et al.,* "Levels of Occupational Aspiration: Some Aspects of Family Experience as a Variable," *ibid.,* pp. 212–214; William H. Sewell *et al.,* "Social Status and Educational and Occupational Aspiration," *ibid.,* 22 (February, 1957), pp. 67–73; Jackson Toby, "Orientation to Education as a Factor in the School Maladjustment of Lower-Class Children," *Social Forces,* 35 (March, 1957), pp. 259–266.

[34] Lipset and Bendix, *op. cit.,* pp. 92–101, 194–197.

TABLE 56

Distribution of Male Workers by Occupational Category and Specified Levels of Education, U.S., 1950

OCCUPATIONAL CATEGORY	Per cent with 4 years high school and up	Per cent with one or more years of college
Nonmanual		
Professional, technical & kindred	85.6	70.3
Managers, officials & proprietors	53.1	26.1
Sales	58.7	27.1
Clerical and kindred	56.4	21.6
Manual		
Craftsmen and foremen	28.5	6.5
Other services (except personal, house)	22.4	5.8
Operatives	20.3	3.7
Private household	17.0	4.9
Laborers, except farm and mine	11.6	2.2
Farm		
Farmers	16.0	4.6
Hired farm labor	10.2	2.5
All categories	*34.3*	*14.9*

SOURCE: Seymour M. Lipset and Reinhard Bendix, *Social Mobility in Industrial Society*, p. 92.

TABLE 57

Estimated Distribution of College Graduates, by Occupation of Father

FATHER'S OCCUPATION	Distribution of college age children	Expected per cent of children graduating from college from each category	Occupational distribution of fathers of total graduating class
Professional and semi-professional	6.5	43	22
Managerial	12.8	19	19
Sales, clerical, and service workers	15.8	15	19
Manual	48.7	8	31
Farm	16.2	6	8
Total	*100.0*		*100*

SOURCE: Lipset and Bendix, *op. cit.*, p. 97.

3. A final limitation on opportunities for mobility is the extent of intermarriage between urban status levels. Studies of "residential propinquity" and marital choice among middle status persons indicate that approximately half of these marriages involve persons from the same or very similar status levels (in terms of religion, family reputation, and occupation of parents).[35] But what is the preponderant *type of intermarriage* (upward or downward) in the remainder of urban marriages? Though the evidence is not always free of contradictions, studies in the United States and Great Britain seem to show that urban males tend to marry more often *below* their status level than above. In Great Britain, this pattern is particularly marked among upper and middle status males. For the United States, a study by Centers reveals a similar pattern (see Tables 58, 59).

TABLE 58

Marital Mobility Patterns Among Occupational Strata of Urban Males, 1945

OCCUPATIONAL STRATUM OF MALE	Per cent who are married up	Per cent who are married at own level	Per cent who are married down	Differences in "up" and "down" marriages, & direction
Business executive	—	15	85	85 down
Professional	7	25	68	61 down
Small business	11	40	49	38 down
White collar	37	23	40	3 down
Skilled manual	24	46	30	6 down
Semiskilled	49	41	10	39 up
Unskilled	60	40	—	60 up

SOURCE: Richard Centers, "Occupational Endogamy in Marital Selection," *American Journal of Sociology*, Vol. 54 (1949), Table 3.

2. Economic consequences

Every manufacturer and distributor in the urban market acts on, or indirectly profits by, the special nature of the urban stratification system and its associated invitation to mobility. The search for status by imitation of specific aspects of other life-styles inevitably creates enlarged markets for status items. Furniture, appliances, clothing, automobiles, magazines, and housing have increased not only in

[35] Glass, *op. cit.*, pp. 326–328; A. B. Hollingshead, "Cultural Factors in the Selection of Marriage Mates," *American Sociological Review*, 15 (October, 1950), pp. 619–627; Richard Centers, "Occupational Endogamy in Mate Selection," *American Journal of Sociology*, 54 (May, 1949), pp. 530–535.

TABLE 59

Marital Mobility Patterns Among Occupational Strata of Urban Females, 1945

OCCUPATIONAL STRATUM OF FEMALE	Per cent who are married up	Per cent who are married at own level	Per cent who are married down	Differences in "up" and "down" marriages, & direction
Business executive	—	55	45	45 down
Professional	20	37	43	23 down
Small business	24	29	47	23 down
White collar	24	40	36	12 down
Skilled manual	48	30	22	26 up
Semiskilled	49	38	13	36 up
Unskilled	63	37	—	63 up

SOURCE: Centers, *op. cit.*, Table 6.

number of units sold, but in the sale of more expensive, more prestigeful models and types.[36] This is due to economic prosperity and
also to changes in consumption habits directed toward status imitation.
Thus, urban civilizations and their peacetime economies are greatly
sustained by a fluid class structure, which is in turn encouraged by
the peculiar dynamics of an expanding urban economy.

3. Decline of class conflicts

Though there are obvious differences in life-style and interests between urban status spheres and status segments, it is very significant
(but not so obvious) that "class conflicts" are becoming less frequent
and less bitter than in previous urban waves, or even as recently as
forty years ago in England, twenty-five years ago in the United
States.[37] An apparent exception is labor-management difficulties in the
form of strikes, lockouts, etc. Yet industrial disputes are more often
settled these days by bargaining than by violence or serious threats
of violence.[38] Even the hostile statements of labor and industrial
leaders seem to be more for newspapers than for one another.

[36] *The New York Times,* November 6, 1960.

[37] For an interesting theory of the mutual opposition of class conflicts
and racial conflicts see Theodore W. Sprague, "The Rivalry of Intolerances
in Race Relations," *Social Forces,* 28 (October, 1949), pp. 68–76.

[38] Arthur Kornhauser et al., eds., *Industrial Conflict* (New York, McGraw-
Hill, 1954); William F. Whyte, *Pattern for Industrial Peace* (New York,
Harper and Brothers, 1951); Neil H. Chamberlain, *Social Responsibility and
Strikes* (New York, Harper and Brothers, 1953); Joseph Shister and William
Hamovitch, *Conflict and Stability in Labor Relations* (Buffalo Dept. of In-
dustrial Relations, University of Buffalo, 1952).

On the whole, however, urban stratification in operation (not in theory) has simultaneously raised invisible status boundaries and yet muted conflicts by a prevalent ideology of mobility. In general, urbanites accept the mixture of fluidity and rigidity in the status sphere; they seem to reserve their hostility for *individuals at any status level* who practice snobbery (*i.e.,* who overemphasize distinctions in a personal manner) or who strive for ascent with "indecent" speed and with inadequate cultural preparation ("he thinks money can buy anything"). Urbanites have come to concern themselves more with security and comfort than with power differences and historical issues of "exploitation." Perhaps this shift in attention reflects an era of prosperity and inflation, and greater ease in status imitation.

4. The role of spatial segregation

As we have previously noted, urban stratification is increasingly accompanied by residential segregation of status spheres. Contacts between status levels seem to be largely temporary, impersonal, and indirect. It is quite likely that this degree of social insulation helps to diminish status conflicts by minimizing personal frictions and frustrations. But such an arrangement is rapidly erasing a sense of "community," which is at best difficult to sustain in such a large, complex entity as the urban region.[39] The insularity and provincialism of many urbanites is by now well known; knowledge of other communities is distorted by ignorance, prejudice, and the attractive inaccuracies of films and other mass media. Even more striking to the social scientist and public administrator, however, is the urbanite's immersion in purely local neighborhood affairs and their relation to a specific style of life (*e.g.,* suburban middle class segments). Los Angeles was once facetiously defined by J. B. Priestley as "six suburbs in search of a city." The modern urban region, especially in the United States might well be defined—though not so humorously—as "a fumbling metropolis deserted by dozens of 'independent' localities

[39] Good discussions and evidence for this phenomenon can be found in: C. Wright Mills, *The Sociological Imagination* (New York, Oxford University Press, 1959), pp. 172–173; Morton Grodzins, *The Metropolitan Area as a Racial Problem* (Pittsburgh, University of Pittsburg Press, 1958); Morton Grodzins, "The New Shame of the Cities," *Confluence,* 7 (1958), pp. 29–46; John M. Foskett, "The Influence of Social Participation on Community Programs and Activities," in Marvin B. Sussman, ed., *Community Structure and Analysis* (New York, Thomas Y. Crowell, 1959), pp. 311–330.

hopefully searching for private Utopias." Consequently, a latent result of urban stratification is an added intensification of problems of *co-ordinating* developments and devising workable planning programs for urban regions.

5. Personal tensions and the status system

It has long been known that urban living creates significant problems of personal adjustment for migrants and their families. A frequent explanation for such problems has been the cultural and social differences between rural and urban communities. Some emphasis has also been given to such factors as poverty and differences in racial and ethnic background. But to these must be added the impact of urban stratification on both migrants and older residents.[40] For many persons, the peculiarities of urban stratification are disquieting; the extraordinary emphasis on mobility, the difficulty of defining limits between status segments, the contradictions between status attributes (morality *vs.* income, education *vs.* occupation, etc.) become sources of anxiety, uncertainty, and insecurity. Only recently has research on this general problem been conducted with fruitful results, sometimes as incidental findings. While it is too soon to draw anything but tentative conclusions, it seems very likely that our understanding of such problems as mental disorder, criminal behavior, marital difficulties, alcoholism, and drug addiction can be deepened by studying the way in which "normal" and "deviant" persons perceive and react to urban stratification.

SELECTED REFERENCES

BARBER, Bernard, *Social Stratification* (New York, Harcourt, Brace, and World, 1957).

CAUTER, T. and DOWNHAM, J. S., *The Communication of Ideas* (London, Chatto and Windus, 1954).

[40] For studies that indicate some effects of class position on deviant behavior see: A. B. Hollingshead and Fritz Redlich, *Social Class and Mental Illness* (New York, John Wiley and Sons, 1958); Richard Cloward and Lloyd Ohlin, *Delinquency and Opportunity* (New York, The Free Press of Glencoe, 1960); Dorothy L. Meier and Wendell Bell, "Anomia and Differential Access to the Achievement of Life Goals," *American Sociological Review*, 24 (April, 1959), pp. 189–201; Ephraim H. Mizruchi, "Social Structure and Anomia in a Small City," *ibid.*, 25 (October, 1960), pp. 645–654.

GLASS, D. V., ed., *Social Mobility in Britain* (London, Routledge and Kegan Paul, 1954).

HOLLINGSHEAD, A. B. and REDLICH, Fritz, *Social Class and Mental Illness* (New York, John Wiley and Sons, 1958).

KAHL, Joseph A., *The American Class Structure* (New York, Holt, Rinehart and Winston, 1957).

LIPSET, Seymour M. and BENDIX, Reinhard, *Social Mobility in Industrial Society* (Berkeley, University of California Press, 1960).

LYND, Robert S. and LYND, Helen M., *Middletown in Transition* (New York, Harcourt, Brace, and World, 1937).

MOGEY, John, *Family and Neighborhood* (London, Oxford University Press, 1956).

OESER, O. A. and HAMMOND, S. B., eds., *Social Structure and Personality in a City* (New York, Macmillan, 1954).

SPINLEY, B. M., *The Deprived and the Privileged* (London, Routledge and Kegan Paul, 1959).

WARNER, W. Lloyd and LUNT, Paul S., *The Social Life of a Modern Community* (New Haven, Yale University Press, 1941).

WARNER, W. Lloyd *et al.*, *Social Class in America* (New York, Harper and Brothers, 1960).

CHAPTER 11

Major Urban Institutions: Economic, Political, and Religious

THE MOST "PUBLIC" and therefore the most discussed aspects of urban social organization are the *major urban institutions*. In the evolving urban environment, these institutions are notable in several respects: (*a*) they are acquiring a greatly extended radius of influence and control—in terms both of area and population; (*b*) they have developed highly formalized and bureaucratic structures; (*c*) they are increasingly interdependent, despite the trend toward specialization; (*d*) they tend to be the practical foci of stability and change in urban regions, and therefore the basic nuclei of regional problems; and (*e*) they appear on the whole to represent groping adjustments to the complexities of dynamic urban regions.

In a sense, urban institutions may be viewed as organized attempts to create essentially rational patterns of land use, services, and their coordination within the limits of societal values—such as democracy, efficiency, equity, etc. However, since urban regions are simultaneously units of national societies in a shrinking world, cultural and social differences among the latter inevitably affect the rational role of evolving urban institutions. A recent United Nations survey indicates, for example, that rapid growth of cities is proceeding without the benefit of fundamental industrial and commercial growth, especially in Asia, Africa, and Latin America.[1] This trend suggests that urbanization

[1] Harland Bartholomew, *Land Uses in American Cities*, 2nd ed. (Cambridge, Mass., Harvard University Press, 1955), p. 119; Julia J. Henderson, "Urbanization and the World Community," in Martin Meyerson, ed., "Metropolis in Ferment," *Annals of the American Academy of Political and Social Science*, 314 (November, 1957), p. 149.

in its earlier stages in the modern world must for a time operate without the aid of responsible urban institutions. Therefore, any analysis of urban institutions should take into account the *stage* of urbanization and the sociocultural differences between societies (*e.g.,* stratification systems, level of technology, form of government, etc.).

Partly through choice, partly as a result of space limitations, we shall emphasize the urban institutions of Western nations and give prominence to the more developed urban regions. Since the full range of institutions cannot receive adequate space in a work of this kind, it seems advisable to concentrate on the most distinctive and significant institutional spheres. These institutions, which the anthropologist, Herskovits, calls "cultural foci," are significant in two respects: (*a*) they comprise the areas of greatest interest, variation, and development; (*b*) they are crucial in the continuing process of interpreting and assessing the desirability and application of new forms and ideas to the urban region.[2]

In the urban setting, the major institutions can be grouped into two categories: (*a*) the basic, sustaining institutions—economic, political, familial, and religious; and (*b*) the supporting or supplementary institutions—*e.g.,* educational, social welfare. This chapter will consider the first category; the second category is the theme of the following chapter. Since the familial institution has already been discussed in Chapter 8—the family is unusually significant because of its primary group *and* institutional character—it will be omitted from the discussion to follow.

Though we have briefly analyzed institutions in Chapter 9 (pp. 172 –173), it may be helpful at this point to define the concept more clearly. This is particularly necessary because "institution" is used in a variety of ways by laymen and social scientists. In the most general sense, institutions refer to organized and widely accepted solutions to the needs of individuals and groups in a community or society. Each institution possesses a set of characteristics or "parts," which give it distinction as a human creation.

1. A specialized function or need, such as provision of physical security, maintenance of order, transmission of accumulated experience.

[2] Melville J. Herskovits, *Man and His Works* (New York, Alfred A. Knopf, 1948), Chap. XXXII.

2. A more or less explicit set of guiding values (mores), which translate "needs" into recognizable objectives (*e.g.,* equality, efficiency, the importance of love, emphasis on youth).
3. A special cluster of social roles and skills, which translate ultimate goals into specific duties and responsibilities for individuals.
4. The development of informal and formal coordination of social roles through formation of groups (primary groups, voluntary associations, and larger bureaucratic organizations).
5. Participation (direct or indirect) of an entire population (community, region, or national society) in this network of values, roles, and groups.
6. A more or less emotional commitment to, or internalization of, institutional values and responsibilities by a substantial portion of a population.[3]

Our discussion will emphasize features 3 and 4 (and to some extent number 2), not only because the bulk of our knowledge of urban institutions refers to these aspects, but also since we can thereby most clearly trace important trends in the operation of institutions in urban regions.

THE ECONOMIC INSTITUTIONAL FRAMEWORK

Cities and urban regions for many centuries have been stimulants to innovation in economic organization. Indeed, modern capitalism is largely the creation of urban groups in Western Europe, based on such specifically urban features as mobile labor, rationalized technology, capital accumulation, "rational" legal systems, individual and group property rights, and instruments for commercial transactions (checks and drafts, bills of lading, contracts, stocks and bonds).[4] During the past eighty years, however, urban regions have become marked by a unique battery of economic organizations, which represent an unplanned, experimental adjustment to metropolitan devel-

[3] For useful analyses of institutions, see F. Stuart Chapin, *Contemporary American Institutions* (New York, Harper and Brothers, 1935), Chaps. I, II; J. O. Hertzler, *Social Institutions* (Lincoln, Neb., University of Nebraska Press, 1949); J. O. Hertzler, *American Social Institutions* (Boston, Allyn and Bacon, 1961), Chaps. III and IV.

[4] Max Weber, *General Economic History* (New York, The Free Press of Glencoe, 1950), pp. 276–313.

opment. These organizations are: the corporate form in industry and commerce; centralized and varied channels of distribution—the department store, the chain store, the mail order house; the advertising agency; various consumer credit facilities; and organized interest groups, such as the specialized trade association, chambers of commerce, and national labor unions.

Such an array of organizational forms, diverse as they may seem, can be profitably analyzed in terms of common problems and objectives in the urban milieu. For example, the basic pursuit of profit tends to require efficiency, optimum size of organization, and specialization in the context of a large, relatively accesible market. The variety of wants among urbanites and their comparative ability to spend present and foreseeable income has undoubtedly stimulated specialization as well. Not only variety, but a constant *increase* in variety of needs and desires, is significant for urban economic organization. The creation of new needs on any scale, however, is dependent on the expansion of leisure, which is perhaps most typical of urbanized life-styles for large segments of the population.

Urban economic institutions cannot be fully understood only as reflections of profit motives, standards of efficiency, and the rational pursuit of progress. Perhaps two other values play supplementary roles in urban economics. As suggested by Galbraith, modern business enterprise (which includes all of the economic forms listed above) is not primarily attuned to the rigors of competition in the classical sense, but instead exhibits a "comprehensive effort to reduce risk." [5] To the producer and distributor in the urban market, risk lies in miscalculating consumer demand, promoting of obsolete products, overdependence on the success of limited types of products, and uncontrolled price variations.

Consequently, Galbraith argues, *advertising* is a necessary technique for controlling consumer tastes and preferences. In a highly efficient economy, productivity tends to outstrip consumer demand; advertising therefore becomes a conscious application of the formula "invention is the mother of necessity." Similarly, *large organizations* make possible a diversification of products, which may provide protection against instabilities in specific sales patterns. *Research and development* in industrial enterprises, while ostensibly aimed at greater efficiency and progress, is, in Galbraith's view, also dedicated to the corporate quest

[5] J. K. Galbraith, *The Affluent Society* (Boston, Houghton Mifflin, 1958), pp. 101–102.

for minimizing market uncertainties, by insuring up-to-date (not necessarily better or cheaper or more efficient) products and methods of production. This process is partly a consequence of competition with similar firms, but also involves "self competition," *i.e.,* to avoid loss of some desired proportion of sales and repute in the urban market. Finally, though it is difficult to document in many instances, reduction of risk is apparent in attempts to control or "administer" prices—whether informally (as in the steel industry) or formally (as in utilities and transportation).[6]

A second value—somewhat related to risk reduction—is the emphasis on *power* or nonlegal controls over segments of the urban economy. In a negative sense, power in the economic sphere consists of attempts to determine economic decisions (wage and price levels, availability of technical ideas) apart from the classical "free play of the market." Theoretically, "market" decisions are made through the independent evaluations of individual units (buyers and sellers). Practically, urban economic power is expressed in a positive way by two widely used methods. The more public approach is through combination, collaboration, or merger of similar or related economic organizations. This is evident in the composite corporation (United States Steel, General Motors, General Foods), the national labor union and federated national unions, the trade association, and the chamber of commerce. "Power through combination" depends on comparatively greater financial resources, superior sources of market information, the increased ability to compete for favorable facilities, and the intangible effects of sheer size (since size and quantity are widely respected, sometimes feared, but rarely challenged effectively by individuals or smaller organizations). In the United States and Great Britain, this form of power is morally (and often legally) barred from extension to violence or open intimidation. This should be compared to the situation in the period 1870 to 1936, when such limits were not widely observed.[7]

Therefore, a second avenue of power has become important beyond measure, as an indispensable supplement to combination: informal influence of administrative and legislative bodies in the political sphere.

[6] Walton H. Hamilton, *The Pattern of Competition* (New York, Columbia University Press, 1940).

[7] Robert A. Brady, *Business as a System of Power* (New York, Columbia University Press, 1943); Henry W. Ehrmann, *Organized Business in France* (Princeton, Princeton University Press, 1957).

Lobbying in the broad sense of representing a specific economic interest before an official or public authority is a major activity, particularly in the United States and Great Britain. Almost every economic interest in urban regions—real estate, industrial corporations, labor unions, retailers, wholesalers, professionals (physicians, teachers, lawyers)—maintains substantial budgets and staffs for acquainting legislators and officials with their respective needs and viewpoints. While lobbying was once regarded as a nefarious activity, in the United States it has become an accepted (if not respected) institutionalized linkage between the economic and political spheres. Federal and some state laws require formal registration of lobbying organizations and itemized accounting of their expenditures. However, in practice, these laws serve to recognize rather than control the activities of lobbyists.[8]

The full story of the role of economic "pressure groups" would fill several libraries, but much of it is scattered in unread scholarly monographs, records of Congressional hearings, and dusty newspaper files. But it is not necessary to digest this mass of essentially repetitive detail to recognize that economic influence groups are meaningful and pervasive responses to major economic and political trends in modern urban regions and their national societies. In general, the specialization and technological efficiency of urban economies create relatively new problems of "surplus" production. Since markets are increasingly complex, economic risks are too high to be left to chance or "natural" resolution. Consequently, some economic interests inevitably seek protection by favorable legislation and administration. Because of the interdependence of urban economies, however, lobbying creates real or imagined threats to other economic interests, and thus an apparently endless cycle of competitive influence ("politics") is characteristic of urban regions. In the United States, for example, where such a process is at its height, influence groups have successfully affected wages, prices, awarding of exclusive economic rights and government contracts, proper channels of distribution, and competition with other nations.[9]

---

[8] Donald C. Blaisdell, *American Democracy Under Pressure* (New York, Ronald Press, 1957), Chap. VI.

[9] *Ibid.*, Chaps. VII, VIII, XIII–XV; Karl Schriftgiesser, *The Lobbyists* (Boston, Little, Brown and Company, 1951); Henry W. Ehrmann, ed., *Interest Groups on Four Continents* (Pittsburgh, University of Pittsburgh Press, 1958); Stuart Chase, *Democracy Under Pressure* (New York, The Twentieth Century Fund, 1945).

The Corporate Form

Small proprietors and partnerships persist as the most numerous form of economic organization in urban regions, but the corporation is doubly significant as contributing a major (and still increasing) share of productivity and dollar value, and as the *symbol* of urban economic organization. Perhaps, then, the extent of corporate organization is a key index to the overall level of urbanism in a society. Generally, newly urbanized societies (India, Africa, the Near East) depend on familial, dynastic, or individualized economic units, while such nations as Great Britain, the United States, Germany, and Canada have had considerable experience in extending private corporate enterprise into virtually every aspect of the urban economy.

To the urban sociologist, the corporation is an excellent example of organizational adaptation to the urban region, as well as an unwitting stimulant to other social changes that have come to be closely associated with urban patterns. There is little question that the corporate form initially reflects attempts to maximize efficiency in financing and directing a variety of economic enterprises. This is accomplished by pooling and coordinating resources, facilities, and skills through the agency of a legally fictitious "person" that is miraculously separate from the identities of any and all individuals associated with it.

However, in practice, the corporation tends to confuse efficiency with impersonality to the point that impersonality comes to mean independence of the local urban region. This is of course recognized by corporate leaders, who try to superimpose personal, noneconomic features on corporate functioning. Most "institutional advertising," [10] the recent practice of "streamlining" financial statements, the facilitation of stockholders' meetings, and the "lending" of corporation executives for local civic duties seem to be designed to restore a quasipersonal flavor to the abstractions of prices, wages, profits, and production figures. But the fact remains that corporations inherently are impersonal and expansive, that in binding together a diversity of supplies, personnel, and areas they have become *extraurban* or *interurban,* absentee owners in a literal sense. One consequence of this impersonality-efficiency-absentee complex is the widely recognized

[10] Leonard I. Pearlin and Morris Rosenberg, "Propaganda Techniques in Institutional Advertising," *Public Opinion Quarterly,* 16 (Spring, 1952), pp. 5–26.

subservience of urbanites to modern economic organizations.[11] Furthermore, this dependence is heightened by the intricate interdependence among economic organizations, which leaves little room for *personal* independence in the economic sphere. Clearly, the extensive corporate structure of urban economics achieves remarkable results, when disturbing conditions are absent. But this organic articulation of the economy accelerates economic chaos in periods of crisis, as the major depressions of the last two generations amply demonstrate.

Corporate efficiency as an ideal points toward an increasingly minute division of labor *within* the corporation and an accompanying system of bureaucracy to coordinate and regularize proper interrelations.[12] Historically, bureaucracy began in military organizations of emerging empires. In the modern urban region, economic bureaucracies are peculiar mixtures of efficiency and nonrationality, of status concerns and technological objectives. Whatever one's attitude toward bureaucracy, the urban corporation is highly successful from the profit standpoint, despite internal problems of red tape and dissident primary groups. However, the *social consequences* of economic bureaucracy deserve more attention than they have received.

Together with technological advances, corporate bureaucracy has largely solved problems of production for urban regions. Scientific research, until recently free of bureaucratization,[13] and increasingly bureaucratized "development" programs have gradually converted bureaucracies from concern for efficient production to a stress on methods of *distribution*. The changing distribution of employed persons from 1900 to 1953 indirectly confirms this trend, as summarized in the accompanying table.[14]

Several obvious but important changes in economic bureaucracies should be noted. First and foremost is a more than 50 per cent decline

[11] Adolph A. Berle, Jr. and Gardiner C. Means, *The Modern Corporation and Private Property* (New York, Macmillan, 1932); James Burnham, *The Managerial Revolution* (New York, John Day, 1941).

[12] Theodore A. Caplow, *The Sociology of Work* (Minneapolis, University of Minnesota Press, 1954), p. 22.

[13] See for example John Jewkes, David Sawers, and Richard Stillerman, *The Sources of Invention* (London, Macmillan, 1958).

[14] J. Frederic Dewhurst and associates, *America's Needs and Resources*, rev. ed. (New York, Twentieth Century Fund, 1955), p. 731; David Kaplan and M. Claire Casey, *Occupational Trends in the United States, 1900 to 1950*, Bureau of the Census, Working Paper No. 5 (Washington, D.C., 1958), p. 7; Reinhard Bendix, *Work and Authority in Industry* (New York, John Wiley and Sons, 1956), pp. 214, 225.

TABLE 60

Occupational Distribution of the Employed Civilian Labor Force in the U.S., 1900–1953

MAJOR OCCUPATIONAL GROUP	Percentage Distribution			
	1900	*1940*	*1950*	*1953*
Professional and semiprofessional	4.3	7.0	7.3	8.7
Proprietors, managers and officials	25.7	18.0	17.4	16.2
Clerical and kindred workers, and salespeople	7.5	16.3	18.9	18.9
Craftsmen, foremen and kindred workers	10.5	11.7	13.0	14.0
Operatives and kindred workers	12.8	18.7	20.8	20.9
Farm laborers and foremen	17.7	7.0	5.1	3.8
Laborers, except farm and mine	12.5	9.1	6.4	6.2
Domestic service workers	5.4	4.6	3.2	3.0
Service workers, except domestic	3.6	7.6	8.0	8.4

SOURCES: J. Frederic Dewhurst and Associates, *America's Needs and Resources: A New Survey* (New York, The Twentieth Century Fund, 1955), p. 731; David L. Kaplan and M. Claire Casey, *Occupational Trends in the United States 1900 to 1950* (Washington, Bureau of the Census, Working Paper No. 5, 1958), p. 7.

in the proportion of industrial laborers (unskilled and semiskilled), accompanied by a steady increase in the proportion of operatives (truck drivers, deliverymen, etc.), and a slight increase in skilled craftsmen (electricians, metal workers, etc.). This reflects increasing mechanization and more recently, automation. Second, there has been almost a threefold increase in the proportion of clerical workers and sales personnel, which now constitute the largest segment of the "white collar" category. Third, while managers, officials, and proprietors have almost doubled their proportion in the labor force, most of this increase has occurred among retail buyers, floor managers, credit personnel, purchasing agents, and officials in wholesale operations. Finally, the substantial increase in professionals (from 4.3 per cent to 8.7 per cent) is largely accounted for by large gains in salaried or bureaucratic professionals—accountants and auditors, chemists, engineers, technicians, and personnel workers. Since the private corporate form constitutes the largest employer of the American labor force (with the exception of the federal government), we may take these employment trends to represent a fundamental stress on skills in processing and distribution, secondarily on those which contribute specialized services (rather than goods) to urbanites.

A more direct confirmation of this shift in corporate effort is the rise of relatively new corporate enterprises, many of which seem to be adaptations to urban conditions of marketing products and personal services.

1. Independent advertising agencies and marketing divisions of manufacturing corporations

The advertising firm achieved prominence as a type in the twenties and early thirties. It is marked by a very high proportion of professional workers—artists, writers—and the willingness to promote a wide diversity of products for its corporate clients. Until very recently, the advertising role complex was performed by virtually anonymous firms and persons, since the product dominated in the economic sphere. At the present, the advertiser or "huckster" is emerging from the background; his character has been etched in popular novels; several firms have achieved a public identity, such as B.B.D. & O.; and the locale of advertising—Madison Avenue—has acquired a symbolic value akin to that of Wall Street.[15]

2. Chain stores

Unlike department stores, which are both older and more varied in merchandise, chain stores try to reach a large segment of the urban population. Their success, dating from the twenties in the United States, rests on perhaps two features: somewhat lowered prices; and the attractive freedom of "self service." It is not at all strange that chain stores have concentrated in just half a dozen fields of marketing—drugs, groceries, auto supplies, low-priced variety goods (e.g., Woolworth's), modestly-priced women's clothing (dresses, shoes), and most recently, department stores. These types of products have a wide and continuous demand, and also require relatively few sales clerks.[16]

3. Mail order organizations

This form of distribution was first directed at customers remote from retail centers—farmers, small town residents. Both Montgomery

[15] Thomas B. Clark, *The Advertising Smoke Screen* (New York, Harper and Brothers, 1944); Martin Mayer, *Madison Avenue, U.S.A.* (New York, Harper and Brothers, 1958); John Gloag, *Advertising in Modern Life* (London, Heinemann, 1959); Eric Field, *Advertising: The Forgotten Years* (London, E. Benn, 1959).

[16] Joseph C. Palamountain, Jr., *The Politics of Distribution* (Cambridge, Mass., Harvard University Press, 1955).

Ward and Sears Roebuck, the leaders in this form, have been able to tap a huge market by mail and phone orders through reduced prices and an increasing range of merchandise. But mail order houses have also entered the urban retail market with distinct success. By creating, in effect, a double-barrelled chain of department stores and mail order centers (often in the same building), Ward's and Sears have become giants in American urban regions (and in other nations, such as Mexico).[17] Urbanites have the option of buying in person, through catalogues in the stores, or ordering by mail. Though it is difficult to identify those most attracted by the mail order department store, many customers seem to be recent migrants from smaller communities, or mobile urban families, who desire the benefits of nationwide service and repair facilities.

4. Sales finance corporations

Perhaps the least recognized innovation in urban economic organization, the sales finance corporation has been instrumental in bridging two forms of consumer credit. During the early part of this century, the major form of credit to individuals was bank loans. Generally, such loans were difficult to obtain and required collateral (property, jewelry, etc.) to protect the lender in case of default. The sales finance corporation, mainly emerging in the twenties, provided credit to the *retailer,* who was thus able to extend credit to the urban consumer. This innovation helped in the mass sale of automobiles, radios, refrigerators, etc., which have since become the most important items in urban purchases.[18]

Since 1945, with the extension of wartime levels of prosperity, consumer credit has been made more fully available by banks, through department store charge accounts, and mail order accounts—all these combining to form the modern system of consumer credit. However, sales finance companies still play a significant part in facilitating sales of automobiles and major appliances in the United States.

[17] A wealth of information is contained in Boris Emmet and John C. Jenck, *Catalogues and Counters: A History of Sears, Roebuck and Company* (Chicago, University of Chicago Press, 1950), especially Chaps. XIX, XXI, and XXVI.

[18] Clyde W. Phelps, *The Role of the Sales Finance Companies in the American Economy* (Baltimore, Commercial Credit Corporation, 1952).

5. Labor unions

Unlike the medieval guild,[19] the labor union is a corporate combination of workers; it is intentionally distinct from and antagonistic to employers. The history of *effective* unionism is relatively short (perhaps from 1850 to the present), though the motivation to form unions can be traced to the eighteenth century in England and the American colonies. Though unions have had political roles, to the urban sociologist their economic significance is based on the attempt to affect (if not control) the *availability and distribution* of workers. The specific motives for this economic role may be varied: material benefits, greater prestige for union leaders, greater share in economic decisions, pursuit of political-ideological goals. In any case, the rise and growing power of unions represent a bureaucratic counterpart to the industrial and commercial corporation.

Though there have been unions of agricultural workers (*e.g.,* the Southern Tenant Farmers' Union), the union is primarily an urban form. Essentially, unions have been virtually the only organizational form suitable for large numbers of otherwise unorganized, ethnically diversified, unskilled (and semiskilled) urban workers in the United States. White collar workers and professionals, on the other hand, tend to view unions as improper and undignified for themselves, since they regard the white collar and professional roles as both prestigeful and constantly expanding in opportunities. Veteran union men, on the other hand, implicitly identify the union as a *protector* against arbitrary employers and the apparently inexorable process of technological advancement. This dual fear, often grounded in fact, helps to explain the "new" emphasis in union objectives—wages tied to cost of living, fringe benefits (health, retirement), guaranteed annual wages, and the union as a respected participant in industrial planning.[20]

A final trend in urban economic organization is a consequence of previously discussed trends. The bureaucratization of the economy

[19] See the detailed discussion in Sylvia R. Thrupp, *The Merchant Class of Medieval London, 1300–1500* (Chicago, University of Chicago Press, 1949).

[20] Philip D. Bradley, ed., *The Public Stake in Union Power* (Charlottesville, University of Virginia Press, 1959); Adolph F. Sturmthal, *Unity and Diversity in European Labor* (New York, The Free Press of Glencoe, 1953); Herbert J. Spiro, *The Politics of German Codetermination* (Cambridge, Mass., Harvard University Press, 1958); Frederick H. Harbison and Robert Dubin, *Patterns of Union-Management Relations* (Chicago, Science Research Associates, 1947).

has in turn stimulated a high degree of occupational specialization. Many people are still surprised that the Census Bureau and other interested agencies can distinguish over 25,000 occupational titles. Whether or not these titles really represent actual differences in skills and duties is a problem for the logician and the taxonomist. But an emphasis on pure skill is prebureaucratic. As economic organizations come to substitute "routine procedures for traditional practices," the previously specific "job" becomes an "occupation" marked by a complex of features relevant to the bureaucratic structure in which the occupation is practiced.[21]

Let us take as an example the occupation of "salesman" for a large industrial corporation. To begin with, the more dignified and preferred title is "sales representative" or "field representative." However, it is difficult to define or locate a distinctive skill (in the traditional sense of acquired ability to produce a material effect more efficiently than those denied special training) among salesmen. Instead, we find a combination of duties, knowledge, and informal relationships which together constitute an occupation. The duties to the firm include maintaining certain levels of sales and preparation of sales orders in the proper manner. These are presumably related to adequate knowledge of one's products and the ways in which they can be demonstrated. The latter "skill" takes on different form in different organizations. Many sales managers emphasize a memorized "spiel"; others encourage more spontaneous demonstrations; some demand "pressure selling"; others prefer a more relaxed approach to customers. Perhaps the key to salesmanship, however, is the ability to develop and maintain cordial personal contacts; with customers by being personally liked, through the aid of expense accounts; and with strategic parts of the salesman's firm (sales manager, secretarial staff, and the shipping department). As an occupational role, the salesman is basically a persuasive mediator. But it is an apparently difficult role to perform. A recent estimate concludes that 90 per cent of the total dollar sales in the United States is made by a mere 10 per cent of American salesmen.[22]

Occupational specialization, however, requires increasing concern for efficiency both in learning specific skills and in developing abilities

[21] Bendix, *op. cit.*, p. 211.
[22] See the authoritative evaluations of William H. Whyte, Jr., *Is Anybody Listening?* (New York, Simon and Schuster, 1952); The Editors of *Fortune*, *Why Do People Buy?* (New York, McGraw-Hill, 1953).

in interpersonal relations with associates and clients. A major innovation has therefore been an emphasis on professionalization of business and commercial roles (technical roles, such as engineer and attorney, had long been professionalized), particularly for middle and top level executives. Increasingly, professionalization has meant a college education, graduate work in university schools of business administration, and a special executive educational program sponsored by industrial corporations. In general, "entrepreneurial" executives (those who have started their own firms) have not stressed the "professional" aspect as much as "bureaucratic" or salaried executives. (See Table 61).[23]

TABLE 61

Educational Attainment of American Business Leaders, by Period and Type of Career

EDUCATIONAL LEVEL	Percentages of entrepreneurs	Percentages of bureaucrats
1831–1875		
High school or less	66	62
College or more	34	38
1876–1920		
High school or less	62	35
College or more	38	65

SOURCE: Reinhard Bendix, *Work and Authority in Industry* (New York, John Wiley and Sons, 1956), p. 230.

POLITICAL INSTITUTIONAL FRAMEWORK

Perhaps the major feature of urban political organization is its relatively slower pace of adaptation to the complexities of the modern urban region. As we have already seen, urban economic structures have been comparatively renovated, or marked by innovation. It may well be that urban leadership and the general population more clearly recognize the *economic* functions of urban areas. On the other hand, it is perhaps easier to persuade urban groups of the necessity for changes in the more rational sphere of the economy, where the benefits can be demonstrated, than in political organization, which must coordinate a wider diversity of essentially nonrational interests. In any case, both political scientists and urban sociologists agree that urban political institutions are generally unequal to their tasks.

[23] Bendix, *op. cit.*, p. 230.

Clearly, the universal trend has been toward expanded services provided by governmental agencies. This expansion is both in *range* of services and in annual *expenditures* for specific types. In American cities, for example, governments have assumed some responsibility for virtually every physical and social need of their constituents— protection, health, education, welfare, recreation, art, housing, utilities, and transportation. During the period 1900-1942, public expenditures rose principally in well established functions, such as health, public welfare, and public works. Since World War II, further increases (excluding those due to inflated costs) [24] indicate the intensified demand of urbanites for public services.

However, if the content of public services has grown more complex, the organizational forms tend to remain faithful to tradition. This is particularly true in those urban areas that are politically subservient to national governments [25]—Washington, D. C., Rio de Janeiro, Buenos Aires, Bombay, and Calcutta. In these urban regions, political control is to a large extent exercised by *national* officials responsible to a federal authority (*e.g.,* Minister of Internal Affairs, a committee from the national legislature, or the President), not to the residents. Consequently, changes in political institutions and programs are possible only by effecting prior changes in the officials or broad policies of the national government.

On the other hand, several significant political innovations have been introduced—or seriously considered—in relatively autonomous urban regions. One trend is a growing emphasis on efficiency and specialization in political-administrative roles. As Gulick, a well-known authority on public administration has rightly concluded, "large scale [in cities] does not allow dependence on simple, inherited, amateur, informal, and voluntary approaches to government."[26] Urban political organization has gone through dynastic control of leading families, to the dominance of political machines, and gradually toward professionalization and bureaucratization. This is reflected in widening use of civil service and merit systems, and the demand for experts in

[24] Solomon Fabricant, *The Trend of Government Activity in the United States Since 1900* (New York, National Bureau of Economic Research, 1952), pp. 77–78, 83; Robert C. Wood, *Metropolis Against Itself* (New York, Committee for Economic Development, 1959), pp. 20–21.

[25] See William A. Robson, ed., *Great Cities of the World* (London, Allen and Unwin, 1954), Introduction.

[26] Luther Gulick, "Metropolitan Organization," in Meyerson, *op. cit.,* p. 57.

public health, crime control, city planning, public education, and industrial development.[27]

In accord with professionalization in urban government, there has been some experimentation in administrative forms. The traditional form consists of a "city council" or "board of aldermen" and a chief executive (mayor), all elected for definite terms. In some instances, the council members elect one of themselves as mayor. But the complexities of urban problems are normally beyond the capabilities of elected officials, no matter how dedicated to government efficiency. During the past fifty years, American cities have tried to improve their urban government in one of two ways.

1. The commission form

Unlike the council-mayor type, the commission form *divides* administrative authority among three, five, or seven elected commissioners, each of whom is responsible for a special group of municipal services. Both legislative and executive powers are combined in each commissioner, thus in practice dispensing with a central executive, and inviting specialized efficiency at the expense of coordination.[28] In general, the system is now quite rare. Even Galveston, Texas, where this innovation first appeared in 1900, has abandoned it.

2. The council-manager form

Earlier examples of this form may be found as far back as fifteenth century Italy, when cities such as Venice hired a *podesta,* or foreign noble, at a high salary to run city services for a city council divided by family feuds.[29] In the modern period, the *city manager* is an administrative expert (with training in either public administration, engineering, or accounting) appointed by the city council to assume complete executive responsibility for all city services.[30] The manager, ideally, is nonpartisan and immune to the appeals of special interest groups, since he is presumed to be a professional rather than a politi-

[27] Orin F. Nolting and Davis S. Arnold, eds., *The Municipal Year Book 1958* (Chicago, International City Managers' Association, 1958), pp. 129–132, 141, 146–165, 228–231.

[28] A brief survey of this form is in Stuart A. Queen and David B. Carpenter, *The American City* (New York, McGraw-Hill, 1953), pp. 312–313.

[29] Max Weber, *The City,* trans. by Don Martindale and Gertrud Neuwirth (New York, The Free Press of Glencoe, 1958), p. 131.

[30] *Municipal Yearbook, 1958,* pp. 241–245.

cian. It is interesting to note that city managers rarely remain in one community until retirement age; part of this is due to the shortage of city managers, and perhaps another factor is an inevitable loss of impartiality, which interferes with his professional role. Nevertheless, the council-manager type enjoys growing popularity, particularly in middle-sized American cities (see Tables 62 and 63).

TABLE 62

Major Forms of Government in American Cities, by Population Category

POPULATION GROUP	Number of cities in table	Mayor-council		Commission		Council-manager	
		No.	Per-cent	No.	Per-cent	No.	Per-cent
Over 500,000	17	16	94	0	0	1	6
250,000–500,000	23	9	39	5	22	9	39
100,000–250,000	68	29	43	14	20	25	37
50,000–100,000	132	45	34	26	20	61	46
25,000–50,000	283	105	37	44	16	134	47
10,000–25,000	800	365	46	117	14	318	40
5,000–10,000	1,146	695	61	114	10	337	29

SOURCE: *The Municipal Year Book 1958* (Chicago, International City Managers Association, 1958), p. 62.

TABLE 63

Distribution of the Council-Manager Form in Each Category of City in the U.S.

POPULATION GROUP	Total No. of cities	Cities with council-manager Plan	
		No.	Per cent
1,000–2,500	3,383	132	3.9
2,500–5,000	1,584	239	15.1
5,000–10,000	1,102	340	30.8
10,000–25,000	804	336	41.8
25,000–50,000	292	149	51.0
50,000–100,000	144	73	50.7
100,000–500,000	94	35	37.2
Over 500,000	19	1	5.3
		(Cincinnati)	

SOURCE: *The Municipal Year Book, 1958*, p. 244.

Political Coordination Problems

Despite experiments with political form and increasing profession-alization, the major problem in urban government is the lack of political coordination between the central city and the myriad communities in urban regions. This has been particularly acute in the last thirty years, as population growth has been most rapid in the suburban and fringe areas (see Chapters 4 and 7). Significantly, most of this "fringe" growth is in substantial communities or municipalities of 10,000 to 50,000 population.[31] These are precisely the kinds of communities that demand a full range of "urban" services and facilities —and yet are too small (and therefore financially unable) to provide these services independently. However, many such communities try "to go it alone," with a resultant inefficiency and confusion that belie the presumed "rationality" of urban civilization.

For example, there is the well-known anomaly of Detroit, which includes within its municipal boundaries the *independent* "island" communities of Hamtramck and Highland Park, each with its own government. Less spectacular but more widespread is the existence of hundreds of separate governmental units within the same metropolitan region in the United States and Great Britain. According to one authority, Chicago had 954 local units, Los Angeles had 319, Philadelphia had 705, Dallas had 63, Boston 112, Madison (Wisconsin) 229, and New York City—1074.[32] As the accompanying map graphically demonstrates, Seattle, a moderate-sized city, is enveloped in a bewildering array of overlapping jurisdictions: counties, water districts, school districts, sewer districts, library districts, housing authorities, etc. In England, the situation is much the same. Within a six-mile radius of Manchester there are 67 different local councils. And in the six largest urban regions (*conurbations*) there is a stupendous total of 232 separate housing authorities, many of them directly competing with one another for housing sites.[33]

The widespread recognition of the urban region as a new *political* entity is on the horizon. In the United States, a few cities are engaged in serious attempts to coordinate government services between central cities and surrounding communities. One such experiment is the "urban county system," which centralizes authority for providing one or more services for all communities in the area (*e.g.*, water, airport, sewage disposal, planning) in an organ of the county in which the central city is located. Los Angeles, St. Louis, and London are among the leaders in this movement. A second trend, which is often

[31] Wood, *op, cit.*, p. 13.

[32] *Municipal Yearbook, 1958*, pp. 41–44; Victor Jones, *Metropolitan Government* (Chicago, University of Chicago Press, 1942), pp. 126–129.

[33] Peter Self, *Cities in Flood* (London, Faber and Faber, 1959), pp. 55–56.

FIGURE 10
Map of Seattle, Washington, Showing 17 Types of Governmental Jurisdiction

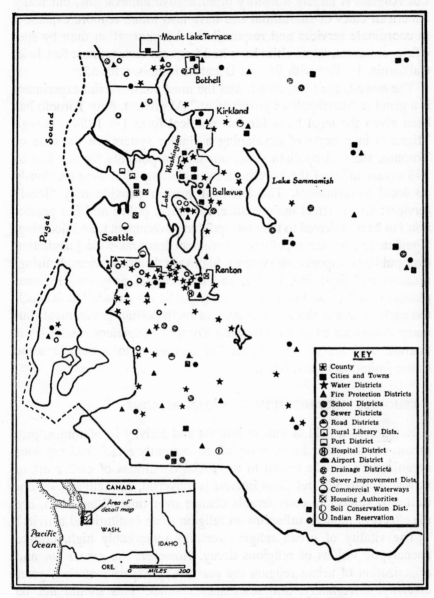

A CHALLENGE: This map of the Seattle area, showing 17 types of governmental jurisdiction, illustrates how complex municipal functions and services are in expanding cities today. A bill was recently introduced in state Legislature to enable Seattle and its environs to establish a metropolitan government to operate on an area-wide basis.

SOURCE: *The New York Times,* Feb. 3, 1957.

hotly contested, is *political annexation* of neighboring communities. Los Angeles is largely a history of successive annexations, but many American cities of substantial size have also found it more expedient to coordinate services and responsibility by annexation than by specific agreements. Some cities have had frequent annexations; San Jose, California, leading with 95 and Decatur, Illinois, with 52.[34]

The newest, the most direct, and the most controversial experiment is a genuine "metropolitan government." At present, only Toronto has been given the legal basis for this political form (in 1954), though Miami is in process of developing a similar system. In the case of Toronto, the metropolitan government is responsible for services to 245 square miles of the Toronto area, including what were previously 13 local governments. The latter at present provide only "local" services: water, street maintenance, sewerage, police and fire protection (to be transferred to the metropolitan government), and licensing. Significantly, the metropolitan government has area-wide jurisdiction over public transportation systems, highways, health services, housing, taxation and financing, justice, and correctional programs, regional planning, and to an increasing extent, public education.[35] It is much too early to assess the achievements of metropolitan government, but many American cities are following Toronto's experiences with great interest, and are engaged in studies that seem to anticipate some future imitation of this form.

RELIGIOUS ORGANIZATION IN URBAN REGIONS

Religion as a field of human interest and activity is, of course, pre-urban. On the other hand, many of the currently established religious organizations can be traced to the social conditions of earlier urban waves. Apparently, religious interest is universal, but religious organization is subject to considerable change over time. What, then, are the effects of modern urbanism on religion as an institutional activity?

The vitality of urban religion remains remarkably high, despite apocalyptic visions of religious decay. However, the *expression* and *organization* of urban religion are marked by experimentation, great diversity, uncertainty, and sometimes conflict. This should not be

[34] *Municipal Yearbook, 1958,* pp. 53–55.

[35] *Ibid.,* pp. 45–49; Robson, *op. cit.,* pp. 376–377; James B. Milner, "The Metropolitan Toronto Plan," *University of Pennsylvania Law Review,* 105 (February, 1957), pp. 570–587; Stephen B. Sweeney, ed., *Metropolitan Analysis* (Philadelphia, University of Pennsylvania Press, 1958), pp. 148–160.

surprising, if the nature of modern urban regions is recalled. Institutionalized religion, in varying degrees in different nations, is enmeshed in two typically "urban" problems: specialization (or perhaps "overspecialization"); and competition from informal or incidental sources of religious interest.

Diversity, Specialization, and Bureaucratization

Throughout the modern world, urbanization is accompanied by some separation of institutionalized religion from other spheres of activity. This trend is particularly clear in American urban regions, where traditional religion is highly compartmentalized as a result of an unparalleled division of labor in the community. Four important consequences have generally followed, though in different degrees in various societies. These are: a growing variety of religious organizations; the assumption of nonreligious functions by religious groups; bureaucratization of religious organization; and a variably visible stratification in religious affiliation.

Once the prevailing established forms of religion become distinct from kinship organization (as in the urbanization of formerly preliterate groups) or the government structure (as in the United States, Canada, and to some extent in Germany and England), urbanites acquire a measure of freedom in their religious affiliations. Any real or imagined dissatisfactions on theological matters, morality, authority, or the personality of clergymen may find an outlet in reduced participation and diluted religious beliefs or formation of new religious organizations. The first alternative has been more prevalent perhaps in nations where one church (Catholic, Mohammedan) holds a continuing monopoly; the second appears in urbanized nations that have no "established" church, as in the United States.

In American urban regions, the number of separate religious groups is staggering—almost 300 denominations and cults.[36] The yellow pages of the telephone directory in most large cities normally list a bewildering alphabetical array of churches, many of which are only vaguely recognizable to nonmembers. Apparently, two major kinds of religious groups account for the greater part of this diversity. The more

[36] Robin M. Williams, Jr., *American Society*, 2nd ed. (New York, Alfred A. Knopf, 1960), pp. 341–344. For descriptions of the variety in religion, see Elmer T. Clark, *The Small Sects in America* (Nashville, Tenn., Cokesbury Press, 1937) and Charles S. Braden, *These Also Believe* (New York, Macmillan, 1949).

numerous type is a series of *cults* and *sects,* usually of an emotional, highly "fundamentalist" faith, which seek to break away from the staid, complacent, established churches (mainly Protestant). With few exceptions, these schismatic groups attract lower status urbanites, particularly those who have recently migrated from rural areas. In this latter category is a considerable number of Negroes. Religious organization tends to be personal and nonbureaucratic. Often each group is distinguished by its name, rather than a special theology. Some examples are: [37] The Seventh-Day Adventists, Jehovah's Witnesses, Church of the Nazarene, New Thought, Theosophy, The I Am Movement, Spiritualist, Church of God, Holiness Sects.

The other type consists of relatively few *well organized denominations* (from a historical standpoint, these are successful survivals of an earlier schismatic movement): *e.g.,* Episcopalian, Congregational, Methodist, Lutheran, Baptist, and Presbyterian. In recent years, both in the United States and England, the Oxford Group Movement (and Moral Rearmament) seems to be developing away from its cultish form toward a less emotionalized organization.[38] In general, the denominational form represents groups with more stable adjustments to urban living than that of cult and sect members.

Competition of Religious Forms

Religious diversity in the "free" situation of American urban regions has meant competition for potential adherents. Often, since theological differences are slight or virtually immune to examination, many additional services have been assumed by religious groups with the hope of attracting and holding members. The weekly sermon comes to be engulfed in pastoral counselling on family matters, recreational programs, social gatherings (teas, suppers, picnics), babysitting services, the newsletter, welfare activities, fund raising, public relations, representation in civic affairs, and sometimes political action. In short, competitive religious groups have tried to provide a vital, attractive religious organization.

[37] W. B. Selbie, *English Sects: A History of Nonconformity* (New York, Holt, Rinehart, and Winston, 1925); Braden, *op. cit.;* Arthur H. Fauset, *Black Gods of the Metropolis: Negro Religious Cults of the Urban North* (Philadelphia, University of Pennsylvania Press, 1944). For the medieval counterpart of this trend, see also Norman Cohn, *The Pursuit of the Millennium* (London, Secker and Warburg, 1957).

[38] Allan W. Eister, *Drawing-Room Conversion: A Sociological Account of the Oxford Group Movement* (Durham, Duke University Press, 1950).

TABLE 64

Social Class Composition of Major Religious Groups in the U.S., 1945–1946

RELIGIOUS GROUPS	Upper class	Middle class	Lower class
National Sample	*13.1*	*30.7*	*56.2*
Episcopal	24.1	33.7	42.2
Congregational	23.9	42.6	33.5
Presbyterian	21.9	40.0	38.1
Jewish	21.8	32.0	46.2
No preference	13.3	26.0	60.7
Methodist	12.7	35.6	51.7
Protestant (unspecified)	12.4	24.1	63.5
Lutheran	10.9	36.1	53.0
Christian (unspecified or Disciples of Christ)	10.0	35.4	54.6
Protestant (various smaller bodies)	10.0	27.3	62.7
Catholic	8.7	24.7	66.6
Baptist	8.0	24.0	68.0

SOURCE: Bernard Barber, *Social Stratification* (New York, Harcourt, Brace and World, 1957), p. 157.

Urban religion, embarking on such a quest, has been forced to follow the well-worn path to increasing bureaucratization. The minister (or rabbi)—and often his wife—is a religious executive, supplemented by assistant or associate ministers, secretaries, governing boards, directors of religious education and music, laymen's committees, and a variety of intradenominational organizations (local, state, regional, and national). Consequently, urban religion in its institutionalized forms is to many urban residents a poor substitute for traditional forms of religion. One typical reaction is passive participation;[39] another is a gradual assumption of a secular attitude that blurs any previously meaningful distinction between the routine and the extraordinary. Still another reaction is the segregation of dissidents into factions jockeying for power. Most important, however, is a tendency toward *stratification,* which is understandable on historical and theological grounds as well.

Several studies clearly demonstrate that urban social classes (in terms of occupational and income differences) are unequally represented in the prevailing variety of religious groups. The accompanying table, based on the composition of major religious bodies in 1945-

[39] John Wicklein, "Lack of Religion Found in Church," The *New York Times,* January 8, 1961.

1946 for the United States,[40] indicates a rather significant tendency for middle class persons to be adherents of Methodist, Episcopal, Congregational, and Jewish faiths, while lower class families seem to be more prevalent in Catholic and Baptist groups. It is tempting to exaggerate the meaning of the differences summarized in this table. But several cautions must be observed. Unfortunately, we have few figures on *historical trends or changes* in the class composition of religious bodies. Furthermore, we cannot interpret this table very satisfactorily until we know that class status strongly influences religious affiliation, that religious affiliation provides opportunities for achieving specific status levels, or that both religious membership and class status are related to some third factor—perhaps income. In addition, membership figures do not tell us about degrees of participation, personal involvement, and satisfaction in urban religious groups.

However, a few tentative conclusions may be drawn. Established religions in urban areas fail to provide satisfying religious services to a substantial number of lower class families, both white and Negro. As a result, cities are breeding-grounds of religious experiments by migratory or unadjusted lower class persons. The "store front" church, the "tent revival," are symbols of a search for a "traditional" religion in the urban setting. Some denominations, notably the Methodist, recognize the consequences of this trend; they find that as they discourage (implicitly or explicitly) lower class whites and virtually all Negroes, these denominations are slowly shifting from the core to the *periphery* of American urban regions (*e.g.,* in Boston, Detroit, Pittsburgh, and Chicago). In Boston only five Methodist churches remain in the innermost zone, five others having closed down in the past ten years.[41] Should this trend continue, and should the class segregation of population likewise extend existing patterns, institutionalized religion in American urban regions may eventually yield two or three separate "religious communities" whose differences will be not merely theological or organizational, but ideological. This might counteract the *functional interdependence* of the components of the urban region with a renewed emphasis on class divisions—not, as Marx predicted, from the contradictions of the capitalist market, but from the subtle monopolies of the "religious market."

[40] See Bernard Barber, *Social Stratification* (New York, Harcourt, Brace, and World, 1957), p. 157. A similar connection between status and religion is demonstrated in Walter Goldschmidt, *As You Sow* (New York, Harcourt, Brace, and World, 1947).

[41] *The New York Times,* March 15, 1959.

The Fragmentation of Religion

Religion in modern urban regions seem to be slowly adjusting to its setting by trial-and-error: by separation and by addition of new services; by general appeals and by narrowed, class-like emphases. But institutionalized religion must also face the fact that there are strong competitors in the urban religious sphere that have no church or temple or bible, that competitors are normal consequences of urban communities and cultures.

Perhaps this situation can be understood by analyzing religion in terms of four distinctive aspects or "parts." (*a*) *Religious beliefs* (or theology) consist of a series of cultural norms that define the nature of a supernatural (or supernaturals), its powers and their expression. (*b*) *Religious rites* or *ceremonies* refer to occasions in which religious beliefs are reinforced by proper use of religious objects—material items that symbolically represent specific religious beliefs. (*c*) *Religious experience* is the individual's feelings of exaltation, "spiritual satisfaction," or excitement, which derive from his contact (direct or indirect) with some supernatural. In this sense, Joan of Arc had religious experiences when she heard the "voices" that encouraged her entrance into the political arena. Similarly, the decision to follow a specific *vocation* (literally a "calling") may be based on an assumed "message" from God or other supernatural agents. (*d*) Finally, for our purposes, religion may develop *religious social organization,* a specialized group dedicated to regularizing contacts with the supernatural by providing expert leadership, properly indoctrinating adherents, and furnishing material and social bases for religious experience.

Traditionally, all four components of religion have been fused into unities known as institutionalized religions. In modern urban regions, however, this fusion is yielding to fragmentation. Of particular significance is a growing autonomy of the first three components from religious social organization—which has the consequence of permitting a greater variety of religious beliefs and supernaturals, and also of expanding the range of situations capable of providing religious experience for urbanites. This process is one aspect of the often noted "secularization of religion," which some believe is the end of religion. But secularization may also be interpreted as "experimentation in religion," in this case by *more direct contact* with the cultural and psychological components of religion.

For example, urbanites seem to be seeking new or "supplementary" supernaturals in such varied guises as Science, Education, political idols (Roosevelt, Churchill, Eisenhower, Adenauer, De Gaulle, etc.) and even in legendary sports figures. To the urbanite, these "supernaturals" possess the advantage of being widely known and yet retaining the sacred aura of "distance" so necessary for reverence.[42]

Religious experience, or its psychological equivalent, is increasingly available in nontraditional forms as a normal aspect of the urban milieu. One important variety is the relentlessly captivating appeal and sensation of the mass media of communication. Urbanites receive a basically nonrational satisfaction or thrill from news stories, picture magazines, favorite television fare, and to some extent from films (but note the attempt to play up the element of "sensation" by wide screens, color, third-dimensional techniques, and even the use of special odors). As a recent survey demonstrated,[43] "missing the newspaper" as a result of a strike meant an interruption to many of a ritualistic, semicompulsive, security-giving experience.

Another major form of urban religious experience is gambling. Here the "supernatural" is the very ancient one of "luck" or "chance." Excepting the professional gamblers, who follow gambling as a vocation, urbanites seem to be extremely vulnerable to the unsophisticated lure of "games of chance"—cards, bingo, horse racing, various sports contests, commercial contests, and even betting on the choice of a number (the notorious "policy game" of New York City, Chicago, and other urban centers).[44]

These subtle and largely neglected sources of religious participation in urban regions are clearly unlike our usual conceptions of organized religion. Moreover, these newer forms seem to reflect some of the characteristic features of urbanization. Almost all of the "religious substitutes" emphasize the primacy of *individual* participation (rather than family or other groups), as well as the *anonymity* of the individual. Furthermore, they require little or no preparation, or deep levels of involvement, for any extended time period. In fact, the diffuseness and lack of visible formalization tend to minimize both

[42] Emile Durkheim, *The Elementary Forms of the Religious Life*, trans. by Joseph W. Swain (New York, The Free Press of Glencoe, 1947), Chap. I.

[43] Bernard Berelson, "What 'Missing the Newspaper' Means," in Paul Lazarsfeld and Frank Stanton, eds., *Communications Research, 1948–1949* (Urbana, Ill., University of Illinois Press, 1949), pp. 111–128.

[44] See Walter C. Reckless, *The Crime Problem* (New York, Appleton-Century-Crofts, Inc., 1950), Chap. XIII.

the effectiveness of community controls and the ability of religious groups to compete for the allegiance of urbanites. Urban religion, therefore, is a study in contrasts; more slowly than the economic and political spheres, it is involved in readjusting once dominant values and organizations to the complex cultural and ecological changes of modern urban regions.

SELECTED REFERENCES

ADRIAN, Charles R., *Governing Urban America* (New York, McGraw-Hill, 1955).

BARITZ, Loren, *The Servants of Power* (Middletown, Conn., Wesleyan University Press, 1960).

CAPLOW, Theodore, *The Sociology of Work* (Minneapolis, University of Minnesota Press, 1954).

Editors of *Fortune, The Executive Life* (New York, Doubleday, 1956).

FISHER, Robert M., ed., *The Metropolis in Modern Life* (New York, Doubleday and Company, 1955).

International City Managers' Association, *The Municipal Year Book 1958* (Chicago, International City Managers' Association, 1958).

JANOWITZ, Morris, ed., *Community Political Systems* (New York, The Free Press of Glencoe, 1960).

JONES, Victor, *Metropolitan Government* (Chicago, University of Chicago Press, 1942).

WOOD, Robert C., *Suburbia: Its People and Their Politics* (Boston, Houghton Mifflin, 1959).

CHAPTER 12

New Institutional Forms: Urban Education and Social Welfare

EDUCATION, THE PROCESS of relaying cultural experience from one generation to another, is a universal necessity, but urban communities are by their very nature both unusually dependent on education and faced with special difficulties in insuring adequate performance of this function. The reasons are fairly obvious. There is, first, the relatively larger number of persons involved in urban education. Perhaps more important is the heterogeneous nature of populations in urban regions: long-term residents and migrants; differences in status levels, occupation, income, religion, nationality, and race. Third, the sheer weight and complexity of culture to be transmitted presents practical problems that are still unsolved in the most "advanced" urban areas. Education, for example, must develop skills in reading, writing, calculation, in vocational pursuits, as well as some general technical and scientific knowledge.

But these technical difficulties are magnified by the extraordinary reliance of urban regions on pervasive and efficient educational processes. Because of its great accessibility and its continually expanding contacts with other communities and societies, the urban region requires the best available information about its own operation and about regions with which it maintains political and economic relationships. More important, this information must be gathered, analyzed, and applied by competent persons as *residents* and as *agents* of urban regions. This is probably the core of the social importance of urban education. Indeed, the world's underdeveloped nations, striving for industrialization and urbanization, recognize the crucial function of education with greater pungency than do "advanced societies," because the former are trying to achieve rapidly improved education with limited resources and personnel.[1] Specifically, educational processes are crucial for the maintenance of the urban region in at least five respects.

1. The most obvious, which was briefly mentioned above, is the necessity for quick, efficient, and meaningful communication among urban groups. In one sense, the urban complex is a network of decision-making processes—decisions on location, production, control, distribution, and exchange of goods and services. As members of formal groups and as individuals, urbanites strive to make intelligent, rational decisions, though emotion and tradition are not completely absent. Urban education provides the necessary tools of communication—ideas, techniques, and acquired interests.

2. Urbanization and the urban way of life largely depend on a vast network of occupations and vocations, each with its own skills, experiences, and problems. With the separation of home and job, the traditional preparation for vocations or trades through the medium of the family is no longer feasible. Indeed, the diversity of needed skills, and the comparative freedom in selecting one's occupation, hinder the role of the family as a direct transmitter of occupational skills. Consequently, a specialized educational system is necessary to transmit vocationally relevant skills. In the urban region, clerical and trades skills are acquired through secondary schools and vocational schools or business and secretarial "colleges," while professional and administrative skills seem to require "higher" educational programs in colleges and universities.

3. It is not sufficiently recognized that the urban economy, which is fundamentally dependent on diversified and expanding demand for urban products, is thereby inevitably affected by the character and distribution of educational programs. Consumer demand (within or between urban regions) reflects not only available income, but the cultivation of tastes and desires for goods and services. In general, the greatest expansion in urban consumer demand has been in products that symbolize *status ascent* or the widening of personal experi-

[1] Lyle W. Shannon, ed., *Underdeveloped Areas* (New York, Harper and Brothers, 1957), Chaps. IV, IX, X; Edward H. Spicer, ed., *Human Problems in Technological Change* (New York, Russell Sage Foundation, 1952).

ence. Larger and better equipped homes, unusual foods, more varied and "better" styled clothing, the use of professional services (physicians, dentists, attorneys, architects, etc.), automobiles, and the steady flow of new appliances—all these are familiar examples of such products.

Essentially, the increasing trend toward consumer interest in these "acquired needs" has been accompanied by the extension of urban educational processes to a growing proportion of urbanites. Advertising, a crucial urban invention, is an obvious and variably effective part of urban education, but the importance of formal public education in conditioning consumer habits should not be neglected.[2] Indeed, teachers and other students often unwittingly create preferences and valuations about food, recreation, clothing, etc.

4. The urban region is simultaneously an *economic* entity and a framework for meeting the *noneconomic* needs of its residents. It is sometimes forgotten that the latter functions soon come to have as much importance to urban residents as the former. In fact, urban Americans seem to give extraordinary attention to such community services as public utilities, schools, library facilities, parks and other recreational areas, etc. in job changes and decisions to move.[3] These increasingly desired services, however, depend on revenues from various kinds of local and regional taxes, as some suburbanites belatedly discover. However, the ultimate source of taxation is current income (not land, as the outmoded real property tax has assumed). Urban income, in turn, is rather directly related to the concentration of highly skilled, professional, and managerial workers. We have already noted that expansion of the higher paid, higher status occupations results from the extension of formal educational opportunities to more and more urbanites. In short, formal education and its immediate consequences are indispensable to the maintenance and enhancement of urban "amenities," which give character to the urban region and motivate urbanites to supply needed manpower.

[2] See Lincoln H. Clark, ed., *Consumer Behavior: Research on Consumer Reactions* (New York, Harper and Brothers, 1958), pp. 13–37, 93–219; David Riesman *et al.*, *The Lonely Crowd* (Garden City, Doubleday Anchor Books, 1953), Chaps. III, IV.

[3] Richard Dewey, "Peripheral Expansion in Milwaukee County," *American Journal of Sociology*, 54 (September, 1948), pp. 118–125; Peter Rossi, *Why Families Move* (New York, the Free Press of Glencoe, 1955); Walter T. Martin, *The Rural-Urban Fringe: A Study of Adjustment to Residence Location* (Eugene, Ore., University of Oregon Press, 1953).

5. Finally, the hallmarks of urbanism—creativity and change in many spheres—can be traced to a developed, specialized educational system. Innovations, which are normally contributed by a small segment of the population (though not necessarily an elite in intelligence or responsibility), stem from disciplined dissatisfaction, independence from traditional restraints, some form of specialized knowledge, and often an unverbalized respect for the value of curiosity, comparison, objectivity, and "progress." [4] Though some urbanites undoubtedly develop these characteristics without much exposure to formal education, most of the widely accepted urban creations have been the rare fruit of education in schools, colleges, and institutes. Increasingly, businessmen, professionals of all kinds, and experts in public and private service—our primary sources of invention—are recruited from those with formal education. By contrast, the innovators in urban areas of 2000 to 5000 years ago were not blessed with formal education; they wrought their contributions out of the practical problems of warfare and religion. [5]

Public education, rarely more than one hundred years old, is a vast, expensive urban experiment in preparing urbanites for the responsibilities and opportunities of urban living. Previously, education was largely informal and intermittent; formal education was limited to a favored minority of professionals (ministers, lawyers, physicians) and merchants, who received their training under private auspices (family or church). [6] With few exceptions, such education was considered inappropriate for females, who needed only the simple domestic skills and a steady devotion to household labor.

The institution of free (*i.e.,* supported by general taxation), public, universal, formalized education has placed a large "finis" to preexisting forms of education, at least at the lower levels. It has become a symbol and a goal for those nations and regions striving to become

[4] See Joseph Rossman, *The Psychology of the Inventor* (Washington, The Inventors Publishing Company, 1931); John Jewkes *et al., The Sources of Invention* (London, Macmillan & Co., Ltd., 1958); H. G. Barnett, *Innovation* (New York, McGraw-Hill, 1953), Chaps. VI, X.

[5] See Lewis Mumford, *Technics and Civilization* (New York, Harcourt, Brace and World, 1934); and Herbert Spencer, *The Principles of Sociology* (New York, D. Appleton and Co., 1897), Vol. 3.

[6] N. Freeman Butts, *A Cultural History of Western Education,* 2nd ed. (New York, McGraw-Hill, 1955); Abraham Flexner, *Universities: American, English, German* (New York, Oxford University Press, 1930).

urbanized or to emulate the fruits of urbanism (literacy, secularism, technical advancements). To the sociologist, public education is marked by a number of specifically "urban" features, which help in understanding the accomplishments and the gnawing problems of modern education throughout the world.

1. Extensiveness

Public education, by law and by custom, is available to all residents of a given age range, regardless of sex, religion, color, and financial status of parents. Though public schools do not achieve full coverage —some families prefer private schools, and some urban youngsters maintain a startling immunity to any formal education—they normally serve such a vast proportion of young people that public education is necessarily a *mass enterprise*.

2. Internal specialization

Despite the large numbers served, urban public education has tended to decry uniformity as an inevitable educational feature. In general, uniformity is greatest at the primary level, with increasing concern for variety and individual needs in secondary and college programs. However, classes for retarded and "exceptional" children, schools for the blind and the deaf, for serious behavior problems (the famous "600" schools in New York City) are increasingly evident in American urban regions. On the secondary level, many cities provide general programs, college preparatory courses, vocational or trade schools, commercial programs, plus adult education courses in "English for Foreigners" to world politics. Comparatively few cities boast municipally owned colleges, but the number is gradually increasing as the pressure for college education comes to exceed the capacities of private colleges and bulging state university centers.

3. Bureaucratization

The scope and variety of educational programs, the rapidly expanding student bodies, and emphasis on improved teaching create problems of organization that help to explain the complex networks of educational bureaucracy. Education has become a community responsibility of intense interest and astronomical expense. Public education is by far the largest expenditure in the municipal budget—about 32 per cent.[7] Consequently, urban education must be planned and reviewed; it must give due attention to hiring and retaining qualified teachers, administrators, and maintenance personnel; it must prepare and house records of its students and their achievements; finally, it must maintain contacts with local government, civic organizations, business firms, and parents. Tests, assignments, awards, meetings, reports become components in the educational establishment; sometimes (the extent is a deliciously moot question) they compete with the learning process.

Educational bureaucracy is understandably concerned with educational techniques and experimentation. Urban education is so extensive and so visibly important to urbanites that criticism may (and does) arise from all quarters. Consequently, to forestall and to answer these criticisms, a recurrent need for novelty and experiment in educational methods is a major theme in urban education. In this respect, the educational bureaucracy is somewhat unique, for bureaucratic systems are normally antagonistic to change, however necessary. Perhaps the dilemma of modern urban education lies in the conflict between bureaucratic forms and the essential dynamics of urban education. In any case, suggested procedures and programs are almost constantly on trial: television classes, teachers' aids, foreign languages in the early grades, the two or three track system, easy or rigid promotion, instruction by ability groups, enrichment programs, teaching machines and "programmed learning," etc.[8]

4. Development of "regional segments" in public education

As urban regions develop, their component areas tend to become more specialized in function, population features, and social class. In the United States, urban education also reflects in some degree this basic sociographic division. While most educational personnel are drawn from middle status groups, schools in the fringe and in many parts of the central city largely serve lower status children. Since these areas generally have limited interest in formal education, and since few of these students aspire to college levels, educational leadership

[7] Bureau of the Census figures, cited by James A. Quinn, *Urban Sociology* (New York, American Book Company, 1955), p. 310.

[8] For a good summary, see C. Winfield Scott and Clyde M. Hill, eds., *Public Education Under Criticism* (Englewood Cliffs, N.J., Prentice-Hall, 1954), Parts II, III, and VII.

has not been encouraged to experiment with programs or techniques. The school systems in such areas tend to be grudgingly content with keeping discipline (if they can) and transmitting minimal skills.

By contrast, suburban school systems are oriented to the needs of students from rising middle class families. In these areas, educational experiment is so prevalent that they are often easily caricatured by critics.[9] Suburban school systems in the United States, it is important to note, are the stronghold of "progressive education."

SOCIAL WELFARE, SOCIAL WORK, AND URBANISM

"Charity," "philanthropy," "social work," "relief," "social welfare" —these are much abused epithets and poorly understood processes in modern communities. Most of the difficulty with these terms can be traced to fixed political ideologies, to acknowledged errors in carrying out these activities, and most significantly, to a failure to understand the historical relation between social welfare and the urban region. Perhaps a first step in clarification is recognizing that charity, philanthropy, relief, and social welfare all refer to a particular *set of functions or services* provided by specialized agencies of the community. Social work, on the other hand, comprises the professional techniques and skills with which these services are performed through responsible organizations designed to regularize and coordinate competent performance. For example, one might drop a coin in the tin cup of a blind man at a busy downtown corner. This is "charity" or "philanthropy," but not social work. It is perhaps altruistically motivated; yet this act tends to be impulsive and soon forgotten. A social work agency may also provide financial aid to the blind man, but this assistance is ideally a result of careful investigation, personal interviews, and a professional interest in the *future* of the person or client.

Social welfare in its various forms has a long history. However, this type of community service was for a long time sporadically provided by groups with other dominant functions (family, church, government). Toward the end of the second "urban wave"—in the seventeenth century in England and the Low Countries—welfare activities

---

[9] William H. Whyte, Jr., *The Organization Man* (Garden City, N.Y., Doubleday and Company, 1956), Chap. XXVIII; John R. Seeley *et al.*, *Crestwood Heights* (New York, Basic Books, 1956); Arthur E. Bestor, *Educational Wastelands* (Urbana, Ill., University of Illinois Press, 1953); Albert Lynd, *Quackery in the Schools* (Boston, Little, Brown, 1953); John Keats, *Schools Without Scholars* (Boston, Houghton Mifflin, 1958).

began to exhibit some specialization, innovation, and some independent status.[10]

Understandably, social welfare has consistently been an urban function. From the eleventh century to the present, urban communities have been characterized by a number of social conditions and problems that to some degree produce community *incapacities*. Most visible are the continuing processes of urbanward migration and consequent pressure of population on available space and services. Second, generally rapid economic and social changes—which are otherwise desired in urban areas—have tended to require personal and family adjustments for which some persons have been unprepared. Particular mention should be made here of the growth of industrial production, the importance of a steady job, the emphasis on more and more acquired skills, the tendency toward increased opportunity for status change and status inconsistency, and the growing variety of consumer products and services.

Third, during the period of greatest urbanization (eighteenth through twentieth centuries in the Western World; the twentieth century in Asia and Africa) the prevailing social organizations were in process of transition to newer, more complex forms. The enormous social consequences of religious deviations and denominations during the Reformation and afterward can perhaps be summarized by reference to the uncertainties and controversies experienced by urban populations in the Ages of Reason and Individuation.[11] A similar picture of transition and crisis can be found among native peoples who have been weaned from tribal religions and obligations after migration to urban centers in Africa, the Pacific, and the United States.[12] Likewise, government structures still tended to be attuned to limited populations and the old municipal problems of physical safety and commercial facilitation. As a result, essentially part-time and volunteer government officials could not easily recognize, much less manage, the problems of continual migration and congestion.

These "transitional" urban features did not immediately stimulate

---

[10] See Walter Friedlander, *An Introduction to Social Welfare* (Englewood Cliffs, N.J., Prentice-Hall, 1955).

[11] Preserved Smith, *The Age of the Reformation* (New York, Henry Holt, 1920).

[12] Laura Thompson, *Culture in Crisis* (New York, Harper and Brothers, 1950); I. Schapera, *Migrant Labour and Tribal Life* (London, Oxford University Press, 1947); Margaret Mead, *Cultural Patterns and Technical Change* (New York, Columbia University Press, 1953).

the search for appropriate solutions. From the sixteenth century till the middle of the nineteenth, with few exceptions, two attitudes effectively hindered any sustained, realistic concern for the deleterious by-products of urbanization (dependency, illness, overcrowding, etc.). One such attitude stressed man's personal responsibility for his troubles; consequently, the community sought to protect itself from assuming the growing burden of unemployment and destitution among urban migrants. The usual consequence was repressive legislation, symbolized in the English Poor Laws. A related attitude during much of the nineteenth century considered "social problems" a natural, inevitable part of social development. The dominant approach was therefore one of "laissez faire" or a refusal to tinker with social processes; in particular, public programs were regarded as impertinent and ineffectual, as persuasively argued by Herbert Spencer in England, by William Graham Sumner in the United States.[13]

Yet by the middle of the nineteenth century, these attitudes were increasingly challenged by "humanitarian" movements sparked by vigorous leadership and more experienced organization. Based on an obvious but deferred application of Christian ethics, humanitarianism launched a devastating critique of urban problems on specific fronts —penal reform, the blind, the mentally ill, the destitute, and the orphaned. But a cardinal shift in attitudes must be noted; humanitarianism viewed migrants and their problems not as "outsiders" and bothersome intruders, but as part of the community and *its* responsibilities.[14] For some decades, this revised evaluation was expressed largely through *private* organizations and programs (*e.g.*, the Charity Organization Society in England and the United States, the YMCA, the Children's Aid Society, and Hull House in Chicago). Gradually, urban communities came to supplement private welfare functions with new publicly financed and administered programs, principally after World War I in the United States, but considerably earlier in England and Germany.[15]

There is much confusion and disagreement about the essential func-

[13] Stuart A. Queen, *Social Work in the Light of History* (Philadelphia, J. B. Lippincott Company, 1922), Part III; Herbert Spencer, *Social Statics,* 3rd ed. (New York, D. Appleton and Co., 1890); W. G. Sumner, *The Forgotten Man and Other Essays* (New Haven, Yale University Press, 1919).

[14] Queen, *op. cit.,* pp. 319–320.

[15] Mary P. Hall, *The Social Services of Modern England* (London, Routledge and Kegan Paul, 1953); Madeline Rooff, *Voluntary Societies and Social Policy* (London, Routledge and Kegan Paul, 1957).

tions that give some identity to social welfare in the urban region. Historically, the services of urban welfare agencies began as supplements to, or substitutes for, established institutions—such as kinship, public government, medicine, and education. Under this conception, welfare services were primarily designed for lower status families and individuals. Specific services most often provided, therefore, were financial assistance, occupational advice, child care and child placement, and treatment of the indigent, disabled, and the sick. As viewed by social workers, social welfare was a means of serving other institutions by helping individuals who had difficulties in using older institutional arrangements. This has been called the residual approach to social welfare.[16]

Perhaps it is useful to relate the residual conception of social welfare to earlier stages in the development of modern urban regions. In these earlier stages, cities were marked by rapid and uncontrolled growth, by precarious economic periods, and by many families unaccustomed to urban conditions. Since 1940 or thereabout, the essentially negative, emergency character of social welfare has lost its former prominence in the thinking and programs of welfare agencies. The trend is now toward consideration of welfare as a normal, specialized institution for a broader range of urbanites. Several new features seem to accompany this modern conception. Perhaps the central innovation is the emergence of responsibility for providing welfare services to the whole community (and region). As this broader service area has developed, more services have been demanded and made available to middle status groups (*e.g.,* vocational counseling and job placement, marital counseling, psychiatric services, etc.) As a consequence, while financial aid is still provided, it is generally receding in importance, in contrast to noneconomic services, for which the client is increasingly expected to pay. In such a shift of attention, wherever possible urban welfare agencies also stress *preventative* programs designed to reduce the financial and psychological disabilities of urbanites.[17] Thus far, however, this ideal has not been successfully translated into well-designed and properly financed programs. Finally,

[16] Helen L. Witmer, *Social Work: An Analysis of a Social Institution* (New York, Holt, Rinehart and Winston, 1942), pp. 24–27, 87–121; Harold L. Wilensky and Charles N. Lebeaux, *Industrial Society and Social Welfare* (New York, Russell Sage Foundation, 1958), pp. 138–140.

[17] Wilensky and Lebeaux, *op. cit.,* pp. 14–15, 147, 171; George R. Nelson, ed., *Freedom and Welfare* (Copenhagen, Ministries of Social Affairs of Denmark, Finland, Iceland, Norway, and Sweden, 1953), pp. 498–499.

modern social welfare has necessarily devoted extraordinary attention to coordination of many specialized services and agencies in the community.

As a genuine product of urban development in the last eighty years, social welfare is marked by the familiar qualities of specialization, bureaucratization, and professionalization. The accompanying chart summarizes the major subdivisions, which are found in virtually every large urban region in the Western world. But this intensive specializa-

TABLE 65

Forms of Specialization in Social Welfare in Modern Urban Regions

BASIS OF SPECIALIZATION	*Illustrative types*
Purpose (or program)	Public assistance, corrections, recreation, vocational rehabilitation
Skill category	Social casework, group work, vocational counseling, psychiatry, community organization
Clientele	Children, adults, the aged, veterans, income category
Auspices and control	Government (federal, state, local, state-local), voluntary (sectarian, non-sectarian, joint-financed)
Geographic location	Geographic limits and boundaries of service

SOURCE: Adapted from Harold L. Wilensky and Charles N. Lebeaux, *Industrial Society and Social Welfare*, p. 248.

tion has not been achieved without two uniquely urban trends. First and more obvious is the development of public and private bureaucracies in social welfare. Lady Bountiful and the dedicated volunteers of the past have little place in modern urban welfare work. Instead we have administrative agencies,[18] increasingly staffed with graded ranks of certified specialists—case workers (junior and senior), supervisors, executive director, home economists, physicians, psychiatrists, stenographers, dictaphone operators, receptionists, and often *interns* in casework. In addition, both private and public agencies operate with that telltale mark of bureaucracies—definite salary scales for each position or rank, and some timetable for salary increments.

A second trend deserves special attention from the urban sociologist

[18] As one student has summarized this trend: "America is the land of the free and the home of the committee." See Edward C. Jenkins, *Philanthropy in America* (New York, Association Press, 1950), p. 33.

and urbanites in general. Urban welfare groups have been compelled to design innovations in organization and coordination of services. As early as the 1880's in England and the United States, the operation of private and public agencies, religious and secular groups, and often of unwittingly competing agencies clearly pointed to the need for *liaison* and regularized cooperation among urban welfare groups. One of the earliest devices, which has come to be basic to welfare organization, was the *social service exchange*.[19] The exchange functions as a clearing-house for all cooperating agencies; it provides a continuous, up-to-date listing of the names of agency clients. This insures in most instances avoidance of duplication, but also enables specific agencies to obtain a broader picture of their client's needs by knowing past (or concurrent) contacts with community agencies.

An extremely important innovation, consciously aimed at co-ordination, is the *council of social agencies*. First used in such areas as Liverpool, Denver, New York, London, Chicago, and Pittsburgh, the council form provides centralized administration and often some planning for member agencies. The exact functions of the council vary somewhat from urban region to urban region. But the most common services are: revamping or combining existing agencies; facilitation of interagency conferences; a source of community and extraregional information for member agencies; advice and co-ordination of public relations; and a concern for professional standards in skills and salaries.[20] In the United States, since most of the member agencies are under private auspices, the council tends to be dominated by the private agencies. By contrast, in Great Britain, each county has its own public assistance committee, which has legal responsibility for overseeing local services in health, assistance, and education.

It is difficult to evaluate the contribution of the council of social agencies. While some coordination of services has been accomplished, many agencies tend to be concerned with maintaining their identity; and it is more than probable that the larger agencies carry unusual weight in council deliberations. Consequently, most councils have not been able to achieve the consensus necessary for genuine long-range planning. Nevertheless, the council seems to be a permanent fixture,

19 Wilensky and Lebeaux, *op. cit.,* Chap. 10.
20 Frank J. Bruno, *Trends in Social Work, 1874–1956* (New York, Columbia University Press, 1957), pp. 192–198.

since it is intimately related to another innovation—the *community chest*.

Fund raising for the numerous private welfare services was in the past a very onerous task. Contributors were plagued by numerous appeals, which tended to be both inconvenient and undignified. Furthermore, contributors could not easily allocate their donations according to the needs of "competing" fund drives. The community chest both simplifies and dignifies fund raising by one combined appeal, normally in the fall. But another coordinating function of the chest is equally important. In arriving at reasonable, workable financial goals, the chest must act as a goad to each agency to prepare justifiable budgets. Indeed, the needs of each agency must be considered in the light of other agencies' programs, as well as in terms of the financial capacity of the community and region. The success of this budgetary coordination depends on close association with the council of social agencies, and also on the relatively autonomous position of the chest, which is usually staffed with professional fund raisers and people with business experience.

SELECTED REFERENCES

COHEN, Nathan E., *Social Work in the American Tradition* (New York, Dryden Press, 1958).

RIESMAN, David, *Constraint and Variety in American Education* (Garden City, L.I., Doubleday and Company, 1958).

WAEFLE, Dael, *America's Resources of Specialized Talent* (New York, Harper and Brothers, 1954).

WILENSKY, Harold L. and LEBEAUX, Charles N., *Industrial Society and Social Welfare* (New York, Russell Sage Foundation, 1958).

WITMER, Helen L., *Social Work* (New York, Holt, Rinehart, and Winston, 1942).

CHAPTER 13

Mass Communications and Urban Leisure: A New Urban Ethic

THE MAJOR ORGANIZATIONAL forms—primary groups, established institutional groups, and the stratification system—of the urban region have created a new and still emerging type of human community, dedicated to the ends of variety, complexity, and productive efficiency. However, these important forms of social organization have had to serve and guide relatively large and mobile populations, as well as continue the normal pursuit of these modern urban goals. Essentially, the underlying problems of urbanization have been to produce "proper" motivation, effective conditions of learning, and a fundamental, meaningful coordination of roles and ideals in urban populations. Consciously or unconsciously, developments in *mass communications* and *leisure* have operated as significant supplements (perhaps as necessary accompaniments) to urban social organization. The major task of this chapter is to outline the special structure and operation of modern mass communication systems and their social and cultural consequences for the urban region.

Mass communication systems are almost wholly urban innovations, principally of the last fifty years. Despite their recency, mass communications have become an integral part of urban living; they are—in one form or another—highly acceptable, even difficult to avoid, and most significant, they are taken for granted by most urbanites. To the sociologist, however, mass communications reveal a special cluster of characteristics in the complexities of urban regions.

1. Scope or Coverage

The range of persons reached by the major mass media today is without precedent. A speaker or performer may be heard by two or three thousand people at best—without the aid of some mass medium. But the daily audience of a local radio station or newspaper may easily be several hundred thousand, or many millions if connected with a radio network or newspaper syndicate. Competitive program ratings for television broadcasts also indicate that considerable proportions of the fifty million television receivers are regularly tuned to specific programs.

2. Uniformity

Although there are obvious variations in exposure, attention, and interpretation of media content, the scope of mass media inevitably raises the level of uniformity of stimuli or reactions among urban consumers. Indeed, marketing and audience research is often devoted to the problem of adjusting media content (*e.g.,* commercials, film stories) to increase the probability of uniform impact on audiences. "Motivation research," which has been a much discussed field recently,[1] is essentially a scientific quest for greater uniformity by discovering and playing on "unconscious" common motives or themes in audiences.

3. Rapidity

The daily newspaper (and news broadcasts on radio and television) is probably the best, continuous demonstration of speed in *collecting* stimuli (news), *editing and coordinating* media content, and finally *dissemination.* Few urbanites care for delayed reporting of news ("there's nothing deader than yesterday's newspaper"), repeats of recent television programs, or even many old movies. Probably few would show any interest in a return to the weekly newspaper. Improved communications and mass production techniques enable the purveyors of mass media to contract space and time in reaching and satisfying their respective consumers. This technical rapidity is an implicit fascination to many urbanites; it inspires confidence and

[1] George H. Smith, *Motivation Research in Advertising and Marketing* (New York, McGraw-Hill, 1954).

dependence, which in turn engender desires for "regular" communication among devotees of each medium.

4. Regularity

From the viewpoint of both disseminators and their audiences, mass communication must be available in a predictable, periodic fashion.[2] Indeed, one useful way of classifying media (or a segment of one medium, such as a specific type of column) is by degree of regularity: hourly (news highlights on radio); daily (newspapers, soap operas); weekly (some magazines, television programs; monthly (magazines); periodically but not with clearly predictable regularity (new films).

5. Exposure during leisure time

In general, mass communications achieve their coverage and effectiveness by aiming mass media to coincide with the largest segments of leisure time. Newspaper circulation and delivery reach their height *before* and *after* regular working hours (from 6:30 to 8:30 A.M. and 4:30 to 6:00 P.M.). Choice television and radio hours, recognized by both audiences and sponsors, are daily from 8:00 to 10:00 P.M. and Sunday evenings. Weekly magazines (*Life, Saturday Evening Post*) are likewise on newsstands and in mail boxes by Friday, so that readers may find time to scan them before they disappear under tables, in magazine racks, or in junior's junk-pile. Furthermore, the expansion of leisure time has been a necessary precondition of the successful *multiplication* of mass media, despite some competition between media—*e.g.*, films and television.

6. "Influence"

Perhaps the key feature of modern mass media is the basic technique employed to direct various aspects of behavior among urbanites. Older, more direct techniques of control—violence, threats, intimidation, bribery—are both difficult to impose (unless some form of despotic government is involved) and highly immoral to most ur-

[2] Bernard Berelson, "What 'Missing the Newspaper' Means," in Paul F. Lazarsfeld and Frank N. Stanton, eds., *Communications Research, 1948–1949* (New York, Harper and Brothers, 1949), pp. 111–128.

banites. Instead, mass communications typically attempt to "influence" the opinions, ideas, and behavior of audiences and publics. The techniques of persuasion, gentle or indirect argument (the "relaxed" or "soft" sell), the subtle appeal to semiconscious motives, even the brash repetitiousness of some commercials, are all designed to appear as "reasonable" and "acceptable" as possible. In short, as the well-known publicist, Edward L. Bernays has phrased it, "the engineering of consent" is the goal not only of public relations in particular, but—in some degree—of all mass communications.[3]

7. Diversity of Influences

While there is considerable diversity in *types of mass media* (film, radio, television, magazines, telephones, books, pamphlets, news-papers) mass communications as an adjunct to urban social organization likewise consists of several *forms* or *contexts* of influence.

1. *Advertising.* The most ubiquitous is advertising, which attempts to influence the process of selection among competing commodities, as well as to develop new needs and tastes for status items.[4] In general, advertising is more or less skillfully grafted on other forms of mass communication, such as entertainment (the "commercial"). There is some controversy among economists and social analysts about the *actual* effectiveness of advertising in influencing, diverting, or increasing sales of particular products, compared with the role of *personal influence.*

2. *Public Relations and Institutional Advertising.* These constitute a second subcategory of mass communications "influence." Instead of direct attempts to focus choices on specific products, public relations functions as a relatively subtle, indirect attempt to create an ac-

[3] Paul F. Lazarsfeld, "Foreword," in Leo A. Handel, *Hollywood Looks at its Audience* (Urbana, Ill., University of Illinois Press, 1950), p. xi; Edward L. Bernays, ed., *The Engineering of Consent* (Norman, Okla., University of Oklahoma Press, 1955); Nicholas Samstag, *Persuasion for Profit* (Norman, Okla., University of Oklahoma Press, 1957); Thomas Whiteside, *The Relaxed Sell* (New York, Oxford University Press, 1954).

[4] Good discussions of advertising's role and effects are available in William H. Whyte, *Is Anybody Listening?* (New York, Simon and Schuster, 1952); Elihu Katz and Paul F. Lazarsfeld, *Personal Influence* (New York, The Free Press of Glencoe, Inc., 1955); Neil Borden, *The Economic Effects of Advertising* (Chicago, Richard D. Irwin, 1942).

ceptable, respectable image of an individual, an organization, or a complex role-cluster (e.g., higher education, private enterprise, or the labor movement). Characteristically, public relations has the task of removing or countering previously "hostile" images or opinions by emphasizing the positive aspects of its sponsors and by avoiding controversial or inflammatory statements.[5] The classic instance of this process is the adept manner in which John D. Rockefeller, Sr. was "transformed" from a "robber baron" into a respectable—if eccentric —philanthropist by Ivy Lee, a publicist with shrewd appreciation of the nature of his audience. Since good will, reputation, etc. are highly subjective and difficult to measure—as compared with variations in sales of products—the impact of public relations cannot be easily evaluated. However, personnel and expenditures in this area have increased substantially since Rockefeller's "sanctification by public relations" and we must assume that those who pay the bills receive (or expect) positive results.

3. *Press agentry,* another form of urban mass communications, should be distinguished from advertising, and especially from public relations, with which it is sometimes identified. Essentially, the press agent is interested in *publicity*—literally "keeping before the public" —for his client. Unlike advertising, press agentry does not seek to influence specific purchases directly; instead, it tries to make its clients dramatically interesting by stressing their individuality and eccentricities, under the assumption that the unusual will be remembered longer and more vividly. If necessary, the press agent can "create" arresting distinctiveness by such expedients as a catchy "stage" name, manufactured biographical items, public brawls, and clients' appearances at elite ceremonial occasions.

4. *Political campaigns.* The organization and operation of mass communications in political campaigns shows some resemblance to both advertising and public relations. However, there are several important differences which merit some analysis. In the dominant type of political campaign, mass communications channels are employed for relatively short periods preceding an election, after which mass media return to their normal commercial and entertainment func-

---

[5] Bernays, *op. cit.,* Chaps. XIV–XVI; Leonard I. Pearlin and Morris Rosenberg, "Propaganda Techniques in Institutional Advertising," *Public Opinion Quarterly,* 16 (Spring, 1952), pp. 5–26; Leila A. Sussman, "The Personnel and Ideology of Public Relations," *ibid.,* 12 (Winter, 1948–49), pp. 697–708; S. H. Walker and Paul Sklar, *Business Finds its Voice* (New York; Harper and Brothers, 1938).

tions.[6] This concentration in time is accompanied by attempts to obtain coverage in all or most media. Campaigns for political office seek to create acceptable images, as in public relations, but media content stress the necessity of a definite act ("vote for. . . ."), unlike public relations. Similar to advertising, political campaigns offer their audiences the possibility of exchange, an urban revival of barter. For choosing a particular brand or candidate, the consumer or voter is promised a desirable effect in return. But while advertising proffers immediate, definite rewards ("brighter teeth") and often some guarantee ("your money back if you are not satisfied that. . . ."), political campaigns are notably and predictably vague about *their* proposals. We have a FTC and a FCC to prevent misrepresentation in advertising. Few people expect political campaigns to observe comparable limitations; indeed, a request for safeguards against the semitruths, fabrications, and broken promises of campaigners would hardly prompt more than a snicker.

Unlike other forms of mass communications, political campaigning is normally marked by controversy, argument, attack, and imputation of ulterior motives. But rarely are political opponents permitted to debate their differences in the same medium at the same time (the Nixon-Kennedy debates were quite exceptional). Consequently, political mass communications tend to be a confusing mixture of positive assertions and critical observations, with pressures for "equal time" to "set the record straight." Fortunately, political audiences do not expose themselves to the blatant inconsistencies of political appeals. Several recent studies show a tendency to select media content congenial to preconceived political choices.[7]

5. *Mass Entertainment.* A very substantial part of modern mass communications is in the form of amusement, entertainment, or recreation for its audiences or publics. Necessarily, the "entertainment" aspect of mass media is superimposed on a commercial advertising base. While the two go hand in hand, they should not be confused. Essentially, mass entertainment media present a contrast to the "serious"

[6] Studies of mass communications in political campaigns are rather rare, but are on the increase. See Stanley Kelley, *Professional Public Relations and Political Power* (Baltimore, Johns Hopkins University Press, 1956); Department of Marketing, Miami University, *The Influence of Television on the Election of 1952* (Oxford, Ohio, Oxford Associates, December, 1954); Paul F. Lazarsfeld *et al., The People's Choice* (New York, Columbia University Press, 1948).

[7] Lazarsfeld, *The People's Choice,* Chaps. XV, XVI; Bernard Berelson *et. al., Voting* (Chicago, University of Chicago Press, 1954), Chaps. VI, VII; Heinz Eulau, "Identification with Class and Political Role Behavior," *Public Opinion Quarterly,* 20 (Spring, 1956), pp. 515–529.

intent of advertising and public relations; they strive to create and maintain a *state of mind* desired (or thought to be desired) by their audiences. Mass media entertain by providing "intangible necessities" of urban life—humor in various forms (radio, films, television, newspaper comics), information and news, human interest, drama, sensation, and vicarious participation in sports.

6. *Public education.* A little reflection is sometimes necessary to remind us that public education (from kindergarten to graduate school) is an increasingly important locus of mass communications. In the urban setting, population size and concentration, diversity of backgrounds, and the complexity of urban culture inevitably remove education from the dominantly "personal" relationship of traditional education—as typified in the country school. The classic pedagogical formula of education—Horace Mann and a boy at opposite ends of a log—is attractive, but quite obsolete. Urban education, with its relatively large classes and variety of courses, depends on mass-produced textbooks, on films and filmstrips, and in the near future, on closed television circuits. These media supplement the role of the teacher, but may subtly place the teacher in a position of subservience to media content. One of the key problems in public education has always been the limits of desirable control over teachers by school boards and organized interests in the community—in selection of textbooks, for example. The increasing use of mass media, which are both expensive and centralized, tends to simplify and impersonalize formal education, to convert the teacher into a mediator between standardized stimuli and students. The "teacher as opinion leader," as disseminator of the content and values in selected mass media, has already been identified.[8] We can only guess at the prevalence of this type.

It should be obvious that public education—particularly with the addition of modern mass media—constitutes a special system of mass influence. Formal education transmits basic cultural skills, but also values, attitudes, and aspirations. Sociologists generally agree that public schools (explicitly or implicitly) sustain or develop *middle class values.*[9] Since urban regions take their character from the middle status categories, public education performs an essential service in

[8] David Riesman, *The Lonely Crowd* (Garden City, N.Y., Doubleday and Company, 1953), p. 83.

[9] See particularly Robert J. Havighurst and Hilda Taba, *Adolescent Character and Personality* (New York, John Wiley and Sons, 1948); A. B. Hollingshead, *Elmtown's Youth* (New York, John Wiley and Sons, 1949); W. Lloyd Warner et al., *Who Shall Be Educated?* (New York, Harper and Brothers, 1944).

reaching the largest number of children. Whatever the deficiencies of public education, it cannot be even temporarily replaced by private education. Those who would close public schools to preserve racial segregation are primarily "rural" in character; they believe middle class values can be properly inculcated by small, almost personal private educational groups. The facts, however distasteful, are otherwise.

Mass communications in modern urban regions operate as relatively private (*i.e.,* not controlled by governmental agencies) systems. Their importance—the effects they produce, the problems they create—depends on the nature of the urban community and the evolving structure of the mass communications sphere. The latter is especially pertinent at this point because it has developed an intricate network of pre-existing and newly created organizations and interaction chains which provide clues to the special position of modern mass communications in urban behavior.

The accompanying diagram is a simplified outline of the major components in mass communications processes. This schematized summary explicitly disregards variations found in specific forms and media of communications. Basically, mass communications is conceived here as organized in terms of *three levels* and *seven substructures* or *role-clusters*. In general, the key to the entire process— in terms of kinds and degree of influence (not in *technical* processes) —is the *intermediary level,* which may be relatively dependent or independent of the policy level, and which is differentially developed in specific communities and in specific forms and media of communication.

1. Media organizations

Normally, privately owned corporations apply technological developments in communications for business purposes. Theoretically, these groups merely furnish facilities for access to audiences and publics. However, a purely objective attitude toward the influence process is not maintained by all media organizations—particularly among the printed media (newspapers, magazines, books). For example, definite political and economic viewpoints may be found in such media as *U. S. News and World Report, The Reporter,* the *New Republic,* the Chicago *Tribune,* and the *Reader's Digest.* With the in-

FIGURE 11
Basic Structure of Urban Mass Communication Systems

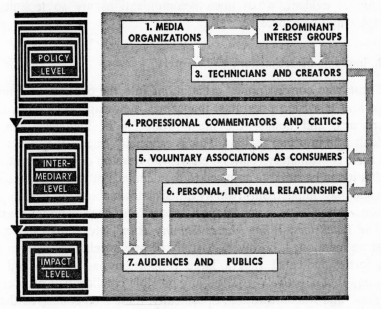

creasing trend toward concentration of media ownership (newspaper chains, interlocking ownership of newspapers, radio, and television), it is likely that the commercial objective will be supplemented by more or less conscious attempts to inspire opinions congenial to those of media owners.

2. Dominant interest groups

As suggested in the preceding paragraph, influence patterns may be determined to some extent by media organizations. More often, dominant interest groups (industry, labor, agriculture, political parties) in the nation or in specific urban regions tend to control media content by (*a*) directly buying time or space in mass media—as advertisers or sponsors; or (*b*) indirectly influencing media owners to favor or reject given types of media content (*e.g.*, salacious stories, crime as adventure, etc.). The latter type of control is covert and informal, and therefore difficult to investigate. But, with such exceptions as "personal journalism" (Harry Golden, for example), media organizations depend on interest groups of some kind for financial support. It is no secret that, in maintaining such support, it often becomes desirable to *anticipate* (rather than follow) the basic orientation of dominant interests. The day of the independent crusader, beholden to no one, is no longer evident, when mass communications are so technically complex and so expensive.

3. Implements: technicians and creators

Those who convert policy orientations into the continuous flow of radio and television programs, magazines, newspapers, lectures, billboard ads, and books—the mass producers of influence—play a difficult role in urban regions. This is especially true of the "creators" and their coordinators (editors, etc.), who develop or direct creativity so that it can be suitably adjusted to the demands of mass communication and mass impact. Surprisingly little is known about this category of persons—despite their importance—apart from such fictional sources as *The Hucksters, What Makes Sammy Run?*, etc. Two exceptions must be mentioned, however. A study of public relations men in the late forties indicated that a large proportion had internalized an ideology that effectively resolved any possible conflicts between "creativeness" and standardization. Specifically, these men conceived themselves as "crusaders" in achieving good will for their clients (usually large business organizations). Consequently, their own skills were regarded as subordinate to the need for persistently functioning channels of mass communication.[10] By contrast, as Spectorsky has delightfully reported on the world of the exurbanites, many writers, illustrators, and advertising men feel uncomfortably cramped by the insatiable demands of media organizations and their sponsors. The exurbanites aspire to artistic creations of a high but unmarketable quality, but they cannot or will not escape from the "treadmill," the "rat race," of wider and wider mass communications.[11]

4. Professional commentators, reviewers, and critics

The conscience or "watchdog" of mass media reposes in the activities of a small grouping of specialized observers—radio and television film critics, book reviewers, and unofficial censors. Because of the staggering output of modern mass media, some form of evaluative sieve, some selector, is needed by the urbanite who tries to be

[10] Sussman, *loc. cit.*
[11] A. C. Spectorsky, *The Exurbanites* (Philadelphia, J. B. Lippincott, 1955).

both up-to-date and reasonably sane. This need is the usual justification for the media critics and reviewers. However, it must be noted that critics do not function in the same manner in all mass media, nor do they seem to exercise the same degree of influence on consumers of the various media. For example, it is doubtful that either newspapers or magazines are evaluated by their readers with the assistance of professional critics, as is often the case in selecting movies, current books, and perhaps television programs. We can only guess at the relative success of specific reviewers in promoting or panning books, shows, and programs.

In general, the role of the critic-reviewer in the mass communications process has been limited to a rather small portion of media consumers, most of whom apply standards of discrimination and careful screening of the available mass media. To this special public, the judgments of a Walter Kerr on drama, a John Crosby on television, a Bosley Crowther on films, and a Clifton Fadiman on books have carried considerable weight. For other urbanites with different or vaguer standards, the critic-reviewer is perhaps less necessary, or merely less apparent. For example, the largest of the book clubs dispense several million books each month to their members. Technically, book selections are in the form of "recommendations" which can be rejected. Actually, book clubs thrive only on the acquiescence of their members. Do book clubs serve primarily as *evaluators* of current books, or as *distributors?* Are decisions about club choices dictated by intrinsic qualities of the books or by shrewd guesses as to what club members will accept?

Two current trends suggest that the critic-reviewer role is being usurped or by-passed by organizations which ordinarily function on the *policy level* in mass communications. Something which has long been suspected in the popular record-radio complex has finally been publicly exposed: the widespread but covert practice among record manufacturers of paying "disk jockeys" to play and otherwise "promote" their products—"payola." Apart from the moral aspect, this reflects an attempt to "streamline" the mass communications system by dispensing with an independent critical phase. In fact, there is some evidence that some record companies have also fabricated to their own satisfaction lists of popularity and sales of current records, and then furnished such lists to disk jockeys as the results of "objective" surveys. To the extent that such practices exist, portions of the record-buying public are inadequately equipped to maintain personal independence of a mass medium.

If the situation in mass recordings seems trivial or peripheral, a related trend in urban mass communications merits close attention. A recent report on history textbooks used in public school systems found that publishers and text writers have produced texts in American history that clearly refuse to present *interpretations* of events or periods. Instead, the texts are written in such a way that "issues are artificially balanced in order to please partisans on every side of each controversy." The result is a "bland uniformity" which leaves little effective choice among competing texts by responsible school officials and teachers.[12] Of course, it is difficult to predict how texts might be selected if a genuine variety were available. But this situation likewise demonstrates that the critic-reviewer role has been implicitly constricted in segments of public education.

5. Voluntary associations as intermediaries

In some instances, the urbanite either *receives* mass communications through affiliation with one or more specialized associations or *discusses* and *evaluates* mass communications (independently received) by participating in such associations. For example, professional people often receive technical and other periodicals through membership in professional organizations. Some of these periodicals are published by the organizations themselves; others are not. Voluntary associations are perhaps more significant as forums for digesting, debating, and interpreting specific items from the mass media. Various types of "fan clubs," civic groups such as the League of Women Voters, business and fraternal groups, and library or musical clubs often function in this manner. But this substructure in mass communications is primarily available in segments of the urban middle classes.

6. Informal contacts and personal influence

The myth of the urbanite as a "mass" cruelly exposed to the direct impact of impersonal mass communications still lingers in modern folklore, perhaps because it is to a very limited extent true. For most residents of the urban region, however, personal and informal

[12] Fred M. Hechinger, "Education in Review," *The New York Times,* February 14, 1960.

contacts or pressures serve as intermediaries or supplements to media content.[13] According to several studies, urban children show a marked tendency to watch television or attend movies with family members or friends.[14] Comic books seem to be read in periods of social seclusion. However, the exchange and discussion of comic books among neighborhood youngsters must constitute a very effective form of personal influence in selecting and evaluating this medium.

Turning to the adult setting, there is a growing fund of studies that suggest that personal influence often plays a decisive role in affecting reactions to mass media. Lazarsfeld and his associates have shown that family and friends are specially important in determining voting behavior of undecided or semiapathetic persons during a political campaign. Indeed, Lazarsfeld concludes that mass media in elections merely activate dormant political interests; that socioeconomic factors and personal influences largely explain consistency and change in urban voting. On the other hand, Janowitz found that primary group pressures on voters generally reinforced the mass media in producing higher levels of voting. Furthermore, conflicting primary group pressures served to *reduce* voting in social categories affected in this manner.[15]

But since mass media are more pervasive in economic contexts, how do primary and informal pressures operate in the related processes of merchandising and advertising? The few investigations of this problem involve urbanites in *status-conscious, middle class areas*. In this segment of the population, according to several independent surveys, specific families informally function as "opinion leaders" or "pace setters" for a given circle of acquaintances. Despite the wide

[13] Katz and Lazarsfeld, *op. cit.*, Part II, Chaps. X, XI, XIII, XIV; Joseph T. Klapper, *The Effects of Mass Communication* (New York, The Free Press of Glencoe, 1960) Chaps. IV, V; Robert K. Merton, "Patterns of Influence: A Study of a Local Community," in Lazarsfeld and Stanton, *op. cit.*, pp. 180–219; E. Jackson Baur, "Public Opinion and the Primary Group," *American Sociological Review*, 25 (April, 1960), pp. 208–219.

[14] Matilda W. Riley and John W. Riley, Jr., "A Sociological Approach to Communications Research," *Public Opinion Quarterly*, 15 (Fall, 1951), pp. 445–460; Eleanor E. Maccoby, "Television: Its Impact on School Children," *ibid.*, pp. 421–444; Eliot Friedson, "The Relation of the Social Situation of Contact to the Media in Mass Communication," *ibid.*, 17 (Summer, 1953), pp. 230–238; Robert V. Hamilton and Richard H. Lawless, "Television Within the Social Matrix," *ibid.*, 20 (Summer, 1956), pp. 394–403.

[15] Lazarsfeld, *The People's Choice*, pp. 74–82; Morris Janowitz and Dwaine Marvick, *Competitive Pressure and Democratic Consent* (Ann Arbor, Mich., Institute of Public Administration, University of Michigan, 1956), pp. 92–94.

TABLE 66

Effects of Primary Group Pressures on the Voting Behavior of Different Categories of Voters

PARTISAN PREDISPOSITION & PRIMARY GROUP PRESSURES	Voting Behavior, 1948–52		
	Pro-Republican vote	Pro-Democratic vote	Persistent Non-voters
Republican partisans under concerted pro-Ike primary group pressures	95.4	2.6	2.0
Non-Republican partisans under concerted pro-Ike primary group pressures	83.6	9.6	6.8
Republican partisans under conflicting primary group pressures	68.8	11.0	20.2
Uncommitted electors under conflicting primary group pressures	36.2	27.1	36.7
Democratic partisans under conflicting primary group pressures	27.2	50.0	22.8
Non-Democratic partisans under concerted pro-Stevenson primary group pressures	12.8	72.3	14.9
Democratic partisans under concerted pro-Stevenson primary group pressures	6.9	80.1	13.0

SOURCE: Janowitz and Marvick, *op. cit.*, p. 94.

and expensive coverage provided by newspapers, radio, and television advertising, Whyte found that such major appliances as home freezers, hi-fi equipment, and air conditioners were concentrated in a few blocks in Philadelphia. Furthermore, few of these purchasers were influenced by salesmen or advertisements. The key to consumer decisions was "word-of-mouth networks," which operate by local standards of appropriate possessions.[16] This principle is sometimes applied by shrewd salesmen (*e.g.*, in selling encyclopedias). But a particularly successful instance was the sales campaign of the gas company in New

[16] William H. Whyte, Jr., *The Organization Man* (Garden City, N.Y., Doubleday and Company, 1956), Chap. XXIV.

York in increasing gas consumption among its customers. A concentrated and highly attractive promotional effort sought out informally influential families who were persuaded to buy gas appliances of various kinds. The informal networks were apparently effective, since gas consumption in the test areas rose appreciably.[17]

Meaning and Effects of Mass Communications

A good deal of controversy in recent years centers on the meaning and effects of mass communications. Manipulators of mass media vigorously interpret their function as agents of progress, civilization, and practical democracy. On the other hand, intellectuals of many stripes condemn mass communications for their poor taste, the apparent premium placed on nonrationality, and the development of drab uniformities of experience. These claims and counterclaims are difficult to evaluate. It may well be that too much attention to the *content* of mass media and to their *intended effects* tends to obscure the *unintended* but extremely important functions of mass media for the vast urban audiences and publics.

A few suggestive studies cast considerable doubt on the efficiency of mass media as molders of opinions and tastes.[18] Paradoxically, urbanites often seem to be more interested in the medium than its content. Thus, political campaigns in newspapers, radio, and television excite public attention, but influence few votes. Sponsors of television programs are beginning to recognize the disconcerting fact that viewers of the most popular shows are often oblivious to the commercials, and cannot identify the product or brand. The only conclusion to be drawn from these items is that urban publics are somehow converting mass communications for their own conscious or unconscious purposes.

It should not be surprising that, from the consumers' standpoint, mass communications are primarily *instruments of leisure,* rather than sober, serious problems for careful resolution. Apparently, urbanites take the simple viewpoint that experiences bearing the label of "leisure" should be treated accordingly. But if mass communications are not clearly instruments of persuasion—as their sponsors hope—what are some of the specific "leisure" functions served by the mass media?

[17] *The New York Times,* September 25, 1955.

[18] See in particular Whyte, *Is Anybody Listening?;* Lazarsfeld, *The People's Choice;* Klapper, *op. cit.;* Robert Alden, "Advertising: Suckers' Birthrate Declines," *The New York Times,* February 21, 1960. A contrary view is taken by Packard, *op. cit.*

Though there are some variations by status level, the following themes seem to recur:

1. Information

With much of his time still committed to the routines of work, voluntary groups, and informal contacts, the urbanite depends on the mass media for easily accessible information on a variety of topics or interests (news, sports, commercial recreation, weather, etc.). The "educational" role of the newspaper and magazine is particularly important; consequently, many urbanites rely on regular deliveries or subscriptions to replace outmoded facts with newer ones.[19] Note that in most instances this information is not world-shaking or related to one's occupation. It is more often superficial, transitory, even frivolous.

2. Desire for meaningful, minor changes

Fads, fashions, vogues, and crazes are part of the acquired needs of urbanites, though many decry the irrationalities of particular fashions. Apparently, both adolescents and adults participate in an informal *status game* [20] (sometimes reaching serious proportions) which provides excitement, anxiety, and some escape from sober responsibilities. The essence of fashion is the *anticipation of change* without much predictability of the *content* of change.[21] Fashions therefore provide the illusion of "movement" and an accompanying excitement. Most fashion changes are comparatively gradual, perhaps because a greater number of small changes is more congenial to urbanites than a small number of drastic changes.

In any case, the attractive superficiality of fashion is a substantial segment of urban leisure and recreation—in clothing, appliances, and vacations. Perhaps a major service of mass communications is the opportunity to obtain quick and extensive coverage of minor and major variations in fashion. This is not only true of the "fashion" magazines (*e.g., Vogue, Harper's Bazaar, Mademoiselle*) but of

[19] Berelson, "What 'Missing the Newspaper' Means," *loc. cit.*

[20] The "status game" is discussed by C. Wright Mills, *White Collar* (New York, Oxford University Press, 1953), Chap. XI; and by Paul F. Lazarsfeld and Robert K. Merton, "Mass Communication, Popular Taste, and Organized Social Action," in Wilbur Schramm, ed., *Mass Communications, 1949* (Urbana, Ill., University of Illinois Press, 1949), pp. 459–480.

[21] A. L. Kroeber and Jane Richardson, "Three Centuries of Women's Dress Fashions: A Quantitative Analysis," *Anthropological Records,* 5 (1940).

newspapers and magazines generally. Advertisements are, over time, "newsworthy" in showing changes in style while apparently offering a specific branded article. Incidentally, the primary mass media of "fashion" are inevitably the *written,* rather than the *visual* or *aural* type, because the former give more time for leisurely appreciation and study.

3. Contact with wider ranges of experience

Mass media content is, by the nature of its creation and dissemination, largely nonlocal or concerned with activities and events outside the normal routine. While urbanites show some interest in purely local items as presented in newspapers and on television (*e.g.,* the local weather report), they seem to prefer mass communications that transcend the immediate and the personal. Often this preference is called "escapism," but such a label assumes special frustrations and dissatisfactions. Whether or not the label is justified, the essential specialization and segregation of urban living do present limitations in experience which belie the insistent urban values of variety, expanded scope, and "cosmopolitanism."

The role of the mass media as intermediary to the unusual or the dramatic has been directly suggested in studies of the attractiveness of daytime "soap operas" to housewives in recent years.[22] Indeed, the great popularity in urban regions of news magazines and "picture" magazines can be understood in this way. In the advertising field, special use is made of inaccessible but attractive personages and places—such as the Tetley Tea Taster, the testimonials of society matrons and film stars, the Rolls Royce in whiskey ads—and also of the bizarre, exotic and unusual—as in ads for Maidenform Bras and Hathaway Shirts. Following this clue, it is not surprising that the most popular programs on television are the "Westerns," the crime and "private eye" category, and the panel show featuring assorted celebrities.

4. Attractive advocacy of middle class values

Despite constant criticism of its uniformity, lapses from good taste, and so on, mass communications as a whole are clearly and openly approved by urbanites. Within each medium, however, there are sub-

[22] W. Lloyd Warner and William Henry, "The Radio Daytime Serial: A Symbolic Analysis," *Genetic Psychology Monographs,* 37 (1948), pp. 7–69.

stantial differences in appeal to existing status levels (*e.g.,* readers of *Harper's* are not likely to read *True Story,* and vice versa). Yet this general acceptance persists, and it probably rests not only on the "themes" or functions previously discussed, but on the implicit or explicit ways in which mass media promote and justify the basic values of middle status groups,[23] and those seeking to simulate those values. Only a few studies have thus far dealt with this aspect of mass communications, but the facts are so familiar that they need only be noted at this point.

Without much exception, the mass media emphasize optimism, "adjustment" and a basic acceptance of modern society. There is an underlying philosophy, expressed in both serious and humorous form, that modern social problems are difficult, but amenable to treatment through education, money, research, and the "good sense of most people." While social criticism is by no means absent from mass media, it tends to be scattered, aimed at specific persons or specialized organizations rather than major institutions, and therefore it tends to be superficial and unexciting to audiences and publics. "Crusades," "campaigns," and "exposés" in newspapers and magazines often serve a recreational purpose rather than stimulate desire for fundamental social or cultural change.

Advertising and mass fiction (found in most media) retain their appeal for urbanites as a constant reminder of the need for (and techniques of) personal striving for "success," mobility, and progress. Indeed, the mass media have essentially converted the *search for status* from a hit-or-miss, amateur interlude to a strategic avocation.[24] It is not too extreme to suggest that modern mass communications constitute a wondrous education for middle-classness, from the inspirations of a Norman Vincent Peale and a Dale Carnegie, to the innumerable tips from advertisers.

Intimately related to the preceding is the widespread concern with such highly regarded middle class values as possession, size, speed— in short, the stress on *quantity.* As delineated in the mass media, these values form a *morality of status.* At the same time, these values are easily measurable, thus providing for the urbanite a continuing picture

[23] This is persuasively presented in John W. Bennett and Melvin M. Tumin, *Social Life* (New York, Alfred A. Knopf, 1948), Chap. XXXI.

[24] Patricke Johns-Heine and Hans H. Gerth, "Values in Mass Periodical Fiction, 1921–1940," *Public Opinion Quarterly,* 13 (Spring, 1949), pp. 105–116; Leo Lowenthal, "Biographies in Popular Magazines," in William Petersen, ed., *American Social Patterns* (Garden City, N.Y., Doubleday and Company, 1956), pp. 63–117.

of his relative status. Part of the fascination of the mass media probably lies in their use as a status "measuring rod."

5. Content for personal relationships

It has sometimes been suggested that the urbanite uses mass communications as a substitute for personal contacts, that mass media serve to limit the desire for social participation. This is probably true of a number of deviant personalities or confirmed isolates. But the available evidence gives little support to this notion among urbanites in general. With the possible exception of television,[25] exposure to mass media does not seem to replace personal contacts. Indeed, the social categories most involved in social interaction (suburbanites, middle class families, and blue collar families)—see Chapter 8—make considerable use of the mass media.

Perhaps this connection rests on the fact that in the urban milieu informal interaction largely depends on items and events beyond the direct experience of the urbanite. Most conversations would sputter into a merited silence if they dealt only with one's aches and pains, what one did recently, and the state of one's children. Instead, social interaction abounds in matters of *indirect* or *vicarious* experience— world news, professional sports, weather reports, and notable or notorious events in favorite media. The urbanite, in effect, must keep abreast of the mass media in order to participate on an equal basis in informal conversation with relatives, friends, and acquaintances.

Mass communications, it is alleged, have combined with mass leisure to produce mass culture, an urban "lowest common denominator" of attitudes and values. If mass culture refers to uniformities of values in media content, this interpretation has some merit.[26] But there is little evidence that mass media have created herd-like uniformities in specific *responses* to media content. Exposure does not insure either *attention* or *acceptance*.[27] In this relatively new sphere of urban

[25] Bennett and Tumin, *op. cit.*, pp. 635–640; Hamilton and Lawless, *loc. cit.;* Frank L. Sweetser, "Home Television and Behavior: Some Tentative Conclusions," *Public Opinion Quarterly*, 19 (Spring, 1955), pp. 79–84.

[26] Bennett and Tumin, *op. cit.*, pp. 609–618; Bernard Rosenberg and David M. White, eds., *Mass Culture* (New York, The Free Press of Glencoe, 1957).

[27] See the interesting discussions of this issue by Herbert Hyman and Paul Sheatsley, "Some Reasons Why Information Campaigns Fail," *Public Opinion Quarterly*, 11 (Fall, 1947), pp. 412–423; Whyte, *Is Anybody Listening?*, Chap. II.

organization, we can instead suggest a subtle process of interactions between urban populations and the various media. To the manipulator of mass media, the process is predominantly "persuasive." To the various publics, mass media present an interesting challenge, combining unequal parts of information and opinion, of sincerity and sensation. The interplay between persuaders and public resembles a semiserious game in which one set of participants "play to win" and the other "plays for kicks." Out of this bizarre form of contact and interchange a new urban ethic has developed—the *ethic* of *ambiguity*.

From the standpoint of both public and mass communicator, the ethic of ambiguity is an ethic of compromise, but each follows its own version of this theme. To the mass communicator, mass media are a shifting amalgam of fact, inference, *non sequitur,* sensation, and special ideology. The "game" consists of devising mixtures that have audience appeal; the new ethic does not demand total fidelity to fact nor unrestricted falsehood.

The audience or public, on the other hand, practices a reciprocal *consumer* ethic of ambiguity and ambivalence. As the "game" is played, resistance and gullibility, the search for fact and the attraction of fantasy, reason, logic, and faith are major ingredients in audience response to media content. To the urbanite, the challenge lies in exposure to the mixed content of mass communication and in selecting personally satisfying segments of fact and fantasy that can be assimilated without destroying the leisure aspect or suggesting immaturity. The peculiar fascination of the advertisement is the delightful danger of being "persuaded" even if one "knows better."

An ethic of ambiguity is understandable, though it certainly clashes with the absolutes of traditional morality and the unswerving guidance of the "Protestant Ethic." For the urbanite, confronted by variety, change, and the probability of soon being either wrong or out of fashion, the ethic of ambiguity is a form of defense against the basic heterogeneity and dynamism of the urban region. Mass communications—properly or improperly defined as an adjunct of leisure—may be interpreted therefore as an *acceptable* locus of ambiguities, as a hedge against change.

But the "game of mass communications" is not always exciting, since creativity is unequal to the demand of repetitive communication. One tires of a favorite program, comic strip, magazine, etc. The ethic of ambiguity is only partly satisfying to urbanites, who are engaged in a search for meaning, order, consistency. In this quest, it seems, attention is shifting from media content to the formal characteristics of mass media (regularity, wide coverage, etc.). The evolving result is a reinterpretation of leisure as "routine," to be planned and organized, rather than a spontaneous activity. It is too early to evaluate the significance of this "routinization of leisure" for urban regional organization. However, if the meaning of leisure becomes indistinguishable from that of work and responsibility (also routinized), and mass communications tend to be vehicles of such a process, the role of urban regions as creative centers may be transformed into that of supertranquilizer. While this interpretation is necessarily tentative, it does suggest that an important clue to urbanism and its future lies in the implicit applications of mass media by urban audiences and in the relation of these new usages to urban organization.

SELECTED REFERENCES

JACOBS, Norman, ed., *Culture for the Millions* (Princeton, D. Van Nostrand Company, 1961).

KATZ, Elihu and LAZARSFELD, Paul F., *Personal Influence* (New York, The Free Press of Glencoe, 1955).

KLAPPER, Joseph T., *The Effects of Mass Communication* (New York, The Free Press of Glencoe, 1960).

LARRABEE, Eric and MEYERSOHN, Rolf, eds., *Mass Leisure* (New York, The Free Press of Glencoe, 1959).

ROSENBERG, Bernard and WHITE, David M., eds., *Mass Culture* (New York, The Free Press of Glencoe, 1957).

SCHRAMM, Wilbur, ed., *The Process and Effects of Mass Communications* (Urban, Ill., University of Illinois Press, 1954).

———, *Mass Communications,* 2nd ed. (Urbana, Ill., University of Illinois Press, 1960).

CHAPTER 14

The Urban Regional System:
A Changing Equilibrium

To MANY PEOPLE from all sorts of occupations and ways of life, the modern urban community seems like a disordered giant, a fascinating but cancerous growth. They are understandably bewildered by its size, by its impetus, its multifaceted interests and forms, and by the numerous problems that daily accompany its functioning. From the viewpoint of the sociologist, however, the primary fact about the urban community is that it is a complex human phenomenon, a human invention in process. Consequently, it must possess some underlying patterns or regularities, however unintended, which require considerable probing in order to fashion a realistic picture of uniquely "urban" order. We may call this set of patterns an evolving system, a persistently imperfect unity, or perhaps a changing sociocultural equilibrium. All refer to the same theme: subtle, dynamic order.

Many sociologists, social philosophers, and other students of urban life have searched for adequate ways of expressing the basic structure of urban systems. As a result, the annals of urban sociology contain a number of provocative but often competing theories of urban organization. We can only attempt to outline a sample of this diversity, in the hope that this will provide useful clues to a modern conception of urban regions as systems of fact and of analysis.

Cultural and Institutional Approaches

Several theories seem to place great emphasis on the major institutions as coordinators of urban systems, particularly in earlier urban waves. Max Weber gave special prominence to *military organization* and its political and economic consequences in classical cities. In the medieval and early modern cities of Europe, however, he noted a decisive shift to the economic focus of commerce and the dominant influence of merchant associations.[1] A similar view has been meticulously detailed by the great Belgian historian, Henri Pirenne.[2] In a most convincing fashion, Fustel de Coulanges interpreted the history of the ancient city as a process fundamentally marked by changes in urban *religion*. The development of cities was first accompanied by community religions, in place of family and tribal deities. With the rise of class conflicts and internal urban revolutions, religion itself receded as an instrument of order. Henceforth, secular government became dominant, guided by varying conceptions of the "public interest."[3]

Still another institutional theory has been available in the works of Oswald Spengler, the poet-philosopher of a troubled urbanism. To Spengler, the city is a late phase in the cyclical workings of world history—the high point of complexity before the inevitable decline to simpler communities based on blood and tradition. The city, in Spengler's view, is organized around the twin structures of a money economy and an expansive science, which together breed democracy and, eventually, disorganization.[4]

Perhaps the most radical and challenging conception of the city, one that sharply diverges from that of Spengler, is the notion of urbanism as a creator of *concentrated institutional functioning,* as a "mobilization, mixture, and magnification" of previous institutions toward a new, "purposive social complexity." In short, according to Mumford, the essence of the city lies in continuous devising of social arrangements for human interaction and spiritual communion. Thus, in a modern translation of the ideas of Fustel de Coulanges and

[1] Max Weber, *General Economic History* (New York, The Free Press of Glencoe, 1950), pp. 316–324, 333–354.

[2] Henri Pirenne, *Medieval Cities* (Princeton, Princeton University Press, 1925), Chap. IV.

[3] Fustel de Coulanges, *The Ancient City,* 10th ed. (Boston, Lee and Shepard, 1900), pp. 167–170, 423–429.

[4] Oswald Spengler, *The Decline of the West* (New York, Alfred A. Knopf, 1937), 2 vols. *Cf.* the discussion in Georg Simmel, *Philosophie des Geldes* (Leipzig, Duncker und Humblot, 1900) and his "The Metropolis and Mental Life," in *The Sociology of Georg Simmel,* Kurt H. Wolff, ed. (New York, The Free Press of Glencoe, 1950), pp. 409–424.

Durkheim, Mumford interprets the city as an expansive religion transcending the realms of economy, kinship, and politics.[5]

Functional Approaches

Unlike institutional explanations of urban structure, the functional approach emphasizes the city as a continual arena of division of labor and specialization on the one hand, and imperfect coordination and degrees of interdependence on the other. Robert Park regarded the city as primarily reflecting competition for space and the consequent development of numerous specialized social types (such as the hobo, the rooming-house resident, the delinquent, and the saleslady). These types inevitably establish *symbiotic relations* with one another, *i.e.,* they come to have indirect dependence on one another in an impersonal, unplanned manner. But Park recognized that these relations were insufficient; therefore, he placed great emphasis on *mass communications* (the newspaper in particular) as a source of superimposed integration.[6]

Students of Park worked out a somewhat modified and yet more detailed functional theory of urban structure. McKenzie, and more recently Bogue,[7] have envisaged the urban region as a *network of economic dominance and sub-dominance;* each urban area, zone, or sector is shown to be bound by one or more economic ties to the central city or the central business district. Even the distribution of population in urban regions demonstrates the effects of economic specialization and interdependence. Thus, in effect, McKenzie and Bogue have interpreted the urban system as an evolving unity whose functioning is mediated by the economic institution through manufacturing, wholesale, and retail activities.

The Verdict is Disorganization

Some students and critics of modern urbanism, on the other hand, are unable to detect a basic urban order. They point to the loss of its

[5] Lewis Mumford, *The Culture of Cities* (New York, Harcourt, Brace and World, 1938), p. 6; and his *The City in History* (New York, Harcourt, Brace and World, 1961), pp. 9–10, 31, 35, 95.

[6] Robert E. Park, *Society* (New York, The Free Press of Glencoe, 1955), Part II.

[7] R. D. McKenzie, *The Metropolitan Community* (New York, McGraw-Hill, 1933); Don J. Bogue, *The Structure of the Metropolitan Community* (Ann Arbor, Mich., Rackham School of Graduate Studies, University of Michigan, 1949).

clear-cut institutional and ecological structure, which was dominant a century or more ago, and they also assert that the city is decaying internally, as evidenced by the urbanite's increasing withdrawal to the suburbs and beyond. Furthermore, Martindale suggests that, unlike past periods of urban glory, the modern city is no longer largely autonomous, or dominant over a region of dependent communities in its hinterland. Instead, he notes a trend toward national (and state) intervention in urban affairs and problems. Somewhat glumly, Martindale offers the prediction: "The age of the city seems to be at an end." [8]

URBANISM, TRANSITION, AND ORGANIC SOLIDARITY

There is some truth in all these explanations and interpretations. But most of these theories contain an implicit picture of some *past* urban order, or of some *desired* order. The basic fact about modern urbanism is its *transitional* nature, its irregular movement toward a newer, more complex structure.[9] In this process, institutions change at varying paces, and inconsistencies crop up with noticeable frequency. Yet, as T. H. Marshall has wisely observed, "human society can make a square meal out of a stew of paradox without getting indigestion—at least for quite a long time." [10] Perhaps we can attempt an interpretation of the "urban stew" by applying two useful conceptions. The first involves the idea of *organic solidarity;* the second emphasizes the importance of unintended, unplanned structures (*latent* structures and consequences) in sustaining this organic solidarity in the urban region.

The nature of organic solidarity in community and society was boldly outlined by the great French sociologist, Emile Durkheim, almost seventy years ago. It is astonishing that this venerable and much cited conception remains so appropriate in clarifying the nature of modern urban regions. Essentially, organic solidarity refers to a complex, subtle type of social organization marked by extensive division of labor and sociocultural specialization, and a set of indirect but

[8] Don Martindale, "Preface," in Max Weber, *The City,* trans. by Don Martindale and Gertrud Neuwirth (New York, The Free Press of Glencoe, 1958), p. 62.

[9] Howard W. Odum, *Understanding Society* (New York, Macmillan, 1947), Chaps. XII, XX, XXIX; Alvin Boskoff, "Social Indecision: A Dysfunctional Focus of Transitional Society," *Social Forces,* 37 (May, 1959), pp. 305–311.

[10] T. H. Marshall, *Citizenship and Social Class* (Cambridge, at the University Press, 1950), p. 84.

effective forms of interdependence. In Durkheim's view, simpler communities are organized around *similarities* in physical type, basic values, and occupations. The problem of social order is comparatively slight, because of a very rudimentary specialization. Consequently, he named this "mechanical solidarity." By contrast, organic solidarity grows out of, and is a necessity in, larger, denser communities, which are more clearly marked by cultural and demographic *differences.*[11]

In applying Durkheim's conception to modern urban regions, several cautions should be noted. First, we must consider organic solidarity as a tentative hypothesis about urban organization. The complexities of urban regions, which we have discussed in Chapters 5–7 and 9–13, are perhaps too advanced to be adequately captured in any unitary conception. Second, organic solidarity refers to a type or degree of social order or regularity, not to necessarily high degrees of *efficiency.* For example, bureaucratic organizations in modern society constitute excellent illustrations of organic solidarity on a limited scale. Yet there is an accumulating fund of evidence that bureaucracies require considerable informal readjustments to satisfy the needs for which they were originally created.[12] Third, by its very nature, organic solidarity does not refer to community of feeling and impulse, as is normally implied in such terms as solidarity, cohesiveness, morale, *esprit de corps,* etc. On the contrary, the bonds that sustain organic solidarity are not primarily emotional or derived from personal contact, but those that are characteristically indirect and nonaffectual.

Typically, organic solidarity in urban regions is not fixed or directly measurable; it is instead a continuous process of growth, complexity, and temporary forms of coordination. Therefore, only the *historical development* of cities (and their regions) provides significant clues to this basic process.[13] Indeed, studies of urban history, along with several theoretical hints from Durkheim enable us to trace with some clarity the *process* by which organic solidarity is created.

[11] Emile Durkheim, *The Division of Labor in Society,* trans. by George Simpson (New York, The Free Press of Glencoe, 1947), Chaps. II, III.

[12] Only a few studies can be cited, notably Peter M. Blau, *The Dynamics of Bureaucracy* (Chicago, University of Chicago Press, 1955); Philip Selznick, *TVA and the Grass Roots* (Berkeley, Calif., University of California Press, 1949); Roy G. Francis and Robert C. Stone, *Service and Procedure in Bureaucracy* (Minneapolis, University of Minnesota Press, 1956).

[13] Two of the best illustrations of this process are provided by Carl Bridenbaugh, *Cities in the Wilderness* (New York, Ronald Press, 1938); and Richard C. Wade, *The Urban Frontier* (Cambridge, Mass., Harvard University Press, 1959).

1. Modern urban regions (*i.e.,* those dating from the eighteenth century) arise within a *pre-existent social and cultural order*—capitalism, scientific technology, forms of political democracy, etc. The individuals and groups that form the first stages of urban organization are inevitably carriers of prevailing morals, aspirations, techniques, and social forms.

2. As urban regions are established, they, of course, may be considered specialized parts of the larger society. But fledgling cities typically develop *internal* specialization, which becomes progressively more complex as population, area, and acquired needs expand. The urban division of labor proceeds along several interconnected lines, in pursuit of originally common ideals, such as efficiency, profit, privacy, etc. Most visible is specialization in production and distribution of goods and services—*occupational specialization*. This is necessarily accompanied by patterned differentiation of urban *land uses,* first for economic, then for social and economic purposes. Soon—as Bridenbaugh has shown for cities in the colonial period—specialization advances in the form of community responsibility for a group of *protective services*—police, water supply, fire protection, waste disposal. Gradually, as normal processes of economic development and urbanward migration operate, the city and its region increasingly reflect noticeable segregation by social status, ethnic background, race, and religion. As a consequence, the ultimate in urban specialization is the multiplication of cultural islands, each with its own touch of uniqueness in aspirations, mores, recent history, facilities for amusement or distraction, and capacity for stability or deviation.[14]

3. This vast and sometimes bewildering medley of specializations would truly be chaotic, indeed impossible, without the simultaneous (yet unplanned) processes of abstraction, rationalization, and generalization. The urban division of labor is extensive in sheer number of specialisms, but also in the widened radius of persons and groups affected. Consequently, an earlier emphasis on the concrete and the particular, so characteristic of traditional ruralites and early stages of childhood, becomes an impediment to those who must daily relate their activities and problems to a larger social canvas. All urbanites

[14] Durkheim, *op. cit.,* pp. 275–277; Amos H. Hawley, *Human Ecology* (New York, Ronald Press, 1950), Chaps. XII–XIV; Harlan W. Gilmore, "The Old New Orleans and the New," *American Sociological Review,* 9 (August, 1944), pp. 385–394.

are not equally engaged in this quest for broader meanings, but the quest itself is typical of persons most conscious of their participation in a highly specialized enterprise. In any case, increasing division of labor is accompanied by the spread of more rational standards, more general principles and attitudes. This is expressed in the extension of public laws and regulations, and the ever encroaching significance of the most universal standard in urban life—money.[15] Since these processes are unpremeditated and somewhat unequally distributed, the results are often superficial rather than profound, amoral rather than moralistic. Perhaps this explains the urbanite's strain toward *sophistication*, which reflects the desire to bathe in the pool of widespread knowledge and "events," no matter how brief the immersion.

4. As specialization in urban regions progresses, a network of *impersonal interdependencies* is produced, not by plan but out of experience. The meaning of a particular job, occupation, service, facility, or material object is inseparable from its links with certain other roles and functions, on which it inevitably depends for personnel, services, or financial support (*e.g.*, the relation of business and industry to higher education and the world of science). The essence of effective specialization is therefore *exchange* between specialists. Consequently, interdependence is reflected in the need to recognize and make adjustments to skills and practices outside our immediate experience, since this accommodation enables each function to be performed with more predictability, more efficiency, and more satisfaction:

"Consequently, even where society relies most completely upon the division of labor, it does not become a jumble of juxtaposed atoms, between which it can establish only external, transient contacts. Rather the members are united by ties which extend deeper and far beyond the short moments during which the exchange is made. Each of the functions that they exercise is, in a fixed way, dependent upon others, and with them forms a solidary system. Accordingly, from the nature of the chosen task permanent duties arise. Because we fill some certain domestic or social function, we are involved in a complex of obligations from which we have no right to free ourselves." [16]

[15] Durkheim, *op. cit.*, pp. 287–290; Simmel, "The Metropolis and Mental Life," *loc. cit.*

[16] Reprinted with permission of the Free Press from *the Division of Labor in Society*, by Emile Durkheim. Copyright 1947 by the Free Press.

It is easy to exaggerate the extent of *recognition* of interdependence. Since extensive division of labor tends to create indirect and impersonal ties, there is often a margin of temporary autonomy for specific groups or roles, *e.g.*, criminal gangs, land subdividers, sweatshop operators, transit companies, etc. However the history of urban regions is in part a record of successful efforts to induce responsibility and limit the divisive effects of autonomy. Many of the urban reform movements—private or public—have been motivated by this very objective.[17] The suburban movement is an excellent example of the quest for autonomy,[18] but the bonds of interdependence remain strong, whether or not the suburbs are annexed. Problems of taxation, zoning, industrial attraction and location, provision of community services—all reflect the essential relations between parts of the urban region.

5. Paradoxically but characteristically, the development of organic solidarity through division of labor, interdependence, and generalization permits—and even encourages— greater freedom for variation in behavior among urban individuals.[19] In a sense, such freedom is the inevitable price of widespread specialization, but it is far from unrestricted licence. Much of this freedom is *ideological* and in the realm of personal morals; it is essentially release from the power of tradition and coercive, localized public opinion. In practice, the result is greater exposure to alternative values, greater experimentation with deviations in *private* behavior, and ultimately, a more acquiescent attitude toward cultural changes in general. In short, organic solidarity tends to enlarge the possibilities of personality development (both useful and dangerous forms, it is true). However, beyond the intangible limits of the private sphere, the urbanite is expected to make a regular, minimal contribution to the overriding division of labor. Regardless of personal opinions, therefore, he follows some occupation (he may call it a rat race or treadmill), pays his various taxes, contributes to one or more charities, and supports numerous commercial enterprises by his patronage. For some urbanites, private variations clearly interfere with specialized participation; but these deviants are almost as exceptional as they are dramatic.

[17] For example, A. Theodore Brown, *The Politics of Reform: Kansas City's Municipal Government 1925–1950* (Kansas City, Community Studies, Inc., March, 1958).

[18] Robert C. Wood, *Suburbia* (Boston, Houghton Mifflin, 1959).

[19] Durkheim, *op. cit.*, pp. 290–303. A very different view of this development is Sigmund Freud, *Civilization and its Discontents* (London, Hogarth Press, 1946).

6. *Latent coordinating structures.* In general, therefore, organic solidarity consists of processes that sustain an emergent but yet unstable social order. This order tends to rest on a rough balance between processes that separate or create dissimilarities (specialization, individual variations) and those that produce connecting links or common experiences (generalization, interdependence, responsibility). Durkheim assumed that organic solidarity was essentially stable and automatically self-regulative, though he recognized "abnormal forms" in which regulation was relatively absent or artificially superimposed (*e.g.,* a rigid caste system).[20] However, it seems probable that the key to organic solidarity in modern urban regions is a set of familiar structures that provide unintended coordination, and thus achieve in some degree the spontaneous regulation required to obtain balance among these component processes.

A major source of latent coordination may be found in the formal, bureaucratic organizations of leading urban institutions, particularly in the governmental and economic spheres. Until very recently, city government was primarily concerned with such obvious functions as police protection, settlement of disputes, care and repair of community facilities (streets, parks). The emphasis was predominantly *negative, i.e.,* to blot out or reduce evidence of disorder; and it was largely uncongenial to concentration of government influence. As urban communities became more complex, the expansion of positive services inevitably altered the role of government in the urban system of organic solidarity. Now the urban region is increasingly unified by the operation of desired and constantly extended public services (education, health, welfare, housing, etc.), which are formally available to all qualified residents as an underlying layer of urban experience. In addition, though the political theory of politicians and laymen is generally averse to such a development, urban government has been compelled to experiment with greater financial and administrative control over this network of public services. The aroused emphasis on efficiency, on accountability and publicity in the governmental sphere, have therefore strengthened the unique, subtle ties of modern regional coordination. Corruption in urban government,[21] which is noticeably declining, merely represents a gap in latent coordination, a failure

---

[20] Durkheim, *op. cit.,* Chap. V and Book 3.

[21] The classic accounts of city corruption are Lincoln Steffens, *The Shame of the Cities* (New York, P. Smith, 1904); and *The Autobiography of Lincoln Steffens* (New York, Harcourt, Brace, 1931). See also Robert S. Allen, ed., *Our Fair City* (New York, Vanguard Press, 1947).

to close one or more informal or unnoticed loopholes in the "connective tissue" between public and private agencies.

Economic organizations in modern urban regions are collectively a web of private government. Indeed, the larger and more influential industries, banks, retailers, and other commercial organizations tend to assume noneconomic roles and broader areas of significance as an accompaniment to their specialized economic functions. If productivity and profit are the explicit aims of these groups, the pursuit of economic objectives normally entails the creation and maintenance of systematic controls or arrangements within each organization and among types of economic organizations, and also an implicit order that enters into and regulates almost every facet of urban living.

The nature of this implicit order is so obvious and routine that we often tend to ignore it. First and most evident, the urban economic institution constantly selects and utilizes a tremendous range of skills and resources that are distributed among the population and land areas of the urban region. Second, with few exceptions, economic organizations provide a regular and virtually uninterrupted flow of necessary and desired services to the entire urban region. This intricate network simultaneously caters to the needs and abilities of each sub-area, social class, racial division, and educational level; it also constitutes the base for the routine functioning of urban family life, religion, recreation, education, public services, and the arts. Third, for most urbanites, the economic institution provides that incalculably important link between the individual, various social organizations, and the community at large—the job. In the urban region, the job is not merely a source of income; it is a donor of status and respect, a psychological mooring-point, and an indirect but effective source of social control of behavior (and probably of attitudes and ideology).[22] Fourth, we are beginning to recognize that economic organizations can (and perhaps must) reflect to some extent the peculiar needs, resources, and values of urban regions, which cannot be fully expressed in such organs as government or the local press. There is, for example, some evidence that industrial and commercial firms make adjustments to the culture and problems of specific urban regions by accepting local mores in race relations—as in department stores and chain drug stores, encouraging a more diversified industrial base,

[22] Theodore Caplow, *The Sociology of Work* (Minneapolis, University of Minnesota Press, 1954); Robert Dubin, *The World of Work* (Englewood Cliffs, N.J., Prentice-Hall, 1958), Chap. XIV; Mirra Komarovsky, *The Unemployed Man and his Family* (New York, Dryden Press, 1940).

locating or relocating offices and plants with some attention to the desires of their workers, and contributing personnel and funds to community programs in welfare and planning.[23]

The urban class system, discussed in Chapter 10, may also be regarded as an unintended mechanism in sustaining organic solidarity. Despite its much noted vagueness, the class structure fundamentally contributes to an implicit order in two ways. On the one hand, it tends to segregate persons and families of similar life-styles from frequent contact with members of other status levels. Inter-class frictions, "class struggles" are remarkably rare in urban regions, to the despair of doctrinaire Marxists and self-selected advocates of particular class ideologies. As a matter of fact, the major instances of friction and violence in modern urban regions exemplify the stubborn remnant of a *caste* system against which Negroes, Mexicans, and Puerto Ricans are in rebellion.[24] On the other hand, the urban class system allows considerable hope (and some probability) of social mobility. The widespread aspiration for upward mobility not only encourages individual achievement and a greater support for urban products and services. It also enhances the prestige of each higher status level, and serves to connect the various levels of status in a personally meaningful manner. Without the leaven of social mobility, the urban class system might be a source of unendurable disillusionment and frustration, and perhaps a prelude to a new caste system—as Spengler predicted on the basis of earlier urban waves.

Since mass communications is still a relatively new addition to urban systems, its contribution to organic solidarity is somewhat unclear at this point. Yet scattered evidence and responsible interpretation by several observers seem to indicate that mass communications is already a moderately significant component of a developing urban order.[25] As we have seen in Chapter 13, the manifest role of mass

[23] A detailed discussion of the relations between industrial organizations and urban areas is the theme of William H. Form and Delbert C. Miller, *Industry, Labor, and Community* (New York, Harper and Brothers, 1960), especially Part II.

[24] Good case studies of urban violence include Alfred M. Lee and Norman D. Humphrey, *Race Riot* (New York, Dryden Press, 1943); Harrison E. Salisbury, *The Shook-Up Generation* (New York, Harper and Brothers, 1958).

[25] Paul F. Lazarsfeld and Robert K. Merton, "Mass Communication, Popular Taste, and Organized Social Action," in Wilbur Schramm, ed., *Mass Communications, 1949* (Urbana, Ill., University of Illinois Press, 1949), pp. 459–480; Morris Janowitz, *The Community Press in an Urban Setting* (New York, The Free Press of Glencoe, 1952).

communications in its various forms is *persuasion* of broad population categories to accept specific products, values, and even personalities. But the accompanying effects appear equally, if not more, notable. If the fragmentary evidence is reliable, urban mass communications is rapidly inculcating an emerging cultural similarity in an otherwise heterogeneous population. This similarity is not deep-seated, as in a folk community based on a traditional close-knit morality. Instead, it is decidedly superficial (but still effective) in the form of an *ethic of ambiguity* (see pp. 275–276). In addition, and probably without conscious intent, mass communications provides a focus of interest and a germ of latent coordination by emphasizing the validity, the attractiveness, and the essential ultimacy of the middle class life-style. Since the modern urban region is in many respects dedicated to the comforts and ideals of middle class families, mass communications supports this complex social system by complimenting those who have attained such a position and encouraging others to aspire to an enticing social or cultural equivalence.

DEVIATIONS FROM ORGANIC SOLIDARITY

Despite these important processes, the organic solidarity of urban regions is far from stable; the incessant and sometimes sudden introduction of cultural and social changes appear to offer a constant threat to complex, precarious order. Urban regions therefore exhibit obvious and widespread gaps or lags in their structure, more than occasional malfunctioning of such critical subsystems as families, public agencies, and distributional mechanisms, and consequently, a continuing repertory of well-known social problems (see Part IV).

To understand the deficiencies in urban order, we must keep in mind that *modern* urban regions are rather novel inventions in the history of the human community and *transitional* systems that face the task of mediating between two forms of community—in Matthew Arnold's somewhat gloomy words, "one dead, the other powerless to be born." Indeed, the transitional nature of urban regions can be grasped by recalling the tenacity of feudal, semifeudal, or theocratic types of community throughout the world. In Western Europe and North America, though feudalism had been in precipitous decline since the seventeenth century, it was not before the first third of the nineteenth century that all of the social and political restraints of a feudal past were removed. In Central and Eastern Europe, on the other hand, the "old regime" was even more persistent; German, Austrian, Hungarian, and Polish cities did not join the ranks of "modern" urban regions until the twentieth century, primarily after World War I. As for Russian cities, a Czarist feudalism has been superseded by Soviet controls, which apparently amounts to putting "old wine in new bottles." Turning to the vast continents of Asia and Africa, to Central and South America, and to the new Pacific nation of islands—Indonesia—we can see that the tentacles of their respective feudalisms are still in process of being loosened, if not removed.

If modern urbanism can be interpreted in part as liberation from an older order, toward what "new" system is it evolving? The bare fact that in general we do not know is the essential dilemma of "transition." Of course, if urbanism were returning to some previous type of system—as largely occurred during the "Dark Ages"—some definite predictions about the future might be reasonably made. But, clearly, the nature of modern urban regions gives little evidence of regression in an *objective* sense (evaluations of tastes, morality, etc. present great problems in interpreting facts, of course), unless one assumes the extinction of urban regions by nuclear warfare. Instead, modern urbanism is marked by a set of characteristics that cannot be distinguished in previous waves of urbanism and that therefore is difficult to evaluate as to its consequences. These features include: the high prestige and considerable autonomy of economic motives and economically oriented organizations; a widespread receptivity to change (both quantitative and qualitative) as a necessary and desirable aspect of experience; the tendency toward urban expansionism in its hinterland by peaceful, indirect means; and a somewhat flexible stratification system, with uniquely vague but attractive opportunities for social mobility.

In this context, the transitional nature of modern urban regions lies in the practical difficulty of assimilating and coordinating these trends in an evolving order without noticeable strain and dissatisfaction. This problem is expressed most basically in the circuitous development of an *intermediate morality* for urbanites, a practical morality distinct from the reassuring rigidities of tradition (*e.g.,* knowing one's place, the code of the gentleman), and yet pointing toward a new and more complex communal morality whose outlines are still far from clear. As we have already noted at various places, the transitional morality of modern urbanism is marked by great aspiration (for

productivity, progress, and possession) and the peculiar ethics of ambiguity and compromise. It is a morality that, in practice, implicitly
assigns responsibility to individual judgment. The "organization man"
is an apparent exception; yet he represents merely the substitution of an
autonomous corporate focus for an emphasis on individual choice.[26]
Furthermore, this intermediate and experimental morality cannot, by
virtue of its special origins, possess the comprehensive range and reassuring certainty of traditional moralities. There is, we must admit,
an unavoidable dash of *anomie* in urbanism, an absence of distinct
norms and standards of evaluation as guides to repeated behavior in
such areas as personal honesty, responsibility for aged relations, advertising, public service *vs.* private interests, and sexual relations.[27]

The transitional morality of urbanism, which contains both latitude
for individualism and a presumably open invitation to *anomie,* is
evident in most aspects of urban life. However, its relative strength
cannot be easily determined. As we learn more about the interrelation of *facts* (rather than opinions) in modern urbanism, we may have
to conclude that transitional morality is a haunting, perhaps annoying,
second melody, not the dominant theme, in the complex, polyphonic
score of urban regionalization. Yet two forms of expression of transitional morality deserve some attention at this point as implicit and
unintended obstacles to organic solidarity. First, there is the continuing growth of powerful, often nonaccountable private organizations bent on achieving their own ends, under the plausible assumption that activities not proscribed by law are therefore clearly ad-
missible and perhaps even praiseworthy. Such groups as labor unions,
real estate developers, contractors, industrial corporations, political
parties, transportation companies, among others, have at times
equated their individual fortunes with the welfare of the urban region
as a whole. Unravelling the merits of such claims would exhaust the
wisdom of many Solomons. But more important, while these groups
press their respective legitimate interests, there is an inevitable competition that strains a precarious urban consensus and sustains the
transitional morality discussed above.

[26] William H. Whyte, Jr., *The Organization Man* (Garden City, N.Y.,
Doubleday and Company, 1956), Parts II, III, V.

[27] Edwin H. Sutherland, *White Collar Crime* (New York, Dryden Press,
1949); Marshall B. Clinard, *The Black Market* (New York, Holt, Rinehart
and Winston, 1952). For a general discussion of "transitional morality," see
Alvin Boskoff, "Postponement of Social Decision in Transitional Society,"
Social Forces, 31 (March, 1953), pp. 232–234.

The second example of transitional morality is more subtle, but no less significant: it concerns the familiar phenomenon of uncontrolled population movements within and between urban regions. Of course, the right to change one's residence is long cherished by urbanites. Freedom to move is basic to the growth of urban regions, and to the typical urban quest for more desirable styles of living. Yet individual (and family) decisions to move are motivated by probable advantages to the individual or family, without much reference to the moves of other residents or to the eventual consequences of such moves for the neighborhood and the region as a whole.[28] To suggest alternative grounds for moving or not moving would certainly invite indignation and anger. However, the rather high mobility of urbanites, which is often preceded by little advance notice (though the desire may have a long history), has extensive effects on such major services as public education, welfare, police and fire protection, as well as on vital sources of taxation. Budgets, programs, personnel, and buildings are normally geared to the recent past and to a future of one to ten years. In short, the availability and quantity of urban community services depend heavily on estimates of needs that are based on recent trends, projections of these trends, and considerable guessing. A great number of individual moves, collectively considered, can therefore confound responsible computation of needs and services. For example, the largest single public expenditure in urban regions is for education. As a result of these population movements, most cities contain some schools that have become too big for their student bodies, while other schools in suburban areas are already fated for obsolescence and overcrowding before the foundations are laid. This situation, repeated in most public aspects of urban organization, stems from urban freedoms that latently challenge organic solidarity and occasionally create local crises (e.g., the Puerto Rican invasion of New York City, and traffic snarls in most major cities).

It appears that urban regions are transitional in another important respect that may help us understand continuing problems of urban order. In general, the major Western cities have developed an increasing independence from ecclesiastical and feudal controls, principally from the thirteenth or fourteenth centuries till the late nineteenth

---

[28] Motives for moving are discussed in Peter Rossi, *Why Families Move* (New York, The Free Press of Glencoe, 1955); Richard Dewey, "Peripheral Expansion in Milwaukee County," *American Journal of Sociology*, 53 (May, 1948), pp. 118–125.

and early twentieth centuries. To the middle classes and the legally emancipated artisans and laborers, the autonomy of the city was the ultimate objective. But political and economic forces that were nurtured by the newly autonomous cities gradually created dominions and empires that have begun to impinge on the relative independence of urban regions. A prime interloper in most European cities has been the *national state,* which has inevitably interfered in the operations of major urban centers (particularly national capitals)—sometimes with needed financial aid, sometimes by political determination of urban legal or economic policy. An excellent example of the latter may be found in the case of London, whose government during the eighteenth and nineteenth centuries was not allowed to acquire adequate responsibility because of a hostile Parliament.[29] On a somewhat reduced scale, Washington, D.C. suffers from frustrated aspirations that can be traced to the refusal of Congress to yield its rule over the nation's capital.

SELECTED REFERENCES

BOGUE, Donald J., *The Structure of the Metropolitan Community* (Ann Arbor, Mich., Horace Rackham School of Graduate Studies, University of Michigan, 1949).

MCKENZIE, R. D., *The Metropolitan Community* (New York, McGraw-Hill, 1933).

MUMFORD, Lewis, *The Culture of Cities* (New York, Harcourt, Brace, and World, 1938), Introduction, and Chap. V.

[29] William A. Robson, *The Government and Misgovernment of London* (London, Allen and Unwin, 1939).

PART IV

Urban Planning
and Social Problems

CHAPTER 15

Social Problems
and the Urban Region

BOTH LAYMEN AND social scientists are concerned by the fact that urban regions continually exhibit contradictory aspects. The catalytic presence of *cultural heterogeneity* seems to be partially negated by growing uniformities in tastes, consumption, and ideas. Creativity in various fields, a hallmark of urbanism, is accompanied by considerable apathy and a taste for the safely familiar. Despite the variety of activities, the vitality and fascination of city living, there is likewise boredom and countless indecisions about use of leisure time ("What would you like to do?" "I don't know. What would *you* like to do?"). If there is expanded productivity—in comforts and conveniences, as well as necessities—poor or dubious health and physical and mental ills are also quite apparent to the urbanite. Finally, the relatively wide opportunities for personal and vicarious achievement share the urban stage with keen feelings, of aimlessness, frustration, and despair (the "quiet desperation" of T. S. Eliot).

The transitional nature of urban regions, which was discussed in the last chapter, seems to provide a helpful way of approaching an understanding of these contradictions and the familiar problems that accompany them. Basically, urban regions have reached a "transitional phase" as a result of three sets of conditions. Most obvious are rapid changes in population, technological capacities, and values. Second, there is the development of relatively autonomous and competing groups in the economic, political, and other spheres. Third, and finally for this brief summary, rather new standards of "humanitarianism," progress, welfare, reform, etc. have added powerful pressures for improved functioning in urban systems. Let us call these the *structural features of urban transition*.

During the greater part of the modern "urban wave," the response to these structural features has been a compound of disinterest, ignorance, fitful and hysterical concern, indecisiveness, and narrowly conceived opportunism. The recent history of any major city provides ample evidence of these responses.[1] As a consequence, despite its material accomplishments, the urban region has accumulated a formidable repertory of basic, critical problems, which have in varying degrees disturbed the more thoughtful urbanites throughout the world. These problems of transitional urbanism may be classified in the following way:

1. Urban congestion and uncontrolled competition for urban space.
2. Personal inadequacy and insecurity.
3. The costs and dilemmas provoked by continual striving for status.
4. The absence of communal cohesion or morality, especially in crisis periods.
5. The failure to promote orderly physical and social development for the urban region as a whole.

Other classifications of fundamental problems are of course possible, particularly since the specific aspects of these problems seem to be interdependent. But whatever classification is used, these constitute almost the entire fund of *modern social problems*. Indeed, in an ever increasing degree, social problems are becoming synonymous with problems of the urban region.[2]

[1] Bessie L. Pierce, *A History of Chicago* (New York, Alfred A. Knopf, 1937–1957), 3 vols.; Blake McKelvey, *Rochester* (Cambridge, Mass., Harvard University Press, 1949–1956), 3 vols.; T. J. Wertenbaker, *Norfolk* (Durham, N.C. Duke University Press, 1931); William A. Robson, ed., *Great Cities of the World* (London, Allen and Unwin, 1954).

[2] Virtually all textbooks on "social problems" and "social disorganization" demonstrate this connection. See such recent texts as Jessie Bernard, *Social Problems at Midcentury* (New York, Dryden Press, 1957); Harry C. Bredemeir and Jackson Toby, *Social Problems in America* (New York, John Wiley and Sons, 1960); Robert K. Merton and Robert A. Nisbet, eds., *Contemporary Social Problems* (New York, Harcourt, Brace, and World, 1961); Marshall Clinard, *The Sociology of Deviant Behavior* (New York, Holt, Rinehart, and Winston, 1957); Paul B. Horton and Gerald R. Lessie, *The Sociology of Social Problems*, 2nd ed., (New York, Appleton-Century-Crofts, Inc., 1960).

Social problems may be defined as repeated and relatively wide-spread human situations which are in some manner recognized as undesirable and as requiring drastic modification. In urban regions, several categories of persons may (and do) exhibit awareness of specific social problems: (*a*) those directly affected by difficulties; (*b*) social scientists, who study such problems as part of their professional pursuits; (*c*) public officials; (*d*) publicists, journalists, and other mass communicators; and (*e*) specific publics reached by the media of mass communication. The question often arises: *how many* must be aware of the significance of situations before we may apply the label "social problems?" Such a question is perhaps unavoidable, but it assumes that social problems are both static phenomena and also numerically decided, as in an election or an "unpopularity" contest.

Serious students of social problems, on the other hand, have made two things relatively clear. (*a*) Social problems have *histories,* courses of development—in scope, severity, degree of public awareness, and attempted solutions. (*b*) As social problems develop, awareness is communicated to broader categories. Often, initial awareness develops among social scientists, certain interest groups, and some mass communicators. Other categories, in varying order, then acquire fleeting or serious concern, hoping and eventually articulating the demand that "something ought to be done."

In general, the existence of urban social problems—or at least the more dramatic and personal manifestations of these problems—is widely recognized. The mass media, the schools, churches, and public agencies have been untiring in attempts to define and illustrate the meaning of crime, juvenile delinquency, gambling, drug addiction, alcoholism, divorce, illegitimacy, labor-management conflicts, racial and religious discrimination, mental disorder, educational deficiencies, inadequate recreation, political corruption, housing problems, slum areas, traffic snarls, the impact of unbalanced local economies and outmoded tax structures, etc. But the causes of such problems, and the factors that explain their persistence, are poorly understood by urbanites. As a matter of fact, social scientists do not yet possess a sufficiently comprehensive explanation of urban social problems, though recent advances in research and theoretical formulations seem promising.[3] Therefore urbanites are understandably confused about appropriate measures or "solutions."

From this continuing conflict of *concern* on the one hand, and be-

[3] Clinard, *op. cit.,* Chap. I; Merton and Nisbet, *op. cit.,* Chap. XV.

wilderment and honest ignorance on the other, several typical reactions to social problems have emerged.

1. Resignation and complacency

Saturated with increasingly banalized accounts of crime, divorce,
graft, strikes, etc., some urbanites seem to develop a protective apathy
about problems that do not directly and personally impinge on their
welfare. Such problems come to be taken for granted, to be noted but
no longer worthy of excitement, indignation, or effort. "That's human
nature," "politics and honesty don't mix," are some typical statements
of this attitude, which approaches social problems as a living folklore,
tangible but not completely real.

2. Manipulation of personality

For many decades, urbanites have been fascinated by the possibility
of fitting personalities to their social environment and thereby reducing those stresses and conflicts which are presumed to cause specific
social problems (such as mental disorder or ethnic discrimination).
Generally, those who confront social problems primarily through contacts with *individual cases* (the clinical setting) assume this approach.[4]
The leading proponents of "personality manipulation" therefore include psychiatrists, physicians, ministers, teachers, and social workers, though there are many in each of these professions who do not
accept the validity or the practicality of this sort of solution.

3. Institutional change [5]

In contrast to the preceding approach, some urbanites find the
source of social problems in imperfect organizational, legal, or ad-

[4] *E.g.,* Robert Lindner, *Must You Conform?* (New York, Holt, Rinehart,
and Winston, 1956); Anna Freud, *The Ego and the Mechanisms of Defence*
(London, International Universities Press, 1946); William Healy and Augusta
Bronner, *Treatment and What Happened Afterward* (Boston, Judge Baker
Guidance Center, 1939); Rollo May, *The Meaning of Anxiety* (New York,
Ronald Press, 1950).

[5] *E.g.,* Robert S. Lynd, *Knowledge for What?* (Princeton, N.J., Princeton
University Press, 1945); Robert M. MacIver, *The More Perfect Union* (New
York, Harper and Brothers, 1948); Carle C. Zimmerman, *The Changing Com-
munity* (New York, Harper and Brothers, 1938); Robert C. Angell, *Free
Society and Moral Crisis* (Ann Arbor, Mich., University of Michigan Press,
1958).

ministrative arrangements—and in the values that underlie these structures. Consequently, various types of reformers, social engineers, community organization workers, and many social scientists place great
reliance on specific alterations in government, economic organization,
school and university systems, etc. The essence of this approach is a
focus on desired changes in *one* institutional sector.

4. The planning approach [6]

This is the broadest, the most comprehensive, and possibly the
most difficult to apply in practice to urban social problems. It is based
on the commonplace observation—a fundamental insight of sociology
—that human affairs exhibit intricate interdependence within a complex group, community, or society. In particular, the planning approach stems from the interrelations of human needs and institutions
in the organic solidarity of modern urbanized societies. It is exemplified in the attempt to view a social problem in terms of its relation to
"normal" structures in the urban region and its relation to other
social problems. Planning, therefore, involves broad knowledge, co-
ordinated programs, and a continuing optimism about the effects of
unfamiliar controls.

To achieve some perspective on urban attitudes toward social problems, we might consider a somewhat simplified comparison of community types in terms of a rough continuum of societal complexity [7]
(see the accompanying table). For our purposes, the extremes of this
continuum should be regarded as reference points for evaluating the
structures and probable trends of modern urban regions.

Focusing briefly on the folk-sacred type, in which the dominant
community form is normally the agricultural village, the major problems are those of *survival,* adaptation to the physical environment,
and to hostile neighbors. Without a developed division of labor, members of this type of community rely on strong traditional values and on
a relatively unpremeditated, trial-and-error approach (*chance discovery*) to group problems. In our sense of the term, social problems are
relatively absent, since tradition provides widely accepted "solutions"
to difficulties in communities untouched by the complex values of ra-

[6] The best sociological discussion of planning is Karl Mannheim, *Man and
Society in an Age of Reconstruction* (New York, Harcourt, Brace, and World,
1940), especially pp. 155–163, 191–199, 222–236, 374–380.
[7] *Ibid.,* pp. 150–155.

TABLE 67

Types of Societal Complexity and Responses to Problems

Societal Type	Folk-Sacred Community	Transitional society	Advanced secular or "State civilization"
Dominant Community Type	Rural village	Urban areas of the 19th and 20th centuries	Large urban regions (stabilized form)
Dominant Social Mechanism	Tradition and chance discovery	Discrete or separate invention	Rationalized planning (authoritarian)

tionality and efficiency. Many preliterate societies (until recently) have approximated this general form.[8]

On the other extreme is a type that has perhaps never yet been fully achieved—the advanced principled-secular or "state civilization" form.[9] Modern totalitarian societies (Fascist, Nazi, and Communist) possess several characteristic features (minute division of labor, bureaucratization, centralized authority, emphasis on science and rational procedures, controlled use of communications media for manipulation of attitudes and values), as well as such related historical instances as the Spartan state and the earlier phases of the Roman Empire. But, to provide a self-consistent and more sharply etched extreme type—and thus perhaps anticipate possible future trends—we might posit a special community form: the stabilized, rationalized urban region.

In such a community, which is an extension of tendencies in modern urban areas, a set of interrelated features might be hypothesized. First and most predictable is the development of the typical urban area as a large land mass, a supercommunity composed of many previously separate communities. Gottmann has already named this

[8] Numerous references to studies of preliterate societies can be found in Felix M. Keesing, *Cultural Anthropology* (New York, Holt, Rinehart, and Winston, 1958); and Ralph Linton, *The Study of Man* (New York, Appleton-Century-Crofts, Inc., 1936). For a handy collection, consult Elman R. Service, *A Profile of Primitive Culture* (New York, Harper and Brothers, 1958).

[9] Howard W. Odum, *Understanding Society* (New York, Macmillan, 1947), pp. 707–708; Franklin H. Giddings, *Civilization and Society* (New York, Henry Holt, 1932), pp. 280–281; Howard Becker, "Current Sacred-Secular Theory," in Howard Becker and Alvin Boskoff, eds., *Modern Sociological Theory* (New York, Dryden Press, 1957), pp. 155–175; Howard Becker, *Man in Reciprocity* (New York, Frederick A. Praeger, 1956), Chap. XII; Alvin Boskoff, "Structure, Function, and Folk Society," *American Sociological Review*, 14 (December, 1949), pp. 749–758.

"megalopolis" and points to its currently most developed manifestation in the urban sprawl from Boston to Washington and environs.[10]

Second, the rationalized urban regional type operates as a single unified system, with centralized services of many kinds and a related structure of centralized authority. Independent suburbs and adjacent but conflicting tax rates or zoning regulations would therefore be absent.

Third, the dominant institution is the political-legal system, rather than kinship or religion, or a privately operated economic sphere (the market, as in transitional urban communities).

Fourth, while status differences persist—and perhaps become even more evident—the rationalized urban region predominantly operates on principles of impartial service and general public welfare. Such an emphasis may derive partially from humane considerations, but more likely it is based on the desire to protect community functioning from the nonrational, parochial interests of competing groups in the region. This rationalized approach is facilitated by a centralized structure of authority, though it is certainly clear that the latter does not *guarantee* the former.

Fifth, the dominant method of treating—and anticipating—community problems is *planning*, a continuous process of controlling, regulating, and coordinating the most significant activities and social processes from "key positions" of knowledge and authority. It is fruitless, at this point in human experience, to evaluate the efficiency and the full moral implications of planning. In general, the world's experience thus far with community, regional, and societal planning has been disappointing. The major reasons seem to be (*a*) inadequate use of existing knowledge; (*b*) poor understanding and faulty cooperation from the majority of citizens; (*c*) wavering sincerity and arrogance of planning officials; and (*d*) interference resulting from the policies of other communities and societies. In the extreme type of the rationalized urban region, it is hypothesized, conditions (*a*) and (*c*) are considerably improved as a result of scientific advances in data accumulation and analysis, and in selection of planning personnel. But the remaining problems elude rational solution in this type.

[10] Jean Gottmann, "Megalopolis, or the Urbanization of the Northeastern Seaboard," *Economic Geography,* 33, (July, 1957), pp. 189–200. This is similar to the term "conurbation," as coined by Patrick Geddes in his *Cities in Evolution,* new and rev. ed. (New York, Oxford Unversity Press, 1950), pp. 14–15.

Consequently, planning is *authoritarian* rather than democratically conceived or approved.

With these polar types as reference points, let us now return to contemporary, transitional urban regions. In response to rapidity of change and the absence of reliable experience in anticipating or controlling change, urban regions have been "experimenting" with several methods of meeting social problems.[11] The complacency-laissez faire complex of attitudes is essentially a survival of the chance discovery approach of the village community. However, the dominant approach until the last few decades has been a reliance on single, narrowly conceived "solutions" to specific immediate problems—what Mannheim has called the stage of *inventive thinking*. Most of the numerous instances of proposed institutional change and personality manipulation have been of this character. For example, we might refer to political reforms (proportional representation, the referendum, improvements in municipal service, civil service and merit systems, revised taxation systems, new housing projects, mental health programs, etc.). Typically, the essence of these measures has been an attack on limited aspects of a particular problem in isolation from related conditions and a concern for "treatment" of already affected persons and groups, rather than prevention of future difficulties.

But the inventive is losing its appeal for urbanites as the persistence (and increase) of social problems involves prodigious financial outlays and also serves to threaten the enjoyment of the "gracious living" so important to the modern urban system of values. In varying degrees, therefore, invention has been challenged by the planning approach. However, since many urban regions share in a political tradition of democracy and long established freedoms, the authoritarian potentialities of planning present further problems. The underlying thread in urban regions as units appears to be the search for a proper blend of planning, invention, and discovery as social techniques—in short, *responsible planning,* or democratic goals pursued by modern, rational-scientific means.[12]

Planning as a Process of Social Change

Planning, and to some extent separate invention, rests on the strategy of mitigating social problems by imposed or controlling

[11] Mannheim, *op. cit.,* pp. 150–155.
[12] *Ibid.,* pp. 363–365.

processes of change in urban regions. It follows, then, that planning must give careful attention to the *general nature* of social and cultural change as revealed in modern urban regions and *modifications* in the "normal" change process that are considered necessary to meet planning goals. Implicitly or explicitly, therefore, the student of urban problems always works with some conception of basic *stages* or *phases* in processes of change. The following scheme may provide a simplified means of summarizing these stages.[18]

1. *Dissatisfaction or problem stage.* Recognition of undesirable situations, of inadequate satisfaction of social needs, or of specific strains that seem menacing, produces attitudes of dissatisfaction among a number of appropriately sensitive persons. The source of these feelings may be traced to the impact of other societies or communities, or the development of internal social difficulties. In this early phase, dissatisfaction is not often dramatic, widespread, or organized.

2. *Innovation.* If dissatisfaction is sufficiently strong, one or more persons may seek to remedy the problem by conceiving a new technique, a new principle of organization, a new piece of apparatus, or a new value (goals, morals, etc.).

3. *The trial appraisal stage.* One of the key phases of change occurs at this point—the presentation of innovations to wider categories for their evaluation and trial. Whatever the worth of an innovation, in order to contribute to change, it must be attractively launched toward its prospective public. Debate, advertising, charismatic personality, the lure of novelty are some of the means by which innovations achieve a trial and therefore the crucial stage of appraisal.

4. *Competitive or transitional stage.* If innovations gain some currency and approval, there is yet the necessity of determining their relation to pre-existing practices, values, and forms. Normally, two alternatives appear: (*a*) the eventual *replacement* of the old by the new; or (*b*) the simultaneous acceptance of the innovation and the established form by different categories of persons. In the latter case, the overall process of change may be delayed by group conflicts. The early history of the United States, for example, was marked by conflicting attitudes toward the Constitution and its system of centralized authority, and a consequent formation of separate, contending political parties.

5. *The integrative stage.* Assuming relatively widespread approval

[18] Alvin Boskoff, "Social Change: Major Problems in the Emergence of Theoretical and Research Foci," in Becker and Boskoff, *op. cit.*, pp. 289–301.

of an innovation, there remains the decisive problem of connecting the innovation to traditional forms and values in other spheres of activity. Since human needs and social structures operate as interdependent chains, the process of change inevitably involves either some modification in the accepted innovation or appropriate readjustments in several established forms. In the first case, which is rather rare, the impact of change has resulted in minimal, relatively insignificant variation. However, genuine and highly significant change occurs in the second instance, as a result of the original innovation, but often from the *derivative changes* prompted by that innovation.

THE STRATEGY OF URBAN PLANNING

We may now explore the interrelations among the three major themes of this chapter: social problems, social change, and planning. The normal progression of social change, as represented by the sequence of five phases, does not operate in a highly rational, consecutive manner in urban regions. Specifically, the process of change seems to reflect difficulties in solving the practical situations connected with phase 4 (the competitive or transitional phase) and phase 5 (the integrative phase). These difficulties largely derive from the numerous innovations in urban life and the rapidity with which they are introduced, the lack of consensus among urban groups and categories about *awareness* of difficulties, adequate goals, and appropriate means of reducing accumulated stress, and the survival in part of a *laissez faire*, individualistic philosophy and a consequent hesitation to "interfere" with the operation of "normal" groups and their unintended effects on the larger community.[14]

Social problems, then, seem to arise and persist under two sets of conditions: (*a*) complex and generally rapid processes of change and (*b*) lack of experience and/or willingness to intervene in an intelligent, systematic manner. Essentially, the *rationale* of urban planning is its potential role in bridging the gap—as efficiently as possible—between adjacent stages of the urban change process. The theory of planning therefore rests on continuing knowledge of human

---

[14] Alvin Boskoff, "Postponement of Social Decision in Transitional Society," *Social Forces,* 31 (March, 1953), pp. 229–234; Alvin Boskoff, "Social Indecision: A Dysfunctional Focus of Transitional Society," *ibid.,* 37 (May, 1959), pp. 305–311.

capabilities and desires, and of altered or improved techniques and facilities for meeting these desires.

Planning also depends on a fundamental strategy or orientation to urban change as a whole. Though this strategy is rarely made explicit, it seems to embody, *first,* a necessary distinction among *demographic, social,* and *cultural* aspects of urban structure and change.[15] But it is the special interrelation of these aspects that is significant for the theory of planning. In simplified form, urban change may be conceived as *historically* traceable to cultural innovations (see Chapter 2) which encouraged *population aggregations* in towns and cities. These in turn have been followed by a number of *social products* (extensive division of labor, bureaucratic structures, specialized publics, etc.). However, *cultural changes*—in the form of mores, laws, tastes, and values—have generally tended to appear less rapidly and with a narrowed scope.

This "lag" in culture should not be confused with the concept of "cultural lag" introduced into American sociology by Ogburn. Cultural lag refers to different rates of change discovered by comparing developments in value systems and in material technology.[16] In the context of planning theory, a comparison is instead made between value systems and *organizational forms.* From this standpoint, social problems may be regarded as products of the discrepancy between complex facilities and pressures, on the one hand, and currently inappropriate values and personal motivations on the other. This may be called *achievement lag,* following Odum.

Achievement lag is a relatively new phenomenon. It results from greatly expanded capabilities for human achievement derived from complex, impersonal forms of social organization, a concomitant change in motivational demands on the personnel and clientele of these organizations, and a continuing inability to satisfy these demands because of adherence to *traditional* value orientations. Implicitly, the newer organizational forms seem to express such implied values as size, efficiency, uniformity, centralized power and authority. Whether these are desirable or not is of course important, but temporarily beside the point. Instead, there is considerable emphasis on

[15] A brief but very useful discussion of these aspects of urban structure is Richard Dewey, "The Rural-Urban Continuum: Real But Relatively Unimportant," *American Journal of Sociology,* 66 (July, 1960), pp. 60–66. See also Boskoff, "Social Change," *op. cit.,* pp. 263–265.

[16] William F. Ogburn, *Social Change,* rev. ed. (New York, Viking Press, 1950), pp. 200–236.

emotion (love, fear), minor and major prejudices, narrow circles of loyalty, individualism, and fatalism of both the optimistic and pessimistic varieties. Achievement lag, then, is experienced as the tension between traditional values and the need for *organizationally* (not materially) appropriate values.[17]

Urban planning often takes for granted the desirability of the major social and cultural changes, but in addition seeks to reduce the human costs of achievement lag. Essentially, planning strategy is twofold. The ultimate objective is a gradual reorientation of traditional values (*i.e.*, cultural change) to enable urbanites to reap the objective benefits of social change with minimal disturbance to their security. However, such cultural changes require further *experiments in organizational change,* since the unplanned social and cultural changes of recent decades clearly have not been accompanied by revelant revisions in values and systems of coordination. The rise of municipal and regional planning organizations since World War I is a material application of this general approach. We shall now turn our attention to planning as a *new urban institution* and try to evaluate as objectively as possible the degree of consistency between planning theory and practice.

SELECTED REFERENCES

BERNARD, Jessie, *Social Problems at Midcentury* (New York, Dryden Press, 1957).

BLOCH, Herbert A., *Disorganization: Personal and Social* (New York, Alfred A. Knopf, 1952).

BOSKOFF, Alvin, "Social Change: Major Problems in the Emergence of Theoretical and Research Foci," in Howard Becker and Alvin Boskoff, eds., *Modern Sociological Theory* (New York, Dryden Press, 1957), Chap. IX.

GLAZER, Nathan and McENTIRE, Davis, eds., *Studies in Housing and Minority Groups* (Berkeley, University of California Press, 1960).

MANNHEIM, Karl, *Man and Society in an Age of Reconstruction* (New York, Harcourt, Brace, and World, 1940).

[17] This type of lag has been analyzed under different "labels" by: Howard Odum, *Notes on the Changing Structure of Contemporary Society* (unpublished memorandum, November 12, 1948); Godfrey Wilson and Monica Wilson, *The Analysis of Social Change* (Cambridge, at the University Press, 1945), pp. 83–116, 125–132; Lowell J. Carr and James E. Stermer, *Willow Run* (New York, Harper and Brothers, 1952), pp 206–207, 321–322; Boskoff, "Social Indecision," *loc. cit.*

CHAPTER 16

Planning as an Urban Institution

MODERN URBAN PLANNING in practice represents a widespread attempt to pursue the objectives discussed in the last chapter through new organizations. Essentially, then, we have been witnessing the birth and early development of a distinctive social institution, marked by relatively new value systems, technical and social roles, recruitment procedures, and patterns of authority. However, planning as a fledgling institution operates in part as an *adjunct* to, in part a *substitute* for, pre-existing institutions, particularly, the political and

TABLE 68

A Comparison of Dominant Values in Planning, Political, and Economic Institutions of the Modern World

Planning institutions	Political institutions	Economic institutions
Nonpartisan	Party emphasis	Politically "opportunistic"
Experts	Laymen	Experts
Continuity of program	Discontinuity	Continuity of program
Future orientation	Immediate present	Present and future orientation
General welfare, tangible and intangible	Power	Tangible profits
Increase of effective radius of co-ordination	Narrow radius	Relatively wide radius

309

economic institutions. Indeed, it is this amalgam of competition and collaboration that helps explain the mixed achievements and limitations of urban planning, and the implicit or explicit resistances it inevitably faces in its formative stages.

The accompanying table summarizes what seem to be the basic value similarities and differences among planning, political organization, and economic structures in Western society. In general, the orientation of planning is more congenial to that of modern economic institutions than to political institutions—especially at local levels. Increasingly, economic units have recognized the need for intelligent "planning" in their respective operations to maximize profits, as well as their competitive position in local, regional, and national markets.[1] On the other hand, political institutions (in the form of charters, constitutions, and traditional offices) tend to represent the political conditions of bygone eras. In practice, some economic groups (businessmen, unions) have tried to alter the orientation of government operations in the direction of a quasi-planning approach, through such innovations as budgeting, forecasting of capital expenditures, estimates of revenue sources, development of relevant funds of data, the use of expert assistance in analyzing and making recommendations about local problems. These conditions—the conservatism of the political sphere, the development of a narrowed thrust toward *economic* planning, the influence of economic on political institutions—provide a fundamental backdrop to planning as an emerging institution.

It is important to remember that the necessity of adapting new institutions to previously dominant ones is a recurrent theme in Western civilization. This process involves changes in pre-existing institutions, as well as in the newly developing institutions. A particularly clear case is the rise of modern capitalism (sixteenth to nineteenth centuries) as a challenge to the political-economic complex of feudalism. The newer institutional components (the corporate form, commercial law, credit instruments, nominally free labor) were in com-

---

[1] Several readable discussions of economic planning in modern society are specially recommended: Kenneth E. Boulding, *The Organizational Revolution* (New York, Harper and Brothers, 1953); Robert A. Dahl and Charles E. Lindblom, *Politics, Economics, and Welfare* (New York, Harper and Brothers, 1953); Carl Landauer, *Theory of National Economic Planning,* (Berkeley, University of California Press, 1947); Karl Mannheim, *Freedom, Power, and Democratic Planning* (New York, Oxford University Press, 1950); and W. Arthur Lewis, *The Principles of Economic Planning* (London, Allen and Unwin, 1950).

petition with manorialism, the system of independent principalities, and with the dominant church. As capitalism developed, its adherents both influenced and were influenced by the rise of national, centralized governments, and likewise the emergence of various Protestant denominations. A similar process may be found in the rise of science (especially in the nineteenth century), in its conflict and accommodation with religion, and its more recent interaction with government and education.[2]

Returning to urban planning as a "new" institution, its major problems (and therefore specific forms of experimentation and adjustment) seem to vary in emphasis from society to society. In the United States, for example, the development of planning is hampered by a continuing lack of consensus on the *desirability* or *necessity* of regional planning and its *goals*. By contrast, Scandinavian countries have long accepted the need for urban planning as a means of insuring the welfare of large segments of their populations. Great Britain has achieved substantial consensus about broad planning goals during the past twenty-five years, though specific programs have sometimes created intense dissatisfactions.[3]

Still another issue confronting the creators of a new institution is the choice and coordination of satisfactory *techniques* for carrying out institutional goals. This is an especially difficult problem for planners because urban planning has arisen in an era of very rapid changes, planners must rely on impressionist evaluations of scattered experiences rather than organized funds of knowledge, and to this very day there is a critical dearth of professional planners, whose role must be filled instead by otherwise capable people from engineering, public administration, architecture, or business. In the past fifty years, therefore, a large number of specific proposals—ranging from a purely physical orientation to dramatic, Utopian social schemes—have been debated, attempted, and partially evaluated by urban

[2] R. H. Tawney, *Religion and the Rise of Capitalism* (New York, Penguin Books, 1947); Amintore Fanfani, *Catholicism, Protestantism, and Capitalism* (New York, Sheed and Ward, 1955); Henri See, *Modern Capitalism* (London, N. Douglas, 1928); Norman Jacobs, *The Origin of Modern Capitalism and Eastern Asia* (Hong Kong, University of Hong Kong Press, 1958).

[3] For useful summaries of the planning movement in Great Britain see M. P. Fogarty, *Town and Country Planning* (London, Hutchinson's University Library, 1948); and William Ashworth, *The Genesis of Modern British Town Planning* (London, Routledge and Kegan Paul, 1954). A detailed account of resistance to planning is Harold Orlans, *Stevenage* (London, Routledge and Kegan Paul, 1952).

planners.[4] This search for appropriate planning techniques, with its accompanying successes and failures, is an enlightening illustration of the problems connected with trying to translate the knowledge and insights of social science into practical situations. We shall consider urban planning *programs* more fully in Chapters 17 and 18.

Intimately related to the problems of consensus on values and planning techniques is the problem of appropriate planning organization and authority. Since planning represents a relatively new set of objectives and a new combination of skills and talents, many of the pre-existing groups in urban government, business, and welfare have not been able to assume responsibility for planning without carrying over values and techniques that are implicitly antagonistic to planning. Consequently, a key step in the rise of planning as a social institution has been the formation of specialized groups designed to facilitate planning as an ongoing function, and also to sustain (and develop) an embryonic "culture" of planning.

Once again, experimentation has been a cardinal feature in two important respects. First, the developing organization of planning has been marked by the emergence of new roles (or new applications of older roles), both official and unofficial. Specifically, urban planning may be analyzed in terms of *administrative, professional, technical, lay,* and *public relations* roles. In recent decades, experimentation has consisted of attempts to operate a planning structure with greater and greater emphasis on the whole spectrum of relevant roles, as we shall see below and in Chapters 17 and 18.

The second aspect of this groping toward a successful institutionalization of urban planning concerns the practical problem of coordinating various roles in the planning process—and especially the crucial one of discovering workable relations between neighboring planning areas and between local and national planning bodies. In short, urban planning—as is the case in any social institution—requires patterns of authority and regulation that are consistent with general planning objectives and the special characteristics of given

[4] See Ebenezer Howard, *Garden Cities of Tomorrow,* rev. ed., (London, Faber and Faber, 1945); José Luis Sert, *Can Our Cities Survive?* (Cambridge, Mass., Harvard University Press, 1942); Lewis Mumford, *From the Ground Up* (New York, Harcourt, Brace and World, 1956); Louis Justement, *New Cities for Old* (New York, McGraw-Hill, 1946); J. Tyrwhit *et al.,* eds., *The Heart of the City* (London, Lund Humphries, 1952); Harvey S. Perloff, ed., *Planning and the Urban Community* (Pittsburgh, University of Pittsburgh Press, 1961).

urban regions. Early efforts in this direction seemed to reflect the survival of two extreme and mutually antagonistic approaches. In such nations as Great Britain and the United States, urban planning was a chaotic mosaic of localisms, without coordination *within* metropolitan areas and virtually innocent of the need for responsible integration *between* areas. The opposing orientation, found in some degree in France and in several Latin American nations, placed major responsibility for specific planning programs in a department of the national government.

Since about 1930, the urbanized nations of the world have recognized the limitations of both solutions to the regulative aspects of urban planning. Out of their more recent experience three modern and partly overlapping systems of authority have emerged. We may refer to these, in an admittedly oversimplified manner, as the British System, the American System, and the Continental System.

The British System

Urban planning in Great Britain, the Netherlands, New Zealand, and Scandinavia [5] has achieved an organizational structure that seeks to combine a faith in democratic values and processes, a concern for the planning needs of relatively small nations, and a solution to the problems of integrating various local programs. Since the development of such a structure has been most fully realized in Great Britain, we can best evaluate this type of approach by a detailed survey of English (and Scots) planning systems.

One key to the British system is the creation of several planning levels. Beginning at the local level, there are five segments of the total urban planning institution.

[5] The following discussion is largely based on: Fogarty, *op. cit.*, pp. 19–24, 61–71, 173–203; J. B. Cullingworth, *Housing Needs and Planning Policy* (London, Routledge and Kegan Paul, 1960); A. J. Brown and H. M. Sherrard, *Town and Country Planning* (Melbourne, Melbourne University Press, 1951); Peter G. Richards, *Delegation in Local Government* (London, Allen and Unwin, 1956), Chap. VI; William A. Robson, *The Development of Local Government*, 2nd ed. (London, Allen and Unwin, 1948); R. J. Polaschek, ed., *Local Government in New Zealand* (London, Oxford University Press, 1956); Central Directorate of Reconstruction and Housing, *Municipal Development Plans in the Netherlands* (The Hague, Government Information Service, July, 1953); Ernest M. Fisher and Richard U. Ratcliff, *European Housing Policy and Practice* (Washington, D.C., Federal Housing Administration, 1936).

1. The local council—borough, district, and small county councils.
2. The large metropolitan council, such as the London County Council (L.C.C.).
3. Joint planning executive committees, made up of various local authorities.
4. Regional offices of the Ministry of Housing and Local Government (formerly called the Ministry of Town and Country Planning).
5. The Ministry of Housing and Local Government in London.

In addition, the British system includes the auxiliary services of:

1. Development councils, usually organized by business groups.
2. University consultants and research organizations.
3. Special commissions appointed by Parliament.
4. Private development corporations operating under charters of official planning bodies.

Since 1947, when the important Town and Country Planning Act reaffirmed and clarified a systematic approach to urban planning, the British system has experimented in allocating specific responsibilities among local, regional, and national levels. Through this law (and subsequent revisions), the national level imposes an obligation on *all local planning authorities* to study their respective needs in housing, transportation, industry, etc., and to conceive a detailed, comprehensive plan for meeting these needs. County councils, which often represent larger cities, and had been granted planning powers since 1929, are now *required* to exercise these functions in consultation with smaller local authorities within their regions. Where county councils do not exist, or where the need for coordination of adjacent community development is clearly recognized, a functional equivalent of the county council is the Joint Planning Committee. In the Birmingham area, for example, 23 local authorities have grouped themselves into six joint planning authorities.[6]

Significantly, the national government does not initiate specific urban planning programs, with one exception to be noted later. A local authority normally secures the services of professional plan-

---

[6] West Midland Group, *Conurbation: A Planning Survey of Birmingham and the Black Country* (London, The Architectural Press, 1948), p. 57.

ners in drawing up a set of planning proposals. In many cases, there is consultation with the Ministry during the formative stages of a planning program. When a given plan is approved by the local authority, it is evaluated either by the Ministry in London, or by *regional* offices of the Ministry. In the latter case, the various national bureaus are represented by two *coordinating commissions,* to which local authorities may apply for information and provisional approval. One such commission, the Distribution of Industry Panel, provides aid and encouragement in matters of economic development. Regional Physical Planning Committees, on the other hand, are concerned with problems of physical planning, such as housing, roads, parks, and greenbelt areas.

If it seems necessary, the Minister of Housing and Local Government may legitimately establish joint planning boards for urban regions marked either by a maze of conflicting authorities or simply inertia with respect to local problems. The members of these boards are appointed by the local authorities concerned, so that planning functions remain faithful to local needs and resources. However, the joint board automatically supersedes the authority of component local councils; it possesses full powers to make appropriate investigations, to devise comprehensive programs, and to implement these programs when the Ministry bestows its official blessing.

The design of urban planning programs is therefore a local or regional responsibility, with the assistance of the national government. However, the ultimate planning authority is by law the Ministry of Housing and Local Government, which must approve any plan before it can be transferred from paper to practice. In general, the Ministry's consultative role in early stages of a plan's preparation eases the problem of securing final approval without protracted conflicts between levels of authority. According to one close observer of British local government,[7] the administration of urban planning processes has been relatively smooth and remarkably lacking in controversy.

The Case of London

A major exception to this system of local initiation, national consultation, and national supervision is the London region. As Robson has pointed out, the chaos of local authorities and the traditionally unsympathetic attitude of Parliament had made planning

[7] Richards, *op. cit.,* p. 115.

extremely necessary but virtually impossible. Consequently, the Town and Country Planning Act of 1947 specifically singled out the London region for extraordinary treatment. The L.C.C. was designated as the key planning authority for the London area, though the small "downtown" City of London was allowed to retain its medieval autonomy on such matters. On the other hand, the Ministry has discretionary powers of initiating surveys and plans, in all probability for the special case of London rather than to impose general controls over British urban planning as a whole. The Ministry has therefore sponsored the famous "Greater London Plan" by Patrick Abercrombie, which spelled out recommendations for decentralizing London's population and industries through the development of 12 (now 15) New Towns. It should be noted also that somewhat similar recommendations were presented by Abercrombie in a plan sponsored by the L.C.C.[8]

The British system, in short, emphasizes areal and regional responsibility for urban planning, with legal (though not always practicable) coordination provided by a national authority.

The American System

Unlike the recent British approach, urban planning in the United States has been largely a local responsibility. Cities are incorporated through charters granted by the various states. In general, state governments have not been sympathetic to urban problems within their borders, nor have they encouraged any comprehensive approach to city and regional planning—either morally or financially. Until recently, the federal government likewise reserved its energies for interstate and international issues. No national agency devoted specifically to urban affairs exists, though there have been several proposals for a Department of Urbiculture in the President's Cabinet. Since 1949, however, as a consequence of housing and slum clearance legislation, the federal government has come to demonstrate some interest and control of city planning programs, principally through

[8] William A. Robson, *The Government and Misgovernment of London* (London, Allen and Unwin, 1939); The Corporation of London, *The City of London: A Record of Destruction and Survival* (London, The Architectural Press, 1951); *Report on Planning in the London Region* (London, The Town Planning Institute, 1956); Cullingworth, *op. cit.*, Chap. VIII; William A. Robson, ed., *Great Cities of the World* (London, Allen and Unwin, 1954), pp. 292–294.

the power to withhold federal funds for local redevelopment programs.[9]

Consequently, urban planning is almost exclusively local in origin
and in responsibility. But this system of local autonomy also reflects
a basically cautious orientation to planning and a hesitancy to develop
efficient lines of authority. Within the typical local (city) planning
structure, therefore, three separable segments operate with variable
degrees of cohesion with one another.

1. *The municipal executive* (including the mayor, the city manager, and the city council).
2. *The planning department or bureau*—a group of professionals
   who are full-time employees of the municipal government.
3. *The planning commission*—a group of appointed, unpaid laymen with legal powers to participate in the planning process.

Formally, the central, legally recognized authority for city planning
is the mayor and his council. Both the planning bureau and the
planning commission have been set up to operate as *specialized*
advisory bodies. The planning bureau has the responsibility of gath-
ering data, developing a Master Plan (to be discussed in Chapter 17),
relating numerous requests to the Master Plan, and presenting proposals for planning projects. In many instances, particularly in cities
under 50,000 population, private planning consultants are hired to
supplement the bureau. Normally, the mayor and council are author-
ized to secure these services, with the advice of the director of the
planning bureau. The planning commission, on the other hand, is
both an advisory and a policy-making agency. It makes recommendations to the executive and the legislative arms for their approval and
financial support. However, such recommendations *originate* as proposals by the planning bureau (or special consulting groups) to the
planning commission, which usually has the authority to accept or
reject plans, and thus determines what is available to the ultimate

[9] Robert A. Walker, *The Planning Function in Urban Government*, 2nd ed.
(Chicago, University of Chicago Press, 1950); Donald Webster, *Urban Planning and Municipal Public Policy* (New York, Harper and Brothers, 1958);
William Anderson, "Political Aspects of City Planning," in Theodore Caplow,
ed., *City Planning* (Minneapolis, Burgess Publishing Company, 1950), pp.
53–79; Robert M. Fisher, *Twenty Years of Public Housing* (New York, Harper
and Brothers, 1959).

planning authority (mayor and city council). Under these conditions, urban planning is in reality an inherently competitive process, a system of checks and balances. Neither the elected officials nor the professional staff of planners play a decisive role in planning.

Since the planning commission seems to exercise "veto power," it has become the key component of local planning and therefore merits closer examination. As a leading student of planning organization has pointed out,[10] the planning commission is a survival of a period in which professional planning was nonexistent and in which the need for planning was ignored by most urban residents. Leading citizens therefore organized themselves to prod city governments to provide a planning orientation and to develop specifically needed programs (*e.g.*, zoning). Indeed, most municipal functions (including police and fire protection, health and welfare services) began in this manner.

However, as city planning became a regular function of local governments, the commission of leading citizens lost its initial and very important role as a public relations arm of planning. As provided by law, the planning commission remains a *policy-making body*. But this role, as it is widely recognized by students of city planning, is an inherently difficult one for the members of planning commissions, for three reasons.

1. By custom, the members are predominantly laymen and representative of the middle and upper status levels—particularly local businessmen. While commission members are conscientious and well meaning, they understandably follow perspectives that reflect their limited (though often highly regarded) experience.[11] Urban planning, however, requires concern for broader viewpoints and experience, especially those of lower status groups and urban minorities.

2. Again, by virtue of their background as laymen and businessmen, commission members rarely possess the interest or the general training that can inculcate a genuine understanding of the nature and scope of urban planning. Normally, therefore, they emphasize the more tangible, discrete aspects of planning. They interpret their function as limited to consideration of physical planning, to "practical" (immediate) problems—such as zoning regulations or a matter of traffic rerouting.

[10] Walker, *op. cit.*, p. 133. See also Webster, *op. cit.*, pp. 102–109.
[11] Walker, *op. cit.*, pp. 153–163.

3. Finally, the planning commission as a unit normally operates with some ambiguity in status and responsibility. Although armed with substantial powers (develop comprehensive plans, review petitions for variations from plans, hiring of the planning staff), the commission tends to be somewhat apart from the regular administrative system and therefore not clearly subject to public control. Commission members are appointed by the mayor or city council, but thereafter they are notably independent; their dismissal or removal can only be on the difficult grounds of incompetence and malfeasance. Furthermore, the laws establishing planning commissions seem to mix advisory and policy-making functions without awareness of the practical difficulties this confusion entails. As a consequence, there are numerous opportunities for frictions and misunderstandings with the mayor and council, and with the professional planning staff.

With this general division of authority, the institutionalization of urban planning often seems like an exercise in futility. In short, the planning structure is self-defeating. The planning staff has its elaborate, long-range blueprints that may seem daring to the cautious layman. The mayor or the city council are busy with the routine affairs of government, and the prospect of re-election; they often view planning as necessary, but the responsibility of other agencies. The typical planning commission is made up of part-time, unpaid lawyers, realtors, and businessmen who regard themselves as guardians of thrift, sanity, and other civic virtues, and who prefer the pace of hesitation to the leaps of bold creativity. A built-in deadlock in urban planning thus prevails until one or more strong personalities comes to sit in the mayor's chair, on the city council, in the office of the planning bureau director, or at the table of commissioners. Sociologists have generally discarded the "great man" theory of history, but the dedicated, highly competent and persuasive personality seems to be the crucial element in converting institutional inertia into a process of achievement. In New York City, for example, city planning was largely stimulated by Mayor La Guardia and the many-titled commissioner, Robert Moses. In Philadelphia, the planning successes of the last decade can be attributed to the indefatigable director of city planning and a dynamic mayor. Similar cases of individual catalysts in planning can be found in many cities, among them Los Angeles, Milwaukee, Cincinnati, and Pittsburgh.

The Continental System

In line with their respective national histories, both France and the Soviet Union can be taken as the clearest illustrations of the rather extreme "Continental" approach to urban planning, which is a survival of nineteenth century forms of administrative centralization. The essence of this planning structure may be found in a highly bureaucratized system of agencies in which initiation of planning is a national responsibility, the desires of local populations are not consulted at most stages of the planning process, and the execution and financing of plans are principally (if not completely) in the hands of a national authority.

France, which is usually numbered among the political democracies, has assimilated the urban planning function into its traditionally centralized administrative system of *departements* and *prefectures,* which are subordinate to the Premier and his ministers. The Ministry of Housing and Reconstruction, aided by an appointed professional planner, maintains regional branches which translate plans initiated in Paris. Municipal governments may advise, submit information, or even criticize such plans; often they are relatively passive participants. For example, in the important task of rebuilding war-ravaged cities, a reconstruction plan is prepared for each city by a planner appointed by the Ministry. Virtually all funds for reconstruction of buildings, streets, and public utilities are from the national treasury.[12]

Urban planning in the Soviet Union has passed through several phases of experimental centralization. Between 1921 and 1940, planning was formally centralized in the State Planning Commission (Gosplan) and the Central Executive Committee of the Communist Party. In practice, however, local city planning was a jumble of uncoordinated programs, of general plans that were executed with unanticipated freedom of interpretation. The pressure for economic achievement and an ambitious program of rebuilding or creating hundreds of cities explain the enormous gap between formal structure and practice. The second phase, roughly corresponding to the forties, reflected three basic innovations in organization: more careful consultation between the State Planning Commission and the local planning authorities; creation of an Administrator of Architectural Affairs to *inspect* planning activities of city planning bodies; the

[12] Leo Grebler, *Europe's Reborn Cities,* Urban Land Institute, Technical Bulletin No. 28 (Washington, D.C., March, 1956), pp. 71, 87–88.

FIGURE 12
The Formal Structure of Urban Planning Organization in the Soviet Union

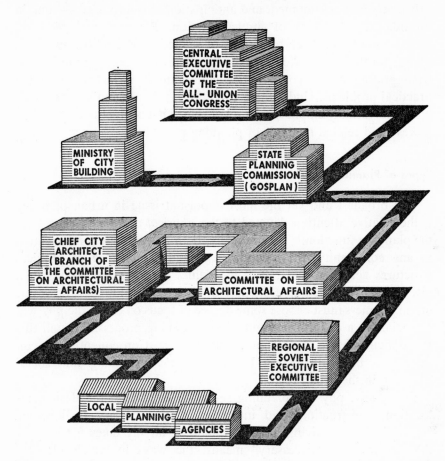

SOURCE: Maurice F. Parkins, *City Planning in Soviet Russia*, pp. 87–88, 98.

reduction of competitive participation in the planning process by hundreds of local government and party groups (a decree of 1948). Despite such measures, Russian city planning did not achieve its current stage of tight, bureaucratic centralization until the early fifties.[13] A simplified framework of control is presented in the following chart.

As a developing urban institution, planning is undergoing experimentation not only in organizational structure and patterns of

[13] Maurice F. Parkins, *City Planning in Soviet Russia* (Chicago, University of Chicago Press, 1953).

authority, but in "planning mores" and distinctive techniques. Unfortunately, the overall goals of urban planning—rational control of urban regional development and anticipation of future needs—contain no inherent strategies of implementation. Planners and planning groups may be inspired by visions of seductive possibilities in urban living, but they must often face the fact that the planning function has been grafted on to communities with long histories and insistent practical problems. Under these conditions, urban planning has developed and variably emphasized a set of somewhat competitive "practical mores" and related methods of planning procedure.

Types of Planning Orientation

The broadest and yet the most important issue in urban planning is the relative attention devoted to the *physical* and *social* aspects of the planning function.[14] Theoretically, both are intimately interrelated in any community; the location, use, and significance of physical structures act upon and reflect the values of organized groups in a given area over a definite time period. As a practical matter, however, urban planners must choose some degree of focus on either the physical or social for a definite segment of the planning process. Though this is a difficult choice, a decision must be made. Consequently, we can identify a basic distinction between *physical planning* and *social planning* in the urban region.

Essentially, physical planning serves to emphasize the design, allocation, construction, and interrelation of necessary facilities or "means" of urban living. Physical planning largely takes for granted the *definition* of "necessary" means, the ways in which physical facilities will be used, and the social consequences of their use. Social planning, on the other hand, is predominantly concerned with the creation, maintenance, or alteration of desired influences on the behavior, values, satisfactions, and interaction patterns of an urban population.

Inevitably, another critical choice confronts the urban planner, regardless of his varying decisions about physical and social aspects. Again, the pressure of specific, continuing urban problems (*e.g.,*

[14] Lewis Mumford, *The Culture of Cities* (New York, Harcourt, Brace, and World, 1938), Chap. VII; William H. Form, "The Place of Social Structure in the Determination of Land Use: Some Implications for A Theory of Urban Ecology," *Social Forces,* 32 (May, 1954), pp. 317–323.

traffic, slum areas, overcrowded schools) demands a selection between tactics: the *corrective* approach and the *creative* approach.

In terms of our distinction in the last chapter (pp. 301–304), the corrective approach is normally on the level of discrete invention; it aims to repair or patch up *existing* cases of difficulty. Since transitional urban communities represent many such cases, it is obvious that they cannot be ignored. But how much effort should be given to treating "symptoms" as contrasted to attempts to search out conditions that can be appropriately altered? The former, while it is necessary, is peripheral to planning; the latter is more difficult, but represents the *essence* of planning as an urban institution.

The actual combinations of decisions on these issues can be presented in a simplified tabular form as the basic "strategic-tactical" kit of the urban planning institution. In the following chapters, we shall review a number of programs that illustrate this variety of planning orientations. We shall also try to evaluate the consequences of the planning institution for the structure of urban regions.

TABLE 69

Classification of Urban Planning Orientations

PLANNING ORIENTATION TYPES	*Applications in urban regions*
Corrective physical orientation	Routine medical and hospital facilities, street repairs, traffic, zoning, downtown redevelopment
Creative physical orientation	Public health programs, subdivision controls, provision of adequate greenbelts
Corrective social orientation	Case work programs (public and private)
Creative social orientation	Well-designed new communities or areas, neighborhood unit approach

SELECTED REFERENCES

ASHWORTH, William, *The Genesis of Modern British Town Planning* (London, Routledge and Kegan Paul, 1954).

GALLION, Arthur B., *The Urban Pattern: City Planning and Design* (Princeton, D. Van Nostrand Company, 1950).

CHAPIN, F. Stuart, Jr., *Urban Land Use Planning* (New York, Harper and Brothers, 1957).

MANNHEIM, Karl, *Freedom, Power, and Democratic Planning* (New York, Oxford University Press, 1950).

————, *Man and Society in an Age of Reconstruction* (New York, Harcourt, Brace, and World, 1940).

MUMFORD, Lewis, *The Culture of Cities* (New York, Harcourt, Brace and World, 1938), Chaps. VI, VII.

WALKER, Robert, *The Planning Function in Urban Government,* 2nd ed. (Chicago, University of Chicago Press, 1950).

WEBSTER, Donald, *Urban Planning and Municipal Public Policy* (New York, Harper and Brothers, 1958).

CHAPTER 17

Corrective Planning

IT SHOULD COME as no surprise that an overwhelming proportion of urban planning has been *corrective* rather than creative in nature. The reasons are fairly clear and are important in understanding the development of planning and its role in the urban region. First and foremost, the rapid and uncoordinated growth of urban agglomerations has produced a vast Pandora's Box of problems, which must be seriously confined to manageable limits before new vistas of urban living can be soberly approached. Indeed, the failure to achieve a measure of success with such urban problems as congestion, traffic snarls, crime, etc. has, in the second place, drained urban finances that might otherwise be allocated to genuinely creative programs. Thirdly, in the formative stage of urban planning administration (roughly 1900–1950), most of the members of planning bodies and commissions were implicitly committed to tangible, immediate programs whose results could be visibly determined by the layman. Fourthly—and perhaps not so clearly—a corrective approach reflects the persistence of traditionalistic, nonrational attitudes among urbanites, instead of the amusingly false picture of the "typical" urban emphasis on rationality, the attraction of new ideas, and "action."

As a consequence of these conditions, we may note an interesting division of labor in the overall planning function of urban regions— at least in the United States. Public (and semipublic) planning agencies have assumed (or been given) responsibility for *corrective* physical planning and *aspects* of *creative* physical planning. The major responsibility for *corrective social* planning—*e.g.*, welfare, rehabilitation, education, and interpersonal relations—remains in the preexistent mosaic of school boards and social work agencies. Creative social planning, which has a long and uneven history as a property of monarchs, politicians, legislatures, and utopian writers, is still not a routine concern of any established, reputable organization. It is largely a reflection of the critical role of individual philosophers, architects, political idealists, educators, and some social scientists. As we shall see in the next chapter, public planning agencies have attempted occasional entries into the difficult area of creative social planning. However, thus far this extension of normal planning functions can be found mainly in European urban planning.

The Master Plan

Corrective urban planning, particularly in the U.S., is a phase in a larger, idealized process of planning, in which creative planning is an ultimate objective. If the immediate problems of urban planning seem to predominate, planners have invented a link between corrective and creative programs in the concept and practical implementation of the Master Plan, or the "comprehensive city plan." [1] Fundamentally, the Master Plan is a graphic summary of present and projected patterns of land use, transportation, community facilities, and financing for an urban region. It represents an attempt to evaluate and select desirable current trends in the physical development of the region, and design changes in specific physical trends for a given period in the future (e.g., 20 years). Consequently, the Master Plan serves as a "measuring rod" for evaluating the significance of any category of community information (birth rates, tax revenues, school population, etc.), any existent public program, or any proposed revisions in community policies. It is important to understand that the Master Plan emphasizes trends and goals, *orientations* rather than detailed blueprints for specific means. Consequently, planning agencies possess a somewhat flexible instrument that provides links and constant guides to thinking and acting, rather than a definitive, eternal, sacred commitment. As information and experience accumulate, the Master Plan can be (planners assert it *must* be) altered to take account of changing events and new conceptions of desirable goals.

In a sense, corrective planning is a preliminary to the planner's fundamental objective—the creation of an urban region that provides the maximum in physical services and social amenities for its residents, *as these are interpreted by a continuing interchange of ideas between*

[1] Mary McLean, ed., *Local Planning Administration*, 3rd ed. (Chicago, International City Managers Association, 1959), pp. 34–35.

urbanites and planners.[2] The role of corrective planning measures, therefore, is to clear up outstanding urban "debts" (unprofitable costs, social and personal wastage, chaotic development) so that newer and more promising responsibilities can be assumed. In other words, before deep-seated changes can be seriously attempted, the possibility of appreciating, financing, and absorbing such changes must be adequately increased by more immediate and somewhat prosaic correctives. The basic sociological problem in corrective urban planning therefore becomes: to what extent do specific corrective measures actually prepare the urban region for the more difficult process of guiding urban development in terms of orderly, comprehensive, and yet practicable images of the future?

We shall review and evaluate in this chapter a representative selection of current forms of corrective urban planning—principally in the area of physical planning. Perhaps we can begin with one of the oldest and most controversial forms: *urban zoning.*

Zoning and its Contributions

Though European cities have long established controls over land use within their municipal borders, the younger and more dynamic cities of the United States were, until recently, so enamoured of sheer growth that considerations of the costs of rapid and uncoordinated growth were ignored. Recognition of the persistent problems of blight, decay, congestion, and wasted or unused land areas finally led to a national conversion to the zoning ordinance as a belated first step toward civic stabilization. Citizens groups, businessmen, architects, and planners were particularly vocal and persuasive in the twenties and thirties, after the pioneer zoning efforts of such cities as New York City and Boston.[3]

As a primary type of corrective physical planning, zoning normally has several basic objectives. First is the necessity of arresting the long-term trend toward purely individualistic, undesirably heterogeneous use of the city's dwindling supply of land. Prior to effective zoning, city lots and parcels were available to either the first or the

[2] Herbert Simon, "Decision Making and Planning," in Harvey S. Perloff, ed., *Planning and the Urban Community* (Pittsburgh, University of Pittsburgh Press, 1961), pp. 189–191.

[3] Theodore Caplow, "Urban Structure in France," *American Sociological Review*, 17 (October, 1952), pp. 544–549; Charles M. Haar, *Land Planning Law in a Free Society* (Cambridge, Mass., Harvard University Press, 1951), pp. 180–195; *Local Planning Administration*, Chap. XI.

highest bidder, without regard for the welfare, safety, or economic effect on neighboring areas.

Second, zoning has often been designed to control or limit the growth of population. This is accomplished by zoning laws that specify maximum densities of population or maximum number of dwelling units per acre.

Third, zoning laws reflect the planner's desire to salvage a reasonable balance among residential, commercial, industrial, and public needs for land in the urban region. Without the guidance of informed zoning, many American cities have an understandable tendency to overestimate commercial land needs—a survival of the widespread economic optimism of 1909 to 1929.[4]

The Limitations of Zoning

Theoretically, these crucial objectives make zoning an extraordinarily promising mechanism—almost the fundamental mechanism—of corrective physical planning. In practice, however, zoning has often achieved little to warm the hearts of genuine planning groups. Several persistent difficulties help to account for this lack of achievement.

One brutal fact inevitably reduces the theoretical potential of zoning: decades of uncontrolled growth present planners with a virtually completed physical pattern that cannot easily (or inexpensively) be changed. Street patterns, location of buildings, etc. are of course not eternal, but they constitute a complex mold for large portions of the central city. Zoning therefore inherits a set of limits that only the irresponsible and the impractical can ignore.

A second important difficulty is the failure to integrate zoning regulations with a comprehensive urban plan. While this situation now receives more attention by planning bodies than in the past, it is often the case that the time-consuming process of developing a long-term plan based on careful analyses is deferred for the more immediate, more tangible, and less difficult process of drawing up zoning ordinances and maps.[5]

[4] See Philip H. Cornick, *On the Problems Created by Premature Subdivision of Urban Lands in Selected Metropolitan Districts* (Albany, N.Y., Division of State Planning, 1938); Haar, *op. cit.*, p. 180.

[5] "Facelifting Cities: Renewal Programs Show New Signs of Life, But Progress Still is Slow," *The Wall Street Journal*, May 7, 1958; Donald Webster, *Urban Planning and Municipal Public Policy* (New York, Harper and Brothers, 1958); Coleman T. Woodbury, *The Future of Cities and Urban Redevelopment* (Chicago, University of Chicago Press, 1953), pp. 641–642.

Zoning laws, in the majority of cases, are limited to municipal boundaries of central cities, or at best, enabling acts permit city zoning authorities to control land use within a narrow band outside the city line (1.5 to 5 miles). Since the greater part of urban population increase has occurred in peripheral areas (in the 5–20 mile band beyond the city proper), this kind of limitation encourages the very difficulties that zoning is supposed to correct. Indeed, one of the consequences of this situation is the development of competing zoning groups, often with divergent objectives. For example, in the New York City metropolitan region, outer suburban areas (such as Norwalk and New Canaan in Connecticut) have designed their zoning regulations to restrict population increase and exclude lower and middle income groups from their areas by requiring four-acre sites. This so-called "snob zoning"—regardless of its intrinsic merits or shortcomings—intensifies the already formidable problems of achieving orderly development in modern urban regions.[6]

A fourth difficulty common to zoning, in the United States and to some extent in Great Britain, is the desire to maintain property values. While this is a legitimate objective, in practice it leads to decisions that invariably delay or even contradict the normal aims of zoning. One of the widespread zoning problems is *nonconforming uses* or *variances*—in short, official permission to continue activities that clearly violate legal specifications for given types of zones (residential, commercial, or industrial). Permitted continuation of nonconforming uses is based on the laudable desire to avoid economic hardships for property owners who invested their resources in buildings before the development of zoning regulations. However, the *removal* of nonconforming uses is generally recognized as an exceedingly slow process, One of the leading planning consultants in the United States (Harland Bartholomew) asserts in addition that failure to reduce nonconforming uses is a major condition in the persistence and spread of blight in areas of transition.[7]

Perhaps another consequence of this concern for protecting existing property values is the practice of "spot" or "piecemeal" zoning, which consists of zoning decisions based on *current* locations of activities and uses, rather than a comprehensive, relatively independent scheme for determining proper patterns of land use.[8] Spot zoning can be iden-

[6] Webster, *op. cit.,* p. 370; *The New York Times,* November 11, 1956; December 16, 1956; March 13, 1960.

[7] Webster, *op. cit.,* p. 404; Haar, *op. cit.,* p. 195.

[8] *Local Planning Administration,* pp. 321–322.

tified in instances where an otherwise homogeneous area (*e.g.,* a predominantly residential area) contains a totally different variety of land use (*e.g.,* a gas station or a bottling plant) that is approved by the local zoning body. Significantly, spot zoning stems from acquiescence to requests from both existing or prospective owners of nonconforming property. To the student of planning, spot zoning not only invites further requests for a patchwork of variant uses; it also serves to interfere with the *corrective* function of zoning, and likewise creates additional obstacles to creative planning.

Still another aspect of the difficulties of zoning is the ever present danger of "overzoning." Whether it can be traced to inadequate surveys of crucial information or special pressures on zoning bodies, the practice of overzoning—or allocating too large a proportion of urban land for a specific type of use—inherently encourages speculation, narrowly conceived interests, and blight. For example, in American cities, zoning officials have tended to reserve unrealistically large areas for business purposes, thus restricting opportunities for residential expansion. It has been estimated, to take an extreme case, that an earlier zoning ordinance for New York City would permit working space for 340 million people in business and industrial zones. The same ordinance, parenthetically, designated residential areas and densities that would have housed 77 million people.[9]

HOUSING PROGRAMS

The city's dual status as a *productive* area and a *residential* entity has often been forgotten. While major efforts have been directed toward more efficient manufacture, processing, and commercial enterprises, the prosaic task of housing urbanites has—until recently—been left to chance and the well-known inadequacies of the private housing market. With few exceptions, the net result in the world's cities has been congestion, greatly deteriorated housing facilities, and the popular "escape to the suburbs." Recognition of the deficiencies of urban housing is almost universal; more than 50 nations have organized national agencies designed to improve the availability and the quality of housing.[10] In addition, numerous local, state, and

[9] Haar, *op. cit.,* p. 180.

[10] *Ibid.,* p. 170; John Graham, *Housing in Scandinavia* (Chapel Hill, N.C., University of North Carolina Press, 1940); Timothy Sosnovy, *The Housing Problem in the Soviet Union* (New York, Research Program on the U.S.S.R.,

regional organizations are currently engaged in mitigating the long-term effects of slums and borderline deterioration.

Surveying the range of urban housing programs, we can fairly conclude that there are several types (or aspects) of housing problems, rather than the oversimplified notion of slums and slum clearance as *the* problem. There is, in accord with this complexity, a formidable network (perhaps "maze" is more correct) of public and private, local and national, professional and lay groups concerned with urban housing.[11] Paradoxically, in a period that presumably emphasizes planning as a comprehensive, coordinated function, the responsibility for planning housing (at least in the United States) is not primarily lodged in the city or metropolitan planning department. Instead, there is a progressive *division of responsibility* (with attempts at articulation) and a bewildering variety of specific programs. In fact, any one interested in modern housing must acquire a bulging glossary of terms that define somewhat distinctive objectives and agencies: urban renewal, urban development and redevelopment, rehabilitation, conservation, and relocation. At this point, however, we shall focus our discussion on the corrective physical aspects of housing planning.

Planning Housing for Growing Populations

As a result of population increase in cities, and also of changes in urban social strata, the housing supply has been inadequate quantitatively and qualitatively unsuitable as well. In Paris, the general absence of new building is indicated by the fact that the average age of its dwellings is more than one hundred years. The French Minister of Construction estimates that the Paris region needs a minimum of 75,000 new dwellings each year to replace unsafe units and accommodate an expanding population. Prior to a planning program, less than 10,000 units a year were built (between 1945 and 1954), though

1954); Edward C. Banfield and Morton Grodzins, *Government and Housing in Metropolitan Areas* (New York, McGraw-Hill, 1958); William W. Nash, *Residential Rehabilitation: Private Profits and Public Purposes* (New York, McGraw-Hill, 1959).

[11] Mabel L. Walker, *Urban Blight and Slums* (Cambridge, Mass., Harvard University Press, 1938); George W. Hartman and John C. Hook, "Substandard Urban Housing in the U.S.: A Quantitative Analysis," *Economic Geography*, 32 (April, 1956), pp. 95–114; Robert M. Fisher, *Twenty Years of Public Housing* (New York, Harper and Brothers, 1959), pp. 17–33; J. B. Cullingworth, *Housing Needs and Planning Policy* (London, Routledge and Kegan Paul, 1960).

this was increased to 50,000–68,000 more recently.[12] The French program now consists of three parts: government loans to stimulate building; the chartering of special companies to build reasonably priced rental units; and government control of speculation in housing sales.

In the United States the urban housing supply has likewise been unequal to demand, especially since 1945. With few exceptions during the late forties and early fifties, the demand for houses and apartments was primarily met by private developers and contractors in fringe or suburban locations. For various reasons, the first waves of postwar housing bypassed considerations of quality and coordination with other community needs and programs. This was the period of "projects," "new subdivisions," and rapidly constructed, artfully advertised "developments."[13]

In general, American cities have not been able to keep pace with the increasing demand for additional (rather than replacement) housing. Local planning bodies in many instances have adequately surveyed housing needs for their respective regions, but appropriate land is either unavailable or is too expensive for local budgets. State and federal subsidies for housing are largely for replacement housing— and this is in most cases for lower income groups.

Somewhere in the border zone between replacement housing and expanded housing is the continuing problem of providing rental housing for middle income urban families. In several metropolitan areas, the major alternative to crowded facilities has been a flight to the suburbs, where, incidentally, rental housing is overshadowed by home owner property and cooperative apartments. Less than ten years ago in the New York City region, there was an estimated *shortage* of about 105,000 dwelling units, most of which were needed in the city proper. At the same time, about 20,000 "excess" dwelling units (mainly houses) were available in the suburbs. During the past ten years, planning for middle income housing *within the city limits* has been obstructed by impossible financial obstacles. However, New York City took a faltering first step in 1958 by constructing a nineteen-story apartment house in Brooklyn for 205 families in the $5,990 to $7,490 income range. This is adjacent to a low-income housing project

[12] *The New York Times*, October 22, 1959.
[13] Compare the discussion of Glenn H. Beyer, *Housing: A Factual Analysis* (New York, Macmillan, 1958) and John Keats, *The Crack in the Picture Window* (New York, Ballantine Books, 1957).

of about 1,000 units. Four more combined (middle and low income) projects in other boroughs are still in the blueprint stage.[14]

Slum Clearance, Redevelopment, and Relocation

Whether considered from a moral, esthetic, economic, or administrative standpoint, the key problem in corrective physical planning is the slum or blighted, irreparable residential area around the city's core, and in scattered nuclei within and beyond the municipal limits. Both in European nations and the United States, urban planners have devoted much thought to this problem, though European city planners have generally been permitted to implement plans earlier and with more effectiveness than their American counterparts. This is perhaps partly explainable by the practice—virtually unknown in American cities—of public purchase of large tracts of land (both within the city and at the fringes) for future housing needs.[15] But most urban planners now agree that slum clearance is basically a *public* responsibility and that state and federal funds are absolutely necessary to finance the huge costs.

Focusing on American cities now, the welter of discussions and planning suggestions on slums has been dominated by a recurrent theme: "the correction of past mistakes alone." Thus, in the pioneer period of American public housing as an antidote to slums (1936–1950), the main emphasis was simply on tearing down deteriorated and unsafe buildings and replacing them with fairly well designed "housing projects" on roughly the same sites.[16] The number of families rehoused in this manner was inevitably small, since the need was immense and the costs were astronomical for what was largely a depression period.

With the housing legislation of 1949 and 1954, two glaring facts were officially recognized: that public housing was *part* of urban planning, rather than a "prima donna;" and that slum clearance must be accompanied by concern for displaced families in the general housing shortage dating from 1945. Consequently, federal subsidies were made available for slum clearance and redevelopment to cities with

[14] *The New York Times*, May 11, 1952; March 23, 1958.

[15] Graham, *op. cit.*, p. 7; Haar, *op. cit.*, p. 209 (footnote 25).

[16] Haar, *op. cit.*, pp. 166–167; Catherine Bauer, "Redevelopment: A Misfit in the Fifties," in Woodbury, *op. cit.*, pp. 9–13.

comprehensive plans. Few cities had such plans in 1954; there was, then, a frenzied period of devising Master Plans to qualify for federal housing aid. By 1958, about 380 cities had submitted one or more detailed redevelopment programs. Yet of the 506 approved programs less than a score have been put into effect because of technical details, bureaucratic delays, resistance of local property owners and resultant lengthy court cases, and problems of integrating housing with highway plans. Washington, D. C., for example, began its first project six years after approval, with an eighty acre development for 1,000 families in apartments and one and two-family houses. The irony of the situation is that during the six year delay, more than 1,000 other dwellings in Washington were added to the ranks of deteriorated buildings.[17]

But, remembering the magnitude of the slum problem in American cities, one of the severest practical problems of planning is finding housing accommodations for former tenants of slum buildings. During the thirties, when there was no housing shortage, displaced slum residents made their own arrangements, which in most cases meant substituting one slum apartment for another. When planners began to see the unsuitability of this expedient, as the housing shortage developed, two other measures were tried as "correctives." One solution gave priority to displaced families in public housing projects at other locations, which had been originally designed to serve the needs of their respective populations. As a consequence, while new housing projects were in construction (taking two to three years), the relocation of slum families was actually intensifying competition for decent housing. The other solution, about which planners themselves are now somewhat disturbed, was to plan and construct housing projects with rather high densities to stem the difficulties of a persistent housing shortage for families with limited incomes.[18] Thus, congestion was not really removed in these areas; it was merely given a superficially different (and very expensive) setting.

Since 1954, the federal government has provided financing for housing projects specifically designed to meet the needs of displaced families (Section 221 of the Housing Act). On the local planning level, this solution still contains several difficulties. Many families from

[17] "Facelifting Cities," *loc. cit.;* Robert Connery and Richard Leach, *The Federal Government and Metropolitan Areas* (Cambridge, Mass., Harvard University Press, 1960), pp. 12–19.

[18] Bauer, *op. cit.,* pp. 13–19.

redeveloped areas are Negro, and this fact reactivates any local patterns of prejudice and discrimination. In practice, the search for adequate relocation areas becomes studded with compromises. To be suitable, such areas should be within a reasonable distance from the central business district and from the subcommunity in which displaced families previously lived. In addition, relocation areas should be relatively vacant, or marked by dispensable, intermittent land uses (*e.g.*, abandoned factories, large, unused lots, run-down, marginal retail stores), so that land costs can be reduced. Finally, the population of adjacent areas must be willing to accept new housing developments for minorities. Several cities, among them Chicago and Atlanta, have been delayed in their relocation projects by local opposition and the sheer unavailability of land that satisfies reasonable planning conditions.

Rehabilitation and Reconditioning

A third approach to housing problems is rehabilitation and reconditioning, which are less dramatic than slum clearance, but yet are extremely important and much less expensive.[19] Essentially, these programs apply to residential areas that have become shabby through neglect and lack of local pride, yet not to the point of presenting immediate "slum" problems. Rehabilitation attempts to prevent advanced stages of deterioration by moderate repairs and remodeling by affected property owners. Several such programs have had the support and technical assistance of local planning departments, but often the major initiative and financing stem from individuals and private civic organizations (such as ACTION and Fight Blight, Inc.). Occasionally, public officials and planning bodies are less than enthusiastic about the possibilities of rehabilitating "marginal" areas. In Washington, D.C., remodeling of the quaintly named Foggy Bottom area (the near Northwest side) was accomplished without official encouragement or financial aid. However, in such cities as Baltimore, Chicago, New Orleans, and Miami, the method of rehabilitation has demonstrated that inner areas of the city can be salvaged without enormous cost for lower and lower middle class families.

[19] Nash, *op. cit.;* Martin Millspaugh and Gurney Breckenfield, *The Human Side of Urban Renewal* (Baltimore, Fight-Blight, Inc., 1958); Chester Rapkin and William G. Grigsby, *Residential Renewal in the Urban Core* (Philadelphia, University of Pennsylvania Press, 1960).

Urban Conservation Programs

A final type of program is an adjunct to planning: urban conservation. Though linked with rehabilitation, either in aims or specific practices, conservation involves a renewed emphasis on enforcement of existing housing code regulations. In many cities over the last decade, revised housing codes have been designed to encourage or require minimum standards of upkeep (*e.g.,* adequate toilets, window screens, hot water, tubs or showers). However, as time elapses and other municipal problems require attention, enforcement of codes often becomes spotty. Legal controls and their proper application are surrounded by an ominous silence—until a crusade arises. Conservation begins when the staff of inspectors is either invigorated or expanded, when code violators are actively sought out, and violators are pressed for compliance; when, finally, the residents of substandard housing really hope for and demand facilities of which they can be proud enough to maintain them in good condition.

TRAFFIC AND TRANSPORTATION

The street pattern of cities is one of the most permanent of man's creations—and normally the most outmoded. If urban regions are inherently dynamic, their street and road networks are embedded in concrete and asphalt molds. But the problem of urban transportation is magnified by the fact that almost one third of the city's land area is invested in a grid of thoroughfares. Consequently, any major change in usage demands corrective measures of staggering proportions.

During the past thirty years, *the* crucial change in usage has been the double-edged adoption of the automobile and the truck. This made possible the modern reclustering of residential and industrial facilities in suburban and fringe areas, the increasing separation of services from their clienteles, an infinitely greater dependence on transportation, and thus a continually burdensome competition for space in the flow of traffic.[20]

Having accepted the automobile as indispensable though troublesome to a high degree, urban planners and their publics in American cities, Paris, London, Rome, Honolulu, and other metropolitan areas are forced to be ingenious within narrow limits. With one or two

[20] The best general discussion is Robert B. Mitchell and Chester Rapkin, *Urban Traffic: A Function of Land Use* (New York, Columbia University Press, 1954).

exceptions they cannot (or will not) control the *use* of cars; certainly, they are unable to stabilize the supply or the demand for cars. Traffic and transportation planning, therefore, has become a desperate attempt to stave off the inevitable *strangulation by auto* until some new and creative approach to urban transportation can be devised.

Perhaps four major types of corrective planning can be noted.

1. Increased efficiency of present thoroughfare systems

Since the investment in existing streets and roads is enormous, a good deal of planning is devoted to maximizing and speeding traffic flow. This is accomplished by: widening streets (a time-consuming process); the use of one-way streets in congested downtown areas; restriction or elimination of on-street parking; the development and improvement of traffic light systems on major thoroughfares, so that the timing of lights is electronically adjusted to changing patterns of traffic density.[21]

2. Rerouting of traffic

Increasingly, city planners are turning to the construction of new thoroughfares as alternative routes for auto traffic. These are the so-called "belt" or "circumferential" parkways, bypasses, expressways, and freeways, which skirt the most congested areas and connect with major interurban highways. The effects of such remedies are difficult to assess, however. In Atlanta, for example, it is widely recognized that the still-to-be completed expressway system is already obsolete. In some instances, downtown traffic congestion has been relieved, though not without causing problems of congestion in other areas. It has also been suggested that the routing of freeways (*e.g.*, in the San Francisco region) has displaced many businesses and homes, thus reducing business and property tax returns to local governments.[22]

[21] *The New York Times*, March 4, 1956.

[22] Urban Land Institute, *The New Highways: Challenge to the Metropolitan Region,* Urban Land Institute, Technical Bulletin No. 31 (Washington, D.C., 1957); James H. Lemly, *Expressway Influence on Land Use and Value: Atlanta 1941–1956* (Atlanta, Georgia State College of Business Administration, 1958); William L. Garrison and Marion E. Marts, *Influence of Highway Improvements on Urban Land,* Highway Economic Studies (Seattle, University of Washington Press, 1958), pp. 53–55; Mel Scott, *The San Francisco Bay Area* (Berkeley, University of California Press, 1959), p. 288; Homer Hoyt, "Expressways and Apartment Sites," *Traffic Quarterly,* 12 (April, 1958), pp. 263–268; *Local Planning Administration,* pp. 198–199.

3. Solutions to parking problems

The dual use of thoroughfares for transportation and parking inevitably interferes with the primary purpose—maximum movement. Consequently, planners have tried to separate these needs as much as possible in the downtown areas. A drastic and, therefore, largely unimitated solution has been attempted in Philadelphia, over considerable protest in the beginning. The city imposed a "no parking" regulation in a square-mile area of the downtown district, with the result that downtown traffic was visibly smoother and the accident rate was almost halved. Another and more popular solution is the provision of public or privately owned parking lots at the fringe of the business district. However, there is some concern that the solution is ultimately as undesirable as the problem. In Chicago's downtown area (and in other cities, too), many blocks are gigantic parking lots, with 60–100 per cent of their land used for cars rather than businesses.[23] Yet in the realm of parking problems, success is highly deceptive. According to one leading traffic analyst, Wilfred Owen:

. . . the more space and the lower the rates (for parking), the greater the inducement to drive into the city despite the inadequacy of its street capacity. . . . Most of America's car owners would rather abandon the city than the car.[24]

4. Mass transit facilities

In the age of the auto, that symbol of apparent individualism, previous forms of urban transportation have tended to wither from neglect and scorn. Yet the suburban trek makes commuting by auto or mass transit (bus, rail, or some variation of these) the only alternatives. A study of New York City's 370,000 suburban commuters indicates that over half depend on railroad lines, while 100,000 come by car, and 63,000 by bus. From an economic standpoint, interurban rail lines are suffering from insufficient business; they can neither maintain or improve commuter service. But from the standpoint of efficiency, rail lines have been found to be superior to any existing mode of transportation. About 48,000 persons can be transported per hour on one rail line, while only 6,700 per hour can be

[23] *The New York Times,* December 16, 1952; "Facelifting Cities, *loc. cit.*
[24] Wilfred Owen, "Shortage in Curbs," *The New York Times,* March 9, 1952.

moved by bus per expressway lane, and a mere 2,250 per hour per car for each expressway lane.[25]

In the last few years, mass or rapid transit has come to be recognized by some planners as the major means of reducing downtown traffic congestion, as well as problems on feeder roads, and the costs of constructing more and more thoroughfares. Philadelphia, for example, has recently inaugurated a program of encouraging suburbanites to use interurban rail lines by subsidizing reductions in commuter fares and simplifying and reducing the expense of transfers from rail lines to city bus and train lines. Other cities are seriously studying the feasibility of operating speedy *monorail systems* from fringe areas to downtown points. Recently, too, a German traffic expert suggested a vast regional subway network connecting the major cities of the Ruhr (Dusseldorf, Essen, and Dortmund), both as a means of rapid transportation and as an air raid shelter system.[26] All such proposals entail huge costs of construction and operation. But it is not yet clear that mass transit facilities will, over the long run, reduce or accelerate congestion. It may well be asked whether or not the most propitious time for obtaining desired results has not already elapsed for some cities.

REDEVELOPMENT IN THE CENTRAL BUSINESS DISTRICT

It is no surprise that the central or downtown area, the oldest part of the city, should be currently scrutinized and diagnosed as requiring extensive physical alterations. Virtually all the major problems of the modern city—traffic congestion, parking facilities, deteriorated or unsightly buildings, housing and community services for minority groups—coexist and intensify one another in the central zone. The result is often an ugliness that repels customers of downtown services and likewise discourages the maintenance of stable neighborhoods near the city's core. Businessmen realize that the downtown district will always be needed, but they cannot ignore the eloquence of comparative sales figures. In several large cities, downtown sales in the

[25] *Local Planning Administration,* pp. 200–203; 219–222; *The New York Times,* February 22, 1959.

[26] City of Philadelphia Urban Traffic and Transportation Board, *Plan and Program 1955* (Philadelphia, Urban Traffic and Transportation Board, 1955); *The New York Times,* March 13, 1960; October 23, 1960; Lewis Mumford, *From the Ground Up* (New York, Harcourt, Brace and World, 1956), Selections 23–25.

last decade of population expansion and enormous spending have tended to decline 5–10 per cent, while suburban sales rose by 20–35 per cent.[27]

Downtown redevelopment faces many problems, however. Some merchants assume a defeatist attitude: "everything's going to the suburbs anyway." Tradition, particularly in the older cities, can delay attempts to revitalize business districts. In Cambridge (England), a modest plan for modernizing a seven-acre tract near the center—notorious for its congestion—has been vigorously opposed in order to preserve the "historical and architectural value of an ancient street [Petty Curl]." City planners propose to provide underground parking, three new ten-story buildings, and a shopping zone reserved for pedestrians.[28]

In the United States, where tradition is somewhat weaker, downtown innovations have met disapproval by taxpayers, who resent the initial costs. But where local planners receive necessary cooperation from business groups, plus financial encouragement from the federal government, revivified and striking business districts have been planned and at least partially rebuilt.[29] Cincinnati is in process of redeveloping 170 acres of a "master-planned central industrial district" in which former slums adjacent to the core are to be replaced by light industrial super-blocks (with adequate parking and trucking facilities), convenient apartment buildings, office buildings, and a new convention center. On a smaller scale, Lowell, Massachusetts, is rebuilding its central business district by constructing three large parking areas, a new civic center, and, eventually, a modern shopping area free from traffic. Philadelphia and its much publicized Penn Center represent a particularly interesting attempt to spruce up a previously ugly complex of railroad walls and outmoded buildings by creating a unified business, shopping, and hotel center around a graceful plaza, in the manner of the older Rockefeller Plaza in New York City. Pittsburgh, with support from local industrial corporations, has cleared large segments of its Golden Triangle for more than fifty new office buildings since 1945. New York City is engaged in a complicated series of projects for the bewildering mosaic known as lower Manhattan.

[27] "Facelifting Cities," *loc cit.*
[28] *The New York Times*, November 22, 1959.
[29] *Ibid.*, May 3, 1953; Charles H. Brown, " 'Downtown' Enters a New Era," *The New York Times Magazine*, January 31, 1960; Special Supplement to *The New York Times*, November 13, 1960; Mumford, *op. cit.*, Selections 11–14, 18.

The basic redevelopment plan calls for several housing projects, near the waterfront, large commercial buildings to replace a patchwork of older buildings, and improvement of pier and docking facilities.

One of the most ambitious sets of proposals for downtown renovation is currently causing much thought among planners. This is the scheme of development currently being translated into reality in Norfolk, Virginia, a venerable yet dynamic city of 300,000 population. While Norfolk is one of the few cities whose downtown areas have maintained (and even increased) sales volume, there is a two-pronged objective in its redevelopment plans: to convert downtown Norfolk into a regional center of *commercial and cultural-artistic affairs*. Essentially, this is envisaged through four interlocking projects. The most basic element is a new loop freeway (100 feet wide) designed to skirt three sides of the central business area and divert traffic from the shopping core. Since the shopping area is in the shape of an elongated rectangle, a system of all-day and rapid-turnover *parking facilities* (operated by public and private groups) is planned at points most accessible to the "long" sides of the area. East of the commercial center and at the opposite edge of expanded parking facilities, the Norfolk plan calls for the replacement of rundown, marginal property and vacant lots by a *civic center,* composed of several public structures. The civic center is also adjacent to the eastern loop of the downtown freeway. Finally, the commercial core itself is to be largely cleared of traffic. Instead, one or two attractive *pedestrian malls,* with a central line of trees and shrubs, and with canopied, non-slip tile walks, has been designed to stimulate business and also to create an esthetic alternative to the current vista of old buildings and the nightly "neon jungle" that resembles a summer amusement park.[30]

AN EVALUATION OF CORRECTIVE PHYSICAL PLANNING

Corrective physical planning is so prevalent and varied in detail that the preceding discussion was necessarily limited to a sampling of efforts of this type. A tremendous amount of money, materials, discussions, and practical compromises has been devoted to the basic problem of arresting blight, congestion, and the deepening ugliness of the urban environment. And yet those who pause to survey the fruits of these programs—urban sociologists, political scientists, city officials, and the professional planners themselves—cannot conclude

[30] *The Norfolk Virginian-Pilot* (Section B), December 6, 1959.

that these extensive efforts have yielded dominantly positive results.

Three or four underlying criticisms are crucial not only to the student of urban planning, but to the thoughtful urbanite as well.

1. Lack of integration

Despite the growth of interest in Master Plans and comprehensive plans, *in practice* much physical planning has been compartmentalized. There has been little serious effort to coordinate the prevailing variety of corrective programs—either with one another, or with a Master Plan. For example, housing developments and highway planning normally are mutually isolated. In general, the lack of coordination may be traced to specialization of authority at the local level and the multiplication of planning agencies on the state and federal levels. It should be recalled that an overwhelming share of funds for corrective physical planning is appropriated by the Congress. Yet neither the Congress nor specially designated federal agencies (*e.g.*, the Bureau of Public Roads, the Housing and Home Authority, the Urban Renewal Administration) has provided any machinery for insuring cooperation and coordination among agencies serving urban planning needs; or requiring that federal funds for various programs be sensibly used by *local* coordination of specific planning programs.[31] With the increasing role of the federal government in urban planning, the alternatives of local or federal coordination are quite obvious, if physical planning is to avoid defeating its avowed purposes.

2. City vs. regional orientation

Because of traditional political barriers, and despite the suburbanization of urban populations, a great deal of urban physical planning treats the corporate "city" as the major unit of planning, rather than the urban region. This is particularly apparent and disturbing in the case of highway plans and housing developments in outer areas. Rarely do the designers of highway routes concern themselves with the larger consequences of new roads for an entire metropolitan area: the attraction of residential and industrial developments near highways in fringe areas and a resultant relocation of demand for urban services. Indeed, any planning program that involves change of land

[31] Connery and Leach, *op. cit.*, pp. 54–55, 59.

use or movement of population and services inevitably has regional implications.[32]

3. Unintended consequences

The preceding criticisms are important in understanding a third critical judgment: that, with some exceptions, the tendency of existing physical planning programs is toward *intensifying* the very problems they are designed to ameliorate. Many cities in the United States are beginning to recognize that the modern traffic jam is not yielding to the frenzied construction of more, wider, better designed highways. In fact, these improved facilities seem to encourage the same (or even greater) concentration of cars in central areas of the city. Continuing delays in improving and extending mass transit facilities likewise aggravate traffic congestion.

Furthermore, many public housing and downtown redevelopment programs also contribute in some degree to urban congestion. As long as housing remains relatively scarce—as has been the case since the early forties—public housing and the prerequisite clearance projects require considerable relocation of displaced families—in most cases, probably by doubling up with relatives or in other inadequate accommodations. But another spur to congestion is the persistent location of public housing in central (or closely situated) areas. Since land is expensive in such areas, large apartment buildings are most economical, but nevertheless preserve congestion. It is significant to note that neither local nor national agencies have encouraged public or private construction of multiple-dwelling units where there is considerably more space—at the fringes of cities. Consequently, and this is the paradox of modern urban regions, while congestion persists near the core, many urbanites in the United States remain attracted to the fringes for single family dwellings and unrealistic quantities of space, thus extending the scope of urban sprawl and devouring land that might be used more judiciously and economically in the future.[33]

As far as downtown planning is concerned, there has been a growing tendency to convert beautification and "opening" of central areas into opportunities to increase the number of large office buildings. Some of these buildings are particularly well designed and interesting additions to the urban landscape. But in such cities as New York,

[32] *Ibid.*, p. 53; Mitchell and Rapkin, *op. cit.*, pp. 178–180.
[33] Connery and Leach, *op. cit.*, p. 15; Nash, *op. cit.*, p. 197.

Denver, Chicago, and San Francisco, the construction of additional buildings may overburden the facilities of the central district and also increase the already bursting traffic load of metropolitan regions. If, on the other hand, the amount of added space for offices outdistances foreseeable needs (as has been suggested is the case in Denver),[34] the new buildings serve to interfere with the satisfaction of other legitimate downtown uses (*e.g.*, hotel space, off-street parking, park areas, or necessary public structures).

4. Symptoms, not causes

By its very nature, corrective physical planning is largely restricted to concern with the concrete, surface aspects of urban problems—symptoms rather than basic causes. In line with this orientation, therefore, existing values are accepted as "givens" by corrective planners, instead of being examined and critically assessed as *components* in urban problems. The unrestricted use of the auto, for example, is one such value that merits close scrutiny, though it is certainly imbued with a sacredness that many would not care to challenge.[35] Yet there is also an implicit acceptance of the worth of "size" and "growth" in urban affairs, without adequate attention to the difficulties these expansive goals entail. In short, corrective physical planning tends to *accentuate* urban trends; its contribution to control of urban change and development is therefore quite limited.

Perhaps the most telling aspect of corrective physical planning, as we have seen it in the United States, is an unwitting emphasis on physical programs for upper and upper middle business and commercial groups, on the one hand, and lower status and minority groups on the other. Highways and downtown renewal bring primary benefits to the former; public housing projects are largely beneficial to the latter. The astonishing fact is that comparatively little corrective planning serves the needs of middle status families, who constitute not only a large segment of the urban region, but also seem to be the most "typical" carriers of urban culture and social organization. A continuous failure to develop the city as an attractive, desirable locale for middle status families helps to explain not only the vast exodus

[34] "Facelifting Cities," *loc. cit.*

[35] A recent exception is John Keats, *The Brazen Chariots* (Boston, Houghton Mifflin, 1959).

to the suburbs, but the apparently stubborn desire to remain in suburban zones despite inconveniences and high costs.

SELECTED REFERENCES

BEYER, Glenn H., *Housing: A Factual Analysis* (New York, Macmillan, 1958).

BREESE, Gerald and WHITEMAN, Dorothy E., eds., *An Approach to Urban Planning* (Princeton, Princeton University Press, 1953).

BRENNAN, T., *Reshaping a City* (Glasgow, The House of Grant, 1959).

CULLINGWORTH, J. B., *Housing Needs and Planning Policy* (London, Routledge and Kegan Paul, 1960).

FISHER, Robert M., *Twenty Years of Public Housing* (New York, Harper and Brothers, 1959).

GREBLER, Leo, *Europe's Reborn Cities,* Urban Land Institute, Technical Bulletin No. 28, (Washington, D.C., March, 1956).

McLEAN, Mary, ed., *Local Planning Administration* (Chicago, International City Managers' Association, 1959).

RAPKIN, Chester and GRIGSBY, William G., *Residential Renewal in the Urban Core* (Philadelphia, University of Pennsylvania Press, 1960).

SELF, Peter, *Cities in Flood* (London, Faber and Faber, 1959).

WOODBURY, Coleman, ed., *The Future of Cities and Urban Redevelopment* (Chicago, University of Chicago Press, 1953).

CHAPTER 18

Creative Planning:
An Application
of Urban Sociology

IF CORRECTIVE PLANNING with its limited objectives has confronted obstacles and opposition, creative planning is understandably more controversial and beset with difficulties. Instead of accepting current modes of social and cultural change, and devising remedies for the problems engendered by these changes, creative urban planning seeks to construct urban regions in which changes can be *consciously selected and articulated* with one another so as to achieve the highest level of experience and opportunity from the urban potential. This is of course an ideal, a projected image, an utopian perspective in the meaning suggested by Mannheim.[1] We have yet to explore the degree to which the distinctive objectives of creative planning have been realized.

But it is first important to recognize that creative planning rests on a cluster of three contributory elements, all of which are necessary for the analysis and appraisal of creative planning.

The Essential Nature of Urban Regions

Implicitly or explicitly, creative planning depends on understanding the basic structure of urban regions in this third "urban wave," as

[1] Karl Mannheim, *Ideology and Utopia* (New York, Harcourt, Brace and World, 1936), Chap. IV.

analyzed by urban sociology and related disciplines.[2] Reviewing the discussion in previous chapters, certain constants or "themes" seem to emerge from sociological studies of urban regions. Since these have been discussed at length, let us briefly restate them at this point.

1. Cities and their regions constitute relatively organized, interdependent networks of population, cultural activities, and land areas —not accidentally juxtaposed fragments.

2. Urban regions, while more highly specialized in function than typically rural communities, nevertheless exhibit considerable diversification. This is evidenced in a typical range of economic specialties (light and heavy industry, finance, wholesale and retail activities, transportation, and communication), and also in the demand for the entire range of *cultural services* men require or come to expect. These services include religion, art, education, recreation, social welfare, health, and public sanitation. In short, the urban region is an enlarged community, not a series of islands connected by roads and bridges.

3. Closely related to the preceding is the complementary relation between residence and family on the one hand, and occupation and place of work, on the other. The sharp separation of the two—the "journey to work"—may be a transitional phenomenon due to rapid urbanization and lack of planning, rather than an inherent urban antagonism between home and plant or office. Consequently, a characteristic differentiation between economic and family functions does not require that they be widely separated *physically* for a substantial part of residents in the urban region.

4. While status distinctions are not rigid in urban regions, they do exist as a consequence of division of labor and differential opportunity to achieve desired styles of urban living. In fact, class differences (however fluid) represent one aspect of the cultural diversity that is so typical of the urban region. Therefore, the organization and services provided by urban regions inevitably develop sensitivity to the needs and desires of specific status categories. Because of the vocal and symbolic preponderance of middle status categories, the urban region appears to emphasize facilities and services for this segment. But there is a relatively large proportion of lower status families,

[2] See Ernest Manheim, "Theoretical Prospects of Urban Sociology in an Urbanized Society," *American Journal of Sociology*, 66 (November, 1960), pp. 226–229.

which are likewise part of the urban order, and therefore contribute to the operation and the problems of urban regions.

5. The urban region is neither comparable to the village nor a highly rationalized, mechanized superplant. It is instead a peculiar composite which draws from these extreme forms of organization, but typically reinterprets these forms in the urban context. More concretely, the urban region represents a complex amalgam of formal, bureaucratized organizations and informal structures. Apparently, urbanites need and support both forms. Indeed, both forms have been "built in" to most urban organizations studied by social scientists.

6. Perhaps another aspect of the preceding feature is the urban mixture of needs and facilities for both *public* and *private* activities. The widespread (and amazingly contradictory) notions of the urbanite as an extroverted, wise-cracking busybody who is always "on stage" or a withdrawn, isolated, lonesome island of quiet desperation probably refer to *extreme deviants*, or persons in the earliest stages of adjustment to urban living. As suggested in Chapters 8 and 9, urbanites seem to desire privacy *and* involvement in various aspects of public affairs.

This appears to mean that urban organization tends to expand opportunities for both specific, individualized activities, and relatively common, generalized motives and affiliations. It is not difficult for us to grasp the need for privacy—as a reaction to rural and small town "grapevines," and the desire for self-expression and creativity. But privacy is complemented by a new and uniquely urban orientation to the public aspect of living, which has two important facets. For the urbanite, the public aspect is apparent in generally available facilities and services, which sustain similarities of interest and basic information despite the diversity of social and cultural milieux. Some examples are police and fire protection, water supply, public education, and such "privately operated" services as media of communication, department and retail stores, and major transportation lines.

In addition to "publicness" of use and availability, there is the increasing sense of *responsibility* as a public phenomenon. This likewise has two aspects: organizational responsibility for providing and improving services (through government agencies, planning bodies, and civic organizations) and personal responsibility to support public organizations by active participation and financial aid. There are of course wide variations among urban regions of the world in the strength of these forms of responsibility. Yet the era of apathy and uncontrolled splinter groups is clearly yielding (though not without reversions) to an emerging urban concept of complex community cohesiveness.

7. Urban regions have rediscovered and perhaps reinterpreted the importance of leisure and the esthetic component as ends in themselves. The desire for pleasant, attractive surroundings as a necessity rather than a luxury is increasingly emphasized—not as a vagrant dream of a distant future, but as a realizable goal in a visible present. This rather new urban focus is a measure of the material achievements of urban technology, of the shift from production to consumption as the crucial aspect of economic organization, and of the accompanying opportunity to become concerned with the amenities of life instead of its harsher aspects.[3] City beautification, the interest in *design* as an instrument of esthetics as well as utility, and the greater concern for urban space for living and recreation all reflect a growing conception of previously neglected values in urbanization.

8. A final theme drawn from sociological analysis of urban regions is the recognition that the physical and ecological structure of specific regions is not inevitable or eternal. Good or bad, orderly or chaotic, the location of groups, facilities, and services in space is an application of *prevailing values*—not of immutable laws of "natural human motivations." Since these values are not identical in contemporary urban regions; since urban values have changed, are changing, and can be changed; consequently, the ecological structure of modern urban regions cannot be accepted as a rigid, unyielding framework for urbanites. In short, urban studies demonstrate that the physical and the sociocultural aspects are inseparable and inherently dynamic in their reciprocal consequences for one another.

Pockets of Inconsistency and Disorder

While urban regions seem to possess an underlying pattern, it is equally evident that urbanization is still a *transitional* process marked

[3] Edward L. Ullman, "Amenities as a Factor in Regional Growth," *Geographical Review*, 44, (January, 1954), pp. 119–132; Christopher Tunnard and Henry H. Reed, *American Skyline* (New York, The New American Library, 1956), especially Parts VI–VIII; Kevin Lynch, *The Image of the City* (Cambridge, Mass., Harvard University Press, 1960); Charles M. Haar, *Land-Use Planning: A Casebook on the Use, Misuse, and Re-use of Urban Land* (Boston, Little, Brown, 1959), pp. 314–315.

by continuing deviations from, or exceptions to, the evolving urban order. These are survivals from earlier social attitudes, and social techniques, that may be interpreted as pockets of inconsistency in an otherwise regular movement toward rational organization and co-ordination. To the urban planner, these constitute underlying problems whose resolution is imperative to creative planning and the future outline of urban organization.

The most obvious and most frequently cited inconsistency is the jumble of competing (or hardly cooperative) formal political authorities in urban regions. Economic and social relations have outgrown traditional administrative limits much as a normal six-year old bursts through recently bought shoes, dresses, shirts, and coats. But it is infinitely easier to buy larger and more comfortable clothes than to obtain expanded and more realistic political units for urban regions.

A particularly crucial element in urban disorder is the inordinate pursuit of technical and social "efficiency" through specialization, social segregation, and division of labor, without sufficient concern for urban coordination and synthesis. To the extent that this general orientation continues, such phenomena as suburban movement inevitably result in slums, traffic problems, increased costs of public services, and lack of understanding between racial and other status divisions in urban regions.

One of the most fundamental aspects of urban difficulties, at least in most of the Western nations, is a continuing *individualistic approach to land use and ownership*. As a reaction to feudal restrictions and as a means of establishing a necessary variety of land uses in early stages of modern urbanization, this attitude is quite understandable and (in its earlier expression) useful. But if permitted to develop unchecked for very long—as was the case in American cities —the practical consequences are often uneconomical and unnecessary development of urban land. This "gold rush" psychology over several generations produces a hardened pattern of land use that is unsuitable for social and economic changes of later periods and, for any immediate period, an acute shortage of land throughout the urban region. Essentially, the limitations in land use impose comparable restrictions on city planners; indeed, the overwhelming proportion of planning under these circumstances is usually corrective physical— with all the shortcomings described in the last chapter.

Though others might be mentioned, a final type of inconsistency stems from a simple fact: a substantial but not easily measured proportion of residents is not clearly urban except in the matter of location. Relatively few urbanites (city or suburban) can trace urban residence in their families more than two generations. This is particularly evident in the heavy currents of rural-urban migration since World War I and in the movement of Negroes and Puerto Ricans to major cities of the U.S.[4]

Consequently, many families in cities and fringe areas carry over values that are inconsistent (though not always antagonistic) with the opportunities and responsibilities of urban living. This is dramatically reflected in the case of persons maladjusted to urbanism—the criminals, a large proportion of the mentally disturbed and disordered, the compulsive gamblers and alcoholics, the chronically unemployed, and those with continually unstable home life. But it is easy to forget that many others are prosaically uncomfortable with or unaccustomed to the peculiar freedom and diversity of the urban region. Statistics on this point are difficult to obtain, yet we can point to such relevant phenomena as disinterest in the facts and issues of community affairs, nonvoting, and the relative disregard of such community resources as museums and libraries. Some will undoubtedly suggest that this is a matter of taste, about which argument is fruitless. However, the important point here is that the insulation of tastes from wider and more diversified forms nullifies the presumed advantages of urban living. It is similar to the incongruous situation of a man entering a restaurant noted for exquisite food and calmly attacking a stale sandwich of peanut butter and jelly, which he has brought for the occasion.

Planning Visions and Ultimate Values

The third component of creative urban planning is abstract, visionary, but nonetheless of decisive importance: a guiding conception of an ideal yet ultimately realizable urban region. At this point, planning largely departs from the realm of facts and investigations for an immersion in the less definite provinces of philosophy and art.

[4] C. Wright Mills *et al.*, *The Puerto Rican Journey* (New York, Harper and Brothers, 1950); Christopher Rand, *The Puerto Ricans* (New York, Oxford University Press, 1958); Oscar Handlin, *The Newcomers: Negroes and Puerto Ricans in a Changing Metropolis* (Cambridge, Mass., Harvard University Press, 1959).

Creative planners try to serve as critics of the contemporary, and as links to the future development of urban regions. Both roles apply a set of ultimate objectives or values that draw on the achievements and failures of urban experience, and also provide stimuli for effort toward positive goals. Since creative planning partakes of broad ideals and social interpretation, it bristles with judgments, evaluations, and assertions: it is therefore typically exposed to debate and controversy, to opinion and fashion, and the scorn of those with myopic vision. What are the goals of creative planning in our era? We shall merely list representative goals with brief descriptions.

1. Orderly development and responsibility.

Mumford and others [5] stress the importance of creating plans that insure smoother incorporation of physical, economic, and social changes in given regions. In addition, there is a growing concern for designing urban regions to achieve greater articulation and reciprocal relations with other urban regions. This conception disposes of the earlier role of cities as insurgent, highly competitive entities for a more mature contribution to the larger society. In short, creative planning seeks to "socialize" the urban region by developing internal responsibilities for stability and external responsibilities for national service.

2. Renewal of internal responsibility

The consensus among urban planners is that the urban region of the future should encourage a consistent and widespread desire to participate actively in neighborhood, community, and regional affairs of various kinds.[6] This goal is based on the prior development of identification and affiliation, rather than withdrawal and alienation. Creative planning seeks to provide the physical setting that restores or expands social participation and community involvement.

[5] Lewis Mumford, *The Culture of Cities* (New York, Harcourt, Brace and World, 1938), pp. 6, 371, 441; Lewis Mumford, "Introduction," in Ebenezer Howard, *Garden Cities of Tomorrow,* enlarged edition (London, Faber and Faber, 1945), p. 38; José Luis Sert, *Can Our Cities Survive?* (Cambridge, Mass, Harvard University Press, 1952); Percival Goodman and Paul Goodman, *Communitas* (Chicago, University of Chicago Press, 1947).

[6] Mumford, *The Culture of Cities,* pp. 483–484; Goodman and Goodman, *op. cit.,* pp. 75–76, 125–126.

3. Livability and general practicality

According to these planning goals, the emphasis is on providing urban regions designed for comfort and convenience for most urbanites, rather than a favored few. The ideal is to create cities in which to enjoy the fruits of modern technology, not their troublesome by-products.[7] In this view, urban areas should become increasingly desirable places to live, as well as work.

4. Flexibility

Contrary to some popular apprehensions, creative planners give great prominence to the need for developing flexible designs and plans. The essence of urbanism, they assert, lies in constant development and the quest for new experiences and solutions to the needs of human association. Since future needs cannot be anticipated in great detail, urban planning should reserve space, facilities, and resources so that changes desired by future generations can be achieved without prohibitive cost and needless frustration.[8] The urban region is conceived not as a monument or museum, but as a continuing frontier in human achievements and satisfactions.

Creative planning, then, is a difficult and evolving combination of basic knowledge of urban trends, a critical survey of urban problems, and a vision of hitherto untapped urban potentialities. In theory and in practice, this type of planning treats the physical and social aspects as inevitably intertwined, a viewpoint that is supported by the social sciences and the arts (both "fine" and "applied"). Furthermore, creative planning explicitly approaches the urban region not only as a product of its society and civilization, but as a model for change, as a leader in the development of modern societies. This ambitious role is often greeted with reserve, suspicion, or the ambivalence of lip service. Consequently, few experiments in creative urban planning have reached beyond the discussion or blueprint stage.

But the limited number of such cases—literally "essays in creative urban planning"—deserves some appraisal. In particular, we should attempt to find in each instance the extent to which plans actually

[7] Henry S. Churchill, "Trends," in Paul K. Hatt and Albert J. Reiss, Jr., eds., *Reader in Urban Sociology* (New York, The Free Press of Glencoe, 1951), p. 680; Clarence S. Stein, *Toward New Towns for America* (Liverpool, University Press of Liverpool, 1951), p. 206.

[8] Mumford, *The Culture of Cities*, p. 441; Stein, *op. cit.*, p. 205.

apply social science, and the practical obstacles in transferring goals into working models. Significantly, creative planning has almost wholly focused on previously undeveloped areas; either establishing new communities, or inserting new, planned areas in the vacant pockets of established communities. Is creative planning necessarily limited to such situations, or may wider applications be feasible in the future?

SELECTED EXAMPLES OF CREATIVE URBAN PLANNING

Radburn, N. J.: A Study in Pioneering and Frustration [9]

It is quite understandable that the first attempt to plan a permanent community in the creative manner should be located in the New York metropolitan area, about sixteen miles from New York City. Radburn was an ambitious gesture, designed to demonstrate the feasibility of establishing a relatively self-contained and orderly "island" in the urban sprawl. Essentially, its planners envisioned an area with a maximum of 25,000 population, with built-in amenities, and with physical features geared to a conception of a balanced, wholesome community.

Under private financing, without government subsidy or loans, Radburn was opened for occupancy in May, 1929. Its residential area was in the form of two superblocks (three in the original plan), each with well-placed clusters of one-family homes (and later some two-family homes), internal park areas available to every family, a separation of pedestrian and automobile routes, and dead end lanes for beauty and isolation from through traffic.

As originally conceived, Radburn was to be a *community,* rather than a suburban appendage. Three elementary schools were planned, one for each superblock, as well as a combined junior and senior high school, and an accessible commercial center. There was even provision for an industrial section at the southwest edge of the super-blocks and yet close to a railroad line and a major highway.

But several available facts were ignored, while the imminence of the Great Depression merely intensified the difficulties of rearing a totally new kind of community. First, the planners had located their community in an area of generally inadequate transportation facilities, either for access to New York City or to other cities in New Jersey. Thus, potential residents with jobs in New York City were not greatly

---

[9] Stein, *op. cit.,* Chap. II.

attracted. Only 400 families took residence there before the war. The painfully slow growth of Radburn was a tremendous financial burden. Furthermore, the old vision of locating employment opportunities nearby was quickly blurred by the unwillingness of industry to move into the area. Looking backward, this is quite understandable: the adjacent rail line was not on a main route; there were no financial inducements; and there was simply no provision in the plan for attracting employers. Finally, because of virtually nonexistent local employment and the costs of residence, Radburn could not develop a balanced status structure. It became—and remains—a homogeneous enclave of middle class commuters.

Despite the defects of its conception and implementation, Radburn provided an early illustration of the potentialities of imaginative urban planning and some necessary cautions to further explorations of the "Radburn Idea." Perhaps the most important contribution was the awakening of community participation through the superblock and the civic associations encouraged by tastefully planned proximity. A measure of the value attributed to this style of living is the return of former residents after World War II, and the number of Radburn children who decided to rear their own families in the setting they themselves had enjoyed in the thirties. Also important is Radburn's demonstration that suitable, orderly neighborhoods could be achieved without the drab uniformity of "packaged" suburbs, and yet with adequate provision for future growth. It is no surprise, then, that the essentials of Radburn are already "classic" and that several European cities have adopted these features in constructing extensive additions to established communities.[10]

The Radburn experience likewise offers very instructive lessons to the creative planner. First, urban plans must give serious attention to the larger region and particularly to the nature of transportation facilities. If the new area is to develop desired social and cultural features, the probable impact of existing facilities must be carefully appraised, and if necessary, an appropriately planned transportation system should be an integral part of a practical scheme. The Radburn experiment demonstrates, in the second place, that such imperative considerations as transportation and a favorable economic base require a congenial framework of cooperation with relevant govern-

[10] *Ibid*, pp. 67–68; Leo Grebler, *Europe's Reborn Cities*, Urban Land Institute, Technical Bulletin No. 28 (Washington, D.C., March, 1956), pp. 58–59.

mental bodies—for information, coordination of activities, and, where necessary, adequate financing. As Stein bluntly remarks in his account of Radburn: ". . . a private corporation has only a gambling chance to carry through to completion the building of a city . . . there must be a certain amount of government cooperation." [11] Finally, to insure a proper range of community services, a creatively planned area must be a politically independent unit, not an appendage of a neighboring and perhaps jealous community. Radburn's residents discovered this essential fact of community living when their plan for a new high school was decisively voted down by their "neighbors" in 1935.

Greenbelt, Maryland: Variations on the Radburn Theme[12]

If Radburn was an outgrowth of private vision in the last gasp of American prosperity, Greenbelt and its sister communities (Greendale, Wisconsin and Greenhills, Ohio) were attempts at creative urban planning by the federal government in the mid-depression years (1935–1938). Unlike Radburn, Greenbelt has continued to grow and to exhibit its potentialities, despite a radical change in ownership. Greenbelt must be viewed as the leading peace-time candidate for successful creative planning in the United States, though it, too, retains questionable aspects found in Radburn.

Located about thirteen miles northeast of an increasingly congested Washington, Greenbelt was planned as a relatively complete community of 875 residential units arranged in a pleasing arc set in a green belt of Maryland. Its original population of about 2,800 was provided with a modest approximation of Radburn principles: the superblock of attached housing units; the separation of pedestrian walks from automobile routes; the use of dead end lanes and service courts; and consistent provision of small play areas near each set of units, as well as larger recreational areas at various points. Because of its closeness to Washington, and as a matter of policy, Greenbelt was at first a community of lower level government employees (about 70 per cent of the community), most of whom were high school graduates. But when an additional 1,000 units were put up in 1941–1942, the typical resident was of higher status in income, formal education, and level of employment in government agencies. By the

[11] Stein, op. cit., p. 67.
[12] Ibid., Chap. VIII.

early fifties, the total population reached almost 7,000 (approximately the projected size of each neighborhood unit in Radburn), many of whom were rather long-term residents in Greenbelt.

However, the nature of the physical setting and a more detailed plan combined to make Greenbelt an improvement over Radburn in several respects. Perhaps the most striking advance was a centrally located community and shopping center, consisting of police and fire departments, the town hall, a large cooperative supermarket, auto repair service, post office, bank, theater, swimming pool, several other stores, and a youth center—all within a half-mile from most units, and just under a mile from the most distant houses. A second feature was the creation of Greenbelt as a political entity with its own government, first under the control of the federal government, and more recently, as a municipality. Consequently, Greenbelt's residents have had considerable direct experience in active government on a number of local problems.[13]

Third, Greenbelt had the important advantage of federal financing, research, and professional planning during the difficult first years of any creative planning venture. In 1951, Greenbelt was sold to a private cooperative of its residents, who operate the community through a city council, mayor, and a city manager.[14]

Fourth, there is the incomparable, long-term benefit of the surrounding greenbelt, which is both a buffer to unwanted urban expansion and an invaluable recreation area for adults and children.

Finally, by mere accident, Greenbelt is four miles from the campus of the University of Maryland, with all the educational and artistic activities a state university normally affords.

Thus, Greenbelt represents the possibilities of an ambitious attempt at initiating an entirely new community with a balanced set of services and facilities. Yet several deficiencies must be noted. Despite the emphasis on the amenities and attractive use of space, Greenbelt's residential units are closely packed together and lacking in the family living space we have come to require since 1945. Perhaps this limitation of indoor family space is a reflection of the depression period, of the small family of that time. Furthermore, in comparison with Radburn, there is greater uniformity of unit design, which contributes

13 *Ibid.*, pp. 147–151.
14 Christian L. Larsen and Richard D. Andrews, *The Government of Greenbelt* (College Park, Md., Bureau of Public Administration, University of Maryland, 1951).

to a "project" look and detracts from the creative planner's quest for beauty.

Once again, no provision for industrial or commercial development was made by Greenbelt's planners. It is, consequently, an area of commuters, adding to the continually troublesome traffic problems of the capital. But a further consequence of its basic dormitory character is a homogenized, one class (middle, white collar), one occupation (federal employee) community—only slightly distinguishable from scores of unplanned residential suburbs that are the objects of so much derision.

The New Towns of Britain: Creative Decentralization on a Large Scale

Without doubt, the most extensive program of creative urban planning is the "New Towns" network that has been transforming the urban regions of Great Britain in the short space of twelve years. The problems of the seven large metropolitan regions (or conurbations), marked by congestion and sprawl, have finally provoked organized attempts at decentralization, and yet the retention of community life. British planners and political leaders, willing to experiment, devised three types of solutions. *Housing estates* (large public housing projects) located in urban fringe areas merely shifted congestion to newer quarters and disrupted local community ties. A second expedient, *satellite towns* built and owned by large cities within an hour's travel time, became suburban appendages and caused little change in either the residential or transportation situation of such conurbations as London. The New Towns, however, fourteen in number to date, give promise of providing solutions that urban regions of the world cannot ignore.[15]

Since eight of the New Towns are in the London region, let us focus on these, recognizing, however, that they are not equally developed or uniformly planned. All but one, Stevenage, is approximately thirty miles from downtown London, beyond congested rings of suburbs and at the borders of a permanent greenbelt of woods, farm land, and parks. Each of the "towns" was designed by a team of planners under the supervision of a Development Corporation, which is responsible to the Ministry of Housing and Local Government and to Parliament.

In view of our previous discussion, the cardinal feature of the New Towns is the *attraction of industrial firms* (mainly from London) to

[15] Peter Self, *Cities in Flood* (London, Faber and Faber, 1959), pp. 88–90.

provide a local employment base. Crawley, for example, had 52 factories and 80 shops by 1956—for a population of about 18,000. Consequently, there is very little commuting to London: 90 per cent of Crawley's workers moved into the community with their factories. On the other hand, Crawley and other "towns" have not been able to attract many large commercial establishments and offices, as in some suburban areas of the United States. But office facilities are being constructed and several government bureaus have set up quarters in the New Towns.[16]

Other features of the New Towns are reminiscent of Radburn and Greenbelt: neighborhood units of superblocks, a greenbelt, neighborhood shops, a centrally located community and shopping zone, and the general separation of pedestrian and motor traffic. But the nature of housing facilities constitutes another step forward in creative planning. Despite the obvious bias toward lower income housing, planners have been able to provide a wider range of facilities than is available in most suburbs. In addition to subsidized housing for working and lower middle groups, there is a growing encouragement of housing for middle and upper income families, developed by private construction firms. Furthermore, some towns undertook to build a fair number of more expensive and attractive houses (either for sale or lease) at the very beginning of town development.[17] To this extent, the New Towns have provided a basis for social variety, even to the point of building special one-story houses expressly for older persons, judiciously dispersed among units for younger families.

In general, the New Towns have been successful in establishing solid roots and in satisfying the social and psychological wants of the loyal and highly traditionalistic Londoner. By contrast with the rapid turnover in the housing estates, where lower status Londoners continue to grumble about the "strangers" who are their neighbors and the lost ties of East End areas, less than 4 per cent of Crawley's families have to date moved away. Part of this stability, which has been achieved in a remarkably short time, is due to the provision of garden plots, to the rapid development of a variety of religious, athletic, and educational associations, to the community Common Rooms for many social functions, and to the closeness of work and home. Adequate community facilities are understandably a problem of new communities; there are yet shortages in playing fields, movie theaters,

[16] *Ibid.*, pp. 59–60; Albert Mayer, "New Ways of Life in Britain's New Towns," *The New York Times Magazine*, January 29, 1956.
[17] Mayer, *loc. cit.;* Self, *op. cit.*, p. 88.

and meeting rooms. But planned towns like Harlow, Crawley, and Hemel Hampstead clearly demonstrate the general direction in which urban planning may fruitfully point.

Brasilia: The Grandeur of a New Capital

A magnificent opportunity to plan a completely new community, literally from the ground up, has recently been taken by the Brazilian government in its decision to construct a new capital 600 miles inland from Rio de Janeiro. Clearly, the design of capital cities presents certain problems, and allows a certain latitude, simply because they differ in function from the more prevalent commercial and industrial cities. In Canberra, newly constructed in 1918, for example, it was decided to create a capital with an uncluttered central area, one strangely planned for golf links and a race track. Completely excluding any industrial development, the plan sharply separated commercial, governmental, and residential clusters to the point of formal beauty and structured inconvenience. The inevitable price has been a considerable traffic problem in a community of about 54,000.[18] To what extent has Brasilia profited by the experience of its Australian counterpart?

Since Brasilia is still in construction, though formally "opened" in April, 1960, it is difficult to evaluate on more than a tentative basis. Indeed, little more than 4,000 federal employees now (1962) live in Brasilia, whereas the projected population is about 500,000. The completed building includes government offices, substantial areas of housing, a hotel, an airport, several broad new highways, plus a huge artificial lake.

The basic quality of Brasilia lies not in its very modernistic architecture, but in a radical deviation from the familiar urban pattern, composed of a core commercial area and a series of rough zones, sectors, and clusters arrayed in amoebic fashion around the core. Brasilia consists of three major parts, which form a unique cross (or in the description of the *New York Times* art critic, "a giant dragonfly."[19] The major "spine" of the city contains a variety of business,

[18] Homer Bigart, "Once-Bleak Canberra Emerging as Modern Capital for Australia," *The New York Times,* February 12, 1961; Herbert W. H. King, "The Canberra—Queanbeyan Symbiosis, A Study of Urban Mutualism," *Geographical Review,* 44 (January, 1954), pp. 101–118; Egon E. Bergel, *Urban Sociology* (New York, McGraw-Hill, 1955), pp. 516–518.

[19] Aline Saarinen, "Brasilia Rises," *The New York Times,* October, 18, 1959.

civic, and recreational buildings. Crossing the spine in the shape of arched wings is a set of residential superblocks, with accessible shopping, schools, and churches. Then at the head of the major axis is a triangular arrangement of the capital's administrative offices. Because of this monumental design, transportation links are especially important. The plan, therefore, calls for a network of highways, cloverleafs, multilevel roads, special pedestrian lanes, and boulevards 400 feet broad.

The boldness of the plan and the obvious attempt to provide a city of dazzling vistas and abundant space mark Brasilia as a city of glamor and persistent interest. It seems to be a huge outdoor museum, a city dedicated to the public aspect. But it remains to be seen what the residential clusters, composed of towering apartment buildings, contribute to the essentials of privacy, family life, and personal involvement in local affairs. We can only guess, secondly, at the ultimate success or failure of constructing a city dependent on auto transportation for its operation. Finally, the purposeful lack of industrial or commercial development may reduce congestion, but it also denies Brasilia a certain balance that urban regions seem to need. Very probably, national capitals constitute a separate type of city. Yet if one compares the specialized with the more balanced world capitals, which type provides better living and more varied experiences? To be more specific, how do Washington, Canberra, Tel Aviv, and Brasilia compare with London, Paris, Berlin, Stockholm, and Tokyo? In other words, to what extent does the governmental function create the basis for *community living?*

SUMMARY

As we review the few serious attempts at creative urban planning, several outstanding features seem to recur. There is, first, the comparative recency of such planning and a consequent incompleteness of execution. Second, creative planners have tended to mix bold visions and questionable retention of past failures. The latter aspect is especially visible in experiments that ignore the need for a balanced economic base, for smoothly flowing transportational and traffic systems, and a setting attractive to a range of status groupings in the urban region. Third, there is a basic quest for restoration of the region as an area of numerous interlocking interests and pursuits, not merely as a place to work and draw income.

Essentially, creative planning has tried to approach the city and its region as an emergent system, in which planning provides crucial connections and strategic additions to effective coordination. Specifically, the essays in creative planning reflect concern for the interrelation of physical, cultural, and social aspects of human groups. In this respect, the planner borrows—or shares—the fundamental orientation of the urban sociologist, who draws from a variety of investigations a conception of the city and the urban region as a recognizable but imperfect system, complex though it may be. On the other hand, in the *execution* of plans, it is often true that greater emphasis is devoted to the physical and cultural dimensions, with a resultant muting of concern for developing social organizations. The planner hopes to create the proper facilities, not the organizations themselves.

Finally, though a *regional* viewpoint and philosophy are consistently expressed in the writings and speeches of creative planners, specific planning programs rarely receive the opportunity to treat the urban region as a practical entity. Instead, planners find themselves projecting their insights and ingenuity on a single functional part of the region—a suburb, a satellite, or perhaps an entire but isolated central city (*e.g.,* Brasilia). Thus far, creative planning and the tentative conclusions of urban sociology are closely parallel lines— but they have yet to meet *consistently* and properly assimilate the unique contributions of one another.

SELECTED REFERENCES

GOODMAN, Percival and GOODMAN, Paul, *Communitas* (Chicago, University of Chicago Press, 1947).

HOWARD, Ebenezer, *Garden Cities of Tomorrow,* enlarged ed. (London, Faber and Faber, 1955).

KUPER, Leo, ed., *Living in Towns* (London, Gresset Press, 1953).

MUMFORD, Lewis, *The City in History* (New York, Harcourt, Brace and World, 1961), Chaps. XVI–XVII.

STEIN, Clarence, *Toward New Towns for America* (Liverpool, University Press of Liverpool, 1951).

TUNNARD, Christopher and REED, Henry H., *American Skyline* (New York, New American Library, 1956).

VIET, Jean, ed., *New Towns: Selected Annotated Bibliography* (Paris, UNESCO, 1960).

Index